STUDIES IN
BIBLIOGRAPHY

STUDIES IN BIBLIOGRAPHY

Edited by

DAVID L. VANDER MEULEN

Volume Fifty-One

Published for

THE BIBLIOGRAPHICAL SOCIETY OF THE UNIVERSITY OF VIRGINIA

BY THE UNIVERSITY PRESS OF VIRGINIA, CHARLOTTESVILLE

1998

Founding Editor
Fredson Bowers (1905–1991)

———

Assistant to the Editor
Elizabeth Lynch

THE UNIVERSITY PRESS OF VIRGINIA
Copyright © 1997 by the Rector and Visitors
of the University of Virginia

Virginia. University. Bibliographical Society.

    Studies in bibliography; papers v.1—
1948/49—
Charlottesville.
       v. illus. 26cm. annual.
Title varies: 1948/49—

    1. Bibliography—Societies. I. Title.
Z1008.V55   010.6275549—3353 Rev.*

ISBN 0–8139–1815–4

The editors invite articles and notes on analytical bibliography, textual criticism, manuscript study, the history of printing and publishing, as well as related matters of method and evidence. Send manuscripts to David L. Vander Meulen, English Department, 219 Bryan Hall, University of Virginia, Charlottesville, VA 22903.

All other correspondence, concerning membership, subscriptions, and other business, should go to Penelope F. Weiss, Executive Secretary, Bibliographical Society, University of Virginia Library, Charlottesville, Va. 22903.

This journal is a member of the Council of Editors of Learned Journals.

Contents

CONTENTS

A Rationale of Collecting

by

G. THOMAS TANSELLE

COLLECTING, IN ONE FORM OR ANOTHER, IS SO UBIQUITOUS, SO MUCH a part of humanity's experience, that it has aroused endless speculation regarding its origins, its motives, its essential nature. There are debates about whether it is instinctive or acquired, about whether it is a rational activity or a mental disease ("mania" being one of the terms often applied to it, sometimes with affection, sometimes not). Most such discussions illuminate some aspect of the subject, but even in their totality they do not encompass all the causes and all the results of collecting. Like every human behavior, collecting is complex enough that there is always something more to be said about it. The attempt to understand collecting not only adds to our knowledge of human nature but also enhances the experience of collecting itself. For whether one collects Renaissance paintings or cigar boxes, Greek antiquities or coffee mugs, rare books or advertising brochures, one's sense of self-awareness is increased by being able to place one's own endeavors in a framework that comprehends the full panoply of related pursuits.

I

To think about collecting in this inclusive way requires, I believe, a definition that makes everyone a collector. I would say, simply, that collecting is the accumulation of tangible things. This definition covers the assembling of natural objects (like fossils and shells) and living entities (like plants and animals) as well as artifacts, the products of humanity; and it leaves open the manner in which the things are acquired, the mental processes leading to their acquisition, and the length of time they are held. Some would object that a definition under which everyone is a collector has insufficient precision to be useful for analysis. I would argue, on the contrary, that only by linking all forms of collecting can we illuminate the fundamental nature of the myriad directions it can take. The kinds of accumulating we are most likely to think of when we hear the word "collecting" are not separated by distinct lines from other types of gathering, and recognition of these relationships helps to clarify them all.

There is, for example, the matter of need. Some might feel that the concept of collecting must involve accumulations that are in excess of what is needed for survival—or, put another way, gatherings that serve no strictly utilitarian function. Collecting, so the argument runs, is a vestige of the instinct for foraging and hoarding found in animals and primitive peoples; when the "need" no longer exists, the hunting and gathering continue anyway and become attached to different classes of objects, now not connected with shelter or bodily nourishment. But such an argument, ignoring the reality of emotional demands, begs the question of what constitutes "need," which is never easy to answer. Even animals' hoarding does not always seem to be realistically related to the necessities of maintaining life;[1] and prehistoric human beings are now thought to have admired and saved certain tools for aesthetic reasons.[2] When one tries to identify human needs, one is bound to hear, in the back of one's mind, Lear's "Oh, reason not the need": the possessions not strictly necessary for bodily survival nevertheless may seem required for establishing a sense of human identity and defining one's place in the world. Nomadic tribes and homeless street-people have their possessions; and those persons or families who lose their accumulated store of objects through fires, storms, robberies, and other catastrophes generally find that their feelings of good fortune in still being alive are naggingly tempered by their sense of deprivation, since they are not as fully alive without the objects that they had made part of their existence. Lord Eccles, in *On Collecting* (1968), observes, "During the blitz on London I saw how simple and profound was the passion for things of one's own. The morning after poor people had been bombed out, they grieved far less for the house or rooms where they had been living than for their things, . . . the things their mother had left them, or their children had given them. The bomb which destroyed their things destroyed part of themselves" (p. 4).[3] It is unwise, then, to complicate a definition of collecting with the idea of need—not only because need is so difficult to pin down but also, and more signifi-

---

1. See, for example, Maurice Rheims's discussion in *La vie étrange des objets* (1959), translated by David Pryce-Jones in 1961 as *The Strange Life of Objects* ("The Collectors' Instinct among Animals," pp. 19–20).

2. In early 1994 the New York firm of Frederick Schultz Ancient Art mounted an exhibition, entitled "Power Tools," designed to illustrate this conclusion, which had been argued by a number of archeologists.

3. Four decades earlier Bohun Lynch, in *Collecting* (1928), had similarly referred to "poor folk who definitely and at any price refuse to part with the possessions of their forefathers" (p. 42); he ended his book by saying, "it is the things that we look at and touch for no practical ends with which, for one reason or another, we can least happily dispense."

cantly, because all forms of amassing objects can in fact be necessities of life, if the role of emotional well-being in physical survival is adequately taken into account. Indeed, it is not unreasonable to claim, as I hope to show, that the possession of objects is for everyone an essential element of life-support.

Another objection that might be raised against the simplicity of my definition is that it does not distinguish random accumulations of objects from purposeful selections. Surely, some will feel, the term "collection" should be reserved for those assemblages that have been systematically built according to a unifying principle and should not be used to dignify the miscellaneous stock of possessions (or even one class of them) that grows up around individuals year by year. It is, in fact, quite conventional to think of "collections" as different from "accumulations," but it is not very satisfactory,[4] because it skirts the question of how, or by whom, the coherence of a "collection" is to be determined. What one person accumulates haphazardly, another will regard as bearing a design; and even the product of a careful plan may turn out to be of interest to another person for an entirely different pattern that can be read into it. In any case, all accumulations are actually selections, and therefore imbued with meaning through that selectivity. Every object that is taken in, that is given entrance to one's house, or room, or personal space, acquires thereby a significance and alters the relationship of everything else within that domain; and every such object is a selection from the vast universe of objects. Some objects, of course, arrive unbidden, but if they are retained (even through inertia, and only temporarily) they are still revealing. Every accumulation, whatever additional significance it may be found to possess, has the unity that comes from its telling something about a human being who lived in a particular time and place. Archivists regularly deal with residues, and they have been wise to recognize that found arrangements of personal papers, in archeological layers that can seem random, carry meaning that is worth paying attention to. Clearly one may wish to distinguish different types of individuals and to separate those who deliberately pursue their own ideas of coherent groupings from those who give no conscious thought to why their possessions are multiplying as they are; but this discrimination will be richer if it is based on an acknowledgment that both types of persons are related, that they are overlapping varieties of "collectors."

4. An example of the unsatisfactory handling of this point occurs in Herbert Read's introduction to Niels von Holst's *Creators, Collectors and Connoisseurs: The Anatomy of Artistic Taste from Antiquity to the Present Day* (1967). After declaring that "purposive collecting" and "mere accumulation of miscellaneous objects" must be distinguished, Read then in fact links them, in their origins and functions, when he says that "possessions in general may be said to give a sense of security" (p. 3).

Still another element of my definition that must logically be dealt with is its limitation to "tangible things." If one is going to take a comprehensive view of collecting, as I am doing, can one not speak of collecting ideas and other intangibles as well as physical entities? The word "collect" can of course be used this way, and regularly is, as when people speak of collecting Carribbean cruises, or performances by Gielgud, or any other experiences—in the same way that Thoreau felt he could own something without taking physical possession of it. Every mindset (in which one "collects one's thoughts") consists of an ever-developing collection of mental routines. Everyone has this kind of collection as well as a collection of physical objects; and there is inevitably a reciprocal relationship between the two, since the mindset (or "temperament") determines which objects one allows to accumulate around one, and the environment created by those objects in turn influences the mindset. But there is a fundamental difference between thoughts and objects, between an internal repertoire of ideas and an external grouping of tangible materials; and this dividing line is more profound than any that may be formulated to separate one kind of assemblage of physical objects from another. (This point can be held even if one wishes to question the existence of the external world, for there is still a distinction between what seems, to any given individual, to come from within and what seems to enter one's consciousness from without.) It appears reasonable, therefore, to exclude mental repertoires from our present definition of a collection but not to eliminate any form of tangible accumulation.[5] Even so, the former remains relevant to the discussion because the latter cannot be thoughtfully considered without recognizing its source in the need of the individual to bridge the gap, to bring what is (or seems) external within one's personal orbit.

Werner Muensterberger, in *Collecting: An Unruly Passion* (1994), works from a somewhat more explicit definition than mine: collecting, he says, is "the selecting, gathering, and keeping of objects of subjective value" (p. 4). Although this definition is careful and useful, my reason for preferring an even simpler one—"the accumulation of tangible things"—is that, in my view, most of the words he uses may be inappropriately restrictive unless they are accompanied by particular explications (and definitions ought to be capable of standing alone). The idea of "selecting," for instance, may seem to imply a conscious and deliberate activity; but all collecting, as Muensterberger well knows (for

5. One writer on collecting who does specifically include experiences in his definition is Russell W. Belk, but his discussions proceed as if he is thinking only of tangible items. See "Collectors and Collecting," *Advances in Consumer Research*, 15 (1988), 548–553 (reprinted in *Interpreting Objects and Collections*, ed. Susan M. Pearce [1994], pp. 317–326); and *Collecting in a Consumer Society* (1995), e.g. p. 66.

his subtitle is "Some Psychological Perspectives"), involves a mixture of conscious and unconscious motivations. Deliberate selections have unconscious causes, and random accumulations are nonetheless selective. Collections may no doubt be classified according to the amount of conscious control they seem to reflect, but the differences among them are matters of degree; and the attempt to understand the nature of collecting must deal with these shifting proportions.

Similarly, to speak of "keeping" a group of things involves permanence, but the length of time one possesses something cannot be an element in determining whether or not one is a collector. The urge to possess must indeed be present, but once possession actually occurs, its longevity is not an essential factor: some people—at all levels of sophistication and deliberateness in their acts of gathering—willingly dispose of their assemblages and start on others; such assemblages, just as much as those held for a lifetime, are surely to be included within the concept of a "collection." And the word "objects" is likely to suggest inanimate entities, yet those who assemble varieties of orchids or breeds of horses must be encompassed by the definition, for they cannot be distinguished, in their motivations or behavior, from those who collect inanimate things.[6] Finally, Muensterberger's reference to "subjective value" is meant to make the point that the desirability of an object to a collector is independent of the market price it would fetch (now or in the future). But why should those who collect for investment (at least in part) or take some pride in the monetary value of what they possess be denied a place in the universe of collecting? If such motives enter (in one degree or another) into a person's gathering of objects, they are simply a part of the total

---

6. When the collecting of living things focuses on human beings, as in a collection of slaves, it of course becomes morally reprehensible. John Elsner and Roger Cardinal, in their introduction to *The Cultures of Collecting* (1994), which I discuss further below, examine the Holocaust as an instance of such collecting. The collecting of people is frequently a metaphor, as when the entomologist narrator of John Fowles's novel *The Collector* (1963) says, "Seeing her always made me feel like I was catching a rarity"—she was "for the real connoisseur" (p. 1). David Vander Meulen has called my attention to June Carter Cash's concept of "klediments" (in her 1979 memoir, *Among My Klediments*), which encompasses people as well as inanimate objects. As quoted in the *Dictionary of American Regional English* entry for "clatterment" (of which "klediment" is a variant spelling derived from regional pronunciation), Cash says, "A klediment can be almost anything that has earned a right to be a part of things close to you. It can be precious antique furniture gathered from grandmother, pieces of china, little handmade doilies, the straw mats on your floor, or the priscilla curtains you made yourself. A klediment can be a thing you love ... A klediment can be a thing you just won't throw away ... A klediment can be a person dear to you." Clearly Cash is talking about something larger than "possessions," for she is not claiming to possess the people close to her; her definition of "klediment" recognizes that each person's intimate environment comprises things one does not possess as well as those one does own. The study of collecting, as I have defined it, helps to show how the latter affect one's way of responding to the former.

psychological underpinning of the assemblage, and they do not affect the more fundamental question of why the various motivations involved led to the particular items present, or to tangible things at all. I make these points not to criticize Muensterberger (for his definition is more thoughtful than many that have been advanced) but to illuminate some of the considerations involved in thinking about collecting.

Muensterberger's book, indeed, may be the most thorough and engaging treatment of the psychology of collecting written for a general audience. (Psychologists have naturally been intrigued by the phenomenon of collecting, for it clearly results from deep emotional drives, and there is an extensive technical literature: the modern tradition of such psychological inquiry goes back to Freud and, perhaps less obviously, to William James—who brought up the subject repeatedly, as in the influential 1892 "Briefer Course" of his *Psychology* where he treated the collecting of "property" as an "instinctive impulse" and the resulting collections as "parts of our empirical selves.")[7] If one wishes to think seriously about the nature of collecting, one has no choice but to ponder human psychology, for collecting often causes people to seem driven by uncontrollable urges that they cannot rationally explain—a fact that has made collecting of interest to a number of novelists, such as, most famously, Balzac (*Cousin Pons*) and, among more recent writers, John Fowles (*The Collector*), Evan S. Connell, Jr. (*The Connoisseur*), and Bruce Chatwin (*Utz*). Muensterberger, a practicing psychoanalyst himself, sees the origins of collecting in childhood traumas. When infants or children have the experience of feeling deprived (even for a short period) of the protection and support of those close to them, they tend to look for relief in their immediate inanimate surroundings and find in controllable physical objects the solace they require. The situation illustrates, in Muensterberger's neat phrase, "the interlocking of biological needs and environmental conditions" (p. 19). Children find in objects a means to keep anxiety under control, and thus they become emotionally attached to one or more items that are associated in their minds with the relief of frustration and mental distress. The holding of these objects, the act of demonstrating that one possesses and controls them, is a pleasurable experience, and one that is repeatedly satisfying because it creates "the illusion of being able to cope" (p. 29).

---

7. James's foreshadowing of recent discussions is also illustrated by his observation that the loss of a collection produces "a sense of the shrinkage of our personality, a partial conversion of ourselves to nothingness" (p. 178). A convenient brief survey of psychoanalytic ideas on collecting appears in the opening pages of Ruth Formanek's "Why They Collect: Collectors Reveal Their Motivations," reprinted in *Interpreting Objects and Collections*, ed. Susan M. Pearce (1994), pp. 327–335. See also the checklist at the end of Muensterberger's book.

Muensterberger's discussion, however one feels about Freudian, or Freud-inspired, or post-Freudian interpretations of human behavior, does go deeper into the psychology of collecting than many of the writings on the subject. Philippe Jullian's *Les Collectioneurs* (1966), for example, though it is in some ways a charming book, remains relatively superficial. At one point he says (in the words of his 1967 translator, Michael Callum), "Every collection is inspired by the same basic factors: fear of boredom, desire for immortality, aesthetic sensibility, vanity, speculation" (p. 74). Similarly, Holbrook Jackson, in *The Anatomy of Bibliomania* (1930–31) offers—under the heading "The Causes of Bibliomania"—sections on "Greed," "Vanity," and "Fashion" (II, 273–289). All these motivations may certainly be involved, in varying proportions, in every individual's collecting, but identifying them does not explain why collecting is the route taken to those ends. There are other ways of passing the time, or securing fame, or satisfying a love of beauty, or feeding one's self-importance, or taking financial risks, or amassing wealth, or following fashion; and the most fundamental question in trying to understand collecting is to ask why it should be the path, rather than some other, that is chosen (consciously or unconsciously) to reach certain personal goals. One may subsequently turn to defining the particular combinations of goals that characterize individual collectors; but such analysis does not reach the deepest levels of the drive to collect. Thus an inquiry like Muensterberger's, which tries to identify the mental processes underlying the more overt motivations, is taking an important step, even if it does not tell the whole story.

That there is more to be said is suggested by Walter Benjamin's characteristically perceptive—but disappointingly elliptical—essay, "Unpacking My Library: A Talk about Book Collecting" (available in Harry Zohn's 1968 English translation in *Illuminations*). One of Benjamin's most penetrating observations is framed as a question: "For what else is this collection but a disorder to which habit has accommodated itself to such an extent that it can appear as order?" (p. 60). The pleasures of the chase and of adding to one's assemblage are framed by Benjamin in the same terms: "The most profound enchantment for the collector is the locking of individual items within a magic circle in which they are fixed as the final thrill, the thrill of acquisition, passes over them." The boundaries of a collection enclose a "magic" space because any object, once "fixed" within it, becomes part of a created order. Benjamin recognizes that collectors deal with "a dialectical tension between the poles of disorder and order," but he does not go much beyond these few sentences in exploring the point. Whether, if asked to expand his discussion, he would have taken the direction I shall take here is impossible to say; but

I do believe that the human need to find order should be thought about as a fundamental—and possibly the most fundamental—explanation of collecting.

I wish to emphasize, however, that this style of explanation is in no way incompatible with psychoanalytical analyses like Muensterberger's. He talks about the individual's need to feel in "control," and such a feeling could also be described as the perception of some degree of order and stability in what previously seemed unyieldingly chaotic. When infants reach out and take charge of objects, they are comforted because they have domesticated what had seemed foreign; by taking physical control of something, they have imposed an order on their relationship to it and thus have made one small part of their environment less mystifying and disorienting. Whether infants require such comfort because of experiences that make them feel abandoned and insecure, or simply because the world around them seems curious or bewildering, can be forever debated. I believe it can be plausibly argued that, even without specific traumas, infants feel the need to bring order to their surroundings through the acquisition of objects, thus setting in motion a lifelong pattern. This hypothesis is not necessarily more universal than Muensterberger's; for if he is right that everyone experiences childhood traumas, then his explanation is also universally applicable. But an hypothesis not dependent on any one category of event (such as a trauma) may perhaps be regarded as more basic.

II

The starting point for thinking about collecting is recognizing the human feeling of wonder that things seem to exist outside the self—the amazement and curiosity aroused by the apparent infinitude of animate and inanimate things that constantly impinge on one's consciousness. And the wonder is not only that these things have an independent existence but also that they seem to have had a pre-existence—that is, to have a history that antedates our awareness of them. The act of reaching out and touching them therefore produces contact both with the environment and with the past. Obviously infants do not consciously have such thoughts, and neither do a great many adults. But philosophers systematically consider the relation of the self to the nonself, and many other people think, and sometimes write, about it in less organized ways. In one fashion or another, at some level of the mind, everyone responds to the puzzle of whether the self is, or can be, connected to what seems to be outside it. The infant grasping and tightly holding a teddy bear, the expert in Old Master drawings pursuing and capturing another example for a collection, and all other acquisitors of tangible things are proving to themselves that they can make physical contact with that outside realm and, by seizing something from it, can subjugate one small part of it and to that extent render it more controllable and orderly. The process gives pleasure by conveying the sense that one is in some measure mastering one's environment, that one is less disoriented in the face of confusion. There is an accompanying and insatiable need to repeat the process, both because one seeks continued reassurance and because each instance brings renewed pleasure.

This process can be analyzed into several components, which include creation of order, fascination with chance, curiosity about the past, and desire for understanding. A sense of order is produced by the act of acquiring a tangible thing because that thing has been removed from one context, immense and inexplicable, and set within a different one, familiar and manageable. Each acquisition takes its place in relation to the other items already present within this context. Susan Stewart concisely captures this point in *On Longing* (1984) when she says that "objects are naturalized into the landscape of the collection" (p. 156). All the relationships among the items may shift somewhat as a result, but the new arrival is not an alien: since the whole is conceptually graspable, the newcomer fits simply by virtue of being there (whereas in the outside world, being there is not enough, for just what an item is fitting into—if it is doing so at all—is not clear). I take it that Benjamin's reference to "the locking of individual items within a magic circle in which they are fixed" is his way of making the same point. Another perceptive writer on collecting, Stephen Jay Gould, uses a similar expression in his absorbing study of eight collectors of fossils (*Finders, Keepers,* 1992, with photographs by Rosamond Wolff Purcell): he speaks of the urge "to bring part of a limitless diversity into an orbit of personal or public appreciation" (p. 10).[8] The "magic circle," the "orbit," imposes a structure on what is placed within it, and the individual repeatedly finds ways of moving more and more things from the outside to the inside of that space, gaining satisfaction each time from the sense of taming another talisman of wildness.

This drive to create order coexists with a fascination for chance. These two are natural partners because the gathering of tangible things entails a constant engagement with contingency, and one is inevitably

8. He also acknowledges the high costs of passionate engagements, incurred by "our uniquely evolved consciousness," and says, "The passion for collecting is a full-time job, a kind of blessed obsession." Notice that Wallace Stevens also uses the adjective "blessed" to make essentially the same point (the famous Stevens passage is mentioned at the end of the present essay).

dazzled by the diverse succession of things that pass one's way. What one gathers is dependent on what one encounters, and one's active seeking is a way of trying to encounter more. But despite one's attempts to increase the odds of finding something, what one actually finds is still a matter of chance. The connection between collecting and gambling has often been made: both involve jousting with fate, an exhilarating activity because it makes one feel unusually engaged with a basic force of life. The desire to find out what will show up next impels the gambler to play one game after another untiringly and drives the collector, with unceasing eagerness, to proceed from one antique shop, or other likely source, to another. Chance fascinates us not only because it produces endless variety but also because we feel that there must be a way to tame it, to pluck from it some reassurances of order. The television program *Antiques Roadshow*, in which people bring their possessions to experts for evaluation, illustrates the randomness in the distribution of objects—and the fact that such randomness is a significant part of the interest the show holds for its participants and its viewers. A large portion of those who bring items for inspection would not consider themselves "collectors," and what they bring comes from the accumulations they live with, including the residues they have retained from previous generations. An amazement that these items now reside where they do is an unspoken emotion of the owners of the items and of the experts as well, just as for the viewers the miscellaneous succession of items has the same appeal as browsing in a shop, where one cannot predict what will turn up next.

A curiosity about the past is also part of the reason that people's attention is captured by this show, as by other parades of objects. Every object acquires an interest quite separate from whatever significance it may have held for its previous possessors, since it is a tangible survivor from an earlier moment, putting one in touch, literally, with a vanished time. Indeed, because an object was looked at and touched by people in the interval (however long or short) between its origin and the present, it provides a link not merely to one past moment but to a series of them. When one observes a tangible thing in this way, thinking of it as a survivor, one gives close attention to all its sensuous aspects, all its physical features, any of which may proclaim something of the origin and subsequent life of the item. This sort of scrutiny, though it may subsume some understanding of the original function of an item, focuses on as many observable details as possible, whether or not they have a bearing on that function. A pitcher is studied not merely as an efficient utilitarian object but also as a tangible thing of a particular shape, material, decoration, glaze, and so on. Items conveying verbal or musical texts, like books and sheet music, are examined not only for those texts and their graphic design but also for other physical elements that mark the objects as products of the workmanship of a given time (such as clues revealing the source and date of the paper or the printing and proofreading procedures followed in the printing shop). Even objects intended solely as visual displays, like paintings and the whole spectrum of *objets d'art*, can be seen as carrying two kinds of exhibitions (not entirely distinct): an aesthetic construct, in which such materials as paint or crystal or porcelain reflect the visions of creators and inspire various (similar or different) visions in observers; and a technical construct, in which the nature of the materials and their manipulation take center stage, regardless of the fact that many of the details thus examined were not intended to be noticed by observers. A sense of this concentration on objects *as objects* is what Benjamin captured in one of his most telling and eloquently succinct statements: that a collector "studies and loves" objects "as the scene, the stage, of their fate" (p. 60). The object itself tells the story of its life.

A desire for understanding is the natural next step that follows from curiosity. When one repeatedly investigates objects in the manner just described, one builds up an inventory of details that form the background against which additional objects are looked at, and in this way a body of knowledge develops.[9] A further fascination of *Antiques Roadshow* is the array of specialists called upon, which not only confirms the fact that no object is too arcane to fall within the expertise of someone but also implicitly teaches a valuable lesson—that all objects, however lowly, deserve to have experts studying them and to be taken seriously as part of the mosaic of the past. Possessing the requisite knowledge for placing an individual item in an historical setting and assessing its quality relative to other similar items is often called connoisseurship—which is simply a form of scholarship. People sometimes think of taste and judgment as the primary traits of a connoisseur, but those qualities must be integrated with solid learning, and that combination is essential for all sound scholarship.

The only way that "facts" become established is through taste and judgment (which could also be called sensitive and balanced evaluation) applied to evidence. The conclusions reached by this procedure stand as facts so long as qualified investigators are not able to find flaws in the arguments, or equally plausible alternatives, or incompatible new evidence: facts are hypotheses that have not been convincingly refuted. Collectors, in one degree or another, all engage in this process, the same one pursued by scientists, social scientists, and scholars of every kind,

---

9. The quantitative element in expertise is recognized by Stowers Johnson in his autobiography *Collector's World* (1989) when he says, "I have found the very volume of a collection deepens experience and betters discriminatory judgement" (p. 203).

whose search for understanding is a search for order. Artists, too, in their own way, propose visions of order, just as we all do through our physical possessions. If one asks why some people become physicists, and others novelists, and others collectors, in their drive to find patterns, I would reply that the question is not properly phrased, since everyone is a collector. Why some become astronomers and others composers is indeed an interesting question, involving individual temperaments and experiences, but it is on a different level from a question about the sources of collecting. However else one tries to come to terms with the outside world, one assembles objects and lives among them in one's own created environment. Martin Conway put this matter memorably when he said that "upon most of us a necessity seems to be laid . . . to obtain possession of objects, not always beautiful, by which our lives thenceforward are conditioned, and our goings out and comings in suffer a daily fettered freedom" (*The Sport of Collecting* [1914], p. 8). Sometimes one's things are related to one's other efforts (as when an art historian collects paintings), and sometimes they are not. But the accumulating of things is always there, manifesting our fundamental search for understanding and illustrating its essential process, the continued attempt to form comprehensible constructions. We all create installations, whether we call ourselves visual artists or not.

The pursuit of understanding through objects has yet another dimension. Since tangible things have lives as well as origins, they take us back to a number of past times, not merely one.[10] Objects not only stimulate us to discover how they came to exist and what their original function was; they also tease us into probing their subsequent status and adventures. Whatever we can learn about how particular objects were regarded over time furthers our sense of understanding our environment by making us more fully aware of the history that every object embodies. We know the recent histories of our current possessions, having lived through various events with them; and we inevitably associate each item with particular successions of events, recollections of which are triggered by the sight, or the thought, of the object. People also know that their things played similar roles for previous possessors and that all other objects as well have survived unique series of events; the desire to learn these stories is an important manifestation of the need for the ordering power of knowledge.

The connections of collecting with narrative have been explored by

10. As Tibor Fischer understood when he made an antique bowl the narrator of his novel *The Collector Collector* (1997). See also Thatcher Freund, *Objects of Desire: The Lives of Antiques and Those Who Pursue Them* (1993); cf. his "The Tales a Table Could Tell," *New York Times Magazine*, 16 January 1994, pp. 22–27, 38–40, 48, 54, 60.

a number of writers. Roger Cardinal opens his essay on Kurt Schwitters, which links collage-making and collecting, with an elegant expression of collecting as narrative: "In its sequential evolution, the collection encodes an intimate narrative, . . . the continuous thread through which selfhood is sewn into the unfolding fabric of a lifetime's experience."[11] This "intimate narrative" resembles the "narrative of interiority" (p. 158) described by Susan Stewart in "Objects of Desire," a chapter in her *On Longing* (1984). Although Stewart may overstate the extent to which such narratives function "to discredit the present" (p. 139), there is no doubt that she is right to speak of the "capacity of objects to serve as traces of . . . events whose materiality has escaped us" and which can be retrieved "only through the invention of narrative" (p. 135). For Mieke Bal, who sees the urge to bring parts of the outside world into a "subject-domain" as fetishistic, it is "the narrative nature of fetishism" that supplies "a crucial motivation for collecting" (p. 105). Although I do not find fetishism a more fundamental explanation of collecting than the search for order,[12] I do think that Bal's exposition of "the plot of collecting" is useful because of its explicit recognition that objects as well as collectors can be regarded as narrative agents (pp. 110–113)—and thus that the stories collected objects tell may be different from the role they play in the collector's own narrative.

The focus of such discussions is sometimes on collecting as a narrative itself and sometimes on the narratives that people find released by objects. The two naturally shade into each other: all the stories we associate with objects have a significant place in our collecting narratives because they form an important part of our relationship with the tangible world. Benjamin, as he was unpacking his library, recounted some of the episodes certain volumes conjured up, exclaiming "what memories crowd in upon you!" (p. 66). Nancy Hale, in the opening chapter of her classic reminiscence *The Life in the Studio* (1969), movingly lingers over the objects left in her mother's studio, recalling their associations with her mother, filtered through her own encounters with them while her mother was alive. The most extended such act of recollection is perhaps Mario Praz's *La casa della vita* (1958), in which the profuse detail of the stories aroused in him by each object matches the richness of his self-

11. "Collecting and Collage-Making: The Case of Kurt Schwitters," in *The Cultures of Collecting*, ed. John Elsner and Roger Cardinal (1994), pp. 68–96.

12. Indeed, I find the logic of the argument unclear. If fetishism is "the *beginning* of the beginning of collecting seen as narrative" (p. 110) and if "collecting is a story, and everyone needs to tell it" (p. 103), then everyone is a fetishist. But why does Bal define collecting in such a restrictive way as to write, "Yet, it is obvious that not every human being is, or can afford to be, a collector" (p. 103)? Bal's essay, "Telling Objects: A Narrative Perspective on Collecting," appears on pp. 97–115 of the Elsner and Cardinal anthology cited in the preceding note.

created environment. This congruence prepares the reader for Praz's feeling, at the end, that he has himself become one of his collected objects. Such an expression of unity with one's collection is a metaphor for the successful pursuit of understanding, the feeling that one has learned so much about certain objects as to make them no longer seem part of a puzzling realm outside the self. One looks at them with a feeling of mastery and deep comprehension.

III

The four aspects of collecting that I have been describing—the creation of order, a fascination with chance, curiosity about the past, and a desire for understanding—are all subsumed under the urge to tame the external world. This general idea, in which collecting is traced to a human need for making the environment seem less threatening and more understandable, has been much in evidence in the past few decades, as intellectual interest in the process of collecting has increased. The trend is symbolized by the seminal anthology *The Cultures of Collecting* (1994), edited by John Elsner and Roger Cardinal, and by the volumes in Routledge's "The Collecting Cultures Series" (1995–   ), edited by Susan M. Pearce. One can only applaud the growing tendency for cultural critics to address this subject, for—given its fundamental role in human life—it has been remarkably neglected (especially so outside the fields of psychology and object-relations psychoanalysis). But if there is a kind of consensus that collectors create stable controllable environments as a way of coping with the chaos of the so-called objective world and defining themselves in relation to it, there is much debate about the details of the process. I hope I can offer some perspective on the discussion by explaining my disagreements with one or two of the major commentators.

One of the better-known essays on collecting is Jean Baudrillard's "Le système marginal" (in *Le système des objets*, 1968). In the words of Roger Cardinal's fine translation (for *The Cultures of Collecting*), Baudrillard says that objects interpose, "in that space between the irreversible flux of existence and our own selves, a screen that is discontinuous, classifiable, reversible, as repetitive as one could wish, a fringe of the world that remains docile in our physical or mental grip, and thus wards off all anxiety" (p. 15). The act of collecting divests objects of their functions and makes them "participate in a mutual relationship" with their owners: the items in a collection "thereby constitute themselves as a *system,* on the basis of which the subject seeks to piece together his world" (p. 7). These statements, and others like them in the essay, are admirable descriptions of the role of assembled objects in human lives, expressing a general point of view about collecting that one would scarcely wish to quarrel with. But the analysis that supports such generalizations has its flaws. For one thing, Baudrillard asserts, late in the essay, that he has been talking about "collecting proper," which he says is "distinct" from "accumulating"; yet he calls the latter "an inferior stage of collecting" (p. 22), thus placing it in the same realm after all and causing the reader to question whether a focus on only a part of the whole spectrum is the best way to search for the fundamental nature of collecting. It remains unclear whether Baudrillard regards "collecting proper" as an activity engaged in by all human beings, or whether he believes that only some reach that "stage" and others remain stalled at a lower level.

The question of the universality of collecting becomes a basic issue through his negative bias, which seems inappropriate if the activity is indeed universal. His comments on the "collecting impulse" of children and his apparent agreement with the view that "an individual who is not some sort of collector can only be a cretin or hopelessly subhuman" (p. 9) suggests that he thinks of collecting as a natural and universal human activity. But if so, it is hard to see why he treats it as regressive. Much of his discussion deals with collecting "as a powerful mechanism of compensation during critical phases in a person's sexual development," as "a regression to the anal stage" (p. 9), as an "escapist" passion leading to a "neurotic equilibrium" (p. 11) and often to a "sexually perverse pattern of behaviour" in which beauty is jealously savored "in isolation" (p. 18), and as a fetishistic activity, a "discreet variety of sexual perversion" (p. 19). If, however, everyone engages in collecting to support "our very project of survival" (p. 7), why should it not be viewed in a positive light? The thought seems to have crossed Baudrillard's mind at the point where he asks, "can one really speak of normality or anomaly here?" (p. 16). This question has the potential to undermine his whole analysis and is not pursued. Instead, he continues to say that "the intercession of objects . . . allows us, albeit regressively, to live our lives" (p. 17), and he ends with the idea that "he who does collect can never entirely shake off an air of impoverishment and depleted humanity." But the essay fails to show why it is not equally possible to see collecting in a diametrically opposite way, not as evasion and escapism but as a human urge to connect with the world, to make sense of it so that one can feel in harmony with it and experience it more richly.

Another writer on these matters, one of the most prolific and thoughtful commentators on collecting and museum studies, is Susan M. Pearce, whose most ambitious work thus far is *On Collecting: An Investigation into Collecting in the European Tradition* (1995). This book, which treats its subject under the heads of practice, poetics, and politics, is notable for its comprehensiveness, its insistent probing, and its command of the literature of the field.[13] Although it suffers from prolixity, it has its eloquent moments. In the particularly sensitive chapter on "Collecting in Time," for example, Pearce says this of objects: "our ability to manipulate them, . . . and their relationship to the thread of memory which they help to constitute, sustains our sense of ourselves as meaningful people passing through time" (p. 254). Scattered throughout the book are sentences that skillfully capture basic ideas about human attention to the physical world, such as the following two: "Objects embody human purposes and experiences, and they invite us to act towards them in ways which may give us what we desire" (p. 166); "Collections are psychic ordering, of individuality, of public and private relationships, and of time and space" (p. 279). Such statements as these—and the point, made in the second sentence of the book, that collecting is a "fundamentally significant aspect" of our relationship with objects, which in turn is "crucial to our lives"—suggest a definition of collecting broad enough to encompass everyone's accumulations.

It is surprising, therefore, that she seems content with a concept of collecting that excludes two-thirds of the population. She begins her series preface, "Nearly one in every three people in North America collects something" (the "Nearly" even implying that the number seems large). Later in the book she speaks of "a third of us" interacting with objects "in ways which result in what we may agree to call a collection" (p. 174). Her preliminary brief definition hints at a requirement of self-consciously purposive selectivity—"the gathering together and setting aside of selected objects" (p. 3)—though this definition would not have to be interpreted in so exclusive a way. But one of her more detailed definitions does make explicit several restrictive elements: collecting, she states, involves "the deliberate intention to create a group of material perceived by its possessor to be lifted out of the common purposes of daily life and to be appropriate to carry a significant investment of thought and feeling, and so also of time, trouble and resource" (p. 23). If only a minority fits this definition, she is faced with the question why those few "choose this way of defining themselves" (p. 174); and her answer, which brings us "as close as we are likely to get to an understanding of what makes a collector," is, "A combination of circumstance, accident and particular traits of personality" (p. 175). This is one of the most unsatisfactory discussions in the book, for this "explanation" could be

---

13. It reuses some material from a previous book, *Museums, Objects and Collections: A Cultural Study* (1992). (These books, incidentally, contain useful listings of writings about collecting.) For other publications of hers, see notes 14 and 18 below.

said to apply to all human actions—certainly to a great deal besides collecting. At various points Pearce seems to be aware of the inhibiting role of her definition. For example, she is forced to say that an accumulation of souvenirs, which she distinguishes from a true collection, is nevertheless "a kind of collection" (p. 245). And interior decor, which she is quite right to discuss, can be taken up only after she apologetically allows for "reservations in the exact correspondence between 'room furnishings' and 'collections' in any pure mode, a purity which is in many ways unhelpful" (p. 257). At this point she should have abandoned her definition.[14]

These comments on Baudrillard and Pearce can serve to suggest what seems to me a basic defect in much of the writing about collecting: the act of collecting is often seen as an aberration, if not a disorder, affecting some portion (frequently a small one) of the human population.[15] This proposition is one that I believe breaks down the more one thinks about it. The relative number of people engaged in collecting is a significant matter, for it determines whether one can reasonably speak of this behavior as an abnormality. Defining collecting so as to include everyone makes sense if two conditions apply: if, first, one cannot form clear-cut distinctions between categories of gathering and, second, one hopes to arrive at the most fundamental understanding of the activity. These two conditions are naturally related, for if one continually finds that attempted categories overlap one another, one should perhaps conclude that there is a broader concept linking them and that one has not found a helpful way of subdividing it. (What one may have identified are some of the characteristics, not always mutually exclusive, that are combined in varying proportions in individual instances.) I am not concerned with terminology: I do not care whether we use "collecting," "gathering," or "accumulating" as the most comprehensive term, or whether we treat all three as synonyms (as I have done here) or find yet another word. What is important is that any concepts we choose to distinguish by separate terms be logically distinct, so that the terminology is an aid to clear thinking and not in itself a cause of confusion.

As I indicated at the outset, it is hard to see how logical distinctions can be made according to how active or purposive or focused collecting

14. In one of her anthologies, *Interpreting Objects and Collections* (1994), she offers a criticism that applies to her own definition: "Forming a worthwhile definition of what makes a collection, and distinguishing it from other kinds of accumulation, is difficult, not least because all such definitions tend to be self-serving and circular, and so leave out much interesting material for reasons which do not bear much investigation" (p. 157).

15. Pearce does say that collectors are "normal members of the contemporary social and family world" (p. 234); but by regarding only a third of the population as collectors she nevertheless makes collecting, by definition, an abnormal activity.

is, or how many hours, days, or years the assembled objects must be retained, or how utilitarian the reasons for retention are—or any similar
attempts to cut up a continuum. What holds all individual acts of collecting together is simply the grasping or receiving of a physical thing, a part
of the material world, and the subsequent segregating of it, through personal possession, from the rest of that world. And it would seem that the
reason people engage in this activity—the most comprehensive reason,
encompassing the others—is their need to feel in control of some part of
the chaos around them, to feel that there is some order in relation to
which they can define themselves. People in general, not surprisingly,
furnish other reasons. Most often, probably, they say that they acquire
certain objects simply because those objects give them enjoyment, but
in so saying they have not fully analyzed the situation. It may be true that
aesthetic satisfaction—which itself may come from the ordering power of
the artistry—is what draws them to one group of objects rather than another; but the desire to possess the objects, and the pleasure that comes
from such possession, stem from the more inclusive urge to achieve a
measure of dominance over the environment. (One can experience aesthetic enjoyment, after all, without physical possession; and one can enjoy
the possession of objects that do not in themselves give one aesthetic
pleasure.) I am glad to see that this general explanation for collecting is
now widely accepted, in one form or another. But it is of course only an
hypothesis, and its acceptance is not crucial to my main point: collecting
is part of the behavior of every person, and by definition it is therefore
not abnormal.

From that basic point, one can move on to consider what makes individual cases different, why some people seem to become pathological
or obsessive in their collecting, why some are more methodical than
others, or focus on certain kinds of objects, or think about the growth in
monetary value of their possessions, and so on. The infinite variety
of combinations and intensities of motivation, being the product of
those great mysteries circumstance and temperament, cannot be fully
plumbed. But each unique history can be examined, and generalizations
can be framed about the patterns these histories fall into. Studies of both
kinds are regularly produced,[16] but investigations on this level do not
often penetrate to the roots of collecting. There is an underlying ground
that unites the diverse accounts, and the detailed histories and analyses
of collectors and collecting take on different meanings and are more

16. For a comprehensive list of such studies in English relating to book collecting, see my
Introduction to Bibliography: Seminar Syllabus (pp. 20–27 and 49–61 in the latest revision,
1996). An extensive list dealing with art collecting can be found in Frank Herrmann's *The
English as Collectors: A Documentary Chrestomathy* (1972; rev. 1996) and in the accompanying exhibition catalogue published by the National Book League (1972).

satisfying when they emerge from an acceptance of collecting as an elemental ingredient of the human condition.

IV

A similarly broad conception of collecting informs one of the best short essays on the subject, John Elsner and Roger Cardinal's introduction to *The Cultures of Collecting*. Their purview encompasses not only private collectors but also the "appointed collectors" of the "social world," such as garbage collectors, ticket collectors, and tax collectors (p. 2). This kind of gathering must be included within the collecting universe I am discussing, and is not easily separable from the rest of it, for those who collect as public officials also inevitably have other private collections of their own, and the two realms can never be entirely distinct. Collecting undertaken as part of one's occupation (the collecting done by museum and library curators, for example, as well as by certain government employees) is ostensibly shaped by institutional policies; but however different a person's professional and personal collections are (often different as a matter of principle, to avoid a conflict of interest), there are bound to be similarities—in approach if not in type of object— because of the link to the same personality. And institutional policies themselves are the constantly evolving products of individuals, whose private attitudes and collecting practices affect their professional judgments.

Elsner and Cardinal's piece serves to remind us that a rationale of collecting should cover not only the functions of collecting for the individual but also its social uses. One could say, of course, that the private satisfactions are themselves the primary public benefit; for by accommodating a basic human need and making individuals feel more in tune with their environment, collecting contributes some degree of harmony and stability to society at large. Another way that collecting has a social function is its role in a market economy. Russell W. Belk, in a book devoted to this subject (*Collecting in a Consumer Society*, 1995), concludes that collecting (which he treats as a form of consumption) is "a relatively healthy activity that invigorates consumer life with passion and purpose" (p. 158). Although his view of collecting is overly narrow (focusing on "inessential luxury goods" [p. 157]) and his criticisms of museums (as elitist bastions of entrenched materialistic taste) are overstated, he does usefully recognize that individual collectors of independent mind, who are not swayed in their interests by market trends, can eventually influence institutional collecting and public exhibitions. And, one might add, this influence in turn affects market prices, which are a powerful force for preservation.

The role of private collecting in the evolution of museum displays points directly to a more fundamental contribution that collecting makes to public life: it affects the way everyone sees the world. One person's set of possessions, whether glimpsed by a few neighbors or more widely shared in a private or institutional setting, is part of the external chaos faced by other people and thus plays a role in their experience of life. However coherent or formless a group of possessions may appear, it inevitably offers juxtapositions that would not have existed without the collector's intervention in the fates of those objects. Since everyone is a collector, what we are really talking about is one of the ways humanity leaves its mark on the environment. The motivations of those whose marks—in the form of their possessions—are still evident may not be understood, and in any case we may not have the same responses as our predecessors to the groupings they formed; but those configurations are part of the given that we have inherited, influencing our own efforts to make sense of what we see and our own assemblages of objects. Whatever understanding we create for ourselves is different from what it would have been if the material world, including other people's accumulations, had been different. This situation is the basis for what we call the advancement of knowledge. What I see in a group of objects may turn out to be the same as what some earlier viewers (including perhaps the collector) saw there, and it is likely to be something I would not have perceived without that particular conjunction of objects. When people repeatedly find the same patterns, they form the consensus necessary to justify calling what they have found a fact (which of course can only be a provisional classification, subject to refutation). In this way collections advance knowledge.

Preservation is the underlying key to such advances, because without the survival of the items repeated viewings of them could not occur. Even though the meanings of objects derive from their contexts and associations, the objects themselves must exist before they can be studied in a context; and the role of collectors in salvaging things, at least for a while, from the destructive stream of time is the fundamental service they provide to the growth of learning. Objects surviving from the past (ancient or recent) sometimes seem suspended in a puzzling limbo without context, but they are nevertheless *there*, awaiting future observation. In the words of Eilean Hooper-Greenhill, "The radical potential of material culture, of concrete objects, of real things, of primary sources, is the endless possibility of rereading" (the conclusion of *Museums and the Shaping of Knowledge*, 1992). Their survival allows them to be our touchstones to the past, placing us in a line of succession that links all those who have touched the objects from the time of their creation to the present. As Elsner and Cardinal say, there is "a past that lies right here"; and collecting, which preserves that past, is important "because it shuns closure and the security of received evaluations" and focuses our attention on what surrounds us, "in all its unpredictability and contingent complexity" (pp. 5–6). In this spirit, they emphasize the usefulness of collecting "against the grain." This frame of mind is characterized by openness and independence, by a recognition that everything is worthy of being saved, not just those things that are regarded as "collectible" by the fashion of a given moment.[17] No collecting is trivial, on either a personal or a public level, because there is no limit to what may have significance for a given individual or within a given milieu.

In the now thriving field of museum studies (which has produced much of the recent writing about collecting),[18] there has been some debate over the relative value of objects versus the value of the knowledge derived from them. Put another way, the question is whether museums should emphasize the acquisition and display of objects or the creation of contextual educational exhibits in which original objects, if present at all, are subordinated to broader historical recreation and ex-

17. This attitude is exemplified in Ivor Noël Hume's statement, "I find . . . the commonplace of yesterday more evocative than its treasures" (*All the Best Rubbish* [1974], p. 9). (His use of "treasures" of course refers to what has been traditionally sought after and has achieved status in the marketplace; he is not suggesting that the "commonplace" items are not also treasures in a different sense.) A similar point of view pervades Howard Mansfield's *In the Memory House* (1993). Although many kinds of objects are neglected, the range of items that people do collect in a dedicated way is immense, as evidenced by any number of journalistic articles focusing on collections that seem unusual or bizarre. See, for example, Lucie Young, "The Possessed: When Too Much Is Not Enough," New York *Times*, 6 February 1997, pp. C1, C6. (This article, incidentally, cites Russell Belk [see note 5 above] as saying in an interview that the conventional estimate of the number of Americans who collect—one in three—is too low; but there is no suggestion that he thinks the definition underlying the estimate should be changed.) For further examples of the wide variety of items that have been considered "collectible," see John Windsor, "Identity Parades," in *The Cultures of Collecting* (see note 11 above), pp. 49–67.

18. Susan M. Pearce's anthology *Museum Studies in Material Culture* (1989) emerged from a conference celebrating the twenty-first anniversary of the 1966 founding of the Department of Museum Studies at Leicester University. Among Pearce's activities on behalf of this field is her editing of a series called "Leicester Readers in Museum Studies." She also edited a volume, *Objects of Knowledge*, published as Volume 1 of Athlone Press's "New Research in Museum Studies." And the Oxford periodical *Journal of the History of Collections*, founded by Oliver Impey and Arthur MacGregor in 1989, developed from a 1983 conference and the resulting 1985 volume, *The Origins of Museums* (also edited by Impey and MacGregor). The general topic of how knowledge has emerged from the assembly of objects persistently recurs in such books. A good example of a detailed study of this point is Paula Findlen's *Possessing Nature: Museums, Collecting, and Scientific Culture in Early Modern Italy* (1994). A recent symposium entitled "The Meaning of Things," sponsored by the Cooper-Hewitt Museum on 25 April 1998, included a paper by Amy K. Levin on "Museum Collecting and Collecting Museums."

plication. This supposed issue is one of those false dilemmas where the two sides are so interrelated that they cannot be separated. Those who take the side of the objects are of course right in the sense that the objects must come first; but stating one's allegiance to objects in the framework of this debate implies that they can be seen independently of the subjective responses they arouse. One cannot complain about explicitly pedagogical displays on the grounds that they yoke objects to a particular present-day viewpoint, for any selection and arrangement of objects inevitably does the same thing; but one can legitimately disapprove of any extrapolation that implies its own infallibility or self-sufficiency. All collectors (individual or institutional) acquire and place objects in relation to some context, which emerges from a combination of temperament and learning; and their imaginative constructs cause observers (who can also be called the next round of collectors) to have insights, and to form collections, that might not have occurred otherwise. This ineluctable process leads us toward the only kind of truths we can have about the past—for while we can never wholly avoid reading the present into a past object, we can make a conscious effort not to, and unless we proceed in this fashion no knowledge is possible.

The way objects convey knowledge has been made clearer in the past few decades by the development of a field, or an approach, called "material culture study." Although it ought to be obvious that we learn about the past through its physical survival, this point in its broadest implications has been little enough regarded in the past that the recent writers on material culture have often been considered proselytizers for something new and have not infrequently met with resistance. By now there have been a number of useful statements on the subject (as well as studies exemplifying the approach), but even the best of them often exhibit a curious disparity in their treatment of objects that carry verbal texts (like books and manuscripts) and those that do not. For example, the art historian Jules David Prown, in his 1982 essay "Mind in Matter: An Introduction to Material Culture Theory and Method" (*Winterthur Portfolio*, 17: 1–19), almost undercuts his perceptive discussion by asserting near the end that artifacts "tell us something, but facts are transmitted better by verbal documents." He is by no means alone in perpetuating the unexamined assumption, implicit here, that words speak to us more unambiguously and truthfully than visual images do, and thus that "documents" (artifacts transmitting verbal texts) are somehow different, in essence, from other objects. Another instance is Gaynor Kavanagh's statement that "to question whether for historians objects have value as evidence or not is perhaps as crass and vacuous as questioning whether documents have value as evidence." Not only does Kavanagh weaken his argument by distinguishing documents from objects, but he proceeds to give the wrong answer to his question: "The plain fact is," he says, "that some have and some have not."[19] But what material culture study must convey, if it is to elaborate its basic insight coherently, is both a recognition of the value of all physical objects, without exception, and an understanding of the ontological sameness of them all. Printed matter is still matter; and what its words seem to be saying (rarely a certainty in any case) must be interpreted in relation to what the whole object is saying.

For these reasons, book collecting is a particularly instructive example of how the assembly of objects contributes to the growth of knowledge. Many people assume that verbal texts can readily be transferred intact from one object to another; to them, the only reason to collect "books" (physical objects) instead of "works" (texts in any embodiment) is an interest in the crafts of bookmaking and in the printing and publishing industries. Indeed, "book collectors" are often thought of as falling into two categories, those who assemble texts (in any edition) to be read and those who bring together specific editions, not necessarily to be read but to be possessed as objects worthy of attention. The latter group is sometimes ridiculed as not seriously interested in the ideas conveyed by verbal works; but anyone who makes such a criticism can only be a person who has not yet learned that books, being physical objects, are most fruitfully read in the same way that all other objects are "read." The field of analytical bibliography, now about a century and a half old, exists to demonstrate that the physical evidence in books can disclose a great deal about how those books were produced, what effect the production process had on the texts, and how the texts were perceived by those who produced the books and those who read them. Scholars in this field, by studying books as physical objects, contribute to printing and publishing history, to scholarly editing, to the history of reading, to the whole process of placing texts in historical contexts.[20] That the makeup

19. "Objects as Evidence, or Not?", in *Museum Studies in Material Culture*, ed. Susan M. Pearce (1989), pp. 125–137 (quotation from p. 126). For further examples of the debates over material culture and of the difficulties people have had in thinking of texts as objects, see footnote 11 (pp. 275–276) of my "Printing History and Other History," *Studies in Bibliography*, 48 (1995), 269–289.

20. Some introduction to this field can be found in several of my essays, such as "Physical Bibliography in the Twentieth Century," in *Books, Manuscripts, and the History of Medicine: Essays on the Fiftieth Anniversary of the Osler Library*, ed. Philip M. Teigen (1982), pp. 55–79; "The Evolving Role of Bibliography, 1884–1984," in *Books and Prints, Past and Present: Papers Presented at The Grolier Club Centennial Convocation* (1984), pp. 15–31; "Issues in Bibliographical Studies since 1942," in *The Book Encompassed: Studies in Twen-*

and wording of texts are affected by the processes of book-production means that the interpretation of texts can never be divorced from the examination of the objects conveying them. Our reading of verbal works and our knowledge of their origins would be impoverished if we had only current reproductions of texts and were deprived of the great store of books that are physical survivors from earlier times. Book collecting therefore advances knowledge in the same way that the saving of all other objects contributes to our understanding of the past. And this understanding, in turn, affects our life in the present—not only in the sense usually meant by this conventional sentiment but also because those objects are a part of the present.

Nabokov's well-known account of his "obsession" with butterflies and butterfly-collecting—originally published in *The New Yorker* (12 June 1948), it became the sixth chapter of *Speak, Memory* (1966)—provides an eloquent illustration of how the strands discussed here come together in individual lives. Butterflies did serve, for Nabokov, as tangible reminders of episodes in his own life, and even the smell of ether, used as the killing agent for one of his earliest childhood catches, "would always cause the porch of the past to light up" (p. 121). His further encounters with butterflies, his repeated acts of observation and pursuit, made him an expert lepidopterist—one who, indeed, contributed to the field through important published papers. His understanding that collecting and rigorous thinking go hand in hand was shown by his ridicule of those who advocated the relaxing of scientific standards for collectors: "Their solicitude for the 'average collector who should not be made to dissect' is comparable to the way nervous publishers of popular novels pamper the 'average reader'—who should not be made to think" (p. 124). Nabokov of course wrote novels as well as scientific articles, and he saw the connections: "I discovered in nature the nonutilitarian delights that I sought in art" (p. 125). He reserved his most moving words for a description of "the highest enjoyment of timelessness" that came to him when he stood outdoors among "rare butterflies":

This is ecstasy, and behind the ecstasy is something else, which is hard to explain. It is like a momentary vacuum into which rushes all that I love. A sense of oneness with sun and stone. A thrill of gratitude to whom it may concern— to the contrapuntal genius of human fate or to tender ghosts humoring a lucky mortal. (p. 139)

---

tieth-Century Bibliography, ed. Peter Davison (1992), pp. 24–36. A more thorough introduction, not yet published, was provided by my 1997 Sandars Lectures, entitled "Analytical Bibliography: An Historical Introduction." A fairly comprehensive listing of the literature of analytical bibliography is included in my *Introduction to Bibliography: Seminar Syllabus* (pp. 169–198 in the latest revision, 1996).

One can have such an epiphany in nature without being a collector of natural things, but whatever accumulations one does have put one in the frame of mind for creating this private sense of belonging. Nabokov's response to butterflies in the wild was undoubtedly reinforced by his experience of placing them in his collection, just as everyone's constructed settings provide patterns for seeing the world.

For some people, the pleasure of amassing objects is increased by knowing that the activity supports scholarship, science, and art; for others, the satisfactions are entirely personal, but the results are nevertheless of public benefit. Collecting is a prime example of behavior in which private desire and social gain are mutually supportive. This symbiosis is not surprising, since the drive that brings about private assemblages of objects is the same one that impels scientists, artists, and scholars to search for meaning on a level that others can assent to, producing in the process the consensus that is knowledge. The paradox that our search for organization and regularity is conducted with passion and primal energy was brilliantly captured by Wallace Stevens in the phrase "rage for order." The woman he describes (in "The Idea of Order at Key West"), striding along the beach singing, not only creates order for herself through her song but also affects the way her listeners subsequently view their surroundings, causing them to see patterns in the reflections of the fishing-boats' lights, which "Mastered the night and portioned out the sea."

This feeling of mastery, however temporary and provisional, is an emotional necessity, and we all are masters of the collections we surround ourselves with, all artists who create worlds with accumulated objects, whether or not we pursue our visions into the public sphere through display, research, or one of the forms we call "art." What Joseph Cornell did, in shaping his inspired boxes out of that vast assemblage of seemingly heterogeneous objects in his Utopia Parkway house, is symbolic of what many others, often in less direct ways, have made of their object-filled surroundings. For Stevens, the rage for order is a "Blessed rage for order" because this drive alone gives us a glimpse of what it means to be at home, to feel secure, in the universe. The collecting we all do, with its varying repercussions, private and public, is our way of venting that rage, of finding ourselves.

Roberto Ridolfi,
Italian Bibliographical Scholar

by

CONOR FAHY

W HILE MANY ITALIAN SCHOLARS HAVE MADE SUBSTANTIAL contributions in this century to the history of the book, there has only been one great twentieth-century Italian analytical bibliographer, marchese Roberto Ridolfi (1899–1991). Ridolfi was more or less a contemporary of Fredson Bowers (1905–1991) but, though he shared Bowers's versatility and intense concentration on the matter in hand, his personality, interests and life-style were very different, more similar in some ways to the earlier, British, generation of leaders in the development of textual bibliography. Ridolfi came from an ancient Florentine family which had played a prominent part for centuries in Florentine and Italian political and cultural life. Apart from service in the First World War, and a brief period in the 1950s, to which I shall return, when he held an appointment at the University of Florence, Ridolfi was never gainfully employed. He lived the life of a gentleman at the family villa of La Baronta, on the hills to the south of Florence. But, like Greg, who likewise had sufficient private means to make it unnecessary for him to seek employment, Ridolfi filled his life with scholarly endeavour. Florence, its history and its culture were central to, indeed, in some senses, his only interests. In this he was typical of many Italians, whose allegiance to Italy is often less strong, or less apparent, than their attachment to the history, culture and well-being of their own ancient locality.

Ridolfi's only formal experience of higher education was a course in chemistry at the University of Pisa, followed at the insistence of his father, who hoped to exploit some thermal springs on the family's land. This course probably helped Ridolfi more than an Italian university education in letters might have done to appreciate the high level of skill necessary for good quality craftsmanship, and to understand the techniques of type-casting and paper-making. He had, anyway, quite a practical cast of mind. But his vocation was humanistic, not scientific. In an autobiographical volume Ridolfi recounts how as a boy he used to wander in the grounds of La Baronta and on the hillside beyond, reciting aloud verses from his favorite poets.[1] His first passion was for lepidoptery. When this faded with the years (and with the disintegration through neglect and the passage of time of his collection of butterflies and other insects), his interests moved to history. Florentine history, naturally, and specifically, family history, since his first subject of study was the figure of a famous Renaissance ancestor, cardinal Niccolò Ridolfi (1501–1550), diplomat, bibliophile and patron of letters. Even though he never published the biography of Niccolò "in nine chapters, with an appendix of documents," which he wrote after three years of work,[2] the research he undertook for this project was crucial to his future career. It revealed to him the riches which were to be found in the largely uncatalogued and often disastrously housed private archives of the ancient Florentine families, to which his family connections gave him unique access. As he later wrote of those years:

Who can recall for me today the quiet happiness of the hours spent over a bundle of letters written to one of those many-sided Florentines of the fifteenth or sixteenth centuries, at one and the same time aristocrats and men of the people, merchants and statesmen, husbandmen and humanists? As if by magic, unheralded, from amongst the pile of missives from bank officials and farm workers would emerge letters from courtesans, painters, goldsmiths, writers, *condottieri*, envoys, princes. And suddenly I would find in my hand the missing link in an historical puzzle, or new facts about famous events or people: *minutiae*, for the most part, but which, in the excitement of the discovery, seem to the scholar like blinding revelations.[3]

Ridolfi's first major contribution to scholarship, which occupied him during the second half of the twenties and the early thirties, was as a describer and cataloguer of some of these archives. A proposal for the recording and conservation of private Italian archives, published in

1. *Memorie di uno studioso* (Rome, 1956), pp. 24–28.

2. *Memorie*, p. 60. However, an article on the cardinal's outstanding library—one of Ridolfi's earliest publications—appeared in 1929. A select list of Ridolfi's scholarly publications, with special reference to the matters discussed in my text, appears at the end thereof. On Niccolò, see now Lucinda M. C. Byatt, "The Concept of Hospitality in a Cardinal's Household in Renaissance Rome," *Renaissance Studies* 2 (1988), pp. 312–320. Ridolfi was proud of the fact that through Niccolò's mother he was directly descended from the great Lorenzo de' Medici.

3. *Memorie*, pp. 75–76: "Chi potrà ridirmi oggi la quieta felicità delle ore consumate sopra un fascio di lettere scritte a uno dei multiformi fiorentini del Quattro o del Cinquecento, a un tempo nobili e popolani, mercanti e uomini di stato, massai ed umanisti? Ecco uscire dal mazzo, maravigliosamente, fra le responsive dell'agente di banco e del contadino, quelle della 'onesta cortigiana', del pittore, dell'orafo, del letterato, del condottiere, dell'ambasciatore, del principe. E lì ecco luccicare a un tratto l'anello che mancava alla catena di un sillogismo storico; ecco cose ignote sopra fatti e uomini noti: piccole cose per lo più, ma che allo studioso sembrano, nel caldo della scoperta, folgoranti rivelazioni."

1928, attracted the attention of Mussolini, and was even the subject of a leading article in *The Times*.[4] The major publication of this phase of his career, a volume of guides and inventories to the private archives of Florence, appeared in 1934, and Ridolfi had assembled the material for three further volumes. But political events (the publishers, the Florentine house of Olschki, were Jewish friends, and Ridolfi was always courageously outspoken in their defence, making no secret of his opposition to Fascism) prevented the continuation of the series, and the material for the remaining volumes later became a victim of the brief occupation of La Baronta by German paratroopers in 1944.

But Ridolfi's work in the private Florentine archives had already set him on the next stage of his career as an historian, which, as he himself notes, lasted more or less for the rest of his active life. Among the riches he had discovered by chance in the course of his work were important new materials regarding two of the greatest figures of Renaissance Florence. One was the Ferrarese Girolamo Savonarola, prior of the Dominican friary of San Marco from 1491 until his death at the stake in 1498, whose tempestuous career as preacher and prophet in the last two decades of the fifteenth century profoundly affected the political and cultural life of the city. The other was the politician and writer Francesco Guicciardini, formulator and executor for many years of Papal policy in Italy, and one of the creators of modern historiography. The next phase of Ridolfi's activity as an historian was devoted to illustrating the lives, and publishing or republishing the works, of these great figures, to whom he later added the third great Florentine of the period, Niccolò Machiavelli. Of the numerous learned publications to which this historical activity gave rise special mention should be made here of Ridolfi's biographies of this trio, published between 1952 and 1960 in a remarkable burst of activity, given Ridolfi's other commitments at the time. These were translated into English and other languages and brought the fruits of his scholarship before an international reading public.

I have sketched Ridolfi's career as an historian, and in so doing anticipated somewhat the passage of time, because it is significant for an understanding of his activities as a bibliographer. It was his work on Savonarola that first made him enter the domain of analytical bibliography. The friar's fiery preaching and his involvement in the return to a more popular form of republican government after the expulsion of the Medici in 1494 gave rise to a flood of printing in Florence, much of it, including editions of single sermons produced soon after their de-

---

4. *The Times*, 2 Sept. 1929, p. 13: "Archives in Italy and England." Ridolfi describes an interview with Mussolini in *Memorie*, pp. 67–73.

livery, undated and even unsigned. To bring some order into this chaos required the careful and accurate analysis of surviving copies. As had been the case with his archival and historical work, Ridolfi received no training as a bibliographer, but was entirely self-taught. He relied, I think, on the lessons to be learned from the *Catalogue of Books Printed in the XVth Century Now in the British Museum* (1908–   ) and from Konrad Haebler's *Handbuch der Inkunabelkunde* (1925). But more than that, he drew also on his previous experiences as an historian. This is Ridolfi's great strength, and modernity, as a bibliographer. He was never worried by doubts about whether analytical bibliography was a science or an art, never bothered about its place in liberal studies, or its function as a "handmaid" of literature, to use Greg's term.[5] To him, a book, in its materiality, was simply an historical document, and analytical bibliography a branch of historical research. Ridolfi's commitment as an historian also helps us to understand the occasional nature of his bibliographical activities. His major contributions to analytical bibliography were concentrated into a single decade, more or less coinciding with the 1950s. For him analytical bibliography was a research tool to be used when necessary, not a lifelong commitment.

Bibliographical problems, as I have said, first entered Ridolfi's ken when his interest was aroused in the activities and works of Savonarola in the late 1920s and early 1930s. They first surface in his splendid edition of Savonarola's letters (1933) and in his contributions to the first volume of the bibliography of Savonarola's works by his uncle, prince Piero Ginori Conti, published in 1939 (another work never completed, because of the war). But the real stimulus came from his decision in 1944, immediately after the end of hostilities in Tuscany, to accept the invitation of Aldo Olschki, son of Leo S. Olschki, to become editor of the leading Italian bibliographical journal, "La Bibliofilia," founded by Leo in 1899, and published ever since by the family publishing house. His editorship of this journal, which was to last for thirty-eight years, exposed Ridolfi to frequent and regular contact with the world of Italian and European bibliographical scholarship, and encouraged him to think again about the bibliographical problems which he had encountered in his work on Savonarola. As he wrote in a characteristic passage of the *Memorie*:

The editorship of *La Bibliofilia* rekindled in me, not my love of the book, which had never cooled, but my enthusiasm for its study. So, despite my age, I went back to school, but my school, then as always, to use Carlyle's phrase,

5. Walter W. Greg, "What is Bibliography?" *Transactions of the Bibliographical Society* 12 (1914), 39–53; 47.

was a library, and once again the books themselves, even when I was studying their history, were my favourite and most valued teachers. From that time on bibliographical articles began to appear more frequently among my publications. As I proceeded further with my studies, I was intrigued to find confirmation of certain precocious methodological intuitions concerning the study of incunables, which had first occurred to me fifteen years previously, when working on the text of fifteenth-century editions of Savonarola.[6]

The first fruits of this period of study and reflection on bibliographical matters, the article "Proposta di ricerche sulle stampe e sugli stampatori del Quattrocento" ("A Proposal for Research on Fifteenth-Century Printing and Printers"), appeared in *La Bibliofilia* in 1949.

As the title of this article reminds us, Ridolfi's interests as a bibliographer centred on incunables, and on Florentine incunables at that. This is simply the result of his own experiences as an historian, and emphasizes the fact that, however strong his interest in the book, both manuscript and printed, his bibliographical studies were contingent on his historical interests.[7] A further reflection of his personal experiences can be seen in the emphasis placed in this study on the attribution and dating of unsigned editions. The attribution and dating of unsigned incunables constitute, in fact, the context of all Ridolfi's contributions to bibliographical method. But it would be incorrect to say that they also define their limitations, because his methodological proposals are often valid for other periods of hand printing.

Within this context, the purpose of the "Proposta" is to stress the need for a multidisciplinary approach. First of all, he comments, those wishing to date incunables ignore at their peril the evidence offered by the contents of the works in question, which can sometimes provide unequivocal *termini a quo* or *ad quem*. This comment may not seem very original to those coming to bibliography from the study of literature,

---

6. *Memorie*, pp. 178–179: "La direzione de *La Bibliofilia* rinfocolò in me, non l'amore del libro, che mai s'era spento, ma lo studio del libro. A quella età, tornai dunque a scuola, ma la mia scuola, giusta una sentenza del Carlyle, è sempre stata una biblioteca; e ancora una volta, in questo studio della sua storia, il libro fu il mio più caro e ascoltato maestro. Da allora le pubblicazioni bibliologiche cominciano a spesseggiare nella mia bibliografia. Di mano in mano che mi addentravo in quegli studi, mi divertivo nel veder confermarsi certe precoci intuizioni di metodologia incunabulistica avute fin da quando lavoravo da filologo, quindici anni prima, sopra le edizioni savonaroliane del secolo XV."

7. He himself was aware of the fact that the concentration of scholarly work on the incunable period was damaging the study of sixteenth-century Italian printing, and excuses himself in the opening paragraph of the "Proposta" for "carrying coals to Newcastle" ("portar vasi a Samo"). In the course of his career Ridolfi in fact made several contributions to the study of the sixteenth-century book, two of which are recorded in the list at the end of this article, but it remains true that his bibliographical activities and thinking were focused on incunables.

but for bibliographers with other backgrounds its advice is timely.[8]

Another line of enquiry for the bibliographical scholar suggested in the "Proposta" is archival research, particularly in legal archives. Here we see the experience of the great authority on the private archives of Florence. But the comment also reveals the broad view of the historian, who conceives of bibliographical studies not as a series of watertight compartments, but as a continuum involving various activities, which together provide the material for the history of printing, itself a part of the history of the book.

The one specifically bibliographical proposal contained in this article is for a study of the phenomenon of offset ("contrastampa" in Italian). The brief reference to offset in the "Proposta" provoked so much interest that Ridolfi was moved to enlarge his comments in the form of an article wholly on the subject, which appeared in the next number of *La Bibliofilia*. This article constitutes the only attempt to have appeared in Italian, and indeed, as far as I am aware, in any language, to describe the nature of offset and the uses to which it can be put in bibliographical analysis.[9] The article's subtitle, "Nuovi sussidi per l'attribuzione e la datazione dei paleotipi" ("New Aids for the Attribution and Dating of Incunables") reiterates the context of all Ridolfi's bibliographical work. Because of his concentration on attribution and dating, Ridolfi focuses attention on those cases in which the offset comes from a different edition, dismissing as of little bibliographical interest cases where it

8. Even within the context of Anglo-American bibliographical studies, however, the advice to bibliographers to take note of the contents of the editions they are examining can have some relevance; see my review, in *Italian Studies* 33 (1978), 121–123, of Leonardas Vytautas Gerulaitis, *Printing and Publishing in Fifteenth-Century Venice* (Chicago, 1976).

9. Significant occurrences of the phenomenon have of course been noted several times in individual cases by British and American scholars; see, for example, William Merritt Sale, Jr., *Samuel Richardson: A Bibliographical Record of His Literary Career with Historical Notes* (New Haven, 1936), *ad indicem*; J. E. Norton, *A Bibliography of the Works of Edward Gibbon* (London, 1940), Appendix I, II (*The Decline and Fall of the Roman Empire*, first ed., London, 1781; 1821 Leipzig ed.); A. T. Hazen, "The Cancels in Johnson's *Journey, 1775*," *Review of English Studies* 17 (1941), 201–203; Hugh Amory, "*Tom Jones* Plus and Minus: Towards a Practical Text," *Harvard Library Bulletin* 25 (1977), 107–111 (first. ed., London, 1749); Arthur Freeman and Theodore Hoffman, "The Ghost of Coleridge's First Effort: 'A Monody on the Death of Chatterton,'" *The Library* 6th ser., 11 (1989), 328–335 (Chatterton, *Poems*, Cambridge, 1794). The offset referred to in these studies, and by Ridolfi, produces a mirror image on the sheet showing the offset, and is to be distinguished from the results of "set-off" (the offsetting of a still wet copy of the first forme onto the tympan sheet or cloth when printing the reiteration), which, if not attended to, will overprint on subsequent copies of the first forme a faint, un-reversed copy of its text. "Set-off" can also at times be bibliographically illuminating, as was brilliantly demonstrated by Peter Blayney (*The Texts of "King Lear" and their Origins. Volume I: Nicholas Okes and the First Quarto*, Cambridge, 1982, pp. 44–45), who used the presence of a special type of "set-off" to show concurrent printing in the Snowdon shop in 1606.

comes from another page of the same edition. In this judgment, however, he is unduly influenced by his special interests. Offset from pages of the same edition can sometimes offer important evidence of such things as the imposition of preliminary matter, the existence of otherwise unrecorded cancels, and the order of sheets through the press. And, in a footnote to his article, Ridolfi himself uses "internal" offset to excellent purpose, as we shall see.

Ridolfi distinguishes two degrees of offset. The first, "that which more properly deserves the name, occurs when a sheet which has just come off the press, or on which the ink is still fresh, comes into contact with another and is offset on it, even if little or no pressure is exerted," the second, "when a page on which ink is no longer wet, but on the other hand not yet completely dry, leaves an impression on another page with which it is in prolonged and continuous contact, as for example when the sheets are bound together in a volume."[10] Instances of the first degree of offset, Ridolfi continues, are those of most use to bibliographers, since they provide evidence of the simultaneous, or almost simultaneous, printing of the pages concerned; moreover, since the ink is still fresh, the offset impression is usually quite easy to read. Examples of the second degree of offset are much less compelling evidence, because of the longer time-lag between printing and offsetting, which Ridolfi estimates as anything between 48 hours and a month; in any case, they are frequently illegible. The latter is the really telling comment here. "Slow" or "tardy" offset, to use Ridolfi's epithets ("lenta," "tardiva"), provided its source can be identified, can still furnish useful chronological and attributional evidence.

In the second half of the article Ridolfi discusses three cases, two of them illustrated with photographs, in which light is thrown on undated and/or unattributed Florentine incunables by the presence of offset, two being instances of his first degree of offset, and one of "slow" or "tardy" offset. A general point emerges from these cases, one which has been mentioned by Ridolfi earlier in his text. In the small, popular editions of few gatherings in quarto format, which form the subject of these examples, offset from another edition occurs exclusively on the first and last pages of a sheet. Ridolfi reasonably concludes that these sheets were stored already folded. In a long footnote (p. 137, n. 2), de-

---

10. "Incunabuli contrastampati," p. 133: "Di contrastampe bisogna distinguerne anzitutto due specie: la prima, che più propriamente merita questo nome, si ha quando il foglio appena uscito dal torchio, o comunque fresco d'inchiostro, venuto a contatto con un altro, lo contrastampa anche se v'è poco o nulla calcato; l'altra quando l'inchiostro già rasciutto di una pagina, ma non ancora completamente disseccato, ne impressiona un'altra posta a riscontro attraverso un lungo e continuo contatto, come accade quando i fogli sono legati in un volume."

voted to showing that some useful evidence can be offered by "internal" offset, deriving from sheets of the same edition, Ridolfi shows conclusively, from the sequence of offsets on the first and last pages of each gathering, that folded sheets of one rather different edition, the *Prediche di Frate Hieronymo da Ferrara* [Florence: Bartolomeo dei Libri, Lorenzo Morgiani, Francesco Buonaccorsi], ad istanza di ser Lorenzo Vivoli, 8 Feb. 1496/7, a substantial Chancery folio gathered mainly in eights and containing Savonarola's Lenten sermons for 1496, were stored already assembled into copies. This detail may be related to the fact that the edition in question was shared by three printers; nonetheless, it illustrates the sort of unprejudiced reasoning Ridolfi brought to the interpretation of bibliographical evidence.[11]

We come now to the period of Ridolfi's other major contribution to Italian bibliographical studies. This was occasioned by the tenure of a post at the University of Florence, where he taught "bibliologia" (analytical bibliography) from 1953 to 1957. This appointment provided further stimulus for his reflections on the methodology of bibliographical research. During the years 1954 to 1956 some of the material which he had prepared for his lecture courses was published, suitably adapted, in a series of articles in *La Bibliofilia*, under the general title of "Nuovi contributi alla storia della stampa nel secolo XV" ("New Contributions to the History of Printing in the Fifteenth Century"). Naturally, the printing in question was Florentine; the articles were later gathered and published, with some additional material, in the volume *La stampa in Firenze nel secolo XV* ("Printing in Florence in the Fifteenth Century"). These articles are notable for the gradual development of what was to become fully fledged only in his little book of 1957, *Le filigrane dei paleotipi* ("The Watermarks of Incunables"), namely, an understanding of the way in which the dating and attribution of incunables can be assisted by paper study. In the "Proposta" of 1949 there is no reference at all to watermarks. Obviously, when writing that article Ridolfi had not yet realised their potential in bibliographical analysis. This was partly due, as he himself explains in *Le filigrane dei paleotipi* (pp. 11–12), to

11. For this edition see Goff S-243; BMC VI pp. 675–676. Ridolfi's work on offset has received further confirmation recently by the discovery in the Bibliothèque Nationale, Paris, reported to a congress at Udine (February 1997) by Edoardo Barbieri from the Università Cattolica, Milan, of a copy of a hitherto unrecorded Florentine incunable (Niccolò Cicerchia, *La passione di Gesù Christo*, [Florence, Lorenzo Morgiani and Johann Petri, 1492]), the existence of which had been postulated by Ridolfi nearly fifty years earlier in "Incunabuli contrastampati," pp. 139–141 (though with a different printer and date), on the basis of an offset in his copy of an edition of Savonarola's *Trattato della orazione*; see also, for the correct printer and date, the third of Ridolfi's "Giunte e correzioni al *Gesamtkatalog der Wiegendrucke*," *La Bibliofilia* 61 (1959), 233–242; 235.

the influence of Konrad Haebler, who in his *Handbuch der Inkunabel-kunde* had expressed substantial scepticism about their usefulness as bibliographical evidence.[12] It is typical of Ridolfi's confident and independent approach to bibliographical analysis that he soon realised this scepticism was unfounded, or at least not justified in the particular cases he was considering. For the vast majority of Florentine incunables had been printed on paper made in the mills at the small centre of Colle di Valdelsa, about 25 miles south of Florence, and something was already known about paper manufactured at Colle; indeed, in the 1950s, when Ridolfi was working on watermarks, some of the old mill structures still existed. Ridolfi did not, like Allan Stevenson at Basel in 1961, climb into the drying lofts of these old mills and commune with the pigeons, but he did use the studies already published, imperfect though they were, on the history of the paper industry at Colle and on the watermarks they contained, and this information, powerfully supplemented by his own observations, enabled him to forge what for Italian bibliographers, and for almost every other bibliographical scholar living at that time, was a new instrument of research.[13]

Ridolfi's developing understanding of the bibliographical use of paper study can be followed in two of the "Nuovi contributi." The first, "Lo *Stampatore del Mesue* e l'introduzione della stampa in Firenze" ("The *Printer of Mesue* and the Introduction of Printing in Florence"), was devoted to a theme dear to Ridolfi's Florentine heart, namely that "printing was not brought to Florence . . . by the 'printer of Mesue,' one of those many foreign printers who introduced the art to almost every other Italian city, but had in reality been 're-invented' by a Florentine goldsmith, Bernardo Cennini."[14] Among the evidence used to demonstrate this thesis, watermarks did not provide the most significant nor,

12. Konrad Haebler, *Handbuch der Inkunabelkunde* (Leipzig, 1925), p. 38.

13. The studies on the Colle paper industry available to Ridolfi, all published around the turn of the century, can now be consulted in *Carta e cartiere a Colle: Miscellanea di Studi raccolti a cura del Comitato Scientifico per l'allestimento del Museo* (Florence, 1982). For Stevenson and the pigeons, see Paul Needham, "Allan H. Stevenson and the Bibliographical Uses of Paper," *Studies in Bibliography* 47 (1994), 23–64; 63.

14. ". . . la stampa non fu portata a Firenze . . . da uno dei soliti stampatori foresti che la portarono in quasi tutte le città d'Italia, lo 'Stampatore del Mesue', ma veramente era stata 'rinventata' da un orefice fiorentino, Bernardo Cennini." The quotation comes from one of Ridolfi's last pieces of writing, his preface to Dennis E. Rhodes, *Gli annali tipografici fiorentini del XV secolo* (Florence, 1988), "the book which I, a specialist in the subject, would most have liked to have offered to fellow specialists," he adds, not without a touch of sadness. In the same preface, Ridolfi records his satisfaction at having noted, in the facsmile reprint of the *Catalogue of Books Printed in the XVth Century Now in the British Museum* (London, 1962–67), a manuscript addition (VII, p. xxxix) in the hand of Victor Scholderer, recording acceptance of the arguments put forward by Ridolfi in his 1954 article identifying the printer of Mesue with Lorenzo Canozzi of Lendinara, printer at Padua.

to tell the truth, the most convincing proofs, but we can already see in his comments on the watermark evidence the first steps along the path of understanding which would take Ridolfi, with his usual rapidity, in a couple of years to a more or less complete grasp of the possibilities of paper study for bibliographical research.

In the first place, Ridolfi, while fully acknowledging the importance of Briquet's magisterial collection of watermark tracings, quickly realised its inadequacies for bibliographical work. He also fully understood the reasons: Briquet's vast repertory was based overwhelmingly on the watermarks found in archival documents, not books; and his use of tracings made the representations of watermarks in his manual too approximate. Ridolfi from the very first used only photographs as illustrations of the watermarks he was discussing. Unfortunately, he said nothing at all in any of his relevant works about the methods used to obtain his sometimes excellent and always serviceable results.[15] To return to his article on the printer of Mesue, what is even more interesting is to see, in a long note on p. 8 of the study, the beginnings of an explicit understanding of what is only implied in his criticism of Briquet's tracings as too approximate, namely, the presence and significance of small differences in watermarks, an understanding which is the beginning of wisdom in paper research. In this note Ridolfi writes:

Even among specialists and bibliographers, it is less well known than it should be that in the fifteenth century the watermarks used by the same mill for the same quality of paper and at the same time could not possess that perfect uniformity which they would have had in our mechanical age; usually they differ from mould to mould in small details. Such differences are not to be regarded as variants denoting diversity of place or time.[16]

15. Some of the reproductions of watermarks in quarto volumes show so complete an image that one feels the copies must have been unbound when photographed. In some cases this was probably because they belonged to Ridolfi. A check in his private library, now in the possession of a Florentine bank, the Cassa di Risparmio di Firenze, shows that he owned copies of all but one of the relevant quartos. Three of the six volumes in question were rebound while in Ridolfi's possession. A fourth volume does not have the monogrammed leather binding of these volumes, but does appear to have been taken out of its vellum binding in modern times and then reinserted. As for the others, a Florentine colleague informs me that Ridolfi was in the habit of making occasional requests to local librarians, which they found it hard to refuse because of the prestige of his name, to remove specific copies of their rare books from their bindings for his inspection; the volumes would then be rebound at his expense.

16. "Nuovi contributi. I," p. 8, n. 2: "Anche presso gli specialisti e i bibliologi, è meno noto di quanto sarebbe desiderabile che nel sec. XV le marche usate dalla stessa cartiera per la stessa qualità di carta e nello stesso tempo non potevano avere quella perfetta uniformità che avrebbero nella nostra età meccanica e che per lo più esse differiscono da forma a forma in piccoli particolari; né queste possono qualificarsi varianti denotanti diversità di luogo o di tempo."

Ridolfi was obviously very close, when he wrote these words, to realising that watermarks are twins; indeed, when he came to prepare this article for inclusion in the 1958 volume *La stampa in Firenze nel secolo XV*, he re-wrote the note to give explicit expression to the concept (without, there or anywhere else, resorting to the metaphor made famous by Allan Stevenson in his article of 1951).[17]

A further step forward is evident in the third of the "Nuovi contributi," "G.W.3851: Antonio Miscomini, non Compagnia del Drago," published in *La Bibliofilia* in 1955. With this article we are back on familiar territory, the dating of incunables *sine notis*. The subject of this third "contributo" is the *Novella di Tancredi principe di Salerno* by the Florentine Girolamo Benivieni (1453–1542), attributed in the *Gesamtkatalog der Wiegendrucke* (III, p. 630) to the Compagnia del Drago at Florence, and dated c. 1497/8. For the identification of the true printer, Antonio Miscomini, Ridolfi relied on typographical evidence; for a preliminary dating, which allowed him to place publication of the edition in the 1480s, he turned to considerations of content. But for a precise dating it was on paper evidence that he relied:

> The paper used in the two gatherings of five leaves which constitute the edition has a single watermark, depicting two crossed hammers inscribed in a circle. Now from my systematic studies of the marks used in the fifteenth century in the Tuscan paper mills I know that the mark in question was in use in the years 1485–1489, but disappeared completely thereafter, being replaced in the same mill in the second half of 1489 by another mark with crossed hammers, but this time inscribed in a mixtilinear figure (approximately reproduced in Briquet, n. 11637; see here fig. 6). But there is more.
>
> If you observe the mark carefully in its first form, you will notice that during the five-year period of its use it underwent some changes, because of the renewal of the moulds, and that the mark which appears in the *Novella* paper belongs to the earliest type, used in the years 1485–86.[18]

Those readers interested in the workings of coincidence will not fail to have noticed that Ridolfi must have been looking at the Colle di Valdelsa crossed hammers in Florentine incunables, and realising the significance

---

17. *La stampa in Firenze*, p. 36, n. 2; and see Allan H. Stevenson, "Watermarks are Twins," *SB* 4 (1951–52), 57–91.

18. "Nuovi contributi. III," 9: "La carta usata nei due quinterni di cui si compone l'edizione ha un'unica filigrana, raffigurante due martelli incrociati e chiusi in un circolo. Ora dai miei studi sistematici intorno ai segni usati nel secolo XV dalle cartiere toscane, risulta che la marca suddetta, in uso negli anni 1485–1489, scompare del tutto dopo questo ultimo anno; nella seconda metà del quale è dalla stessa officina sostituita con quella dei due martelli similmente incrociati ma in una formella mistilinea (approssimativamente riprodotta dal Briquet, n. 11637; vedi qui la fig. 6). C'è anche di più.

"Osservando minutamente la marca nel suo primo stato, si vede che durante il quinquennio suddetto subì qualche mutamento, col rinnovo delle forme e che quella della *Novella* appartiene al primo tipo, usato nel 1485–86."

of their "slight changes" for his research, at more or less the same time that Allan Stevenson, in the Pierpont Morgan and other American libraries, was becoming familiar with the ebb and flow of the Basel bull's head and cross-on-mounts watermarks, which were to form the basis of his dazzling demonstration of the date and place of printing of the *Missale speciale*.[19] While postponing to a later stage a comparison between the two scholars, let me assuage curiosity by saying now that there is no evidence of contact between them; indeed, it seems that in their activity as paper scholars they were totally unaware of each other's existence.[20]

To return to the passage quoted above, it is clear that in consequence of his observations of watermarks in Florentine incunables, Ridolfi had succeeded in imposing a certain order on what seemed, when he was working on the first "contributo," a confusing succession of marks having more or less the same motif. This step forward resulted from his having carried out "systematic studies" of the Tuscan watermarks in Florentine incunables, as a result of which he had been able to form his own watermark catalogue, limited in scope to local marks, but much more relevant than anything he could get from Briquet. With this material, he had come to realise that when a couple of moulds became worn out with use, the papermakers of Colle would replace them with another pair in which the same watermark motif was used, but sufficiently differentiated to enable the paper made with this particular pair of moulds to be identified. Thus, the proliferation of similar but not identical marks, which had led Haebler and others to reject the study

19. Stevenson's study of these two watermark types occupied more or less the whole of 1954, from February, "when the news broke that the Pierpont Morgan Library had acquired a copy of the 'Constance Missal,'" to December 30, when "I kept my tryst with Constance" in the Pierpont Morgan Library. "Within twenty minutes—or was it half an hour?" Stevenson adds, "I knew beyond peradventure that some of the paper in the *Missale speciale* was the same as the main paper in the Henricus Ariminensis" (*De quattuor virtutibus cardinalibus* [Strasbourg, c. 1473/4]; see Allan Stevenson, *The Problem of the Missale Speciale*, London, 1967, pp. 28–31).

20. Ridolfi's *Le filigrane dei paleotipi* is listed in the Bibliography of the 1968 edition of Briquet's *Les filigranes*, edited by Stevenson (Charles Moise Briquet, *Les filigranes: dictionnaire historique des marques du papier dès leur apparition vers 1282 jusqu'en 1600: A Facsimile of the 1907 Edition with Supplementary Material Contributed by a Number of Scholars*, edited by Allan Stevenson, Amsterdam, 1968, 4 vol.), but it is not clear whether this Bibliography was compiled by Stevenson. In any case, Ridolfi's book probably owes its inclusion here to the review by Victor Scholderer published in *The Library* in 1958 (see below, and note 36). More to the point is the fact that there is no mention of Ridolfi in the pages (xxviii–xxix) in which Stevenson talks about Italy and Italian paper historians in his article "Briquet and the Future of Paper Studies," prefaced to Charles Moise Briquet, *Briquet's Opuscula: The Complete Works of Dr C. M. Briquet without "Les filigranes"* (Hilversum, 1955). It may be significant that the works of all the scholars mentioned in this section of Stevenson's article had been published, like the two volumes mentioned above, by the Paper Publications Society. I have not come across the name of Stevenson in any of Ridolfi's works, nor was *The Problem of the Missale Speciale* ever reviewed in *La Bibliofilia*.

of watermarks as a tool for bibliographical research, turned out to be the very feature which made them useful.

Ridolfi's mature thinking on watermark evidence is contained in the little booklet of 1957, *Le filigrane dei paleotipi*. Here he gathered the more or less scattered observations of the "Nuovi contributi" into a coherent exposition. He begins by stating that what makes watermark evidence a valid tool in the dating of unsigned editions is the fact that incunable printers did not keep large stocks of paper, but bought (or were given by those commissioning their work) the quantity of paper necessary for the printing of each book, or group of books. This understanding is a fundamental step forward. As usual, Ridolfi gives no indication of the source of his insight; we must assume that it is the result of his own observations, both of the paper supply in the books themselves (they were, after all, his main teachers, as he himself says), and of the few documentary sources available to him, such as the diary of the printing establishment in the Dominican convent of S. Jacopo at Ripoli, on the outskirts of Florence.[21] As he puts it:

> However, in comparison with manuscripts, the printing of books entailed a far greater consumption of paper and continual purchases by the printers. But, in order to avoid the inconvenience and risk of warehousing this paper themselves, and more particularly, the consequent unproductive immobilization of capital, always in short supply in the fifteenth-century printing industry, they habitually bought from the mills only that quantity of paper which was strictly necessary for the printing of the books which were on the press at any time. Indeed, as we learn from documentary sources and from the examination of the paper in these books, often they bought this paper in several lots, especially if they were printing a substantial work.[22]

From these considerations Ridolfi deduces the following principle: "one can be absolutely sure that the paper used in an edition is more or less contemporary with the date printed at the end of that edition."[23]

21. See Emilio Nesi, *Il diario della stamperia di Ripoli* (Florence, 1903). Recent discussions of this press and its documents include Susan Noakes, "The Development of the Book Market in Late Quattrocento Italy: Printers' Failures and the Role of the Middleman," *Journal of Mediaeval and Renaissance Studies* 11 (1981), 23–55, and Melissa C. Flannery, "San Jacopo di Ripoli Imprints at Yale," *Yale University Library Gazette* 63 (1988–89), 115–131.

22. *Le filigrane dei paleotipi*, pp. 13–14: "La stampa dei libri richiedeva invece, a comparazione dei manoscritti, un consumo di carta enormemente maggiore e continui acquisti da parte degli stampatori; i quali, per evitare l'ingombro e i rischi della giacenza in un magazzino, ma molto più per fuggire l'inutile ristagno, o come oggi si dice, l'immobilizzazione dei capitali, dei quali essi nel secolo XV sempre patirono penuria, usavano comprare dalle cartiere volta per volta la quantità strettamente necessaria alla stampa dei libri che avevano sotto torchio: anzi, più spesso, come si apprende da documenti di archivio e dall'esame della carta medesima, soltanto per una parte di tale fabbisogno, specie se si trattava di un'opera piuttosto voluminosa."

23. *Le filigrane*, p. 14: "si ha l'assoluta certezza che la carta usata in una edizione è pressoché sincrona alla data segnata in calce a quella edizione."

Here, however, in attempting to distance himself from the calculations of Briquet, which are based on the far slower consumption of paper in the manuscript period, Ridolfi has exaggerated, or better, has drawn too sweeping a conclusion from the material with which he was familiar, that is, mainly popular editions comprising few sheets, and produced by local printers. His principle is frequently violated, most obviously in the case of editions whose printing for some reason or another is protracted over a period of years, and for which some of the paper has been bought before printing began. In addition, possibly because many of the editions he was dealing with were relatively small, Ridolfi makes no explicit distinction between runs of paper with the same watermark, which are likely to belong to a single purchase of paper, and single sheets with other watermarks, which are likely to be the remains of purchases made on other occasions, and thus not necessarily "more or less contemporary with the date printed at the end of that edition."[24] Indeed, his principle has to be applied with care even in the cases he had in mind; in this context, it would be interesting to re-examine the specific instances of dating by paper evidence brought forward in his publications of the 1950s, to see if they stand up to a more sophisticated analysis. It is perhaps significant that Stevenson, who probably knew more than Ridolfi about the practices of the Renaissance paper industry, was more cautious in his claims regarding the contemporaneity of paper manufacture and paper use, declaring that stocks of paper used in printing were "ordinarily . . . secured within one, two, or three years after manufacture. . . ."[25] Nonetheless, Ridolfi's principle shows that he was fully aware of the main fact of life concerning paper supply in early printing, namely, that printers and publishers normally could not af-

24. For example, his principle does not apply to the printing at Verona in the period 1619–22 of a large folio volume of nearly 800 pages, the *Musaeum Francisci Calceolarii*, for which the Veronese apothecary Francesco Calzolari Jr., who commissioned the volume, bought the paper required in four successive lots from two papermakers of S. Martino Buonalbergo, centre of the Veronese papermaking industry, beginning in January 1619. But before the second lot, purchased between 29 March and 3 June 1619, had been used up, printing was interrupted for fifteen months, because of the death of the author. When it was resumed, in autumn 1621, the remaining part of the second lot was used first, two years after its purchase, before the third and fourth lots were bought in 1621 and 1622. The volume was published at the very end of 1622. The papers involved can readily be identified by their watermarks, and comprise three major runs, involving $185\frac{1}{2}$ of the $199\frac{1}{2}$ sheets which make up the volume. But in the remaining 14 sheets we find a mixture of several watermarks, which are doubtless remnants of paper stocks which the printer had accumulated from other jobs; see *Printing a Book at Verona in 1622: The Account Book of Francesco Calzolari Junior*, ed. Conor Fahy (Paris, 1993), pp. 51–52. For the concept of runs and remnants see above all Stevenson, *The Problem of the Missale Speciale*, Chap. VI, "Runs and Remnants," pp. 71–99; 94–95.

25. Stevenson, *The Problem*, p. 94. However, for a significant enlarging by Ridolfi of the time interval to be assumed for paper evidence see below.

ford to lay in stocks of paper against potential future consumption, but bought or were supplied with paper for specific jobs, as and when required.

It is natural, given Ridolfi's interests, that he should immediately draw a corollary from his principle, which is "that an edition *sine anno* is to be assigned to the same period as a dated edition in which an identical watermark can be observed."[26] This leads him to the central point of his exposition, an explanation of the reasons for, and the modes of, the similarities and differences between watermarks of the same motif and design:

It is well known that in the fifteenth century, as in the centuries before and after, in every paper-mill the vats containing pulp were provided with at least two moulds, each with its network of wire threads, the horizontal ones (wire lines) thin and very close together, the vertical ones (chain lines) somewhat thicker and much further apart; on one side, usually positioned so that the watermark ended up exactly in the middle of one half of the sheet, was the mark, also made of wire thread, which left an imprint (the watermark) on the paper, visible when held up to the light because the wire of the mark made the paper thinner. The design of the mark was normally identical in each mould of the pair, in so far as the manual nature of the operation and the quality of the material used permitted. If they wanted to employ the same symbol or sign for another pair of moulds, to be used at another vat, paper manufacturers usually took care to distinguish the new mark by some detail of the design or by its size. . . .

When, after a period which varied from one to two years, a pair of moulds needed to be renewed, in the new pair the same symbol or sign would be used, but with some difference in design or size, or with the addition of some particular design detail.[27]

26. *Le filigrane*, p. 14: "Ne consegue il corollario che un'edizione *sine anno* è da assegnare allo stesso tempo di un'altra datata, nella quale si osservi un'identica filigrana."

27. *Le filigrane*, pp. 22–23: "È ben noto che nel secolo XV, come del resto nei precedenti e nei seguenti, a corredo di ciascun tino di pasta ogni cartiera aveva almeno due forme con il loro traliccio di fili metallici, fittissimi e sottili gli orizzontali (vergelle), più o meno distanti e un po' maggioretti i verticali (filoni); da una parte, per lo più in modo che venisse a trovarsi nel giusto mezzo di una delle metà del foglio piegato in due, era fissato il marchio, anch'esso di filo metallico, che doveva lasciare sulla carta la sua impronta (cioè appunto la filigrana) visibile in trasparenza per il minore spessore del foglio corrispondente al rilievo del marchio. Il disegno del quale era generalmente identico in entrambe le forme della coppia, per quanto lo permetteva l'esecuzione manuale e la qualità della materia adoperata; mentre quando si voleva usare per un'altra coppia di forme, addette ad un altro tino, lo stesso simbolo o segno, si aveva assai spesso cura di differenziarlo in qualche particolarità del disegno o nelle dimensioni. . . .

"Quando la coppia di forme in uso veniva sostituita, dopo uno spazio di tempo variabile da uno a due anni, nella nuova coppia di forme si ripeteva lo stesso simbolo o segno, ma con un disegno alquanto diverso o di diversa misura, o con l'aggiunta di qualche segno particolare."

This is Ridolfi's most mature expression of his understanding of watermark diversity. He describes three sources of differentiation in watermarks having the same motif: 1) watermarks are twins, because the moulds used in their manufacture are twins, but they are dissimilar, not identical, ones; 2) a watermark with the same motif can be used in the moulds of another vat, but it will be distinguished "by some detail of the design or by its size;" 3) when worn-out moulds are replaced, the mark will be repeated, "but with some difference in design or size, or with the addition of some particular design detail." There is also a fourth source of differentiation, previously mentioned by Ridolfi, and it is far from being the least important for his method; this is "the deformations produced by usage in the delicate design of wire thread," from which it follows that "even the images produced by the same mould vary in the course of time in ways which are more or less visible."[28] In other words, a watermark decays in the course of its relatively short life, it presents itself to the bibliographer in a series of successive states, which offer him another element capable of establishing a chronological succession. This sequence of states of the same watermark is all the more precious in that in practice it is often difficult to distinguish between Ridolfi's second and third type of differentiation. Indeed, it can sometimes be difficult to distinguish, on the basis of design alone, between all three types of differentiation, as twins can differ quite substantially in size. The fact is that the only sure way of identifying twins is to find them in a substantial run of paper.

Ridolfi has now arrived at his conclusion:

> ... it is obvious that, because they were hand-made, watermarks with the same motif were always likely to contain small differences of design; new marks, with new motifs, appeared only when the mill increased its capacity by acquiring further vats, or changed hands. This said, it is equally obvious that two sheets of paper whose watermarks are identical down to the smallest detail were manufactured in the same mill, at the same vat, in the same mould, in a period of time which in no case exceeds two years. Even if one takes the maximum time-span, this is already a very satisfactory approximation. However, the time-span can be reduced further in the case of watermarks which are deformed, or have breaks, or show the effects of wear. On occasions I have been able to reduce it to as little as a few months.

It is clear, then, that by examining dated or clearly datable editions and recording the succession of watermarks and the process, where it exists, of their distortion, one can give a date to editions *sine anno*.[29]

28. *Le filigrane*, pp. 19, 22: "... le deformazioni prodotte dall'uso nel tenue disegno di duttile filo"; "... perfino le impronte prodotte dalla medesima forma variano col tempo più o meno visibilmente. ..."

29. *Le filigrane*, p. 24: "... è ovvio che, sempre a causa della esecuzione manuale, pic-

Quod erat demonstrandum. Ridolfi concludes the first part of his booklet, which constitutes undoubtedly the most acute contribution to analytical bibliography made by an Italian scholar, with a proposal, speedily dubbed utopistic by colleagues (as indeed it was, at the time), for the compilation of a general catalogue of incunable watermarks, preferably photographic, organized by place of printing, and based on the examination, not just of every edition, but of all the accessible copies of every edition. The second part of *Le filigrane* comprises a discussion of one particular mark, a Greek cross in a circle, which was used in a mill at Colle di Valdelsa for the last twenty-five years of the fifteenth century (the dates come from the inspection by Ridolfi of printed editions, but the identification of the place of origin of the mark is derived, characteristically, from a document). Ridolfi charts the successive differences in the mark, of which he claims to have identified about fifty versions, deriving from at least twenty-four pairs of moulds, and adds: "Among these versions, those observed in dated editions, or in editions which can be confidently dated, allow us to date all the editions *sine anno* in which the marks occur."[30] The booklet ends with a "little catalogue" of editions containing this mark, followed by a series of twenty-three photographs, illustrating thirty-eight marks.

The name of Allan Stevenson has already occurred several times in these pages. It is clear that in their work on paper research he and Ridolfi arrived more or less simultaneously at exactly the same conclusions about the usefulness of watermark evidence for dating editions *sine anno*; yet each seems to have been completely unaware of the other's existence.[31] The different life-styles and *formae mentis* of the renowned Florentine aristocrat and scholar, and the more-or-less failed American college professor, hit the eye.[32] When one comes to compare their works,

cole diversità di disegno sarebbero state inevitabili: segni affatto nuovi, con nuovi simboli, s'introducevano soltanto se la cartiera si arricchiva di nuovi tini o se passava in altre mani. Ciò posto, è parimente ovvio che due fogli di carta aventi marche identiche in ogni minimo particolare sono uscite dalla stessa cartiera, dallo stesso tino, dalla stessa forma, in un periodo di tempo mai superiore a due anni. Così, se pur si prende il massimo periodo di durata, l'approssimazione sarebbe già molto soddisfacente. Tale approssimazione può essere però ulteriormente ridotta in caso di deformazioni o di rotture e anche per le piccole alterazioni prodotte dall'uso. Talvolta ho potuto ristringerla a qualche mese soltanto.

"È manifesto, dunque, che seguendo, attraverso lo spoglio di tutte le edizioni datate o sicuramente databili, la successione e le eventuali deformazioni dei marchi si potranno datare le edizioni *sine anno*."

30. *Le filigrane*, p. 33: "Tra le dette varietà, quelle osservate in edizioni datate o sicuramente databili, ci permettono di datare tutte le edizioni senza anno nelle quali ricorrono."

31. See above, note 20.

32. For information on Stevenson's life and works, see Paul Needham's splendid article cited above, note 13.

however, the advantage clearly lies with the less obviously successful and gifted Stevenson. For Ridolfi, analytical bibliography was one among many scholarly interests, pursued with great flair, but also with an aristocratic *sprezzatura*, straight out of Castiglione's *Book of the Courtier*, which led him to be brief in his exposition, and reticent about the techniques and methods employed. It is also true that in Ridolfi's work these techniques and methods, including paper research, were means to an end, not ends in themselves. Perhaps in different circumstances he would have developed further his brilliant deductions about the way offset and watermark evidence can assist the bibliographical scholar, and would have given the same penetrating attention to other aspects of bibliographical analysis; but, as we shall see, fate conspired to place obstacles in his way, and after his brief experience as a teacher of analytical bibliography, he turned back to his historical studies. His edition of Machiavelli's *Mandragola*, published in 1965, was based on a recently discovered manuscript, not on the printed editions; Ridolfi's discussions of these editions, and the other bibliographical articles he published in the 1960s, contain no new insights into the methodology of bibliographical research. Stevenson was more limited in his scholarly interests than Ridolfi, but also more single-minded. He devoted all his intellectual energies to paper research, and wanted nothing more than to pass on his knowledge to his readers. The point comes over forcefully when we compare the 400 pages of *The Problem of the Missale Speciale* with the 45 pages of Ridolfi's little work. Stevenson is incomparably more informative than Ridolfi, both on paper research and on paper production. In *The Problem of the Missale Speciale*, as well as a long discussion of the likely time-span between the date of paper manufacture and of its use in printed books, and a description of how watermarks are made, we have a series of practical and useful pieces of advice for the bibliographer, about such things as the vital distinction between runs and remnants, the existence of sewing dots (those invaluable aids to distinguishing incunable watermarks), the practice of placing twin watermarks in opposite halves of the mould (certainly a feature of Venetian paper in the Renaissance, as Stevenson knew it to be of Basel paper), and the gradual sideways movement of marks in the mould, if not attached to a chain-line. None of this information can be obtained from Ridolfi's contributions, which, for all their brilliance, are disappointingly silent, perhaps deliberately, about techniques and methods. Stevenson, on the other hand, does his best to tell all. For anyone wanting to learn how to begin and how to prosper as a paper scholar, Stevenson is the man.

No-one has yet written the history of Ridolfi's course at the University of Florence. Even the dates are uncertain. According to Maria Jole Minicucci, it ran from 1953 to 1957, but one who had been a student in the first year of the course recently put its start as 1952. It was never well attended. Indeed, in one year there was only a single student.[33] Perhaps this was the reason, or one of the reasons, why in 1957 the post held by Ridolfi was abolished. With it went the Centro per lo Studio dei Paleotipi ("Centre for the Study of Incunables"), which Ridolfi had set up in the university, and of which his booklet, *Le filigrane dei paleotipi*, was the first and only publication. A few years later, in 1963, Ridolfi refounded the Centre in the Biblioteca Nazionale, Florence, with Maria Jole Minicucci, a member of the library staff, as collaborator, but its activities were cut short, this time for good, by the disastrous flood of November 1966, which seriously affected the library buildings. The only one of its projects to survive this final setback was a typewritten index, compiled by Minicucci, to the 2460 illustrations of type published between 1907 and 1939 by the Gesellschaft für Typenkunde des XV Jahrhunderts in parallel with Konrad Haebler's *Typenrepertorium der Wiegendrucke* (Halle 1905–24). This index, which integrates and corrects the previous partial indexes of Madsen and Juchhoff, has been deposited with Ridolfi's library in premises belonging to the Cassa di Risparmio di Firenze.[34]

The termination of his appointment at the University of Florence and the subsequent vicissitudes of the Centre for the Study of Incunables more or less put an end to Ridolfi's activities as an analytical bibliographer. If man had not done so, nature would soon have stepped in, because as he advanced in years, Ridolfi's eyesight began to fail; by the time of his death he was completely blind. In his lifetime his remarkable if limited contribution to analytical bibliography was little understood in Italy, where until recently this particular branch of the discipline of book history has not been much cultivated.[35] The originality of

33. His name was Roberto Abbondanza. Ridolfi himself records how the *bidello* (janitor), with a typically Florentine play on the student's surname, would open the door of the lecture room each week and introduce the lone student with the announcement: "Di studenti c'è Abbondanza."

34. On the last years of the Centre see Maria Jole Minicucci's two studies, "Roberto Ridolfi incunabulista: contributo alla storia degli studi paleotipici in Italia," in *Studi offerti a Roberto Ridolfi*, ed. B. Maracchi Biagiarelli and D. E. Rhodes (Florence, 1973), pp. 1–76, and "Roberto Ridolfi, maestro di studi incunabulistici," in *Per Roberto Ridolfi* (Florence, 1992), pp. 15–27.

35. It is ironic that Ridolfi was not very happy with my article, "Introduzione alla bibliografia testuale" ("Introduction to textual bibliography"), published in *La Bibliofilia* in 1980, which heralded the recent revival of interest in analytical bibliography in Italy. Indeed, had it not already been accepted on behalf of the journal by the acting editor while Ridolfi was ill, I doubt whether he would have published it.

Le filigrane dei paleotipi was not appreciated, either in Italy or else-where. The book did receive a friendly review in *The Library* from Victor Scholderer, the Italian specialist of the British Museum Library and a friend of Ridolfi's, but it is typical of the imperfect appreciation at that time, in all but a very few bibliographers, of the importance of paper research that Scholderer calls attention, not so much to the first, methodological, part of *Le filigrane*, but to the discussion of the crossed hammers mark from Colle in the second part. I suspect this is why Ridolfi's book is listed in the Bibliography of the Stevenson edition of Briquet's *Les filigranes* (1968), not in one of the sections "Evidential value of watermarks" or "Methodology," but in the geographical sec-tion "Watermarks in Early Printed Books—Italy," with the comment: "Mainly concerned with Colle wms."[36] A proper appreciation of Ridolfi's stature has come only in the 1990s, with the maturing of a new interest in analytical bibliography among Italian book historians and textual critics, coinciding as it has done with the reassessment, occa-sioned by his death in 1991, of Ridolfi's multifarious contributions to Italian culture.[37] In addition to the specific lessons contained in his bibliographical studies outlined above, present and future generations of Italian bibliographers can learn from Ridolfi's activities as an his-torian a more general lesson. Analytical bibliography is part of an his-torical discipline, and while it must begin with the consideration of the printed book as a material object, its results have little value unless immersed in the context of the cultural, economic, political and social forces at work in the production of printed books.

36. Scholderer's review appeared in *The Library* 5th ser. 13 (1958), 143–144. *Le filigrane dei paleotipi* is item B86, p. *42, of the 1968 edition of Briquet's *Les filigranes* (see above, note 20).

37. Among contributions dealing wholly or in part with Ridolfi's bibliographical work, or containing appreciations thereof, are the two studies (more informative than critical) of Maria Jole Minicucci mentioned above, n. 33; *Roberto Ridolfi: un fiorentino alla Baronta. Testimonianze di Alessandro Olschki, Luigi Balsamo, Eugenio Garin, Giovanni Spadolini, Indro Montanelli* (Florence, Leo S. Olschki, 1992); Giuseppina Zappella, "Il formato nella descrizione del libro antico: valore bibliologico e scelte catalografiche," *Biblioteche oggi* 11 (September 1993), 52–62; Paul F. Gehl, "Watermark Evidence for the Competitive Practices of Antonio Miscomini," *The Library* 6th ser. 15 (1993), 281–305; Luigi Balsamo, "Bibliologia e filologia umanistica," in *Sul libro bolognese del Rinascimento*, ed. Luigi Balsamo and Leonardo Quaquarelli (Bologna, 1994), pp. 7–26; Conor Fahy, "Roberto Ridolfi e lo studio bibliologico della carta," *La Bibliofilia* 97 (1995), 35–57; Luigi Balsamo, "Ridolfi bibliologo e *La Bibliofilia*" (forthcoming in *La Bibliofilia*). There has been no opportunity to men-tion earlier another aspect of the output of this talented man—Ridolfi's outstanding gifts as an essayist, which kept his name continually before the Italian reading public for many years as a renowned regular contributor to the *terza pagina* ("page 3") of the quality Italian press, traditionally devoted to literary and other cultural topics.

SELECT LIST OF PUBLICATIONS OF ROBERTO RIDOLFI

"Della questione degli archivi privati in Italia e della sua risoluzione," *La Bibliofilia* 30 (1928): 205–209.

"La biblioteca del cardinale Niccolò Ridolfi (1501–1550): nuovo contributo di notizie e di documenti," *La Bibliofilia* 31 (1929): 173–193.

L'archivio della famiglia Guicciardini (Florence: Leo S. Olschki, 1931). 142 pp.

Donato Giannotti, *Lettere a Piero Vettori pubblicate sopra gli originali del British Museum da Roberto Ridolfi e Cecil Roth con un saggio illustrativo a cura di Roberto Ridolfi* (Florence: Vallecchi, 1932). 212 pp.

Girolamo Savonarola, *Le lettere ora per la prima volta raccolte e a miglior lezione ridotte da Roberto Ridolfi* (Florence: Leo S. Olschki, 1933). cxciii, 268 pp.

Gli archivi delle famiglie fiorentine, Volume I (Florence: Leo S. Olschki, 1934). 246 pp.

Studi savonaroliani (Florence: Leo S. Olschki, 1935). 318 pp.

Principe Piero Ginori Conti, *Bibliografia delle opere del Savonarola, Vol. I. Cronologia e bibliografia delle Prediche con contributi storici e filologici di Roberto Ridolfi* (Florence: Fondazione Ginori Conti, 1939). 176 pp.

Francesco Guicciardini, *Le cose fiorentine, ora per la prima volta pubblicate da Roberto Ridolfi* (Florence: Leo S. Olschki, 1945).

"Proposta di ricerche sulle stampe e sugli stampatori del Quattrocento," *La Bibliofilia* 51 (1949): 1–8.

"Incunabuli contrastampati: nuovi sussidi per l'attribuzione e la datazione dei paleotipi," *La Bibliofilia* 51 (1949): 131–144.

Vita di Girolamo Savonarola, 2 vols (Rome: Angelo Belardetti, 1952). 410, 306 pp. Engl. transl. by Cecil Grayson (London: Routledge and Kegan Paul, 1959).

Vita di Niccolò Machiavelli (Rome: Angelo Belardetti, 1954). 502 pp. Engl. transl. by Cecil Grayson (London: Routledge and Kegan Paul, 1963).

"Nuovi contributi alla storia della stampa nel secolo XV. I. Lo "Stampatore del Mesue" e l'introduzione della stampa in Firenze," *La Bibliofilia* 56 (1954): 1–20.

"Nuovi contributi alla storia della stampa nel secolo XV. III. G.W.3851: Antonio Miscomini, non Compagnia del Drago," *La Bibliofilia* 57 (1955): 1–11.

"Nuovi contributi alla storia della stampa nel secolo XV. V. Note sopra Bartolomeo de' Libri," *La Bibliofilia* 57 (1955): 89–104.

Memorie di uno studioso (Rome: Angelo Belardetti, 1956). 251 pp.

Le filigrane dei paleotipi: saggio metodologico (Florence: Tipografia Giuntina, 1957). 45 pp.

"Giunte e correzioni al *Gesamtkatalog der Wiegendrucke* (Parte prima, I)," *La Bibliofilia* 59 (1957): 85–100.

La stampa in Firenze nel secolo XV (Florence: Leo S. Olschki, 1958). 156 pp.

"Giunte e correzioni al *Gesamtkatalog der Wiegendrucke*. III. Circerchia: Passione di Gesù Cristo," *La Bibliofilia* 61 (1959): 233–242.

Vita di Francesco Guicciardini (Rome: Angelo Belardetti, 1960). 560 pp. Engl. transl. by Cecil Grayson (London: Routledge and Kegan Paul, 1967).

"Composizione, rappresentazione e prima edizione della *Mandragola*," *La Bibliofilia* 64 (1962): 285–300.

"La seconda edizione della *Mandragola* e un codicillo sopra la prima," *La Bibliofilia* 66 (1964): 49–62.

Niccolò Machiavelli, *La Mandragola, per la prima volta restituita alla sua integrità a cura di Roberto Ridolfi* (Florence: Leo S. Olschki, 1965). 232 pp.

Studi sulle commedie del Machiavelli (Pisa: Nistri-Lischi, 1968). 178 pp.

Vita di Niccolò Machiavelli: quinta edizione italiana ancora accresciuta e in parte rifatta (Florence: Sansoni, 1972). 656 pp.

Studi guicciardiniani (Florence: Leo S. Olschki, 1978). 344 pp.

FISTS AND FILIATIONS IN EARLY CHAUCER FOLIOS, 1532–1602

by

JOSEPH A. DANE

THYNNE's 1532, double-column folio edition of Chaucer is the first of the series of black-letter folios constituting the early "vulgate" Chaucer.[1] The interest of Chaucerians in these editions has been two-fold: for some, they provide a record of canon-formation, with each subsequent edition adding to its predecessor.[2] For others, the interest is almost exclusively textual-critical, with the value of each edition based on the off chance that it may be an independent witness for manuscript readings now lost. The following article looks at what might be called the extra-textual tradition of these editions—their page layout, line composition, and the mysterious marginalia typeset in the early editions' texts of the *House of Fame*.[3] Examination of these elements first provides evidence for printer's copy used in the various editions (a question often obscured by editorial concentration on textual matters) and secondly illustrates a process of rationalization, whereby printers reinterpreted details of their tradition they understood no better than we do.

The history of this series of editions was sketched as early as the eighteenth century, and finally presented with uncommon clarity by Thomas R. Lounsbury in 1892.[4] What is generally accepted today is the following: the

---

1. The principal editions (several with variant issues) are as follows: the 1532 Thynne edition (STC 5068); an edition of 1542 adding the Plowman's Tale (STC 5069–5070); an undated edition where the Plowman's Tale is moved to precede the Parson's Tale (1550? STC 5071–5074); the Stow edition of 1561 (STC 5075–5076.3); two editions credited to Thomas Speght of 1598 and 1602 (STC 5077–79; STC 5080–81). I will use the now standard abbreviations adopted by the Variorum Chaucer, although I have reservations (expressed in my conclusion below) about what these abbreviations sometimes mean: TH1, TH2, and TH3 (= the Thynne editions of 1532, 1542, and 1550); ST (= Stow's edition of 1561); and SP1 and SP2 (=the two Speght editions of 1598 and 1602).

2. See, e.g., Walter W. Skeat, "Early Editions of Chaucer's Works," *The Complete Works of Geoffrey Chaucer*, vol. 1 (1894): 27–46. On the manuscript sources for the many additions to the canon made by Stow, see esp. Bradford Y. Fletcher, "Printer's Copy for Stow's Chaucer," *Studies in Bibliography* 31 (1978): 184–201.

3. I am not concerned here with the typography; see my *Who is Buried in Chaucer's Tomb? Studies in the Reception of Chaucer's Book* (1998), chap. 3: "Toward a Typographical History of Chaucer."

4. Thomas R. Lounsbury, *Studies in Chaucer*, 3 vols. (1892), 1: 265–280, based in large part on Francis Thynne, *Animadversions uppon the Annotacions and Corrections of some imperfections of impressions of Chaucers workes* (1598), ed. G. H. Kingsley, rev. J. F. Furnivall (1875). See more recently the excellent bibliographies by Eleanor Prescott Hammond, *Chaucer: A Bibliographical Manual* (1908), 116–127, John R. Hetherington, *Chaucer, 1532–1602: Notes and Facsimile Texts* (1964), and the discussion by Charles Muscatine, *The Book of Geoffrey Chaucer* (1963), and Derek Pearsall, "Thomas Speght (ca. 1550—?)," in Paul G.

1542 and 1550 editions (TH2 and TH3) are set from the 1532 edition; the
Stow edition of 1561 (ST) is set from the 1550 edition; the Speght edition of
1598 (SP1) is set from the 1561 edition; the Speght edition of 1602 (SP2), although a reprint of 1598, is to some extent based on the 1561 edition as well.
This simplified description shows that the relation between the various editions is not strictly linear, but sometimes "leapfrog," although even the most
careful scholars of these editions occasionally imply otherwise.[5]

The complex relations among the later folios need clarification, particularly in view of the recent collations provided by the Variorum Chaucer. And
in the initial sections below, I focus on what can be conjectured as the printer's
copy for the two Speght editions—an entity to be distinguished from the
various textual-critical entities known as "copy-text."[6] I will suggest that the
printer's copy for a great part of the 1602 edition is not simply *a copy* of the
1561 edition, but *the same copy* previously marked up to serve as printer's
copy for the 1598 edition.

Printer's Copy for the Two Speght Editions: Prose Sections

Since the 1602 edition contains revised versions of much of the preliminary matter from the 1598 edition and two texts not in Stow's 1561 edition
("Chaucer's Dream" and "Flower and the Leaf," fols. 355–368), some form of
the 1598 text served as printer's copy for these sections in 1602. If we consider
the 1602 edition alone, it might seem improbable that Speght would use the
1598 edition to set these sections, then use a 1561 edition as printer's copy for
the remainder of the edition. Yet the bibliographical evidence from prose

---

Ruggiers, ed., *Editing Chaucer: The Great Tradition* (1984), 71–92. See also: W. W. Greg,
"The Early Printed Editions of the *Canterbury Tales*," *PMLA* 39 (1924): 737–761; Alice
S. Miskimin, *The Renaissance Chaucer* (1975), 242–261; and Tim William Machan, "Speght's
Works and the Invention of Chaucer," *Text* 8 (1995): 145–170. The importance of Louns-
bury is often underestimated, but the influence of his narrative and the infectiousness of
his style are easily seen, as in the following statement on the relation of Speght to William
and Francis Thynne: "In return Speght spoke with the profoundest deference of the
Thynnes, father and son" (273); the sentence finds its way into Pearsall virtually unchanged:
"He speaks with the profoundest deference of the Thynnes, father and son . . ." (Pearsall,
85). The word then finds its way into a recent volume of the Variorum Chaucer: "Perhaps
in deference to Thynne . . ."; Malcolm Andrew et al., *The General Prologue*, Variorum
Chaucer II, 1 (1993), 100.

5. "They are set up, line by line, from their predecessor, diverging from it only insofar
as the text undergoes the usual mechanical degeneration at the hands of the compositor"
(Pearsall, "Speght," 71).

6. See the brief notes in G. Thomas Tanselle, "The Meaning of Copy-text: A Further
Note," *SB* 23 (1970): 191–192. No specific document exists in the sense of those studied long
ago by Gavin Bone, "Extant MSS. printed from by Wynkyn de Worde," *The Library* ser. 4,
12 (1931): 284–306, or more recently by James E. Blodgett, "Some Printer's Copy for William
Thynne's 1532 Edition of Chaucer," *The Library* ser. 6, 1 (1979): 97–113, and by N. F.
Blake, "Aftermath: Manuscript to Print," in Jeremy Griffiths and Derek Pearsall, ed., *Book
Production and Publishing in Britain, 1375–1475* (1989), Appendix A: "Caxton Prints for
which a copy-text survives or which were used as copy," 419–425 (Blake's word "copy" has
the meaning "printer's copy").

sections proves that he did precisely that. And even though there is no *a priori* reason to assume Speght acted rationally, if Speght had a copy of the 1561 edition readily available—the one used to set the 1598 edition—this procedure makes perfect sense.

Because the collations so far done by Lounsbury and by Variorum editors have been confined to the verse sections, the only kind of printing influence that has been detected is a "page-by-page" set-up or what Andrew calls "articulation" (meaning, I think, headings, section breaks, etc.). It is easy enough to determine, say, that the 1598 edition is set from the 1561 edition (since the page length is the same), but since the 1602 edition employs a longer column, it seems to have no relation in terms of page layout to the earlier editions.[7]

A comparison of the uncollated prose sections is, however, decisive. Throughout most of the prose, the 1598 edition is a perfect, line-by-line reprint of the 1561 edition. And since the 1561 and 1598 editions are so similar, any apparent relation of the 1602 edition to either seems to prove nothing. Consequently, some Chaucerians have concluded that the printer's copy cannot be determined for individual sections (so Plummer, *Summoner's Tale*, 85). Yet examination of the compositing details in these prose sections proves absolutely that the 1602 edition used the edition of 1561 as a printer's copy, just as did the 1598 edition.

Although the 1598 edition is a line-by-line reprint of the 1561 edition, at the end of sections of prose that line-by-line correspondence occasionally grows slack. The reason is fairly obvious. The purpose of a line-for-line reprint is not primarily to aid a compositor (that it actually interfered with the 1598 compositor's work is shown by the erratic spacing between words occasionally necessary to keep the line-by-line correspondence).[8] It is rather an aid for the printer in casting off copy—something that can be done very precisely if compositors are instructed to reproduce the copy line for line. A compositor working this way can relax when approaching a section break, since there will be some leeway in the setting of the final line preceding a new paragraph. Consequently, in prose sections, the line-for-line correspondence between the 1598 and 1561 editions every few pages tends to drift apart toward the end of paragraphs and section divisions. I have checked those particular sections where the two editions differ, and here, the 1602 edition

7. The volumes of the Variorum consulted here are the following: Derek Pearsall, *The Nun's Priest's Tale* (1984); Thomas W. Ross, *The Miller's Tale* (1983); Donald C. Baker, *The Manciple's Tale* (1984); Helen Storm Corsa, *The Physician's Tale* (1987); Beverly Boyd, *The Prioress's Tale* (1987); Donald C. Baker, *The Squire's Tale* (1990); Andrew et. al., *General Prologue* (1993); John F. Plummer III, *The Summoner's Tale* (1995). In his notes (267, n. 26), Pearsall cites collations by Moorman on the General Prologue; I assume these are what is included in the published version, although Ransom seems to be claiming to have thoroughly revised them (Andrew et al., *General Prologue*, xv). Ransom's statement is none too clear here, and I am uncertain as to whose "Collations," Ransom's or Moorman's, were checked by Dr. Levy. I will refer to this edition simply as Andrew's. On the setting of the 1598 edition, see Pearsall, "Speght," 79, 84–85, with reference to collations contained in his excellent edition of *The Floure and the Leafe and The Assembly of Ladies* (1962).

8. Aesthetically, the prose sections of the 1598 edition seem badly set as a result. The spacing in the 1602 edition is far more uniform.

often comes into perfect line-for-line correspondence with the edition 1561.[9] (Had the 1602 edition been set from a copy of the 1598 edition, we would expect the two to agree in line composition against the 1561 edition at the end of paragraphs; but they do not.)

In determining printer's copy, the evidence from line composition is more decisive than evidence from accidentals or substantives. In the prose sections, Speght indisputably printed from a copy of the 1561 edition in 1602 just as he did in 1598. Any agreement in accidentals grouping the 1598 and 1602 editions against the 1561 edition is thus the result of the same compositorial or house style being imposed on the printer's copy of both; any agreement in substantives producing these same groupings (SP1 and SP2 against ST) must be coincidental or the result of contamination—either the result of specific corrections introduced from the 1598 edition into a copy of the 1561 edition, which in turn served as printer's copy for the 1602 edition, or, more probably, the result of a correction introduced into the copy of the 1561 edition that was then used as printer's copy for both the 1598 and 1602 editions.

The preliminary matter of the two editions presents a different situation, since much of this appears only in the 1598 edition and not in that of 1561. The Life of Chaucer and all sections in roman type of the preliminaries of the 1602 edition are set directly from 1598. Although the 1602 edition is not a line-for-line reprint, specific correspondences in layout can be seen in the italicized marginal notes (see for both editions sig. b2r and the marginal note on Canterbury College at the top of sig. b3r). These show that the printer's copy for the 1602 edition was a copy of the 1598 edition, not, say, the manuscript that was itself the basis of that earlier edition.

One might assume, then, that *all* the preliminary matter in the 1602 edition would be set from the 1598 edition, but that, surprisingly, is not the case. Much of the preliminary matter differs in content (for example, the dedicatory letter to Cecil and the section "To the Readers"). Clearly, behind these is a manuscript, not the 1598 printed text. More surprising is the case of the introductory letter from Thynne to Henry VIII (reprinted in all sixteenth-century folio editions since the 1532 edition), where Speght follows what seems an unnecessarily complicated procedure. The number of lines per column in 1602 is different from the number of lines in 1598 and 1561. Comparing the 1550, 1561, 1598 and 1602 editions shows very clearly that the 1602 edition used the 1598 edition for its heading—a margin-to-margin heading in three sizes of roman type: both the typeface and the layout are identical in the two. In addition, the ornament running across the top of the page is the same (the 1602 version having an additional section). It seems preposterous that Speght in 1602, after using the 1598 edition for the Life of Chaucer and for the very heading to the letter of Thynne, then shifted to a 1561 edition for the printer's copy of the text of that letter; yet he did precisely that. The

---

9. See, e.g., the first paragraphs of "Pars secunda penitencie" of the Parson's Tale in ST and SP1 (sig. S5r). The second paragraph of SP2 (1602, sig. R6r) is a line-for-line reprint of ST, not SP1. See also, ST and SP1, sig. T2va. Again, SP2 (sig. 2va) agrees with ST only. The same correspondences exist in the *Testament of Love.*

evidence from the layout and line composition is unambiguous. Unlike prose in the rest of the volume, the preliminaries of the 1598 edition are not re-printed line for line from the 1561 edition. And for the most part, the three editions of 1561, 1598, and 1602 vary in layout here. But at the end of paragraph sections in the letter to Thynne on sig. C5v, the line lengths and breaks for the 1602 edition are identical to those of 1561 and bear no relation to those of 1598. This cannot be fortuitous; the prose of the 1602 edition, both in text and in its preliminaries, was set from the 1561 edition *whenever a 1561 text was available*. The only reasonable explanation for this is a readily available copy of the 1561 edition already in the possession of the press.

As noted earlier, variation in substantives and accidentals[10] is less important in determining printer's copy than matters of page layout and line composition. And as far as I know, none of these prose sections—either those of the text or the preliminaries—has been thoroughly collated for such variation. In those prose sections I have collated, I have found no substantive disagreements in the three editions (although I presume they exist, and that the Variorum editors will in the future find them). If and when such disagreement is found, it will indicate something other than printer's copy: because the 1561 and 1598 editions generally correspond line for line, any corrector set to the task of introducing the readings from a copy of one into a copy of the other would have a relatively easy time of it.[11] As for accidentals, the only pattern of variation that could challenge the above hypothesis would be the overwhelming agreement of SP1 and SP2 against ST. The collations I have done show only what is expected: general agreement of SP1 and SP2 in accidentals; general agreement of both with ST; numerous cases of ST and SP1 against SP2; numerous cases of ST and SP2 against SP1.

Textual-Critical Evidence of Printer's Copy for SP2: Verse Sections

The collations of the Variorum editors for verse sections of the *Canterbury Tales* support the conclusions above, although some of their claims are unnecessarily understated. All are based to some extent upon Pearsall: "The conclusion seems clear that SP2 was reset from ST . . . but SP2 has been so extensively edited that the evidence cannot be so decisive as it usually is with early printed editions" (*Nun's Priest's Tale*, 114). Only Baker in his edition of the Squire's Tale is categorical about the 1561 edition as printer's copy; yet the evidence is far stronger than other editors seem to believe.[12] In only

10. The distinction is that found in W. W. Greg, "The Rationale of Copy-Text," *SB* 3 (1950–51): 19–36. Although much criticized, it is of crucial importance in twentieth-century Chaucer editing; see below, n. 29.

11. This accounts in part for the general agreement of the prose sections in these editions: errors in a line-for-line reprint of prose will be much more apparent to compositors and proof-readers than in ordinary reprints of prose, or even in line-for-line reprints of verse.

12. Baker, *Squire's Tale*, 106; Baker cites as reference the somewhat variable statements in Pearsall, *Nun's Priest's Tale*, 114, Corsa, *Physician's Tale*, 78, and Boyd, *Prioress's Tale*, 102. Cf. Plummer, the most recent Variorum editor: "Because ST and SP1 are nearly identical, one cannot demonstrate beyond doubt which of the two served as copytext for SP2"

one or two instances is the substantive variation such as even to suggest that either printer's copy or textual source for the 1602 edition was anything other than a copy of the 1561 edition, and even these examples are capable of alternative explanation. Original manuscript readings supposedly "restored" in 1602 are, as Pearsall states, "commonplace" and "widely attested."[13] The manner of presenting statistics in these volumes occasionally implies some uncertainty about the printer's copy or copy-text for the 1602 edition. But at least for the Tales already collated by the Variorum editors (the General Prologue is a special case), there should be no hesitation whatsoever, as examination of the exceptions cited by these editors quickly reveals.[14]

(*Summoner's Tale*, 85); and Corsa, *Physician's Tale*, "The making of SP2's text . . . remains a mystery" (79).

13. *Nun's Priest's Tale*, 114. Pearsall claims that such restorations occasionally involve complete lines. If that were true, it would be decisive evidence of a textual source beyond that of the 1561 edition. But the sole example Pearsall cites involves line 4117:

> When humors ben too habundant in a wight:
> certes this dreme, which ye haue met to night
> Commeth of the great superfluitie
> Of red color that is in you parde. . . . (1602 edition)

The third line here seems to replace what in all editions from Caxton to SP1 is some version of the following: "I tel you trouthe ye may trust me." The full context of this supposed restoration shows that the authentic line does not come from an independent source. See, e.g., the 1532 reading:

> Whan humours ben to habudant in a wight
> Certes this dreme / which ye haue met to night
> I tel you trouthe / ye may trust me
> Cometh of superfluyte / & reed colour parde
> Whiche cause folke to drede in her dremes.

The 1602 edition produces a reading (recorded in earlier sources) by *cancelling* a superfluous line, not by adding a line.

14. Baker, *Manciples Tale*, 68: "Whatever the exemplar from which SP2 was set up, either ST or SP1, SP2 contributes 25 variants from SP1." The figures are misleading, and Baker provides only two instances where SP2 agrees with SP1 in substantive variation against ST: at line 105, Stow has "in pearth," a misreading of a thorn, easily corrected to "in this world" (SP1 and SP2) (many manuscripts read "in this earth"). The clear error "criyng" at 301 requires no source to correct to "crye." A similar error occurs at 262, where SP2 corrects a clear error "prien" to "wryen" (a reading that also appears in MS); the error involves only the reading of a scribal *w* as *p*. See also, the correction at line 105, the first line of the tale—a correction likely to come not from manuscript but from SP1. Corsa, *Physician's Tale*, 78–79, claims that SP1 and ST diverge substantively ten times, and that in six of those instances, SP2 reads with ST (lines 59, 82, 190, 216, 271, 276). This to me certainly implies that SP2 does not read with ST at 125, 138, 165, or 190. But that is not the case. SP2 agrees with ST in all ten instances. I agree with the conclusions of Boyd, *Prioress's Tale*, 102, which are those of Pearsall; but the reference to the Variorum Table of Correspondences ("SP2 agrees with ST in 95 variants and with SP1 in 93") is misleading in that such agreement is only with Hg (the readings to which the Variorum editors are more or less committed as original). As far as I can determine, every example Boyd cites is evidence that the printer's copy for 1602 was ST, and there is no evidence of mixed agreement (i.e., agreement with SP1 against ST). See finally Baker, *Squire's Tale*, 106: "In 7 of the 8 divergences of SP1 from ST, SP2 reads with ST; the sole exception is at line 440, where

Where some question remains is in the General Prologue. The evidence presented by Lounsbury in 1892 and the more detailed collations recently published by Andrew show that the situation is not the same as in the texts of the Tales. To begin with, printer's copy, which editors of other *Canterbury Tales* sections describe simply as ST, must be defined more carefully, since Stow's edition contains two versions of the General Prologue, one with woodcuts (STw) and one without (ST).[15] Andrew quite correctly concludes that the only version "behind" the 1598 edition is ST, not STw (Andrew calls this a "copytext," 94) and the same is true for the 1602 edition; that is, particular readings of STw can be disregarded.[16] I extend this here by suggesting that we are dealing not with a textual copy-text (ST rather than STw) but more likely a specific copy of ST—a specific copy that may have served as printer's copy for both Speght editions.

More than in the Tales, the General Prologue shows apparently mixed filiation—a conflation of ST and SP1. Andrew follows Lounsbury and concludes: "It seems then that ST and SP1 had nearly equal influence on the GP text of SP2" (100). The influence Andrew notes here is textual, and the word "equal" misleading. The statistics Andrew provides supporting this statement actually show that these two texts (ST and SP1) influenced SP2 in demonstrably different ways.[17] Printer's copy for SP2 is ST. Any substantive agreement of SP1 and SP2 against ST is coincidental, or possibly the result of an

---

SP2 has a unique reading." The evidence is unanimous: since the SP2 reading at 440 is unique, this is not an exception to the notion of ST as printer's copy.

15. The revised STC lists three issues here; the title pages and the two versions of the prologue distinguish STC 5075 from 5076. STC 5076.3 has a different colophon; one of its listed copies contains woodcuts, the other (apparently) does not. The abbreviations STw and ST in this context should be construed as referring simply to the printed pages containing the General Prologue.

16. Andrew's statistics supporting this are much more decisive than Andrew claims, and the apparent evidence for mixed agreement is illusory. Andrew enumerates 23 substantive differences between STw and ST (95), and concludes "ST is clearly the copytext for SP1" (96). On four of these, SP1 seems to agree with ST. But only one of these involves substantive variation (*and/and a* at 558): *plaien/plain* (236) is a spelling variant; *meserable/miserable* (435) is another accidental variant elevated to a substantive; *out of/out oft* (487) is another accidental. Andrew is the first Variorum editor to discuss in detail the problems of the definition of a variant (122–124). Nonetheless, the statistics themselves are by nature uncritical, and many of the supposed substantives tabulated are products of easily correctable accidental variation. See, e.g., the following instances of variation between STw and ST: *ensired/espired*; *porte/sporte*; *pleasaunt/pleasaunce*; *no/not*; *he/she*.

17. The evidence for "equality" Andrew presents is in the following statistical statement: SP2 and ST agree against SP1 58 times; SP1 and SP2 agree against ST 60 times (Andrew, 100). But again, Andrew's analysis (which is careful and detailed) actually yields a somewhat different statement, with none of the illusory balance of the above: where SP2 and ST agree against SP1, 2 cases involve SP1 omission, and 23 involve SP1 additions; where SP1 and SP2 agree against ST, 26 cases involve ST omission, and 14 involve ST additions. Obviously, the influence of each text on SP2 is different. I believe the conclusion to be drawn here is the following: the agreement of SP1 and SP2 against ST is random; the agreement of SP2 and ST against SP1 is systematic (most involve SP1 additions); the implication is that ST is printer's copy for SP2.

editorial change made in the particular copy of ST that served as printer's copy for both.[18]

Lounsbury noted that Speght states in his introductory note "To the Readers" (1598) that he did not involve himself in the edition until late in the printing process: "three parts thereof alreadie printed." The various sections of the book should thus differ textually, reflecting Speght's care (or interference) (Lounsbury, 270–271). What Speght's work amounted to is unknown, but it could well account for the apparent mixed textual affiliation of the General Prologue. The copies Speght refers to when he claims the text is "by old written copies corrected" ("To the Readers" 1598) or "by old copies reformed" (1602), are probably no older than 1561 (so Pearsall, "Speght," 86–87).

The Problem of the Fists

The editions under discussion here have a long-noted oddity that bears on the tradition of printer's copy for these editions. The earlier folios contain some typographically peculiar marginalia in the *House of Fame*; in the 1561 edition, these typographical marks seem to be replaced for the most part with marginal fists, and they are again confined to the *House of Fame*.[19] The 1598 edition has no marginalia of any kind, but the 1602 edition marks proverbs and sententiae with marginal fists throughout (the two texts printed from the 1598 edition, texts not found in the 1561 edition, are unmarked). Hetherington is one of few bibliographers to address these marginalia:

The earlier Chaucer folios themselves contain some markings which could be regarded as anticipating the formal and practical use of the first. Curiously, in each edition these only appear with *The House of Fame*. In 1542 and 1561 they only occur in the 'middle' margin. In 1550 they seem to be 'end of line' rather than marginal. I have not found any single line to be marked in more than one edition. (8–9)[20]

No explanation of these marginal marks has been offered beyond this. And the only sixteenth-century books where I am aware of having encountered

18. See, e.g., the apparent agreement of SP1 and SP2 against ST at line 147: only when variants are considered singly do SP1 and SP2 agree; there is no agreement if the entire line is taken as lemma. The agreement at line 176 (*pace* for ST's *space*) is quite possibly the consequence of SP1 following a marked copy of 1561, not a matter of a 1598 reading being introduced into that copy. Many of the more radical differences are cited by Lounsbury, 275–276; but of these fifteen, only two show agreement of SP1 and SP2 against ST. And most of the more substantial variants in Andrew show the same thing (see, e.g., line 73). The agreement of SP1 and SP2 against ST often involves individual words, and such agreement is quite possibly the result of a gloss (*called/clepyd*, line 121; *wenden/goon*, line 21). Again, this is perfectly consistent with a single marked-up copy of ST serving as printer's copy for both Speght editions.

19. There is at least one exception to this in Stow, and there may be more. On fol. 243r of ST (sig. Y3r), there are five small ornaments in the inner margin. I have not found these elsewhere in the edition.

20. The statement that these marks occur in the 1542 and 1561 editions only in the middle margin is not accurate.

similar marks in any significant numbers are the Great Bibles from the early
1540s printed by Grafton and Whitchurch (Grafton is the printer responsible
for the 1542 Chaucer, although not named in the colophon). Here, they appear sporadically in the Kalendar, varying in location from edition to edition,
and disappearing from later editions.[21]

In the first Thynne edition of 1532, three marks occur, all easily repro-
ducible on a keyboard: on fol. 316, *House of Fame*, lines 837, 848 and 858:

(:):)   (:):)   (:(:):)

In 1542, this same section is marked at lines 848 and 853:

(:) (:)   (:) (:)

In 1550, the most heavily marked version, no marks appear in this section.[22]

In the 1542 edition, in the middle sections of *House of Fame*, there are
two more marks of this kind—a *punctus elevatus* (I represent this mark below
with a modern question mark) within parentheses at lines 1108 and 1127.
Toward the beginning and end of the work, several other differently constructed marks occur: three small joined o's, a leaf, and a fist in lines 77, 83,
98 respectively. In the final section, the mark consisting of three o's recurs at
line 1947, and right-pointing fists appear in the interior margin, set with the
left column of type, at lines 1923, 1955, 2130, and 2140.

I will state now that I am not about to offer an explication of the specific
function of these marks. I am certain that if some dozen or so lines in any text
were marked entirely at random, most bibliographers, textual critics, or literary critics worthy of their profession could come up with reasons why those
particular lines (and only those lines) were of significance. My argument here
is rather that the very tradition of these marks was in itself stronger than their
perceived function and that only in 1602 were they finally rationalized. In
short: sixteenth-century printers had no clearer idea of the original function
of these marks than we do.

With that caveat, several aspects of these marks should be noted. I begin
with the 1542 edition. Here the right-pointing fists appear in the interior
margin, but they are set within the borders of the left column of type. They
thus point to lines in the right column, not to the left-column lines in which
they are clearly set. Are they pointing the wrong way? The last two marginal

21. See the 1539 Bible (STC 5068), and the series of Great Bibles printed by Grafton
and/or Whitchurch from 1540–1541 (STC 2070–2076). Ornaments constructed from type
sorts much like those in the Chaucer editions appear frequently in the prefatory matter,
with no discernable relation from edition to edition. For a convenient overview, see Francis
Fry, *A Description of the Great Bible, 1539, and the Six Editions of Cranmer's Bible, 1540
and 1541, printed by Grafton and Whitchurch* (1865), plates 2–4. Later Bibles printed by
Whitchurch in 1549 (STC 2079) and 1550 (STC 2081) do not contain a calendar; these contain sporadic ornaments and marginal fists, but nothing similar to those discussed here.
Stephen Tabor of the Clark Library has pointed out to me as well the signature marks
indicating half-sheet collation noted by David J. Shaw, "Quire and Sheet Numbers in
Sixteenth-Century France," *The Library* ser. 6, 17 (1995): 311–320.

22. For ease of reference, I cite these by the line numbering in Larry D. Benson, ed.,
The Riverside Chaucer (1987).

fists seem to point to line 2154 in the right column—a line about stamping for eels (!, see note in Riverside 990)—and a line in the spurious continuation reading "Of that god of Thondre." Eel-stamping may be noteworthy, but these fists almost certainly originate as responses to the lines in the left margin: "With boxes crommed ful of lyes / As euer vessel was with lyes" (lines 2129–30) and "For al mote out late or rathe / Al the sheues in the rathe" (lines 2139–40). Each involves an apparent example of *rime riche,* and such a rime type may well have attracted editorial concern. In the second couplet, the rime is clearly an error (for *rathe* read *lathe*). In the first, the rime depends in part on the meaning of *boxes*—if, that is, *boxes* belongs here. MS. F reads *boystes,* MS. B *bowgys.* I haven't a clue what lines 2129–30 mean or what Thynne in 1532 thought his variant meant: the Riverside gloss at p. 373 suggests a rime on *lies* and *lees:* "With containers full of lies as ever vessel was with dregs."

The other odd mark, the joined o's at line 1947, is also not a mark for a reader; the reading "In sommer whan they ben grene" reads in other copies "In sommer whan they grene bene." This mark is quite possibly a compositor's rendition of what was intended as a mark of transposition.[23] Like the fists at the end of the text, this is something produced during the printing process, and represents (or originates in) notes to a printer or editor. Taken together, these marks are not in any way coherent guides for a reader; for any reader taking them seriously would be alternately baffled by the text in the vicinity or left wondering what the fuss was all about.

The 1550 edition contains many complex and bizarre-looking marginal marks and ornaments. Again, they are confined to the *House of Fame.* In some cases, they appear like those in the 1542 edition (there are numerous instances where they are constructed with type sorts, rather than ornamental sorts). For the first two books, these consist almost exclusively of marks formed from parentheses, the *punctus elevatus,* and colons: many are as easily constructed on a keyboard as from a typecase and include the following, at lines 171, 520, 704 and 930:

):((?)   )?((?)?(?)

At the end of the second book, with the beginning of a new quire (3G), these become much more elaborate, formed by multiple commas, inverted commas, colons, etc. Among these are the marks at lines 1185 and 1128 and 1467:

(,:,:,:,:,)   (:()?)   (:) (:) (:

These are consistently well formed and quite carefully done; they are not a haphazard collection of sorts, but formed, for example, with alternating commas and right-facing or left-facing inverted commas, all within parentheses. The following occurs at line 1429:

(,:':,:':,:':,:)

23. For early printers' marks of transposition, see the examples in Peter W. M. Blayney, *The Texts of King Lear and Their Origins,* vol. 1: *Nicholas Okes and the First Quarto* (1982), 224, fig. 17d, 225 n.1, and 237, figs. 31f.

I have conjectured a number of functions for these: annotations for inexistent notes, illegible corrections for text, casting-off marks for a projected edition. Most of my conjectures, however, contain the word *inexistent* or a near variant: there are no annotations; the lines marked are in no obvious need of correction; the intervals would not be appropriate for casting off copy. The precise function of the (lost) original marks that inspired the compositor for the 1550 edition to create these variant marks is quite simply lost.

The distribution of these marks does, however, reflect the physical structure of the book, and thus not what must have been the distribution of whatever marks were in the printer's copy (an annotated copy of the 1532 edition). The pattern of their distribution is a product of the creation of this edition. The more elaborate marks appear only in a single quire, 3G, and the independence of that quire is shown by the initial line, which erroneously repeats the last line of quire 3F and thus makes the catchword inaccurate; some sort of interruption occurs here. Another indication that these are products of processes at the printing house is the presence of marks in quire 3F. They occur only in particular formes: 3F2r/3F5v and 3F3r/3F4v. They do not occur in the reverse formes: 3F2v/3F5r and 3F3r/3F4r. All this indicates that whatever these marks may have represented or have been thought to represent, their presence in the 1550 edition is a function of something in the printer's copy that one compositor could have interpreted as "something to be printed" and another could have interpreted as "something to be ignored" (the hypothetical compositors could of course be one compositor working under a different directive).

When we look at the edition of 1561, we can see another step in the apparent rationalization of an oddity in a printer's copy. For this edition, the printer's copy was a copy of the 1550 edition, containing the bizarre printed marginalia in the *House of Fame*. The 1561 edition puts fists in its text of *House of Fame* (and in no other text). *Pace* Hetherington, there appears to be some relation of these fists to the marks in 1550, and it might be argued that in some cases, they represent an interpretation of the marginalia of 1550.[24]

In the first two books of *House of Fame*, there is no apparent correspondence. There are a number of fists at lines 250ff., but no mark corresponds to them in the 1550 or 1542 editions (at the end of the first book). There are none in the 1561 edition on sig. 3e2r–3e3v (an entire inner and outer forme), whereas numerous marks appear in this section in the 1550 edition. From the beginning of book 3, there are numerous fists in the 1561 edition, and many marks in the edition of 1550. There is some correspondence here: a mark oc-

---

24. See, however, the downward pointing fist at "So gyue hem ioye that it here" in the 1561 edition; there is a leaf there in 1542, but nothing in 1550. Yet 1542 is not the printer's copy, and it may be that relations between the 1550 and 1561 placement of marginalia are products of pure chance. Anne Hudson, "John Stow (1525?–1605)," in Ruggiers, 60, rightly concludes that the 1550 edition is the source for that of 1561, but collates, unnecessarily, against various earlier 'issues' of 1542 and 1550 for press-variation. There is no likelihood that divergences among various issues in terms of press variation will be any greater than divergences in individual copies of the same issue, since issue is not defined by variant sheets.

curs at line 1169 in the 1550 edition and an upward-pointing fist in the 1561 edition; another mark at line 1206 might correspond to an upward-pointing fist in the same line in 1561, and another mark at line 1217 might correspond to an upward-pointing fist at line 1219 in 1561. So also at line 1465, an upward-pointing fist in the 1561 edition is at least in the vicinity of a strange mark in the 1550 edition at line 1467; a downward-pointing fist at line 1479 might correspond to another mark in the 1550 edition. But of the eleven fists that follow, there is only a rough correspondence in one or two cases.

A few additional peculiarities about the fists in the 1561 edition are noteworthy. To begin with, there is only one such fist in the typefont, a right-pointing fist. This is set to point right on only one occasion. In all other uses, the fist appears between the two columns, set with the left column of print, and points either up or down. There may be a correspondence with the text, but trying to find one appears to have the intellectual validity of the *Sortes Virgilianae*. What can be said is the same that can be said of the 1550 marginalia: they respond to something noticeable in the printer's copy, but not something the compositor fully understood or interpreted in any intelligible way.

What happens in the two Speght editions is a response: in the 1598 edition, no marginal fists appear, although Speght claims in his introductory note "To the Readers" that he has marked all sentences and proverbs. In 1602, marginal fists appear *throughout* the book (with the exception of the two texts that the 1598 edition added to the contents of earlier editions: "Chaucer's Dream" and "Flower and the Leaf"). And they are perfectly rationalized—marking sentences and proverbs, precisely what Speght claims on his title page and in the preliminaries.[25] Because they are rational, they have no relation to any of the marginalia in earlier editions.

The history of these marks confirms other evidence for printer's copy, supporting the hypothesis of the retention of particular books or manuscripts as printer's copy, first for the editions of 1542 and 1550, and second for the edition of 1602. There is no doubt concerning the general relations of the 1542 and 1550 editions: the collations show that both were set from the first Thynne edition (1532). How, then, does the 1550 edition happen to have so many marks, some of which correspond exactly to the 1542 edition? And why do both editions have marks that are formed typographically like the three in the 1532 edition?

The only explanation for this is that the 1550 and 1542 editions were set not simply from what a textual critic might call TH (the text of the 1532 edition) but rather from a specific copy of that edition, a marked-up copy.[26]

25. In "To the Readers" (1598) Speght claims as one of his eight "undertakings": "Sentences noted." But this is not included among the seven "Additions" listed on the title page and the sentences are in fact not noted in the 1598 edition. The title page of 1602 states "Sentences and Prouerbes noted" and Speght adds to the earlier dedicatory letter to Cecil of 1598 the statement that he has "noted withall most of his Sentences and Prouerbs."

26. I have done some checking of press variants in various copies of this edition, and the conjecture of a single material printer's copy for both editions would be refuted if the 1550 and 1542 editions were shown to differ on the variants that exist in different copies of

Such a specifically marked copy would explain all apparent correspondence with these two editions as far as particular extraneous marginalia are concerned. The relations of the various printers involved in the two editions are close. According to Isaac, the printing of the 1550 edition, in all its issues, is done by Nicholas Hill, who shared type with Whitchurch and Grafton (Grafton is responsible for the 1542 edition); the printers named in the colophons (Bonham and Reynes for 1542; Bonham, Kele, Petit and Toye for 1550) are part of a consortium..[27] These close relations provide additional support for the notion of a single marked-up copy of the 1532 edition used as printer's copy for both editions. Had another copy been chosen as printer's copy, there would be no reason to suspect any correspondence between the 1542 and 1550 editions as far as the marginal markings are concerned, unless there was a printed mark in the 1532 edition at the point of these correspondences.

The marginalia also help describe the nature of the printer's copy for the 1602 edition. The 1561 edition served as printer's copy for this edition, and its marginal fists may well have provided the inspiration for the fists in 1602, just as the incoherence of their placement could have inspired the rejection of the fists in 1598. The marginal fists in the 1602 edition, thus, do not represent the marginal fists actually printed in its printer's copy (otherwise they would correspond to those in the 1561 *House of Fame*) but rather indicate lines marked by hand in that copy. This would explain why no such fists appear in those sections of the book set from the edition of 1598—only the printed source text (ST) was marked, not the source text for these two poems. It also can explain why Speght claims in 1598 to have marked the text's proverbs ("Seuenthly, sentences noted"), when only the 1602 edition is so marked (see n. 25 above). The printer's copy used in 1598 may well have been so marked, just as Speght claims, but those marks were not introduced into the printed text (as marginal fists) until that copy was used again as printer's copy for the 1602 edition.

CONCLUSION

In 1892, Lounsbury examined lines from the General Prologue, looking primarily for evidence of Speght's claim that he had consulted earlier manu-

---

1532. They do not so differ in any I have checked so far. See my "On 'Correctness': A Note on Some Press Variants in Thynne's 1532 Edition of Chaucer," *The Library* ser. 6, 17 (1995): 156–67.

27. Frank Isaac, *English and Scottish Printing Types, 1535–58, 1552–58* (1932), see Appendix: William Bonham, Robert Toy, and entry under Richard Kele, Richard Grafton, 29–39, Edward Whitchurch, 40–50, and Nicholas Hill, 88–91 (for 94T, see figs. 50 and 88a). The type identification and size is the same (94T; see figs. 50 and 88a), and the two are very similar (the upper case is different). See, however, the notes by Hetherington, 3–4, and discussion in Muscatine, *Book of Geoffrey Chaucer*, 23–24. The Variorum editors often refer to unspecified evidence in favor of the later date for the third Thynne edition (1550, instead of the 1545 date in the first edition of STC), but none has detailed what that evidence is. See, e.g., Andrew, 94. (I believe the reference is to Hetherington, 3–4, although Andrew, unlike other Variorum editors, does not include Hetherington in his bibliography). Isaac's work is cited by Muscatine, but not by any of the Variorum editors.

scripts. Although his conclusion was negative, in the process Lounsbury discovered many of the variants that provided an outline for the printing history of these editions, and in particular, the relation of the 1602 edition to the earlier editions of 1561 and 1598. Lounsbury concluded: "A full examination, which has never been made and hardly seems worth making, would be necessary to settle the matter beyond all dispute" (277). The examination "hardly worth making" has now, with the work of the Variorum editors, begun in earnest. Most of the collations confirm the evidence provided by details of layout and line composition, but the interest of editors in possible original manuscript readings contained in these late editions has obscured what the evidence for many of them shows and what Lounsbury suspected: clear and exclusive dependence of later editions on earlier editions whenever those editions were available.[28]

The examination of layout and composition suggests a few areas in which editorial language regarding sources for certain texts could be clarified. Manuscript sigla refer to readings contained in specific material objects. But the sigla for printed editions (TH, ST, SP)—sigla I have of necessity adopted here—refer to entire editions, individual copies of which have different readings, either due to ordinary press-variation, or more significantly to the intervention of an annotator. In the present case, one could imagine, say, a copy of the 1561 edition, in which all the readings of the 1598 edition had been entered, or in which numerous changes had been made that were eventually to become the 1598 version (in terms of textual substantives, the two might be identical). Any text copied closely from this might resemble the 1561 edition in details of layout and perhaps in accidentals, but in terms of substantives, it would duplicate the 1598 edition. A textual critic might reasonably claim that the 1598 edition served as 'copy-text' or 'base-text'. And under certain understandings of these terms, that could be the case. But it would not serve as 'printer's copy' in any sense—whether we mean by that phrase a physical object in the press room, or more abstractly an edition, one of whose representative copies is in the press room.

Evidence for actual printer's copy is more likely to come from extra-textual matters than from the level of textual substantives of interest to most editors—a level to which modern Chaucer editors have found themselves increasingly committed, especially since the publication of Manly and Rickert's Table of Variants in 1940. Yet the precise definition of a substantive and the textual-critical value of such substantives varies considerably (the transposition *he said*/*said he* is common in Chaucer texts and by definition classi-

---

28. The reluctance of editors to give up the notion of such manuscript sources can be seen as manuscript readings hypothesized by one scholar become actual historical manuscripts for another. Where Pearsall spoke of possible manuscript *readings* in Speght (readings he characterizes as "commonplace"), Corsa, citing Pearsall, speaks of specific manuscripts: "The difficulty in such research, however, is increased by Speght's inconsistent use of more than one manuscript" (Corsa, 79, with reference to Pearsall, "Speght," 87). There is no evidence that Speght used *any* manuscript, unless we include as manuscript hand-written notes (perhaps his own) in a copy of the 1561 edition.

fied as a substantive; but the textual-critical value of such variation is no more than that of accidentals).[29]

The books examined here show that details of layout persist quite apart from their textual or intellectual functions, just as the use of black-letter itself for medieval texts persisted as the implications of that typeface changed dramatically. Later printers were faced not only with making sense of a text growing increasingly archaic and inaccessible, but with making sense of at least one mystery of their own making.

29. John M. Manly and Edith Rickert, *The Text of the Canterbury Tales*, 8 vols. (1940); Andrew, 122–24, and notes on 122. Andrew is the first Variorum editor to provide a clear presentation along with examples of what Manly-Rickert and later Variorum editors define as a variant. Some points of value can also be extracted (with difficulty) from an earlier study by Kurt Rydland, "The Meaning of 'Variant Reading' in the Manly-Rickert *Canterbury Tales*," *Neuphilologische Mitteilungen* 73 (1972), 805–814.

THOMAS USK'S "PERDURABLE LETTERS":
THE *TESTAMENT OF LOVE* FROM SCRIPT TO PRINT

by

ANNE MIDDLETON

> Th' entent of al these maters is the lest clere understanding, to weten, at th'ende of this thirde boke. . . . Yet if these thinges han a good and a sleigh inseer, which that can souke hony of the harde stone, oyle of the drye rocke, [he] may lightly fele nobley of mater in my leude imaginacion closed.
> (*Testament of Love* III.i.137–143)[1]

thentent of al these maters is the lest clere understanding/ to weten at thende of this thirde boke ful knowing thorowe goddes grace/ I thinke to make neverthelater/ yet if these thynges han a good and a sleight inseer/ which that can souke hony of the harde stone/ oyle of the drye rocke/ may lyghtly fele nobley of mater in my leude ymagination closed. (f. 351r, col. 1, l. 48– col. 2, ll. 1–8)

As is well known, no manuscript of Thomas Usk's *Testament of Love* has come to light. The work survives only because William Thynne printed it in his 1532 folio Chaucer edition, and until 1844, when Sir Harris Nicolas demonstrated that its biographical details were at odds with documentable facts of Chaucer's career, it was accepted, with few demurrers, as Chaucer's work.[2] As is also well known, the text of the *Testament* as it appears in Thynne exhibits a sequence of abrupt displacements of text in the third book of the work. These occur in midline and midsentence, and radically disrupt logical and syntactic sense and clear exposition—a state of affairs that implies a disordering of printer's copy.[3]

1. Except where noted, I cite Skeat's edition, in *Chaucerian and Other Pieces*, ed. Walter W. Skeat (Oxford: Clarendon, 1897), pp. 1–145; notes pp. 451–484. Thynne's text, however, is worth citing, for the passage offers a small conspectus of the difficulties that confront an editor:

2. Henry Bradley's entry on Thomas Usk in the *Dictionary of National Biography* (vol. 20, pp. 60–62) remains the best succinct account of Usk's career, and of the main events in the discovery of Usk's authorship. Its biographical information is valuably supplemented by Ramona Bressie, "The Date of Thomas Usk's *Testament of Love*," *Modern Philology* 26 (1928), 17–29.

3. Henry Bradley, in *The Athenaeum* #3615 (February 5, 1897), p. 184, first described these displacements, identifying six separate disjunct segments. Skeat adopted this account in his edition, and offers a hypothesis (pp. xix–xxii) about the misarrangement of the printer's copy to explain the disorder and justify the sequence of his reconstruction. Ramona Bressie (note 2 above) was to my knowledge the first to discover that Skeat's reconstruction of the order of displaced text in Book III erred in reversing the positions of chapters v and vi (see

That this massive disordering of expository sequence and sense went virtually unremarked from the sixteenth through most of the nineteenth centuries testifies revealingly to the uses made of the work during the interval in which it was taken to be Chaucer's. The work seems to have been read during these centuries chiefly for its contribution to a biography of Chaucer, and as a complement to *Boece* in exhibiting its author's eloquence in the grand manner, adorned with classical allusion and elegant apostrophe.[4] For these purposes the first two-thirds of the *Testament* (through the end of Book II) provided virtually all of the apposite material. Its biographically encoded *consolatio* (the main task of the *Testament* through II.iv, roughly corresponding to the function of Boethius's Book I) ceases a little more than one-third of the way through Usk's work; the turn toward "remedie" in the middle third of the work provides, with frequent evocation of antique historical example and analogy, the arts, and natural philosophy, the framework in which Love, the visionary instructor throughout the *Testament*, offers the disconsolate persona a course of moral and eschatological edification: the project of the remainder of Usk's Book II is an approximate counterpart to the functions of Books II and III of Boethius's *Consolatio*. This second movement of Usk's work yields to sustained philosophical argument in Book III, which retains its Boethian cast only in the dialogic framing of its exposition, but bases its arguments in detail and at length on a different Latin source text, St. Anselm's *De Concordia Praescientiae et Praedestinationis et Gratiae Dei cum Libero Arbitrio.*

With Book III Usk's work becomes more decisively what it has been pointing toward with its preceding allusive gesturing: a synthetic enterprise of some intellectual ambition and originality, of a kind as yet mostly "unat-

---

p. 28, n. 1 of her article), though she does not explain either how the acrostic, disrupted by the transposition she proposes, might be restored, or what mechanics of disruption could account for either Skeat's arrangement (which she finds as baffling as I do) or the revision of it she proposes. Her tentative solution to the latter problem is to postulate the loss of text after III.i, since this book alone of the three "lacks a lyrical chapter after the Prologue," and since at II.iv.121 Love forecasts matter about a "king" to be treated later "whan I shew the ground where moral virtue groweth"—yet in Bressie's view the king remains unmentioned when Love's exposition reaches that topic in Book III. My account below addresses both of these issues.

4. In his biography *John Gower: Moral Philosopher and Friend of Chaucer* (New York: New York Univ. Press, 1964), John Hurt Fisher provides a valuable discussion of the causes and effects of the attribution of the *Testament* to Chaucer, and the impacts of the early reconstructed biographies of Chaucer and Gower on the definition of critical reputations and agendas in the study of major and minor Ricardian writers. Fisher's entire first chapter (pp. 1–36) is germane to the present essay; see esp. pp. 21–24. One particularly noteworthy effect of the long-standing attribution of the *Testament* to Chaucer was its role in sustaining the image of Chaucer as dissenting, if ultimately reconciled, son of the church: Usk's euphemized "biography" represents the author's earlier missteps and others' misreading of them as "heresy" and later reassimilation to Love's law and sect; these references were sometimes read literally by early readers as admissions of earlier lapses of religious faith and disavowed early adherence to Wycliffite belief. These remarks, however, occur within the fictional figuration of the work as Love's corrective pedagogy, and cannot be read as representations of their author's religious views.

tempted yet in prose or rhyme" in English: a complex account of the will and its constancy, drawn in detail from Anselm.[5] In Book III Usk appropriates Anselm's discussion of the human will as it operates within the divine moral and eschatological economy into the service of a broadly analogous argument about worldly integrity of purpose and loyalty in public or civic service—in effect a transmutation of theology into ethics and political theory: service of the earthly and heavenly "king" are uneasily merged in a distinctive and original idealistic discourse. It is an ambitious enterprise, and some would hold that its syncretic argument is at best only partly successful. But whatever its intrinsic merits as a piece of political-philosophical reasoning, for my purposes here it will suffice to emphasize its reception—or rather the lack of one: the argument of Usk's Book III was apparently of insufficient interest in the interval of more than three centuries between Thynne's printing and the later nineteenth century to permit any reader to notice fundamental ruptures of its expository logic and syntax in at least four places.[6]

5. While Usk's use of his source materials is not to my purpose here, it is worth remarking that while Anselm's discussion of these matters builds in part on the exposition of the fundamental problem of divine prescience and human free choice in the *Consolatio*, its philosophical bearing is quite different from that of Boethius. It is concerned with divine justice and the soul's salvation, as well as with the earlier philosopher's interest in a diffusely Platonic mode of what might be called general theological metaphysics. More central to Anselm's concerns than the metaphysics of fortune and foreknowledge is the difficult moral theology of the will, both divine and human, a discourse that became still more diversified in its terms, and controverted in its implications, in the years between Anselm and Usk. Thus, even though the Anselmian vocabulary Usk deployed in Book III is not in itself markedly more arcane than that of Boethius on the same topics, the distinctions it makes for Anselm are finer, and the implications differently drawn out. For detailed discussions of Usk's use of Anselm in Book III of the *Testament*, see George Sanderlin, "Usk's *Testament of Love* and St. Anselm," *Speculum* 17 (1942). 69–73, and Stephen Medcalf, "Transposition: Thomas Usk's Testament of Love," in *The Medieval Translator*, vol. 1, ed. Roger Ellis (Woodbridge, Suffolk: D. S. Brewer, 1989), pp. 181–195; for an account demonstrating that this work of Anselm is the specific source of Uks's "wexing tree" image in that book, see Lucy Lewis, "Langland's Tree of Charity and Usk's 'Wexing Tree,' " *Notes and Queries* 240, no. 4 (Dec. 1995), 429–433.

6. In partial extenuation of the printer's errors at these junctures, and his failure to notice them in setting copy, it should be said that the diction and general register of Usk's Book III are more rarefied for long stretches than any other text in Thynne's massive volume. As Thynne apparently lacked familiarity with some of Usk's legal terms (e.g. "torcencious" at I.vi.131; Skeat p. 28), the sixteenth-century printer also had little experience or knowledge of the terms of philosophical argument to guide him through what he would certainly have considered "scole-matere" of "gret difficulte" (had he taken the time to "read" it, in the modern sense of that term). Moreover, in preparing the Usk for printing, Thynne apparently had no second source for cross-checking, as he did in setting comparably abstruse material in the Chaucer corpus. As James E. Blodgett points out, Thynne used Caxton and at least one other manuscript for the text of *Boece* (to take one discursively close comparison), and he had similar second or multiple points of textual reference for much of the rest of his massive edition; see Blodgett's chapter "William Thynne" in *Editing Chaucer: The Great Tradition*, ed. Paul G. Ruggiers (Norman, Okla.: Pilgrim Books, 1984), pp. 35–52 (notes, pp. 255–259), esp. p. 45. In the face of the difficulties peculiar to Book III, Thynne did his best to "read" it, and present it, within the norms of what he apparently believed the work in general to be: a "gentil" and eloquent treatise on refined love, with a strongly Boethian cast—in other words, as a work testifying that *Troilus* stood at the "stremes hede"

Largely in consequence of this inattention, the general bearing and purpose of Usk's *Testament* as a whole—its design, and designs upon its primary intended recipients, whoever they may have been, as a rhetorical and communicative act within an articulated world of discourse—remained unexamined, beyond the capacious conviction that the work was "Chaucerian," even though the definition and implications of that affinity were not more closely specified. Only when the *Testament* was loosed from its critical moorings as a work of Chaucer were these intentional and performative dimensions of the work attended to, and then almost entirely to the discredit of its actual author.

Once firmly dissociated from the works of the father of English literature, its posture seen no longer as either pious or playful self-reference but unbecomingly motived emulation, the *Testament* was doubly orphaned as an object of literary-historical inquiry. It was newly culpable on two counts: for a prose style that only now came to be considered, by the first scholars to attempt to read it closely, pretentious and turgid; and for obtrusive, even abject, political designs of self-exculpation and ingratiation in the eyes of the powerful (generally understood to be the royal circle, however that might be defined). Like a lost or bastard child (as Plato famously says of a text circulating free of the intent of the living mind and voice from which it issued), the *Testament* was disabled by this textual isolation from giving a coherent account of itself. Despite (or perhaps because of) the gestures of literary as well as political self-explanation that pervade the text, the work was seen as little more than an assemblage of such gestures. The systematic designs of the work and its author upon the world of philosophic and poetic fiction (the chief discursive registers with which it associates itself throughout) seemed once again obscure, explicable only in terms of failed careerist or imitative aspirations. Usk's fall from political grace (he was executed, shortly after his new political master, Nicholas Brembre, March 3, 1388, as one of the London adherents of the royal faction purged during the brief ascendancy of Richard II's magnate opponents, the Lords Appellant) has, it seemed, closed off the legibility of his ambitious literary venture.

The intellectual reception of this work in longer retrospect is secondary, however, to the task of this essay. Rather, I wish to offer here a conjectural account of the *kind* of material text the printer had in hand: its format, layout, and ornament—all aspects of its *ordinatio* as a complete book—in order to discover unnoticed aspects of its designs as a verbal and material object, and the legibility of those designs to Usk's contemporaries and to Thynne. I

---

of a tradition. This discursive gap has some bearing on the textual treatment of Usk not only by his printer but also by his only published editor to date. Where Skeat lacks awareness of Usk's direct Latin source (as he does throughout most of Book III), and where the editor's account of the text requires semantic awareness beyond a sound sense of Middle English idiom, his identifications of lapses of sense, and his emendations, are often as unsteady as those one might want to attribute to the printer—or (the explanation Skeat and Bradley preferred) to the deplorable state of the manuscript the printer used. Examples discussed below will further bear out the way discursive obstacles were transmitted in the form of mechanical errors.

attempt here to enlist textual and codicological information and inference in the service of literary history, to ascertain their utility for historical understanding of the worlds of textual production and aspiration in which Usk moved and through which his book was made and preserved to the sixteenth century. I propose here to "read" the bibliographical codes rather than the philosophical argument of Usk's work, to demonstrate that the recoverable features of the material text functioned as metapoetic aspects of the *Testament*, and to show that the terms of art and connoisseurship by which they were to be noticed and understood are also verbally indicated, and amply supported and justified, in the author's proffered terms of art and gestures of self-exegesis.

On the face of it, this is a quixotic and paradoxical task: to pursue the legible, if elusive, account of itself that the material text of a work distinctively offers, yet in this case in the absence of the chief item of direct material evidence: the manuscript book of the *Testament*. It is, moreover, a venture founded upon error: this inferential reconstruction begins in, and is enabled by, more than one *felix culpa* of a textual rather than political character—the errors of Thynne's printer in the ordering of text, and then those of Skeat in reconstructing the correct sequence. Yet this largely reconstructive and descriptive account of a vanished material text does not engage more than glancingly the minutiae of textual criticism *per se* at the level of individual lections, and contributes little toward the much-needed new edition—though the description offered here may contribute to some systematic rather than piecemeal hypotheses about how some of Thynne's manifestly erroneous lections came about. Rather, this exercise enables us to "read" through the mishaps that befell the material text in transmission some information both about Usk's literary designs and about their immediate fortunes and standing within a few years of his death, and also to recover the terms and limits of Thynne's "reading" of the bibliographical codes of this purportedly Chaucerian work. We can thus infer how Thynne regarded this text, not only as a valued piece of Chauceriana, but also as a piece of fine bookmaking whose codes of physical presentation he could at least admire and attempt to preserve in his own layout of the text, even as he nevertheless failed to read in them the many layers of textworker wit that informed Usk's deployment of them. Not *although*, but *because* it betrays at best partial understanding of Usk's work, Thynne's print representation of it discloses much about the character of the lost manuscript, and about the many signals it provided, through its physical format and manner of presentation, of the arts of perspicuous viewing and reading on which the lost manuscript book implicitly depended for its address and immediate reception, and to which it explicitly adverts in its self-advertisement.

By thus "reading" a material text that no longer survives, I also propose a revised understanding of the implied audience immediately addressed by the work, and of the mode and language through which Usk asserted his purpose and its performative claims—both of which have long dominated both historical and philological accounts of the *Testament*. All authorities thus far agree that Usk meant with this work to ingratiate himself with those "on whom [his] fate might depend"; critics to date have differed chiefly in the degree of disgust this (stipulatively) ulterior yet all-too-transparent motive excites. While I do not ultimately disagree with this claim as a general description of the work's intentional design, I dissociate the present account from much of what has often followed from this observation—and not simply in my rather more benign view of the ethics of Usk's enterprise. These I find no more unworthy than those implicit in, say, Chaucer's "Envoy to Scogan" or *Legend of Good Women*, or Gower's "In Praise of Peace" or *Confessio Amantis*: all texts, I suggest, which participate in a larger conversation among men of letters about their shared condition as thinkers and actors in a world in which they were ultimately dependents—a conversation to which Usk's work eloquently testifies, and to which it contributed significantly.[7] More fundamentally, I identify differently from most scholars heretofore who those were "on whom Usk's fate might depend": these addresses were in the first instance, I claim, other members of the clerical class, not the magnates, burgesses, or royal patrons who might employ them—the latter usually imagined by modern critics to be the intended readers of this work.[8]

More fundamentally still, I dispute the purported *ulteriority* of the work's motives, and of the terms of its intentional artfulness. These are, I shall show, in plain view, and plainly, pervasively, and wittily legible in this remarkably

7. Paul Strohm, in "Politics and Poetics: Usk and Chaucer in the 1380s," in *Literary Practice and Social Chance in Britain, 1380–1530*, ed. Lee Patterson (Berkeley: Univ. of California Press, 1990), pp. 83–112, imagines Usk producing the *Testament* "in a state of undoubted isolation" (p. 105). In this essay, and in another complementary to it—"The Textual Vicissitudes of Usk's Appeal," in his book *Hochon's Arrow: The Social Imagination of Fourteenth Century Texts* (Princeton: Princeton Univ. Press, 1992), pp. 145–160—Strohm offers the most nuanced and attentive reading that Usk's career and writings have had recently, or perhaps ever. His focus in both essays is Usk's political self-positioning through skillful textual interventions. While Strohm offers excellent discussions of the broad generic frameworks of each of Usk's two main textual initiatives (his approver's appeal against his former employer, London mayor John Northampton, and the *consolatio* of the *Testament*), it is largely extraneous to his purpose to discuss at length other literary and bibliographical codes to which Usk adverted with the *Testament*. The present essay intends chiefly to complement Strohm's work with an examination of these additional facets of Usk's textual self-fashioning, rather than to contest work of unparalleled value in restoring Usk, and the medium of his art, to serious, sympathetic, and detailed consideration. I shall, however, propose here that we might usefully further qualify our notion of what Usk's "isolation" might have meant, both as a description of his social situation, and as a factor in the production of his ambitious literary venture. While Usk seems not to have succeeded as he might have wished in reshaping his political reputation, his textual environment— that is, a discursive field that encompassed poetic, legal, and bibliographical codes, the chief means through which Usk's imagination articulated its purposes, as I shall argue here— was, I believe, rich in companionship, shared expertise and professional "language" (in an extended sense of the term), and moral and material support. That this kind of "friendship" proved ultimately inefficacious to save him from his political destiny is a fact of some importance for literary as well as political and cultural history—but this inference did not escape the men of letters among those contemporaries who survived him.

8. This exercise tends to corroborate the view of May Newman Hallmundsson, "The Community of Law and Letters: Some Notes on Thomas Usk's Audience," *Viator* 9 (1978), 357–365, though it greatly amplifies the technical means and bearing of the work in this context.

intricate text and book—above all to Usk's fellow "clerics": textworkers and bibliophiles who blend without distinction into the several other occupations covered by this capacious and fluid term in the later fourteenth century. The category encompasses scriveners as well as versifiers, ecclesiastical and legal odd-job and regular-service men of several sorts: in a lifetime, and in rapid alternation, one man might be described accurately under several of these headings. The *Testament*, I suggest, speaks in the first instance to such men, and in their craft-languages—that is, to those who serve, not to the king, lords, or knights as prospective "patrons." It speaks, in short, to others of Usk's kind, to those for whom documentary and bibliographic high literacy is a means and medium of service, whose self-image and skills, and terms of art and connoisseurship, are acquired "on the job" (whatever the job may be), whose positions and self-representations are for all that largely under-authorized, and for whom these common facts of life are matters of complex self-awareness, as the founding conditions of what would in retrospect be called literature. Usk's art in the *Testament*, I suggest, shows most clearly in his witty and complex engagement with the terms and values of these textworkers' common vocation (and the problems of their necessary self-advertisement) within that capacious yet elusive and precarious category of being: men *of letters*.

Usk's self-representation in the *Testament* wittily realizes this common-place identity of the verbal artist in the most literal way possible: an acrostic formed by the initial letters of each chapter spells out Usk's name in a petitionary message that extends across all three books of the work: (I) MARGARETE OF (II) VIRTW HAVE MERCI (III) ON THIN VSK. Only with the nineteenth-century conjectural reordering of the displaced segments of the text as it appeared in Thynne was the acrostic message and authorial signature recovered, confirming the attribution of the work to Usk—an attribution earlier conjectured by Henry Bradley, who recognized in some features of the euphemistically occulted "biography" of the persona of the work events that accorded with some of Usk's actions as scrivener of, then as appealer against, London Mayor John Northampton in the fraught London political climate of the 1380s. Since then there has been little attention to the text *per se*, which has seen no new published edition since Skeat's in the 1897 supplementary seventh volume to his six-volume *Works* of Chaucer (which remains the only published edition to this day, and is therefore by default my text of reference here). Skeat's conjectural account of the disordering of the printer's copy is still, therefore, the only one readily available.[9] I have

9. Three unpublished Ph.D. dissertations, to my knowledge, have undertaken to provide a sounder text of the *Testament*, and to correct Skeat's mistaken reconstruction of the displaced text in Book III: Ramona Bressie (Univ. of Chicago, 1932), Virginia Bording Jellech (Washington Univ., St. Louis, 1970), and John Leyerle (Harvard Univ., 1977). The last two of these re-edited the text, and Jellech's, perhaps as the more readily available of these two, has become to some recent scholars the text of reference; Leyerle reports (personal communication, May 1996) that he is preparing an edition for publication, as is R. Allen Shoaf. Jellech's dissertation, which I have consulted, seconds Bressie's correction of the sequence of text in Book III, but does not deal systematically with the mechanics of text-

learned much from, and largely agree with, the work of those scholars who have since undertaken to correct Skeat's reconstruction, but here I use Skeat's text heuristically, in the service of a different enterprise: to discover the bibliographical and metapoetic signs of Usk's effort to engage the attention of the "sleigh inseers" and "good bookamenders" he seeks, and to prompt reconsideration of the milieu and semiotic systems within which he made his bid for "frendes," and of the immediate fortunes of these efforts.

I

Skeat conjectured, somewhat perfunctorily, that Thynne's source text might have consisted of ten quires of 8, laid out in what he calls, without further specification, "the usual way," and that the displaced portion of Book III represented one quire of 8 plus one of 2, both refolded, the latter cut along the spine and the whole resorted in a complex pattern that is difficult to understand, still less reconstruct. Working in two directions simultaneously—from the dimensions of the displaced segments as identified by Skeat, and from the beginning of the work to the first point of disruption—I sought to derive a page and quiring format that could account for Thynne's erroneous ordering of text, and the point at which it occurred—to determine, in other words, what "the usual way" of formatting and quiring a vernacular prose work in manuscript was for Skeat.[10] An adequate account of Thynne's manuscript

---

disarrangement or the format of the lost manuscript. Bressie, in the 1928 article cited above (p. 28, n. 1), was the first to discover that (to state the case somewhat inaccurately for the moment; we will refine it below), Skeat's edition reverses the correct order of the fifth and sixth chapters of Usk's Book III, but she did not pursue the implications of this correction for understanding the quiring and other formatting features of the lost manuscript. Rather, because the text was still in her view defective at some of these points of disruption, she conjectured substantial loss of text from Thynne's edition; as will be seen below, I consider this hypothesis unnecessary to account for Thynne's text, and for the formal features of the lost manuscript that immediately underlay it. Her correction of Skeat's reconstruction is the more impressive in that she discerned from Usk's arguments alone, without reference to his Latin source text, the correct continuity of the text of Book III: her work predates by more than a decade the discovery, published by George Sanderlin in 1942, of the St. Anselm source text for much of Book III. As we shall see below, the continuities and discontinuities in Usk's use of his source confirms Bressie's account of the correct order of text.

10. Skeat's account of the mechanics of internal disruption within the sequence of misplaced segments was, as Bressie noted, less troublesome to this purpose than his puzzling characterization of the relative volume of the disrupted portion in relation to the preceding continuous text. As she observed—and as a mere page count of Skeat's edition should have revealed—the total volume of displaced printed text was not, as Skeat's claim seemed to require, a little more than 1/10 the size of the undisrupted preceding text of the work to that point, but more like 1/5 (displaced text, as rearranged by Skeat, continuously fills pages 118–143 of Skeat's 145–page text). If only one quire of 8 and a bifolium were involved in the displacement, then each page of the manuscript would have had to contain about 70 lines of Thynne's text as printed in a rather compact typeface, and the disruption would then have been preceded by five similar quires, not ten. In that case, the source manuscript would almost certainly have been laid out as a relatively small double-column page, which seemed to me an unlikely disposition of a vernacular prose work of that length—especially if it came to the printer's hands detached (as its unbound state implies) from a larger mis-

should be able to propose a rearrangement of the discontinuous blocs of text that would not only yield continuous sense (as in broad terms Skeat's reconstruction did), but also lend itself to systematic bibliographical description of the entire lost volume. It would, that is, be able to explain how the continuous preceding manuscript text was both laid out on the page and disposed into quires so as to put the first interruption—if not at the end of a quire, at least at the end of a leaf—at a point 76.5 of Thynne's printed lines into Book III, chapter iv.[11]

In attempting to determine a size module for a page, and hence for a quire, in the manuscript used by Thynne, I used the number of lines of Thynne's text as *a basis for description and comparison,* as a unit of measurement to describe chapter-lengths; I call these units Th-lines. (Appendix A lists these.) I did not, of course, assume that Thynne's lines of print each corresponded directly to a line of manuscript; rather, the Th-line simply represented a regularity of amplitude which would have a counterpart in the product of regular scribal hand or hands in the manuscript. Scribal abbreviations, even if not replicated in Thynne, would, I presumed, nevertheless have been used consistently over the long course of the scribe's work, and therefore themselves exhibit a regularity that would warrant the use of line-counts of Thynne's text to serve as a basis for division and comparison of textual units.[12] For this purpose, I took Skeat's reconstructed division and sequence of chapters in the disordered portion of Thynne's text as provisionally correct (since it makes superficially good syntactical and logical

---

cellany. If on the other hand Skeat simply misspoke, and the misordered portion occupied not one but two quires and a bifolium, following ten similar undisrupted quires, this would imply a manuscript page-format containing about 36 of Thynne's lines, in more plausible single-column format.

11. While it was my initial hypothesis that a work of this length came to Thynne's hands as a book (even if an unbound one) rather than in a miscellany, the more fundamental question was not its contiguity with other works, but its presumptive internal integrity and format. (In a continuous prose text with catchwords—for as I shall show below, Thynne's source had catchwords—*misbound* manuscript text seemed unlikely; therefore only an *unbound* manuscript text could have allowed the disordering of quires by the printer.) Whether I was naive or unjustified in my initial assumption—that double-column format would be an unlikely disposition of a vernacular work of this kind and length, especially as a free-standing text—I must leave to more experienced codicologists to judge. As this essay will suggest, however, the only other format that readily lends itself to explaining the displacement of text in Book III would be a layout much like Thynne's: a double-column page with about 48 lines per column, and hence 192–195 of Thynne's lines per leaf—a layout, in short, much like the large Ellesmere manuscript. (Thynne's format for the *Testament* is a two-column page of 48 lines, as it is for all other prose works in this large folio edition: Chaucer's *Boece, Astrolabe,* and the Parson's Tale, for example.) But like other formats I attempted, this one had far less explanatory power in accounting for other features of Thynne's text, so I do not present it schematically here.

12. Only after deriving a plausible tentative hypothesis about the general format of the manuscript could one examine Thynne's text for signs that implied compression or elision of text in the source manuscript, or any other indication of irregularities of amplitude in scribal hand or usage, especially toward the ends of manuscript quires, and toward the end of the work—a hunch that would eventually prove useful, as did the presumption of scribal abbreviation in the manuscript.

sense of Book III), until it could be shown otherwise. In the event, I was able to confirm Bressie's and Jellech's revision of Skeat's reconstruction, but to somewhat different ends than the recovery of continuous expository sense. In the interim, however, Skeat's error proved to be heuristic *felix culpa*, forcing into view the quiring scheme of the lost manuscript.

My only other initial hypothesis concerned the initial letters of chapters that bore the petitionary acrostic. I conjectured that Thynne's source must also have had some visual formula and ornamental program for featuring the acrostic chapter-initials—the only element of Thynne's *mise-en-page* that enabled the recovery of the acrostic.[13] Thynne does not number the chapter divisions within the three Books of the work, as Skeat does in his edition; it is therefore highly unlikely that his source had numbered chapters, for such unambiguous indication of sequence would very likely have prevented the massive disordering of text in Book III, as well as the printer's failure to identify the correct chapter divisions at II.x and III.iv. Although the printer marks the three-book division of Usk's work by many signals, using headings and closings (e.g. "Thus endeth the seconde booke, and here after foloweth the thirde boke") and running page heads, and a disposition of text such that each of the three Books begins at the head of a column on a recto page, he identifies the *Testament*'s chapters as such only by large feature initials, in nearly all cases (except of course where they come at the head of a column, as they do with remarkable frequency, especially early in the work) also preceded by an interval of space, equivalent in vertical dimension to a line or two of type.[14]

Because Thynne scarcely ever further subdivides Usk's prose into paragraphs by indenting—as he does, for instance, with Chaucer's Parson's Tale— these acrostic initials are virtually the only visual indicator of textual segmentation below the level of book-division.[15] It therefore seemed reasonable to

13. I use the term "initial" for a letter that falls at the beginning of a line of text, and indicates—by larger size, placement within an inset space-block, or different typeface such as bold, or by any combination of these—the beginning of a unit of text; I reserve the term "capital" for letters of whatever typeface that are actually in the upper case of that face. In Thynne, sentences do not always begin with capitals, and sometimes the textface capital is the sole marker of new unit; see Appendix C. For the distinction, and the complex distinctions it marks in liturgical manuscripts, see Andrew Hughes, *Medieval Manuscripts for Mass and Office: A Guide to Their Organization and Terminology* (Toronto: Univ. of Toronto Press, 1982), p. 103.

14. This is the general typographic formula for dividing prose that Thynne used, following Caxton, in presenting Chaucer's *Boece*, and in *Treatise on the Astrolabe*: in those works, chapters are not numbered, but receive a feature initial (or the space for one; see below), in a feature-block two or three lines in height, and of equal width, integrated into the upper right corner of the text-block. In Chaucer's two free-standing prose works, these subdivisions also have headings: in *Boece*, there are extensive *incipits* of the corresponding Latin text; in *Astrolabe*, sections of text have descriptive headers in English, most of them at least a clause in length. Similarly, the text of the Parson's Tale is divided with topical Latin phrasal headers, "De Ira," "De Invidia," and the like, and the immediately ensuing text occasionally (though not usually) begins with a small feature initial similar to those used in beginning Usk's chapters.

15. Thynne's text of Usk sometimes runs for more than three double-column pages with no readily visible subdivision apart from the chapter-capitals and/or a one-line space.

infer that in these respects—the use of feature initials, and the comparative lack of other internal segmentation within chapters—Thynne's textual disposition was somehow guided by that of his source.[16] A subordinate conjecture, therefore, was that the initial capital of each Book in the manuscript text might have been especially large and prominent: Thynne awards these three book-initials far more elaborate woodblock capitals than he gives to other chapter-initials—or indeed, as we shall see, to any other unit-initials anywhere in his huge folio volume. I hypothesized, and resolved to test the hypothesis in my reconstruction, that these acrostic initials might also have fallen at the heads of pages, for maximum visual impact, drawing the reader's attention to the acrostic as a diacritical ornament of the work as well as an adornment of the physical page.[17]

Because in addition the chapters of Book III are on average about 44 of Thynne's lines longer than those of Book II, and about 40 lines longer than those of Book I (see Appendix A)—and also because, as noted, they present continuous argument that is not only intrinsically difficult, but relatively inert and unpointed rhetorically, in comparison with the exposition of the first two books—it becomes easy to imagine how textual displacement occurred, and remained long unrecognized as such, in the setting of Book III. Facing a manuscript lacking division into units any smaller than the chapter, and without other internal visual signal except infrequent catchwords, the typesetter failed to notice a displaced quire until he had progressed far into setting it. The oversight is still more easily forgiven when one recognizes that for the next three hundred years no other readers seem to have detected it either.

16. This inference is further supported by the printer's behavior in allocating space and woodblock ornament to the chapter-initials (for a complete list, see Appendix C). Especially in the first two-thirds of the work, he set aside space for large initials, even where he apparently lacked at the outset of the job a sufficiently full array of decorative woodblock letters for the purpose. At three places in Book II—at II.iii (for the initial R), v (W) and x (M)—the printer allocates a block of space 3 lines high and equally wide for a feature initial that never materialized; the letter wanted is indicated by a capital from the text font used as a guide-letter, holding a place for the expected ornamental block in the center of the feature block (in much the same way that guide-letters are lightly inscribed in the space set aside for the later ministrations of the painter or limner in manuscript books). In five other places the printer marks a chapter division by a line-indent of a space one or two letters in width—and also in all but one instance by a preceding space vertically equivalent to one line of type—but the chapter-initial used is merely a capital of the text-font: at I.iv (A), x (F), III.ii (N), iii (T) and iv (H, preceded by no separating vertical spacing). The increased frequency of errors in chapter-divisions in the latter part of the work offers some evidence—to be discussed systematically below—that the ornamental program of the manuscript may have changed a little more than halfway through the work, in such a way that the decorative marking of chapter-initials had become less visually distinctive, even while remaining systematic: once in Book II (where he supplied two erroneous divisions instead of the one correct one) and once in Book III (an instance unnoticed by Skeat and all readers since, as we shall see), within the portion of displaced text, the printer erred in identifying the chapter initial. Yet the fact that the chapter-divisions were with one exception correctly indicated all the way through the displaced portion of text in Book III also suggests that this feature of the manuscript's *ordinatio* was maintained in some visually distinctive fashion all the way through the text. Where the printer seems to have become confused, I shall suggest, is at points of transition between one decorative code and another in the general program for marking the chapter-initials.

17. On the diacritical use of acrostics, anagrams, and other signatory or self-referential devices in late-medieval vernacular texts, see my essay "William Langland's 'Kynde Name':

As Skeat discovered, Thynne erred in Book II in identifying some of the acrostic-bearing chapter capitals; while Skeat corrected these in his edition, he himself erred, as I shall show, in reconstructing not only the sequence but also the division of chapters in Book III.[18] Yet each of these errors, both Thynne's and Skeat's, enabled unsought and finer-grained conjectures, not only for confirming earlier scholars' corrections of Skeat's reconstruction, but—more important for my purposes—facilitating the recovery of what counted for Thynne as the chief bibliographical codes that influenced not only his formatting but possibly even his selection of Usk's text as an important piece of Chauceriana. These inadvertences offered unexpected access to a virtual, if not actual, bibliographical "reading"—quire by quire, page by page, if not word by word—of a manuscript book that no longer exists, and to the world of discursive codes that defined its legibility and expressive form to its intended primary users.

II

The labor of approximating a description of Thynne's source scarcely lends itself to narration except as a long process of trial and error, in search of those general text-modules of page and quire that would alone yield Thynne's disposition of text, both erroneous and correctly restored, and no other. Because this untidy and often-repeated exercise in what one bemused observer of the messy process termed the "lower mathematics" makes better reading in summary than reproduced play-by-play (its main findings are presented schematically in Appendices A, B, and C), I shall first state in summary form its outcome: my derived general description of the absent manuscript. I shall then review the inferential sequence by which it was derived.

The normative page of Thynne's source of the *Testament*—the pattern

---

Authorial Signature and Social Identity in Late Fourteenth-Century England," in *Literary Practice and Social Change in Britain, 1380–1530*, ed. Lee Patterson (Berkeley: Univ. of California Press, 1990), pp. 15–82.

18. Thynne's (or his printer's) manner of resolving his failure to detect the correct capital to represent the chapter head of II.xi, "Every soule of reson hath two thinges of ster . . ."—which in the printed text begins a new sentence without a capital and appears in Thynne without intervening spatial division as line 41 in col. 1 of a verso page—is revealing of what he took to be the relevant signals in his source. It is revealing, too, that he was aware of it at the point of marking off copy, and not at the typesetting stage: having noted that he had missed a signal of chapter-division at a point where he evidently expected one, he took steps to make up the deficiency, using cues he apparently considered normal in the manuscript, and he reproduced these cues with his rectification. He chose as chapter-dividing capitals the letter C that heads f. 348v, col. 1 ("Certayn (qd I) amonge thynges . . .") and the letter T that heads f. 349r, col. 2 ("Trewly lady to you it were a gret . . .")—one letter preceding (by 40 lines) and one following (by 104 lines) the correct chapter initial—thus redividing the two chapters x and xi, as presented in Skeat, into three, and obscuring the acrostic at this point (MCTRCI instead of MERCI). As will be seen in the quiring diagram (Appendix B), in my conjectural reconstruction of the manuscript the letters C and T would also have fallen in page-initial position in Thynne's source (at the head of 1r and 4r of their quire of 8, instead of at the beginning of f. 2v of the quire, where the correct chapter-division would have occurred).

that was used for ruling and planning the entire manuscript book, and that remained nearly constant through scribal production from beginning to end of the work—contained a fraction more than 24 of Thynne's lines. It was disposed in such a way as to serve Thynne through nearly half the work as a remarkably reliable guide in marking off a manuscript that he would present in print in a double-column format of 48 lines, the layout he also used for other Chaucerian prose works in the volume. Because the manuscript design seems to have served Thynne's printer so neatly and well so far into the work, as well as for additional reasons discussed below, I inferred that the actual manuscript page ruling was, if not for 24 lines, then something very close to it, probably no more than 27.[19] The hand or hands were probably fairly regular and professional—a feature perhaps unsurprising in a work that was composed by a professional scribe and may never have travelled far from his circle.[20] The inferrable amplitude of the hand—expressed as the number of characters and word-spaces per manuscript page—varies scarcely at all from the beginning to the end of the work, and its slight variation occurs in clearly describable stages. The module of less than 24.5 lines (that is, the number of lines of Thynne's text that corresponds to a page of his conjectured source) remains remarkably constant throughout Book I and the first two full quires of 8 in book II, creeping toward 25 by midway through Book II, and to slightly over 25 by the end of Book II, attaining by the end of Book III an average of 26.28 in the final quire.[21] These specifications

19. Though it may not be useful to compare presentations of prose and verse texts—and in any case more widely experienced codicologists than I will be able to furnish more apposite comparisons for the book format I conjecture here—I note that this ruling resembles that of the Holloway fragment of *Piers Plowman C*, and less exactly that of other early C manuscripts; see Ralph Hanna III, "Studies in the Manuscripts of Piers Plowman," *Yearbook of Langland Studies* 7 (1993), 1–25, esp. 2–5. M. C. Seymour, "The English Manuscripts of *Mandeville's Travels*," *Edinburgh Bibliographical Society Transactions* 4, part 55 (1966), 167–210, describes several manuscript books of the fourteenth and fifteenth centuries made in the page-format I conjecture here: between 22 and 28 lines. The page-sizes of these vary from a small 130 x 90 mm, with a ruled text-block of 90 x 55 mm (a 24-line page), to 255 x 180 mm, with a text-block of 180 x 120 mm (a 28-line page); most fall in the range of 210-220 mm high x 140-145 mm wide, with a median text-block size of 145 x 95 mm. These comparisons, while limited in range, at least indicate that the size and arrangement I hypothesize here is not an unusual one for vernacular manuscript books, and was a common one in use for copies of Mandeville's prose work.

20. It has been conjectured that Thynne's source may have been an autograph; see, for example, Paul Strohm, "Politics and Poetics," p. 105. Compositions showing the author's or compiler's careful spatial planning of text layout are not unknown in the fourteenth century; see, for example Lucy Freeman Sandler, "*Omne bonum: Compilatio* and *Ordinatio* in an English Illustrated Encyclopedia of the Fourteenth Century," in *Medieval Book Production: Assessing the Evidence*, ed. L. L. Brownrigg Los Altos Hills, Calif.: Anderson-Lovelace, 1990), pp. 183–200; see also discussion below of the implications of the design program of the manuscript.

21. The amplitude of the hand quire by quire may be calculated by using the figures in Appendices A and B together. This slight but regular change in ratio between the necessarily constant amplitude of the printed text and the average number of manuscript lines and pages that I conjecture it represents might be explained in several ways, some of which must await both a general account of the quiring and my reconstruction of the displacement of text in Book III. One possibility would be a change of scribal hand at Book III

suggest a page size of about 210 x 150 mm, with a text-block of about 150 x 100 mm.[22]

The quire structure, too, is remarkably regular throughout. Though the manuscript book may have remained unbound—and certainly was unbound when Thynne used it—it shows signs (discussed further below) of unitary planning as a volume, laid out and assembled in uniformly ruled quires of 8; the few exceptions to this rule in turn lend themselves to simple statement in the form of rules.[23] In order to account for the quiring pattern that emerged from my explanation of the Book III displacements of text, I conjectured that each of the three Books of the work began with a new quire, and quires were abbreviated as necessary at the ends of each book by the common practice of subtracting bifolia or single leaves at the end of the unit. This plan would also have assured that an especially elaborate, and very probably painted, first-chapter capital for each Book (one which might have occupied an initial block of at least twice the vertical and horizontal dimensions of

---

or in the latter chapters of Book II, to a second scribe who could fit slightly more text into the same previously ruled page, an explanation which for the moment presupposes what I shall shortly show: these inferable regularities imply forethought in the design of the entire book as a single program and product. For further discussion, see Appendix B, Note on Book III.

22. This estimate of page size is based not only on the range of page-dimensions for English vernacular prose in books of similar line-ruling, as described by Samuels (above), but also on my own conjectures, based on statistical norms derived from the characteristics and amplitudes of the five professional scribal hands of the early fifteenth century discussed, and shown in actual-size photographic reproduction in the illustrative plates, in A. I. Doyle and M. B. Parkes, "The Production of Copies of The *Canterbury Tales* and the *Confessio Amantis* in the Early Fifteenth Century," in *Medieval Scribes, Manuscripts, and Libraries: Essays Presented to N. R. Ker*, ed. M. B. Parkes and Andrew G. Watson (London: Scolar, 1978), pp. 163–210. Different as these five hands are in individual characteristics, their amplitude—as described by the number of letters on average per horizontal centimeter, combined with the average number of lines of text per vertical centimeter—is remarkably similar. Across all of the illustrative plates, these hands range from about 1.6 to 1.8 lines of text per vertical centimeter, and 4.5–4.85 characters, including spaces, on average per horizontal centimeter, thus suggesting a range of amplitude in the professional text-hands used in vernacular books at the close of the fourteenth century—a range within which, I propose, one might conjecturally approximate a text-block size that would contain some 24–26 of Thynne's lines (which on average contain about 44 characters per line, or about 1056 characters, including spacing and diacritics, per 24 lines). If a conjectured normal page of the manuscript contained 24 to 26.28 lines of Thynne's text, and the scribal hand of Thynne's source were of a size and character similar to those described by Doyle and Parkes, then to contain the same number of characters as this text-module in Thynne, a text-block ruled to contain 24–27 lines of text would have to be about 100 cm wide (cf. 75 in Thynne), and 135–150 mm high. These dimensions fall in about the middle of the range of those page-formats of 22–28 lines in the Mandeville manuscripts described by Samuels, the dimensions of which in turn suggest for the Usk manuscript a normal layout protocol in which a page-width is about equal to the vertical dimension of the text-block, with a page-height at least one-third larger than the width: i.e. about 210 x 150 mm.

23. See Appendix B for a general quiring description, and contents by chapter. I propose below a shift in decorative program in the latter half of the work that might further affect both the slightly increased volume of text per page in this part of the text, and also help to account for the printer's errors and other irregularies in indicating chapter divisions correctly, which are also confined to the later half of the work.

those devoted to other acrostic chapter-capitals) would occur on the first page—and the flesh side—of a new quire.[24]

In a text of this page and quiring design, the dislocated text would begin at a point 72–81 lines into chapter iv (in fact, after 76.5 of Thynne's lines) of Book III—at what we may now specify as the end of a regular quire of 8. The displaced text, moreover, would fill exactly three quires, followed by a final quire of two leaves: a bifolium in which three of the four sides contain the remaining text (80.6 of Thynne's lines) of the final chapter of the work.

Thus far, neither the page nor quiring arrangement in this conjecturally reconstructed manuscript book is unusual in any way: as we have seen, many surviving vernacular books of the late fourteenth or early fifteenth century share these features of the *Testament*'s general bibliographic design. From this combination of page and quiring features, however, a noteworthy and wholly unexpected further patterned regularity of the lost book emerged: the *acrostic capital of every chapter in the work would occur naturally in page-initial position*, in the upper left corner of the text-block.[25] Moreover, except in a very few instances (exceptions which all occur in the last third of the manuscript) all of these acrostic capitals would have fallen naturally on a flesh-side of the leaf.[26]

24. Here Thynne seems to have taken his cues about the bibliographical codes appropriate to the presentation of the *Testament* from the *mise-en-page* of his manuscript: the two largest woodblock decorated initials used anywhere in his huge folio volume are assigned to the acrostic capitals of Usk's Prologue (M) and Book II.i (V): ornate capitals seven lines high. For the head-letter of Book I, the acrostic initial to chapter i (A), which begins the next recto page following the Prologue, he uses an initial five lines high—the same size decorative capital he uses to begin *Romaunt of the Rose*, to head the books of *Boece*, and as the first letter of the *Astrolabe*. For the head-letter of Book III, the acrostic initial to chapter i (O), he uses a decorated capital four lines high—the same one, in fact, he had used to begin the Parson's Tale. (For a summary listing of Thynne's treatment of chapter-initials, see Appendix C.) In Books II and III, Usk's first chapter also serves the function of a prologue, not only to its Book, but as an additional general statement of purpose, method, and design of the whole work, amplifying the initial Prologue. In making sure that each of these begins at the head of col. 2 of a recto page, Thynne may have registered this further general prefatory and metapoetic function of these initial chapters, as well as the division of Books—for he did not thus apportion text, for instance, at the book divisions of *Boece*, which occur in mid-column. In other words, Thynne's care in securing these printerly elegances in disposing major divisions of text may approximate, with the means afforded by his own general *mise-en-page* for prose works in the volume, those of the manuscript before him, and his sense of the principles of its *ordinatio*.

25. For a complete listing of the placement of chapter-initials within the quire in my reconstruction, see Appendix B. In Books I and II, the acrostic chapter-initials fall on a recto page in 15 instances and on a verso page 9 times, while in Book III all chapters but the first begin on a verso page. In the normal quiring I have described, only five (with a sixth possible) of the 34 chapter-initials would fall on the hair-side of a leaf. These apparent exceptions allow further inference about the book's design program; discussion of their implications follows my account of the displaced text in Book III.

26. The bibliographical implications of these hair-side capitals will be considered more closely below. For the moment, let it suffice to note that the hair-side chapter-capitals, as conjectured from the normal quiring pattern I propose here, would with normal folding and assembly of the quire occur in the two places in the work where large-scale printer error in the segmentation of text also occurs; see Appendix B. In Book III, the first of two chapter-

It is difficult to attribute this extraordinarily consistent pattern to mere statistical chance, and also hard to avoid its clear implication: that the page-module of the book was a factor in the design of the work that intersected at some stage of its realization with the production and shaping of the verbal text. That is, the semiotics of the spatial and scribal *ordinatio* of the book and those of its composition as a verbal artifact were in some fashion, and at some stage of its making, linked in its production as a book. As an object of unitary physical as well as conceptual design, it proclaimed its maker's intent through the disposition of its physical space and acrostic signature as well as through its rhetorical style and philosophical "content," and as a book it invoked and rewarded several kinds of sophisticated awareness of the arts of textual design simultaneously.

To ascertain further features of this impressive program of book design, and to understand their relation to other aspects of Usk's declarations of form, method, and purpose, we will need to examine more closely that portion of the text that offers the one glaring exception to these regularities: the displacement of text in Book III. Through a reconstruction of the mechanics of its occurrence, and the design principles implicit in the correct restoration of textual order, it will also be possible to discern additional details of the physical disposition of the manuscript book—and ultimately to elucidate the terms of Usk's literary self-presentation and self-exegesis. At this point not only Thynne's *culpa* but Skeat's became for my purposes *felix*: nothing short of a detailed re-examination of the textual as well as discursive and argumentative logic involved in these sections of the work—the sections that both Skeat and Thynne evidently found its least interesting part, but which most

---

capitals that falls on a hair-side of a leaf is iv (H); it is at the conclusion of that quire, at 76.5 of Thynne's lines into chapter iv, that the first disruption of text occurs—with an erroneously chosen next quire, as we shall shortly see. In Book II, all hair-side chapter-initials would have occurred within the last two full quires of 8, according to the most probable quiring pattern for this Book, between chapters x–xiii; it is for that reason that in Appendix B I suggest a local alteration in the quiring pattern—still regular, but subdividing eights into fours—that would have prevented these occurrences, *if* the maker of the manuscript book had wished to do so. It was within the first of these two quires that, as Skeat discovered, Thynne failed to identify the chapter break between x and xi, choosing the wrong capitals to denote chapter division, thus reapportioning x and xi as Skeat (correctly) divides them, into three, and obscuring the acrostic at this point (MCTRCI instead of MERCI). The three chapters thus erroneously created were 176, 144.5, and 72 lines long, instead of the 216 and 175 lines of the correct two-chapter division of these 391 lines of text; it should be noted at this point that both divisions of this body of text—Thynne's as well as the correct one—share a factor of 24, plus or minus less than one of Thynne's lines, for each unit. At least as significant as their length, however, for understanding the error of Thynne (or that of his printer Thomas Godfrey) in the chapter division of Book II is the position within its quire of the one chapter signal the printer missed: that of chapter xi (E), which would have occurred either on f. 2v or f. 6v of its quire (see Appendix B). Thus far in the manuscript this is an unusual position for a chapter division. By this point in the work Thynne had good reason to expect divisions to occur on ff. 1 or 5, on a recto page, or failing all these, a flesh side of the leaf. Thynne's solution to the problem—to choose instead chapter-division initials, C and T, that headed recto pages of the first and fourth (or in an alternative quiring the fifth and eighth) leaves of their quire—shows his understanding of the norms of his source so far.

concerned me—could possibly have offered the almost fortuitous access their editorial work affords to the terms of design and craft-knowledge displayed by the manuscript of the *Testament* and advertised by its author, as well as to the arts of reading and "appreciation"—entirely continuous with those of its making—that as a manuscript book it elicited from its readers, and received at least in part from Thynne.

III

Skeat's correction of Thynne's disordered text in Book III led him to postulate *six discontinuous segments of text,* which I shall label DS 1 through DS 6, *following the order in which they occur in Thynne,* not the order in which Skeat places them in his restoration.[27] In Skeat's reconstruction, which followed Bradley's, the correct sequence of these six displaced segments is DS 5, 3, 6, 2, 4, 1. The total volume of displaced material constitutes about ⅗ of the total length of Book III. The largest segment of uninterrupted text within the disordered portion, DS 1, is approximately ⅓ the length of this displaced portion (420.5 of the total of 1241 lines—exactly the volume of text that would be contained in a quire of 8 ruled to accommodate just over 26 of Thynne's lines per page), i.e. ⅕ of the length of the whole of Book III; I therefore conjectured that it represented the last full quire of the manuscript. This postulate could not, however, explain the disturbance within the other two hypothesized quires that would produce the text-order reconstructed by Skeat. In every format I attempted, the remaining discontinuities would fall about the middle of a page, not (as it seemed the facts of the case to that point demanded) at the end of a leaf—yet I could discern nothing at any of these junctures that would form a basis for eyeskip by the printer, or suggest the omission of text.

As Ramona Bressie first discerned, however, Skeat's reconstructed se-

27. The following is keyed to Thynne's text (Th), and followed by the location of the segment in the Skeat edition (Sk):

DS 1 (420.5 Th-lines): Th f. 354r, col. 2, l. 11: "fole have I not sayd . . ." (Sk III.vii.94f, p. 135), through Th f. 356v, col. 1, ll. 4–5 "syth god is *þe* greatest love and the" (Sk III.ix.46, p. 143).

DS 2 (88 Th-lines): Th f. 356v, col. 1, l. 5 "ne ought to loke thynges . . ." (Sk III.vi.97, p. 131), through Th f. 356v, col 2, l. 44: "blysse in thynkyng of that knotte." (Sk III.vi.161, p. 132) [ends chapter in Th and Sk].

DS 3 (194.5 Th-lines): Th f. 356v, col. 2, l. 46 "Nowe trewly lady I have my grounde . . ." (Sk III.v.8, p. 124) [begins chapter in Th and in my reconstruction, where it heads my chapter 6], through Th f. 357v, col. 2, l. 48 "the wexyng tre of whiche ye first meved." (Sk III.v.157–158, p. 128) [ends chapter and leaf in Th, chapter v in Sk, chapter 6 in my reconstruction].

DS 4 (120.5 Th-lines): Th f. 358r, col. 1, l. 1 "Very trouth (qd she) hast thou nowe . . ." (Sk III.vii.1, p. 132), through Th f. 357v, col. 1, l. 25 ". . . shal bringe out frute that is" (Sk III.vii.94, p. 135).

DS 5 (286 Th-lines): Th f. 357v, col. 1, ll. 25–26 "nothyng preterit ne passed . . ." (Sk. III.iv.56, p. 118), through Th f. 360r, col. 1, l. 24 ". . . ioy euer to onbyde." (Sk III.v.7, p. 124).

DS 6 (128 Th-lines): Th f. 360r, col. 1, ll. 24–25 "Nowe lady (qd I) that tree to set fayne wolde I lerne." (Sk III.vi.1, p. 128), through Th f. 360v, col. 2, l. 9 ". . . & yet al=way use ye" (Sk III.vi.96–97, pp. 130–131).

quence reversed the correct expository order of the fifth and sixth chapters of Book III. So far as I am aware, every scholar who has addressed the problem of the text-order of Book III has concurred in her revision of Skeat's reconstruction, and since I too agree with it, I can summarize her findings briefly here, in order to proceed to its implications for understanding the material text Thynne's printer had in hand. Bressie based her argument on the expository logic of the content of these discontinuous segments of text: the first disruption occurs at a point 76.5 Th-lines into the fourth chapter. Skeat rightly perceived that the next segment continuous with it was DS 5, which, according to his division of chapters, completes the fourth chapter and continues with the first 8.5 lines of the next, a short paragraph in Skeat's edition that begins with the letter I and supplies the acrostic initial of his chapter v. In this short paragraph, Love introduces the much-discussed expository figure of the tree, grounded in "free arbitrement of thinges," and producing the "spire, that by processe of tyme shal in greetnesse sprede, to have braunches and blosmes of waxing frute in grace. . . ." Lady Love's gradual explication of this philosophical figure continues through this portion of the work into the seventh chapter. Bressie noticed that the persona's first eager response to this intriguing figure, his expressed desire to learn "that tree to sette" (a wish he articulates in the first sentence of Skeat's DS 6, which in the reconstruction of his edition begins chapter vi and supplies the acrostic initial N), prompts Love's stern insistence that he must first learn the nature and preparation of the "grounde" for it. Hence Love's exposition of the "spire" she mentions at the end of DS 5 is deferred at her behest until she first explains the "grounde" of "purpos," properly set "there vertue foloweth"; this exposition occupies all of what Skeat's edition designates chapter vi, consisting of DS 6 and DS 2 in sequence. Bressie correctly saw that this portion, DS 6 + 2, should follow directly after DS 5, Love's introduction of the tree figure, and that Skeat's DS 3, the portion of his chapter v that followed its first 8.5 lines, should properly follow it in the logic and rhetoric of Love's development of the tree figure. DS 3 begins with the persona's clear acknowledgment of the correctness of Bressie's reconstructed expository order: "Nowe, trewly, lady, I have my grounde wel understonde; but what thing is thilke spire that in-to a tree sholde wexe? Expowne me that thing, what ye thereof mene" (II.v.8–10; Skeat p. 124).

Bressie's restoration of expository sense and logic is clearly correct; expressed in terms of textual mechanics, it has a similarly clarifying effect: the corrected order of Skeat's six putatively discontinuous segments is now no longer DS 5, 3, 6, 2, 4, 1, but DS 5, 6, 2, 3, 4, 1. As Bressie saw—though she did not further pursue the textual mechanics of her discovery—with this rearrangement there are no longer six discontinuous segments of text to account for, but only three: DS 5 + 6, DS 2 + 3 + 4, and DS 1—and hence only four discontinuities, not seven, to explain, all of them occurring in mid-sentence within chapters. Once one has reduced Skeat's six units of displaced text to three in this way, it also becomes apparent that the other two units are, like DS 1, a quire in length—and that as set by the printer their integrity as quires was intact, not, as Skeat's account requires, further compromised by internal reshuffling of leaves. The contents of these three quires are closely similar in length (414, 406, and 420.5 Th-lines, respectively), a finding that strongly corroborates the initial hypothesis that DS 1 represented one full quire: it is now apparent that the other two continuous portions of displaced text also represent full quires, which I shall designate r, s, and t. If these were quires of eight leaves, each page contained 25–26 Th-lines of text.[28] From this revised reconstruction of text-sequence emerges a simple explanation of the printer's error: it reveals that only one erroneous move, and not several compounded, led to the massive displacements discernible in Thynne. It allows a clear physical explanation of the order of text between the first and last discontinuity in Thynne, and will eventually support in fuller detail the general hypothesis I have offered about the page and quiring features of the manuscript. It also enables, as we shall shortly see, one further necessary revision in the division of chapters in Book III—and hence in the disposition of acrostic-bearing initials within quires—which in turn facilitates still finer-grained inferences about the *ordinatio* of the manuscript, and its legible meaning to its contemporaries and to Thynne. But first and foremost, it discloses a clear and simple explanation of the one printer's misreading that led to this large-scale disordering of text.

The revised arrangement of text allows the gross mechanics of the printer's error to be easily described: the last and the third-from-last quires of eight in Book III were reversed. That is all; there was no misfolding or inversion of quires, as Skeat's explanation proposes, nor was there loss of text, as Bressie suggests. When the printer reached a point 76.5 lines into chapter iv, he reached the end of a quire in his manuscript. He had also just passed the end of a stint in typesetting: the initial displacement of text occurs on the first page of a new quire (Q) of Thynne's volume—the last of the six full folio quires of six leaves he would set (the text spills over to fill one more complete leaf, plus one recto column, of the following quire R). At this break in his work, perhaps in the course of arranging the next stint of manuscript material to be set, he mistakenly identified as the next quire of his manuscript what was in fact its last full quire of 8 leaves (t), instead of the antepenultimate one (r) that would have given the correct continuity of text. The finer

<hr>

28. While the difference between these three quires in the total number of Thynne's lines each contains is marked, even the greatest disparity, that between s and t, represents a difference per page of less than one 1.1 line (an average of 26.28 of Thynne's lines per page in quire t, as against 25.375 Th-lines per page in the preceding quire). Moreover, since quire t had on average the highest density of Th-lines per page in the manuscript, exceeding the next highest, quire r (25.88) by 0.4 Th-lines, it may represent the scribe's effort—in the event unsuccessful—to make the final full quire contain all, or nearly all, of the remaining text. In fact 80.6 Th-lines of text were left over, which in the manuscript required three of four sides of a final bifolium; similarly, Thynne's text overflowed the end of a quire by one full two-column leaf plus one full column. As will be seen below, Thynne could have contained all but this last column of the *Testament* in the six full quires he allotted to it, had he eschewed the unusual full-leaf framed title page he chose to use to begin the work—but this choice evidently was meaningful to him; see below for the implications of Thynne's efficiency in marking off his copy, and implications of his choices of layout format for understanding the *ordinatio* of the lost manuscript.

mechanics of this key mistake are also easy to infer—and here Skeat's conjectural emendation at the relevant juncture is inspired: the error turns on a
misread catchword.

At the first dislocation—where in Skeat's segmentation DS 5 (beginning
my quire r) ought to begin, but instead in Thynne DS 1 (my quire t) follows
the end of the preceding quire—Thynne's text reads thus:[29]

> ... Thou shalte (qd she)
> understande/ that in heven is goddes beynge/
> although he be over al by po wer/ yet ther is
> abydinge of devyne persone/ in whiche hevene
> is everlastynge presence/ withouten any mo =
> vable tyme there //* Fole have I nat sayd toforn
> this/ as tyme hurteth/ right so ayenward tyme
> healeth and rewardeth. ...
>
> (f. 354r, col. 2, ll. 6–13)

The transition from what I conjecture was the end of the next-to-last quire s
(set by Thynne in correct penultimate position in the book, though now
flanked on both sides by the contents of quires that had exchanged places)
to the text that should have followed at the first point of dislocation (i.e. the
juncture at which DS 4 is followed by DS 1) in Thynne reads thus (I use //**
to mark the point of disruption; in the correct ordering of quires, text from
this juncture on should correctly have followed //* in the passage above):

> and al
> though frute fayleth one yere or two/ yet shal
> suche a season come one tyme or other / that
> shal bringe out frute that //** is nothyng preterit
> ne passed ther is nothyng future ne comyng/
> but al thynges togider in that place be pre =
> sent everlastynge without eny mevynge/ wher =
> fore to god al thynge is as nowe: ...
>
> (f. 358v, col. 1, ll. 22–29)

In his correct suturing of text at this juncture, where my quire s should
be followed by quire t, Skeat (p. 135) guessed—rightly, I believe—that the
juncture //** in the second passage above was in the manuscript followed
by the phrase "[is parfit]." If this was the case, then this phrase, or simply the
word "perfit," was the catchword at the end of quire s. At the end of the quire

---

29. I use //* to mark the point of juncture between the last lines of continuous text of
III.iv at the end of the quire and the beginning of the wrongly chosen quire t (i.e. DS 1). The
single slash / represents the mark Thynne uses in setting Usk's prose in type. Since he seems
to use it somewhat more liberally in printing the *Testament* than he does in any of Chaucer's
prose texts—Melibee, the Parson's Tale, or the Boethius translation—it may have been a
feature of his source manuscript; its occurrence in these texts warrants more systematic
study. It appears to represent the *punctus elevatus*, identifying clausal boundaries according to rhetorical and performative rather than grammatico-logical principles. As a diacritic
originally used in monastic and liturgical texts, and adopted into more general use in the
later middle ages, it may register both Usk's sense of Love's discourse as "song," and his
representation of his vocation and composition as secular counterparts to performed devotional service. On the origins and use of the *punctus elevatus*, see M. B. Parkes, *Pause
and Effect: Punctuation in the West* (Berkeley and Los Angeles: Univ. of California Press,
1993), pp. 69–73, 153, 306.

where the first disruption of textual order occurred (quire q in my general description), 76.5 Th-lines into III.iv, that catchword must have been some variant of the phrase "[is no] preterit," or simply its final word.[30] It is also likely that one or both catchwords—and possibly these terms in the body of the text as well—were written using the usual abbreviations for the syllables *per, pre,* and *ter* that were very common in scribal hands in wide use in about 1400. To a sixteenth-century eye, these abbreviations—which derived from common practice in university books and extended in the latter fourteenth century into documentary and administrative usage (and Thynne's output included little from these venues)—would probably be difficult to differentiate, making the words "perfit" and "preterit" look very much alike.[31] Little

30. The word "preterit" was of course chiefly a term from grammatical discourse (as in this context was its companion term, which may possibly have been spelled "past(e)" in the manuscript and expanded by the printer as "passed") and would have been relatively unfamiliar to a non-clerical textworker in the sixteenth century. The strangeness of the term, in a discourse that is properly about time considered metaphysically or theoretically, not as the medium of historical events, would have added to the potential for error in the printing shop at this juncture; this offers another of many occasions on which local discursive estrangement produced large-scale mechanical consequences.

31. Thynne's text throughout this section makes it certain that some abbreviations of this sort appeared in his source—and that he did not always expand them correctly; see for example the two different renderings of "instrument" in the following passage, both of them representing a tilde-n abbreviation, elided either by the printer in expansion, or by the manuscript's scribe in transcribing the text before him. Because this passage also illustrates succinctly how discursive estrangement generates desperate mechanical correction, both by Thynne and by Skeat, I cite it fully here; it occurs at the other major point of disjuncture in Book III, between DS 6 and 2 (i.e. between my quires r and s). The disjunct lines as they appear in Thynne, here reconnected (with */ /* representing the suture, and italics indicating my expansion of the abbreviation Thynne uses and presumably found in his copy text and retained), read:

> This istrument [sic] may
> ben had/ although affect & usage be left out of
> doyng/ right as ye have sight & reson, and yet al=
> way use ye */ /* ne ought to loke thynges with resonnyng
> to *prove*/ and so is instrumet [sic] of wyl/wyl: and
> yet varyeth he from effect & vsing bothe.
> (f. 360v, col. 2, ll. 6–9 */ /* f. 356v, vol. 1, ll. 5–7)

This is the sort of thing that has fostered Usk's reputation for tortuous and turgid prose, with only partial and uncontextualized justice. Skeat emends "ne ought" to "[nat]" (correctly, in my judgment) but introduces a comma after "loke," followed by an unnecessary "[ne]" before "thynges," which together vitiate the ME sense of "loke" operative here (i.e "undertake," "set about" [to do something]), and hence of the whole clause, by making the only semantically possible sense of "look" in the emended construction "behold, gaze"—which is surely incorrect in this explanatory context. The sense of the passage, all of it translated from Anselm's *De Concordia* III.11, is: "The instrument may be possessed, even when its 'affect' (here affection or inclination) and usage are not operative: just as you have [the faculties of] sight and reason, yet you do not always put these to use by undertaking to prove things by the use of reason; so likewise the instrument-of-willing is will, yet it differs both from the effect (i.e. inclination or 'affection') and the use of the will." My own understanding of the Anselmian texts has been greatly assisted by the English translation in *Anselm of Canterbury*, vol. 2: Philosophical Fragments, ed. and transl. Jasper Hopkins and Herbert Richardson (Toronto: Edwin Mellen Press, 1976).

more than confusion of these two catchwords would be required to explain the printer's erroneous choice of quire t rather than r at this juncture.

Other small local features further abetted his mistake at this point. The word "tyme" occurs in the last line immediately preceding both quire breaks—i.e. in the one preceding the correct next quire, and in the one immediately preceding the quire that the printer chose instead. Faced with two out of three remaining quires that each began with a word he could not confidently expand as "perfit," or make sense of as "preterit," the printer retreated in some bafflement to a fallback position in construing the immediate and local verbal continuity of the text—and proceeded to set the quire of his manuscript which not only began with what looked like the right catchword, but also used the word "tyme" twice in its second line.

Apparently without recognizing his error, the printer finished setting quire t, which should have been his manuscript's last full quire (and for that reason may not have closed with a catchword, since all that followed it was a bifolium). He now had only two quires of 8 left, each of course presenting yet another impasse of immediate verbal continuity with the preceding sentence fragment, since both were wrong at that point. Both offered unpromising headwords, neither of which made a plausible continuity with the incomplete sentence in the last line of quire t, "what wonder sith god is the gretest love and the . . .": quire r, mistakenly rejected at the first point of discontinuity, began with the problematic ". . . [nothing] preterit," and s offered the equally inauspicious ". . . nat to loke thinges with resonnyng to prove." The printer also had, of course, the final bifolium, the text that should have followed the end of the quire he had just set—but that was very obviously final, since it closed with an unambiguous *explicit,* and a couplet to boot:

> Charyte is love/ and love is cha=
> ryte/god graunte us al therin to be frended.
> And thus the Testament of Love is ended.
>
> (f. 361r, col. 1, ll. 38–40)

Caught among bleak and narrowing possibilities, the printer may have again looked for clues to connection in similarity of local verbal details and rhetorical gesture—this time, perhaps, reasoning backward from the obvious *explicit* bifolium to the end of each of the remaining quires, to ascertain which of the two might sound more convincingly like a final cadence. It may have been on these grounds that quire r seemed to offer the greater likelihood of serving as a peroration: as we have seen, much of it "expownded" the elaborate organizing figure of the "waxing" tree, and its final pages reached the point of explaining the "affection" of the will—a theme that accorded well with three remaining pages extolling divine wisdom, and the "grace and frute that I long have desyred." At the end of quire s, on the other hand, the printer found Love still berating "Usk" for his dull wits, as she was doing when quire t, which he had just set, began (no surprise, for these two points are in the correct order of text immediately adjacent)—and this seemed hardly the right tone with which to approach the final moments of a long and high-minded dialogue of instruction and comfort.

I can offer no more precise hypothesis than this to explain why quire s was, at this point of diminishing possibilities for coherence, correctly identified as the penultimate rather than final regular quire of the book—but so it was, and the last quire of 8 set was the one that properly ought to have ensued at the first point of bafflement; it was then followed by the conclusion, easily identifiable as such by its request for the reader's prayers for the author, as well as by its tidy couplet. The printer's sole error—though it grossly and massively disrupted the sense of the text—amounted to one incorrect choice at a routine point of textual disjuncture. Yet despite its pervasive damage to local syntax and general logic in Book III, he never fully recognized this error for what it was, and attempted instead to patch over its remaining traces by desperate—and entirely local and mechanical—conjecture. In the face of unpromising alternatives, he seems to have fallen back on local rhetorical characteristics, rather than the customary scribal and bibliographical signals, at the ends of quires to reorient himself in setting the remainder of the text. In short, even in the face of temporary uncertainty, it appears that the printer never ventured continuously to *read* the text for elementary syntactic and semantic coherence at the level of the sentence, to say nothing of larger argumentative continuity.

More surprising—and in the long run more telling—is not that the printer failed to do so (this task belongs after all to the philologist's, not the printer's, craft-repertory), but that apparently no one else until Skeat and Bradley did so either: in the intervening centuries no one records noticing the fundamental expository and syntactic illogic that resulted. We must conclude that the only feature of Book III that interested readers in the ensuing centuries was its tribute to Chaucer, taken entirely out of context. The deeper textual and discursive logic by which this important praise was framed—and hence, I wish now to suggest, its diacritical meaning as a gesture within the intentional design of the *Testament* as work and act—went unnoticed, as did the elaborately metapoetic purposes served by the disposition of Usk's work as a book, both in general and in detail.

Yet if the foregoing account, drawing out the bibliographical implications of Bressie's and Jellech's revised reconstruction of the correct text-sequence, is convincing, it nevertheless remains incomplete. In order to recover the *ordinatio* of Thynne's source as well as the expository logic of its content—and to discern where these two levels of composition intersected in Usk's design—we must examine more closely the textual and rhetorical positioning of the one feature of Book III that seems to have interested Thynne and most readers since: its fulsome compliment to Chaucer. In order to examine the role of this seeming digression in the otherwise firm expository continuity of Book III, we must reconsider where its fifth chapter, as restored, properly begins.

As we have noted, it is not fully accurate to describe the foregoing reconstruction of text-order as a simple reversal of Skeat's chapters v and vi. Strictly speaking, the revision proposed thus far reverses the order of Skeat's postulated DS 6 + 2 and that of DS 3, not that of the whole of Skeat's chapters v and vi—for as we have seen, the first paragraph of Skeat's chapter v is defined as the last 8.5 Th-lines of his DS 5; it also supplies the necessary acrostic initial I for . . . THIN VSK. Yet on several grounds—syntactic, expository, rhetorical, as well as textual, and in relation to Usk's use of sources—this seems another incorrectly identified chapter-division, which unlike those in Book II remained undetected by Skeat. By all of these criteria a far more convincing chapter-division is a clear turn in the dialogue that occurs 40 Th-lines earlier, and likewise supplies the necessary I acrostic-initial. That juncture lies a page earlier in Skeat and in Thynne, where both, in my estimation, failed to discover the correct point of division between Usk's fourth and fifth chapters, at line 241 of Skeat's chapter iv. In both Thynne and Skeat it falls in the middle of a paragraph (indicated below by / /), which in Skeat reads in its entirety:

'Now sothly,' quod I, 'this have I wel understande; so that now me thinketh that prescience of god and free arbitrement withouten any repugnaunce acorden; and that maketh the strength of eternite, which encloseth by presence during al tymes, and al things that ben, han ben, and shul ben in any tyme. / / I wolde now (quod I) a litel understande, sithen that [god] al thing thus beforn wot, whether thilke wetinge be of tho thinges, or els thilke thinges ben to ben of goddes weting, and thereof take his being, than shulde god be maker and auctour of badde werkes, and so he sholde not rightfully punisshe yvel doinges of mankynde.' (III.iv.236–247; Skeat p. 123)[32]

The juncture I have proposed as a chapter-division marks a clear break between steps in the logical and rhetoric of exposition, a turn from summary understanding of what has just been expounded to naming the next topic for inquiry. The division is further corroborated by the redundant marking of speaker ("quod I") in two successive sentences: this is not Usk's practice elsewhere in this work, and would be unnecessary for clarification except across a chapter-division. Equally telling, however, is the fact that the division I propose between the fourth and fifth chapters also marks a discontinuity—the first since the beginning of the third chapter of Book III—in Usk's use of his Latin source.

Usk derives Love's lengthy course of pedagogy in Book III almost entirely from Anselm's *De Concordia*. The first of three long blocks from it (which

32. While editorial emendation, to say nothing of a systematic rationale for it that would be required for editing, is entirely beyond the scope of the present essay, occasional "hit-and-run" identification of erroneous transcription, whether by Skeat of Thynne, or (conjecturally) of errors by the printer in reading his copy, offers useful glimpses of features of the absent manuscript. In line 244, "his" should almost certainly be emended to "hir" to give correct sense: "therof take hir [i.e. their] being"; the referent is "things" which take their being from God. Here, it would appear, scribal *r* has apparently been misidentified by the printer as long-*s*. I would eliminate Skeat's addition of [god] as an emendation in this passage; the only correction necessary here is in word-division, thus "sithen that al thing thus be forn-wot" (Th: "sythen that al thyng thus be forne wot"; word-division in Thynne here and frequently is somewhat ambiguous)—i.e. since all things thus are foreknown. Though this further correction has no direct bearing on the present argument, it illustrates Skeat's presumption that the discussion of foreknowledge and free will is in Usk's hands more theologically centered than in fact it is; Skeat was, however, unaware of Usk's source, which here he follows very closely.

together account for some 23 of Skeat's 45 printed pages of Usk's Book III), closely and continuously translated from the start of Anselm's Book I, chapter 1, begins at the head of the third chapter of Usk's Book III. Usk signals the beginning of his lengthy appropriation of a Latin source with a variant of a device he uses frequently in the work for this purpose: Love commands "Usk" to start taking dictation: "Then gan Love nighe me nere, and with a noble countenance of visage and limmes, dressed her nigh my sitting-place. 'Take forth,' quod she, 'thy pen, and redily wryte these wordes . . .'" (III.iii.1–5; Skeat p. 111).[33] From this point, Usk works steadily and methodically through Anselm's chapters 1–5, translating almost continuously and quite fully, condensing in places, but virtually without major breaks in expository continuity[34] He renders Anselm's chapter 5 without substantial elision, from line

33. Similarly, at the transition discussed above at the end of Usk's chapter 5, after Love has expounded the "grounde" and proceeds to gratify "Usk's" second request, expressed at the beginning of chapter 6, to learn more of the "tree," she once again commands him to "take good hede to the wordes." Her injunction signals Usk's return to his Latin source, to resume direct translation from *De Concordia*—there from Book III, chapter 6. As has been noticed, Usk's "wexing tree" is rooted in an analogy expounded in that chapter, which Usk elaborates; see Lucy Lewis, "Langland's Tree of Charity and Usk's 'Wexing Tree'" (cited above). Lewis is chiefly concerned to disprove the widely repeated view that Usk is indebted to Langland for this elaborate tree metaphor; she does not consider—nor will I here, though I believe the question may be worth opening—the possibility of mutual influence between the two writers in developing a complex analogical figure that does considerable conceptual work for both, though with different emphases and results for each. More apposite to the present inquiry is Usk's elaborate yet evasive marking of his textual debts, through the disposition of his fictive dialogue—an internal indication of the *ordinatio*, and informing "literary theory" of his work. Another example, heralding Usk's use of a different source (thus far unidentified, but almost certainly Latin verse), occurs at the head of II.ii:

> In this mene whyle this comfortable lady gan singe a wonder mater of endytinge in Latin; but trewely, the noble colours in rethorik wyse knitte were so craftely, that my conning wol not strecche to remembre; but the sentence, I trowe, somdel have I in mynde. Certes, they were wonder swete of sowne, and they were touched al in lamentacion wyse, and by no werbles of myrthe. Lo! thus gan she singe in Latin, as I may constrewe it in our Englisshe tonge. (II.ii.1–8; Skeat p. 49)

This unusual explicitness in marking (some, not all) of his literary indebtedness differs from the procedures of both Langland and Chaucer, and warrants attention in its own right as an aspect of Usk's "literary theory."

34. Usk's one noteworthy departure from his source in this long stretch of continuous translation illustrates the extreme care and wit with which he adapted his Latin sources throughout, and bears comparison with his handling of examples in Boethius in the first two books. As Skeat notes, at several points Usk replaces a political or moral anecdote drawn by Boethius from Roman history with one of comparable antiquity and exemplarity from British history: Hengist, King John, "Henry Curtmantil." In bending Anselm to his purpose, however, Usk pointedly avoids rather than invites national or contemporary application with his choice of illustrative instance. At the beginning of *De Concordia* I.3, Anselm offers two cases to explicate the distinction between absolute and conditional necessity in statements of futurity. For the former. Anselm uses (as does Boethius) the traditional example of the sunrise: if I say that the sunrise will occur tomorrow, it does so by necessity. Anselm's example of contingent necessity, however, may have seemed an all-too-modern instance, best avoided in the years following not only 1381, but, still closer to home, Usk's role in London unrest over rival factions and mayors: ". . . if I say, 'Tomorrow there will be an insurrection

111 (in Skeat's text) of his own chapter iv, where the Latin text begins its new chapter with the Job example: Anselm introduces it as a pre-emptive answer to a possible objection, while Usk puts it in the mouth of "Usk" who here intervenes to "allege authoritees grete, that contrarien your [i.e. Love's] sayinges" (III.iv.110–111; Skeat p. 119). With what I consider the concluding sentence of Usk's fourth chapter, Usk reaches the end of Anselm's chapter 5. He now departs briefly from the continuity of his Latin source for the first time since he began translating extensively from it: what I consider the first sentence of his fifth chapter, beginning with the acrostic-bearing I ("I wolde now (quod I) a litel understonde . . .") translates the first paragraph of Anselm's chapter 7.

Usk uses no more of *De Concordia* 1.7 than this sentence, however. He now momentarily departs from Anselm altogether, to introduce his famous and fulsome praise of Chaucer, put in the mouth of Love, who commends to "Usk" the treatment of the requested "mater" presented by "the noble philosophical poete in English" in "a tretis that he made of my servant Troilus": "His better ne his pere in scole of my rules coude I never fynde." Much of the purported awkwardness often noted in the placement of this compliment vanishes with the redivision of chapters. This extensive tribute to an admired contemporary now introduces Usk's account of the upright will as the "grounde" of right loving, instead of occurring, as Skeat's chapter division would have it, almost as an aside or afterthought, an additional contemporary authority somewhat awkwardly hailed in, "alleged" merely to finish off an abstruse distinction between the human and divine sense of temporal seriality.[35] In its newly featured position at the head of a chapter it marks a

---

among the people' it is not the case that the insurrection will occur by necessity." Perhaps not, but it seemed to Usk prudent to replace this Anselmian example of future contingency: "For if I say, 'tomorrow love is comming in this Margarites herte,' nat therfore thorow necessite shal the ilke love be . . ." (III.iii.166–168; Skeat p. 115). Usk makes sure that no unpleasant aura of recent history clings to his high-minded philosophical account of ideal affinity; his "British" past is adorned by the decent patina of age.

35. Much discussion of this "florid compliment" (Bradley, *Athenaeum*, 184 [see n. 3 above]) has emphasized its supposedly clumsy placement in the work: it is "introduced in an awkward manner which suggests that it was written for a special purpose" (Bradley, *DNB*, 20.61). Since it has heretofore seemed so patently "dragged in," at the end of a chapter and apparently without contextual prompt, its purely ingratiatory motives have been considered all too plain, and entirely to Usk's discredit. It has further been inferred from this placement as a purported afterthought that the response of any right-thinking contemporary of Usk to such sycophantic praise is a foregone conclusion: "We may be pretty sure that Usk's praise occasioned Chaucer much more embarrassment than pleasure." This reading of Usk's motives, and of his contemporaries' likely reading of them, in turn shapes the interpretation of Gower's compliment to Chaucer in much the same terms as Usk's. When at the end of *Confessio Amantis* (*2941–57) Gower's Venus bids Amans farewell and sends her greetings back to Chaucer ("as mi disciple and mi poete"), with the exhortation that the latter should forthwith "make his testament of love" we are asked to regard this allusion as to Usk's discredit, through which Gower "playfully" "quizz[ed] the poet about his disreputable admirer" (Bradley, *Athenaeum*). This entire chain of inferences admits of radically different possibilities—for example, that Gower, in all his works a self-proclaimed devotee of love as a bond of virtuous civil affinity, genuinely admired the *Testament*, and that the removal of this passage in the later redactions of the *Confessio* marked, not a changed relation of Gower

point of transition in Usk's independent use of Anselm's argument, from the exposition of the divine perspective on temporal events to an account of the world of human experience and action, and the central role of the upright and constant will in that realm. Anselm's treatise makes that transition in a chapter (vi) of *De Concordia* omitted by Usk, with a brief consideration of divine justice in allowing "our first parents" to fall; in its place Usk's Love "alleges" her own authority: Chaucer's "tretis," and the exposition of this thorny problem already expounded by "my servant Troilus."

The corrected chapter division renders this praise of Chaucer no mere sycophantic digression, but rather the hinge between the two main movements of Usk's argument, from metaphysical to moral philosophy—surely Chaucer's two great distinctions as a thinker and writer in the eyes of contemporaries in the 1380s.[36] Whatever its further motives in the world of

---

to Chaucer, but a shared averting of the eyes in sorrow at the brutal end of a fellow man of letters (the tiny joke in "So that mi Court it mai recorde" [*2957] acknowledges, without rancor and with some affection, Usk's self-presentation in the *Testament* as scrivener of Love). And more: that Gower not only admired the *Testament* but understood it, as a serious engagement with their common and precarious condition as men of letters—with, that is, the ethical quandaries concerning how the will's real commitments can be understood, where literary ambition, personal integrity, an ideal of service, and social-political dependence intersect—and that he commended it as such to a fellow-poet who appeared of late at a standstill in his own art, having lately begun, and not yet finished, yet another May-morning love-vision in a too familiar mode. And yet more: that Usk's compliment to Chaucer is purposeful in terms of the *Testament*'s own literary project, and Usk's self-created role in this work as in the first instance a literary rather than political aspirant, and no more (and no less) a plea for notice and intercession than Chaucer's tonally complex "Envoy to Scogan," which has not caused similar embarrassment about or on behalf of Chaucer in modern critical accounts.

36. It may have had the further advantage of keeping the exposition distinct from Christian theology as such—that is, solidly in the decorously and safely "classicizing" discursive realm so carefully maintained by the rest of Usk's small changes in his Boethian model, and firmly within the realm of civil rather than divine philosophy. It is beyond the scope of the present essay to devote to this Chaucer compliment the analytic attention it deserves; one point, however, has some bearing on this argument, for it concerns the textual genre with which Usk allies *Troilus*, and with which he wishes the *Testament* to be associated—and also the literary register with which Thynne evidently associated Usk's text: that of idealized "love"-discourse. Usk's tribute honors Chaucer's "witte and good reson of sentence," his "noble sayinges" and "gentil manliche speche, without any maner of nycete of storiers imaginacion"—that is, his seriousness as a moral philosopher and his diplomatic eloquence, not narrative invention, and not "sentement." These, in Usk's view, are the distinctive excellences of the "tretis" of Troilus; the "love" Troilus serves, and which he invokes in the speech to which Usk refers explicitly in this tribute, is a Boethian strength and refinement of commitment identified by Usk as a civil, not a private, virtue and "affection." Usk here plainly identifies the Love expounded in the *Testament* as the same literary commodity that engages the sustained philosophical interest of both Gower and Chaucer in the very years in which Usk was writing: not as an occasion for witty Petrarchan oxymoron ("the usual ridiculous contradictions"—Skeat, p. 481), but a code in which to converse about the theory and practice of political and social ethics, in shared writerly circumstances that combine verbal articulateness and sociopolitical dependence. It tells us much about how Usk reads *Troilus*, and how we should read him. For excellent and apposite accounts of "love" within coded political and literary discourse generally in the Ricardian era, see Patricia J. Eberle, "The Politics of Courtly Style at the Court of Richard II," in *The Spirit*

patronage and mutual acknowledgment among vernacular writers, with this gesture Usk indicates his own careful and independent suturing and redirection of Anselm's treatise to his own purposes: when he returns to *De Concordia*, it is to Anselm's Book III, and Usk's use of it is from that point "grounded" (as Anselm's is not) in the analogical image of the tree, greatly amplified by Usk in his own fifth and sixth chapters. The compliment to Chaucer—falling, as it does, far past the most densely clustered of Usk's verbal allusions to *Troilus*—thus serves, like Usk's own petitionary and signatory acrostic, an important diacritical function in the work. This strategic and independent deployment of a graceful compliment to a "modern classic" of serious vernacular philosophizing to serve an important suturing function in his own ambitious argument is indicative of Usk's care throughout his own composition to align the disposition of his work as text with its substantive argumentative articulation and self-positioning gestures. It now remains to examine the further signs of this formal attention in the work's bibliographical disposition.

With the foregoing proposed redivision of chapters in Book III, we may now return to the further textual implications of this restoration of both continuity and chapter-articulation. As we noted above, if the quires we have posited as the regular format of the manuscript were of eight leaves, then the contents of the three displaced quires imply that each leaf contained about 25–26.5 Th-lines of text. The revised chapter division discloses that chapter-lengths in the third book (and as became apparent when this hypothesis was applied to quiring the entire preceding contents of each Book of the work) fall into multiples of this module. The redivided chapters illustrate the general principle. My correction reassigns all of the last 48 lines of DS 5 to Usk's fifth chapter as I now redefine its boundaries—that is, the contents of two manuscript pages. This fifth chapter now consists first of the 39.5 Th-lines that Skeat had assigned to the conclusion of his chapter iv, followed by the first 8.5 lines he assigns to the beginning of his chapter v. It continues with all 129 lines of DS 6 (which begin Skeat's chapter vi), then all 88 lines of DS 2 (which in Skeat end chapter vi), to define tthe corrected fifth chapter as now 265 Th-lines in length—probably 10 full sides or pages of a manuscript quired in eights. The redefined sixth chapter consists solely of DS 3, and is 197 lines

---

of the Court, ed. Glyn S. Burgess and Robert A. Taylor (Cambridge: D. S. Brewer, 1985), pp. 168–178, and Lee Patterson, "Court Politics and the Invention of Literature," in *Culture and History, 1350–1600*, ed David Aers (London: Harvester Wheatsheaf, 1992), pp. 7–41; for an account of Usk's relation to Chaucer in this vein, see David R. Carlson, "Chaucer's Boethius and Thomas Usk's *Testament of Love*: Politics and Love in the Chaucerian Tradition," in *The Center and Its Compass: Studies in Medieval Literature in Honor of Professor John Leyerle*, ed. Robert A. Taylor, James F. Burke, Patricia J. Eberle, Ian Lancashire, and Brian S. Merrilees, Studies in Medieval Culture 33 (Kalamazoo: Western Michigan Univ., 1993), pp. 29–70. The continued transmutation of this broadly coded discourse of courtship, dependency, and the quest for patronage under the guise of the amatory has also been widely discussed by scholars of sixteenth-century literature; it may have some bearing on how Thynne regarded Usk's text in assimilating it as Chauceriana; see, for example, Arthur F. Marotti, "Love Is Not Love: Elizabethan Sonnet Sequences and the Social Order," *ELH* 49 (1982), 396–428.

long. The redefined fourth chapter is now 314 lines long: the 76.5 lines (3 pages) that began in the preceding quire, before the first displacement of text, plus 237.5 more (9 pages) in DS 5.[37]

Working backward from the reconstructed quires of eight to postulate that its preceding quires were similarly assembled and ruled confirms the astonishing inference that these chapter-length modules suggest: that the acrostic chapter-initial almost certainly always fell in page-initial position—and therefore that the acrostic was a featured aspect of the design of the book *at the point of composition of the text*. It follows, in other words, that the amplitude of the expository composition and the *ordinatio* of the material book were planned simultaneously, and by one hand—Usk's. It is important to underscore here the *durchkomponiert* character of this entire integrated textual performance: the patterns inferred here imply that the amplitude of the prose composition had to be continually adjusted so as to support the chosen overall physical disposition of the book's divisions and the acrostic that marked them. Its overall page-format possibly differentiated levels of ornament for these initials as the message proceeded across the three books from the honored and probably symbolic addressee (the enigmatic "Margarete") in Book I, to the petition (Book II), then to the name of the humble petitioner and author.

Usk's care with these features of layout and ornament imply that he considered them aspects of the work's expressive and communicative form, a sign of the kinds of books to which he wished his own to assert a pleasing and thought-provoking resemblance. It also—and by no means incidentally, in view of the widespread assumption that Usk wrote this work in isolation and impoverishment—implies that Usk either himself knew the limner's as well as scrivener's art, or knew how to find and put out text to such artisans and to plan the campaign of work of an entire book around this complex integration of crafts. As we shall see, he was not alone among governmental bureaucrats who commanded these constituent skills of text-production. Nor does Usk leave these compositional beauties of his work entirely to the fortuitous notice of his contemporaries. He prominently declares the aesthetic principles, textual logic, and terms of connoisseurship of an impressive piece of manuscript book-design by witty inscription in the rhetorical self-exegesis of the *Testament*—especially, as we shall see, in the elaborately allusive proems to each Book. The artfulness of this work as both a material and a verbal composition is repeatedly advertised in passages of self-explanation at key points of expository, compilatory, and rhetorical transition; it remains to examine the relations between these two levels and forms of self-clarification in the *Testament*.

The tribute to Chaucer is one such complex linkage between the biblio-

---

37. Even with this redivision III.iv is still the longest chapter in the work (though not so long as Skeat's division makes it): longer by nearly 50 lines than any other chapter in Book III, and exceeding by over 30 lines the next-longest (I.vi). This lack of visual segmentation in the manuscript for very long stretches, together with the lowering of the ornamental level of the acrostic initials in the third book (proposed below) may have further increased the likelihood of misdivision of chapters.

graphic and metapoetic levels. This compliment to an admired contemporary man of letters also serves to specify the *forma tractandi* and *forma tractatus* of Usk's own work, to mark its distinctive philosophic ambitions, to declare a point of independence from his actual source in the act of professing allegiance with an admired and similarly "classicizing" model, and to indicate a new movement in his argument, from metaphysical hypothesis to worldly ethics. Each of these levels of signification subtly comments on the others; at such points (and they are many in the *Testament*) it is difficult to separate signifier and signified, figure from ground. Usk's own description of the intricate multiplicity of his designs can hardly be bettered: "In this boke be many privy thinges wimpled and folde; unneth shul leude men the plites unwinde" (III.ix.76–77; Skeat p. 144).[38] To discern the full intricacy of these "plites," we may return one more time to the "folds" of the material text Thynne had before him. In those seemingly anomalous hair-side chapter-initials, in Thynne's erroneous chapter-divisions, and other small slips between script and print, we may detect more of the coterie wit of Usk's design, as a textworker's display piece addressed to the connoisseurship of other men of letters.

We have noted in passing a few exceptions to the inferentially derived larger descriptive "rules" of the book's make-up, all of them occurring in the latter half of the work. Three will require our attention: the printer's two erroneous chapter-heads in Book II; the increased frequency in the latter half of the work with which chapter-initials fall on the hair-side of a leaf, or a verso page (or both); and the possible occurrence (heretofore unremarked) of chapter-initials in other than page-initial position within the final reaches of the work. These, I shall suggest, are linked phenomena, and have implications for understanding the ornamental program by which the chapter-acrostic was marked throughout the manuscript book—a program whose explicit rationale and terms of connoisseurship Usk describes in his Prologue.

In the quiring scheme I propose, the acrostic initial falls on a flesh-side of the leaf without exception through II.ix—that is, in the first 20 of the work's 34 chapters (considering the Prologue a chapter for this purpose); two-thirds of these occurrences are on a recto page. By contrast, in the last 14 chapters of the work—chapters x–xiv of Book II, and all nine chapters of Book III— four have chapter-initials that would by regular quiring fall on the hair-side of the leaf; even more striking is the occurrence of 11 of these 14 on a verso page, including all but the first chapter of Book III. All three of the printer's

---

38. Kathryn Kerby-Fulton reads this remark as a way of telegraphing to a coterie audience the kind of insider's appeal, reception, and appreciation Usk sought for his work; from this and many other such elusive cross-references and intersections of the occupations and avocations of men of letters, she demonstrates the existence of a capacious and lively culture of reading and writing, and mutual commentary, in late fourteenth-century London. See Kathryn Kerby-Fulton and Steven Justice, "Langlandian Reading Circles and the Civil Service in London and Dublin, 1380–1427," *New Medieval Literatures* 1 (1997), 59–83; for the resemblances among several forms of literary self-exegesis and poetic "autobiography" in this period, see also her essay "Langland and the Bibliographic Ego," in *Written Work: Langland, Labor, and Authorship*, ed. Steven Justice and Kathryn Kerby-Fulton (Philadelphia: Univ. of Pennsylvania Press, 1997), pp. 67–143.

erroneous identifications of chapter-initials occur within this second portion of the work: the two identified and rectified by Skeat in the misdivision of II.x, the other the one I have proposed for the redivision between the fourth and fifth chapters of Book III. It would have been possible (see Appendix B) within this general quiring scheme to avert all hair-side acrostic-initials by slight adjustments in the quiring layout—*if* that had been a desideratum in the making of the book. Yet there are good reasons for supposing that in the latter portion of the work this was no longer the case, even if it had been to that point a regular feature of the book's design. We may best approach this question by considering these anomalous placements of chapter-initials in the latter portion of the work as designed variations in the general program of ornament for the acrostic.

When Thomas Godfrey, Thynne's printer, first misidentified a chapter-division, shortly after II.x, it may be that his mistake inadvertently registered a change in the manuscript's ornamentation plan at this point in the text—a change at the level of page-layout and elaboration rather than quiring. At some point after II.vii (after, that is, the acrostic had spelled MARGARET OF VIRTW) the decorative program may have lowered its elaboration by one or more levels, shifting from feature-initial blocks intended for painted decoration to letters enhanced only by red or blue color, or simply by pen-flourishes—forms of ornament for which the provision of flesh-side page surface was less important.[39] Possibly this reduction in ornamental decorum happened in two stages, with a second downward shift in the ornateness of decorated initials at the end of Book II (after the acrostic had finished spelling HAVE MERCI) leaving all of Book III to indicate the name of the humbly petitioning would-be recipient of "Margarete's" favor—ON THIN VSK—in letters still less ornate than those preceding. Thynne's printed text certainly suggests such a three-level distinction in the overall decorative scheme, for it registers its own downward shifts in decorum at just these two points.[40]

39. It seems significant that Godfrey began to misidentify chapter-divisions just past this point in the work, a mistake possibly compounded by the fact that the later chapters of Book II are of more irregular lengths than the norm to that point: they either occupy an odd number of pages, causing more frequent verso chapter-divisions, or they are shorter than the norm heretofore, or both. In any event, by Book III, the printer seems to have reoriented himself to the revised program for indicating chapter-initials: despite the fact that *all* acrostic initials but the first in Book III occur on the verso of a leaf, the printer misidentified only one of them in that Book (and Skeat followed the error). It should also be noted here that the only two almost certain exceptions to the general "rule" that chapter-initials fall in the upper left corner of the page occur in quires s and t. In both, the first chapter-initial of the quire falls after more than three full sides of text, but less than four full pages: the sixth chapter of Book III begins 88 Th-lines into the quire; the eighth, 91 Th-lines into its quire, implying that both the N of THIN and the S of VSK may have occurred halfway down a verso flesh side (f. 2v of the quire in both cases). This irregularity (in both cases made up with the following chapter-initial, which would have occurred in normal page-initial position) lends itself to various interpretations; see Appendix B.

40. Except for the first letter of Book III, the initial at the head of II.x (shortly after which the printer first misses the correct chapter-division)—the M of MERCI—is the last in the work to be allotted by the printer more than a 2-line high bold initial: there, as at two earlier points in Book II (chapters iii and v, the R and W of VIRTW) he allocates a block

Usk indicates on the first page of his Prologue an exact awareness of at least three distinct levels of visual adornment of texts available to the accomplished textworker: diacritical gradations not only of bibliographical style but of laboriousness and skill, expense and value: "colours riche," "red inke," and "coles and chalke" (i.e. black and white) (Prologue 14–22; Skeat p. 1). The levels of verbal and imaginative arts, rather than scribal or limner's crafts enlisted in the making of the book, are of course the primary figurative referent here: the "colours" are presumably those of elevated rhetorical style and figuration, while Usk equates "red ink" with verse rhythm or meter as an ornament for pointing a composition and making it memorable; "coles and chalke" mark the humbler mode of his own prose endeavor—a practical medium that may nevertheless "yeve sight, that other precious thinges shal be the more in reverence." Usk loads this threefold distinction of levels still further by suggesting its loose correlation with the triad of Latin, in which "clerkes endyten . . . for they have the propertee of science," French, in which "Frenchmen . . . endyten their queynt termes," and English "our dames tonge"—realized in its full plainness and "leudeness" in prose. Here as often in the work, the bibliophile's, the textworker's, the translator's, and the verbal maker's terms of art are used to signify moral and rhetorical categories, and vice versa: compositional values and textual and bibliographical codes are mutually implicated. It is not beyond Usk's inkhorn wit to indicate thus what he intended to have realized graphically in the bibliographical program and decor of his book: that its central "precious thinges"—"Margarete" and all she represents—will receive more lavish tribute in visual ornament than the name and mission of the petitioner, inscribed in the mere black-and-white of pen flourishes, the visibility of the latter a tribute to the "better colours" that limn the precious Margarete in its "blewe shel." Yet as this false-modesty topos indicates, such differentiation of levels of style and ornament articulates a single endeavor: to "yeve sight" to the intentional design of the whole, as a signed petitionary act of a textworker who thus, and far from incidentally, displays to the "sleigh inseer" his thorough acquaintance with, and technical command of, all aspects of his craft. In the very act of disavowing his own aspiration to wield "queynt knittynge colours" in this work, Usk marks him-

---

of space for an ornamental letter three lines high, which never appeared. A further lowering of the level of ornament is marked in his disposition of initials in Book III: after the ornamental woodblock letter that heads this Book, the next three chapter-initials—i.e. all three chapter-heads that preceded the dislocation of quires—are merely textface capitals, indented a space or two from the margin and separated from the preceding chapter either by spacing or by hanging-indented text at the end of the preceding chapter. Within the disordered quires, chapters are indicated only by two-line-high inset bold initials, and in the last quire set by the printer (which should have followed at the point of initial disruption) the first chapter-division (that of the fifth chapter) is, as we have seen, misplaced— deferred by 40 lines, though to another point that provides an I as chapter-head. If his lack of a sufficient range of decorative large initials was the printer's sole reason for resorting to textface capitals or the plain two-line-high bold initials that predominate in the last half of the text, one would have expected a more random distribution of these replacements; it seems more reasonable to infer that the manuscript *ordinatio* guided his choices to some degree.

self as a connoisseur and designer, if not a direct practitioner, of every level of the textmaker's art.

What specific kind of book was Usk's *Testament* designed to be, or to resemble? The question awaits a more expert codicologist's attention (which I hope here to invite), but a few tentative answers suggest themselves. This is a relatively small-format book, in overall size and page-format much like that of many other vernacular books of around 1400.[41] It is thus highly portable and personal. Yet unlike many other vernacular books of this size and arrangement—most of those known to me comparatively unadorned and practical in their "production values"—its regularities of design imply some expense of forethought and labor in programmatic and unitary production as a book intended to be "read" and valued as an object, returned to and savored, opened, unfolded—literally ex-plicated—reflectively by a reader approaching its matter in and through its manner, its *ordinatio* as such. In this respect its compositional ambitions as a book more closely resemble those of larger folio manuscripts of Usk's contemporaries (the Ellesmere, and the carefully-arranged larger Gower manuscripts, come to mind; the slightly smaller *Troilus* manuscripts, such as the ornamented Corpus manuscript, may offer a closer analogue). It is in this sense something of an oxymoron as a book of vernacular prose: personal in scale and mode, yet relatively refined and ornate as a made object.

The presence of a signatory acrostic also links it with some Latin texts of the fourteenth century, notably Higden's *Polychronicon*.[42] Usk certainly knew this work, since he appropriates extended figures from it early and often in the *Testament*. His first such appropriation is in the service of self-exegesis, adapted to indicate the mode of his own work, and the kind of wit it will exhibit throughout:

Yet also have I leve of the noble husbande Boece, although I be a straunger of conninge, to come after his doctrine, and these grete workmen, and glene my handfuls of the shedinge after their handes; and, if me faile ought of my ful, to encrease my porcion with that I shal drawe by privitees out of the shocke. (Prologue 110–114; Skeat p. 4)

41. One might call its dimension and folding a "late-medieval octavo," though that terminology is used more commonly in the parlance of print bibliography. For the application of similar shorthand, the "late-medieval quarto," to the vernacular-book layout containing some 35–40 lines per page, and a page dimension of about 11¼″ x 7¾″, see Ralph Hanna, "The Manuscripts and Transmission of Chaucer's *Troilus*," originally published in *The Idea of Medieval Literature: New Essays . . . in Honor of Donald R. Howard*, ed. James M. Dean and Christian K. Zacher (Newark, Del.: Univ. of Delaware Press, 1992), pp. 173–188; I cite it from its slightly revised form in Hanna, *Pursuing History: Middle English Manuscripts and Their Texts* (Stanford: Stanford Univ. Press, 1996), pp. 115–129 (p. 117).

42. In an essay on Thomas Usk and Adam Usk—"Private Selves and the Intellectual Marketplace in Late Fourteenth-Century England: The Case of the Two Usks," *New Literary History* 28 (1997), 291–318—Andrew Galloway discusses Thomas Usk's use of Higden in the *Testament* in his own strategems of self-presentation. I am grateful to him for allowing me to see this essay in manuscript, and also for a personal communication (discussed in the following note) on the *mise-en-page* of acrostic letters in Usk manuscripts.

His own work, Usk here artfully proclaims, will be something of a *cento* drawn from the leavings of "these grete workmen" among his illustrious contemporaries (albeit largely as unattributed self-help—"by privitees"—for "a slye servaunt in his owne helpe is often muche commended"), as well as from the "noble husband Boece": here Usk conjures a pun (Boaz/Boece) out of Higden's gleaning figure to name the primary fictive modality of his own enterprise, the expository dialogue. Yet Higden's acrostic is simply signatory ("Presentem cronica compilavit frater Ranulphus Cestrensis monachus"), not, like Usk's, also petitionary, and it disposes the acrostic initials at chapter openings "wherever they fall on the page."[43] Acrostics with an additional diacritical function—that is, those that articulate by their placement the form or intent of the work itself, as well as spell a signature or other message—are more often ornaments of stanziac verse compositions. Usk is, moreover, self-referentially witty in calling attention to his acrostic: in his prologue (chapter i) to Book II he again frames his advertisement of formal design in the form of a humility *topos*: "But bycause that in connynge I am yong, and can yet but crepe, this leude A.b.c. have I set in-to lerning; for I can not passen the telling of three as yet" (II.i.112–114; Skeat p. 49).[44] It appears we must seek further for the analogues invoked by this formal disposition, and by the thoroughgoing bibliographic design, of his work.

Strange as it may seem, these properties of the book ally it more closely with religious service-books of various sorts designed for personal use, than with vernacular manuscripts of either prose or verse. With its acrostic head-letters of each chapter in page-initial position, and a probable further differentiation of the decorative program of these initials along the course of the acrostic, as it proceeded from naming the symbolic honoree, to specifying the act of virtue sought, to the petitioner's identity in the maker's signature, the visual disposition of the page alludes broadly to the differentiated means by which the levels of segmentation of text were marked in psalters, books of

43. Andrew Galloway, personal communication. He refers here to Higden's autograph manuscript of the *Polychronicon*, Huntington Library MS 132, which "shows Higden's late alterations and additions including some to the acrostic." Galloway observes, however, that in this manuscript "when Higden alters his acrostic from its previous version, inserting his Christian name 'frater Ranulphus' after 'compilavit' and before 'Cestrensis,' the new acrostic initials do tend to fall at the tops of pages." On the other hand, he adds, this effect may be "just coincidence," and would require further study of whether there were changes in the chapter-divisions as Higden revised. My thanks to Andrew Galloway for sharing his research on Higden with me; inferences from it are of course solely mine.

44. There is some likelihood that this remark also adverts to Usk's sporadic use of rhythmic, but non-alliterating, prose in *clausulae*: working "three wordes togidre," or variants of this phrase, are common in the alliterative verse corpus for distinguishing this poetic practice from mere clausal rhythm as adornment, and specifying what makes it formal verse; see Ralph Hanna, "Alliterative Poetry," in *The Cambridge History of Medieval English Literature*, ed. David Wallace (Cambridge: Cambridge Univ. Press, forthcoming 1998). Usk's self-awareness about this form of "art-prose," and his apparent sense that it was a rough English equivalent to the *metra* of Boethius as an ornament and elevation of philosophic exposition, warrants much further study; here it should only be noted that it occurs chiefly in those portions of the *Testament* that most closely imitate the organization and style of the *Consolatio*, rather than in Usk's adaptation of Anselm in Book III.

hours, and breviaries made for personal use.[45] However loosely, the book's format provocatively alludes to the formal protocols and diacritical markers of books of prayer, petition, and devotion of various intricately organized kinds, and invites comparison of its maker's textualized speech-act with those individual liturgical rehearsals of praise and confession that such books enabled. In other words; by this means the maker manages to imply that his book might be regarded as a kind of "service-book," albeit realized in a largely secular, civic register: it is, in effect, a visible, and endlessly repeatable, act of devotion to an ideal of constancy, an exemplification and performance (as praise or prayer is "performed") of the motions of the rightly directed will, albeit in royal or civic rather than divine "service." As a testament, it instantiates what it also recommends to the user of the book: perfect service impelled not by fear or favor, but solely by "love." If this was the perceived mode of the book to Usk's contemporaries, it becomes possible to imagine that "moral Gower" might have meant in earnest the commendation, made in the voice of Venus to Amans as she sends him back from his long and now-terminated visionary love-quest to the ordinary world, to "gret wel Chaucer" and urge him to "make his testament of love."

However startling, this analogy of the *Testament* with personal performance of liturgical devotions is not in the least far-fetched: one need look no further than Usk's own self-exegeses in the work to find its rationale. It has been remarked that Usk's range of devotions on the block as he faced his death—impressive even to the Monk of Westminster, who was otherwise no admirer of Usk and all his kind—implied "near-professional" competence and familiarity with the central clerical "reading and singing" repertoire: "the Placebo and Dirige, the Seven Penitential Psalms, the Te Deum, Nunc dimittis, Quicumque vult" (the Athanasian Creed), and "other hymns that bear upon devotion in the hour of death."[46] The resemblance of this array to the "limbs" by which Langland's Will labors in his vocation has also been observed.[47] Similarly, in the *Testament* Usk presents his ultimate purpose not as petition but "joye," to which he hopes to gain access by "the key of David." In a pose remarkably like Langland's fictive self-representation as one who "solaces himself" with his "makings," Usk suggests from the beginning of his work that the mode of this enterprise is to be understood with reference to the psalmist, and more broadly as an act of performed devotion: "Lo, David sayth, 'thou hast delyted me in makinge,' as who sayth, to have

45. See Hughes, pp. 103–107.

46. The phrase "near-professional" is that of Paul Strohm ("Textual Environment," p. 159), who discusses Usk's many-sided textual and performative competences in this connection; the account of Usk's repertory of devotions at the place of execution is that of the Monk of Westminster: *The Westminster Chronicle 1381–1394*, ed. and trans. L. C. Hector and Barbara F. Harvey (Oxford: Clarendon, 1982), pp. 314–315. For this and other observations on the "reading and singing" repertoire, I am greatly indebted to Katherine Zieman, whose Ph.D. dissertation ("Reading and Singing: Liturgy, Literacy, and Literature in Late Medieval England"; Univ. of California, Berkeley, 1997) discusses the relations of this repertoire to the framing of literary and other textworkers' arts and vocation in this period.

47. Most recently and cogently by Kathryn Kerby-Fulton and Steven Justice ("Langlandian Reading Circles," n. 38 above).

delyt in the tune, how god hath lent me in consideration of thy makinge"
(Prologue 61–64, Skeat p. 3). Here he adverts to Psalm 91:1–4; in the first
chapter of the third book, the third of the three prologues in which Usk
declares the modes and intentions of the work, he explains his purpose in
bringing his work to fulfillment with the "most certayn" number three (as
history itself is completed with the end of earthly time and the reign of
"joye"), and once again adverts to the language of formal devotion.[48] "But
yet at the dore shal I knocke, if the key of David wolde the locke unshitte, and
he bring me in, which that childrens tonges both openeth and closeth"
(III.i.159–161; Skeat pp. 105–106). The primary allusion is to one of the "O"
antiphons—"O clavis David, et sceptrum domus Israel, qui aperis et nemo
claudit, claudis et nemo aperit: veni, et educ vinctum de domo carceris,
sedentem in tenebris et umbra mortis"—further enriched, it appears, with an
association of that passage with Psalm 8:2, "ex ore infantium et lactantium
laudes perfecisti," the first psalm of Matins of the Office of the Blessed Virgin.
The entire prologue (i.e. chapter i) of Book III bristles with such allusion: in
the passage used as an epigraph to this essay ("hony of the hard stone, oyle
of the dry rocke"), Usk quotes Deuteronomy 32:13, a verse from the *Canticum
Moysi*, one of the six Old Testament canticles that followed Psalm 150 in
most English psalters; it is immediately followed by a passage that invokes
Isaiah 12:3, from the *Canticum Isaye*, another of these six (possibly with associations of still other verses I have not identified), linking it in turn directly
to the "key of David" passage:[49]

But for my book shal be of joye (as I sayd), and I [am: Skeat] so fer set from thilke
place from whens gladnesse shulde come; my corde is to short to lete my boket ought
cacche of that water; and fewe men be abouten my corde to eche, and many in ful
purpose ben redy it shorter to make, and to enclose th'entre, that myn boket of joye
nothing sholde cacche, but empty returne, my careful sorowes to encrese . . . .: good
lord, send me water in-to the cop of these mountayns, and I shal drinke thereof, my
thurstes to stanche, and sey, these be comfortable welles. And yet I seye more, the
house of joye to me is nat opened. . . . (III.i.140–154; Skeat p. 105)

It is in moves like these, rather than in Usk's use of the extended tree
figure that has thus far been the primary focus of attention in considering the
relations between the *Testament* and *Piers Plowman*, that we must look for
the most significant intertextualities—or at least similarities in conceptualiz-
ing the writer's compositional and social-performative identity—with Langland's poem. For both, the language of liturgical service is also a language not
only of spiritual self-realization, but also of literary and social self-explanation
and self-justification, an inexhaustible fountain of tropes for only "autobiog-

____

48. Usk retrospectively compares the modes of the three books of the work to the three
ages of the world: Book I parallels the time of Deviation (from the Fall to the Redemption,
analogous to his own fictively narrated political mishaps), Book II the time of Grace, which
offers the "true way in fordoinge of the badde" (i.e. constant service to the "Margarete"),
Book III a prophetic hope of "rest" in a time of "joye" (see III.i; Skeat pp. 101–102).

49. On the place of the Old Testament canticles, as well as the Magnificat, in the
Psalter, see John A. Alford, "Rolle's English Psalter and *Lectio Divina*," *Bulletin of the
John Rylands Library* 77 (1995), 47–59.

raphy" or self-exculpation that ultimately mattered to these makers: that which declared to users the modality of their work. Yet in assessing Usk's deployment of this language, it is equally important to note the insider's self-deprecatory humor in its homely elaboration here: the conceit of the "boket" diving repeatedly into an out-of-the-way "welle" and coming up short, at the end of a "corde" always in danger of being further shortened in its laborious but largely futile pursuit of the nourishing "waters" of "joye." If this speaks of and from the abjection of the man of letters dependent on patronage, it does so not from a posture of desperation or isolation, but wittily and gamely for the recognition of others in the same crowded boat—or "boket."

Was this manuscript book an autograph? Thus far I have spoken of it in ways that imply Usk's "hand" in its making, if not literally as its scribal hand, then at least in its production, in some fashion direct enough to assure that its textual amplitude and its bibliographic disposition on the page were coordinated to produce the unusually regular occurrence of its chief diacritic in page-initial position, and often enough on a flesh side of a leaf to realize the ordinational effects of this arrangement—a state of affairs that at least implies some tinkering and adjustments in the text by Usk at the point of preparing fair copy, if not more direct and personal involvement in the actual book that came to Thynne's hands. We cannot, of course, answer this question in the absence of the manuscript (though if the book were to come to light it could quickly be ascertained, since Usk's approver's appeal, still preserved in the Public Record Office, ostentatiously proclaims its writing by Usk's "owne honde").[50]

Analogies, however, are not far to seek for the autograph production of elaborately planned decorated books in this period.[51] James le Palmere, treasurer's scribe in the Exchequer, planned and wrote in his own hand a three-volume encyclopedia of his own devising, and his integrative work in its making included putting out the text to pen-flourishers and painters who

---

50. Andrew Prescott reports to me (oral communication, May 8, 1997) that his reinspection of the Usk appeal in its situation among the records that led to the actions taken against Northampton and his followers suggests that this document is indeed, as it states, in Usk's "owne honde." I hope soon to inspect a photograph of this document, with a view to the possibility of ascertaining whether any of the more systematic mistakes in Thynne's construing of the lost manuscript could be attributable to any equally systematic habits in that hand. This exercise, however, would require a far more minute examination of the entire Thynne text—and in effect a trial act of re-editing it in its entirety—which I have not yet ventured, since at least one new edition of the text is shortly to be published.

51. Future study of the text of the *Testament* in this connection should probably attend to the size of the text-modules drawn from known sources, and the amplitudes of the "bridgework" between them: the opening segment of III.5, for example, which includes Usk's elaborate compliment to Chaucer and also forms a transition between two large segments of more direct and continuous translation, from Anselm's Book I to Book III, is exactly 48 Th-lines long, equivalent in this manuscript to both sides of one full leaf. In other words, it may be possible to infer from closer study of the material text how Usk built his work, much as it is a matter of substantial interest that Langland's C-version additions are almost all in modules of about 100 lines; see Ralph Hanna, "On the Versions of *Piers Plowman*," in *Pursuing History*, pp. 201–243, esp. 239.

completed the decorative initials to Palmere's specifications, as Palmere continued work on the production of text; some of the decorative work on the manuscript postdated Palmere's death in 1375.[52] Like Usk, Palmere was a Londoner and the son of a tradesman (his father was a mercer, Usk's a cap-maker), but like Usk's, Palmere's own occupation, and whatever patronage or preferment he received, was founded on his writing and textual skills. Like Usk's composition of the *Testament*, Palmere's work on his massive encyclopedia can only have been an avocation, an alternative and somewhat ostentatious deployment of his marketable abilities, perhaps to advertise their possessor as a man of versatile and useful talents. But their exercise at a high level of successful integrative operation would also have been a matter of pride, self-esteem, and ultimately sheer personal pleasure, as it always is for a skilled and proficient craftsperson of any trade: not simply an instrument and medium of employment and potential advancement, but also those of a *jeu d'esprit*, sheer self-delighting self-display: "thou hast delighted me in making."

These material and discursive signs suggest that Usk worked through the production of the *Testament* in an environment in which, if gainful employment was always that of a dependent, and hence to some degree precarious (a fact of life that many of his contemporaries also registered in writing), the exercise of its constituent skills was neither isolated nor unregarded, and was well-populated with knowledgeable appreciators near at hand. It was their attention and admiration primarily, and only secondarily that of agents who might more accurately be termed political or dispositive, that, I believe, Usk sought to engage with the *Testament*. In terms of ultimate effects, this might be considered by some a distinction without a difference: the right "sleigh inseers" within the textual bureacracy could put in a good word for a man of talent at least as effectively a great landowner or knight—perhaps more so, since they knew and could assess the skills and qualities of character involved in literate employment. But it makes a great deal of difference to our understanding of the conception of the means, agency and "art" available to men of letters in the later fourteenth century, and the terms of their shared self-awareness as "professionals," however multiform their actual appointments over the course of a career.

Did Usk actually find in these circles of textworkers the contemporary appreciation he sought? The lack of a surviving manuscript of the work, let alone multiple copies of it, may not constitute a meaningful answer to this question. Especially in view of Usk's brutal execution in 1388 (the Westminster Chronicler reports that it took thirty blows of the axe to dispatch him, surely cruel and unusual punishment in an era, and among a host of similar executions in the same season, when a single stroke usually sufficed), and the fraught political factionalism that never wholly ceased to revolve around the king in the last fifteen years of the century, it is unlikely that anyone who possessed a copy at that point, or who had encountered the work in

52. See Sandler, "*Omne bonum*," cited in n. 20 above.

the making, would have had any reason to promulgate its further copying. If it was chiefly admired by, as it had been designed for, fellow textworkers, themselves as ultimately dependent as Usk had been on royal favor and its shifting fortunes, the *Testament* would already have done, for Usk and these "frendes," all the ideational and ideological work it could do: testified elaborately to their common condition, shared hopes, and—much more important—the terms within which they could articulate the common grounds of their self-respect. Beyond that, it could only be a souvenir, preserved among the papers of those to whom it recalled the man who had inscribed his name and petition in its very structure. Indeed, the care invested in its making as a material text would have made it all the more difficult to reproduce, as well as largely devoid of discursive interest much beyond these circles. Surely at best caviare to the general by virtue of its complex, almost frenetic, allusiveness to the constituent repertory of "clerical" (but not in the first instance ecclesiastical or religious) art, it would also have been hard to copy in such a way as to retain its material terms of art as well: to recall an analogous instance, the *Pearl* manuscript—sole witness to all its texts, and quite possibly a humbly-made copy of a more expertly and expensively designed illustrated and decorated exemplar—is to acknowledge how narrow is the gap between rarity and complete annihilation of textual testimony, and how little can be inferred from sheer numerical attestation.

Better testimony, therefore, is that of Usk's contemporary makers, in their own work: Gower's, for one, and possibly even Langland's (if an *ignotum per ignotius* may be taken in evidence). In addition to "Gower's" fictively-displaced injunction to "Chaucer" (the quotation marks signifying, as they have in discussing the *Testament*, the represented maker in the work), there is also a haunting echo of Usk's *apologia pro vita sua* in Langland's last representation of Will's justification of his anomalous enterprise. In the waking encounter in London, inserted between the first two dreams of the poem, at the head of Passus V of the C-version, the same "singing and reading" repertory that had marked Usk's pious last moments constitutes the tools of Will's elusive trade, which like Usk he defends by analogies drawn from the parables. The Pearl of Great Price figures for both as the ultimate ideal object of value in this anomalous vocation, the obscure object of clerical desire; the Dishonest Steward ("a slye servaunt in his owne helpe is often moche commended") is also invoked by Will's use of the wily "servaunt's" plea of exemption from manual labor, to dig I am unable, to beg I am ashamed—a text adduced repeatedly by clerical wits since at least the twelfth century in defense of the distinctively non-laborious and irrevocable character of their vocation. Besides its own richly self-referential wit, this one Langlandian representation of a judicial proceeding against the maker-protagonist—a passage almost certainly written within no more than a year after Usk's execution—may have gained additional resonance by recalling to fellow textworkers another recent encounter by one of their number with censorious juridical authority, with far less happy results: while Usk went to the block for his textual service to the wrong powers, in Langland's fictive version

"Will" escapes sanctions to dream and "make" the rest of the poem.[53] Nor was Langland the only one of Usk's contemporaries to frame a declaration of authorial intent in the fictive form of a high-stakes encounter with punitive regal will and authority: the *Legend of Good Women* and the *Confessio Amantis*, both produced in the later 1380s, likewise stage the implications of these writers' recognition of an uneasy and shifting dependency that always underlies their resilient subjective sense of the intellectual and spiritual integrity attained through the exercise of "clerical" arts.

If this was the "reading" Usk received from contemporaries, it is not difficult to imagine that his book came to survive among their effects as a kind of keepsake; it was among such family "heyrelomes" that it may have attracted Thynne's notice as a piece of Chauceriana. While from the point of view of modern literary scholarship and textual culture Thynne and his printer were astonishingly indifferent to the *content* of Usk's text (had it been otherwise someone would certainly have noticed the massive displacements in Book III), we have in the foregoing signs copious evidence that Thynne "read" with some care and perception the various niceties of visual *ordinatio*, and general bibliographical signs of value and care that his source manuscript provided—and not merely for the mechanical marking-off of text toward the spatial and workshop planning of his own massive folio production. Perhaps more fundamentally, we can discern in Thynne's presentational choices thus far his "reading" of the complex bibliographical codes, both large-scale and minute, that indicated the work's generic affinities and aspirations, and expressed its intended value and "meaning" as an object by means that were both physically and culturally legible. Though no philologist or literary critic—or for that matter even a self-conscious connoisseur of books as such, though he was proud of his assiduous searches for Chaucerian material to print—Thynne appears nevertheless to have been keenly conversant with the broad craft-language and aesthetic capacities of his own occupation, an astute observer and interpreter of its terms of art.[54] His conversational capacities in this kind, moreover, seem to have extended some way into the "history of the language"—that is, into an intuitive grasp of the conventions of what amounted to the antecedent stage of his own practice: the London manuscript book-trade, and its expressive forms and media. As we have had occasion to notice at many points in this essay, insofar as the *Testament* was realized and transmitted as a work in this "language," Usk was a self-conscious user of it, and he found in Thynne a very good reader indeed.[55]

53. See my essay "Acts of Vagrancy: The C Version 'Autobiography' and the Statute of 1388," in *Written Work: Langland, Labor, and Authorship*, ed. Steven Justice and Kathryn Kerby-Fulton (Philadelphia: Univ. of Pennsylvania Press, 1997), pp. 208–317.

54. On Thynne's search for further Chauceriana, and the intersections of his efforts with both his own royal service and the activities of other contemporary printers, see Blodgett, "William Thynne" (cited in n. 6 above), *passim.*

55. Besides his lavish use of large woodblock capitals, on a scale otherwise unequalled in this large volume, Thynne used other bibliographical codes to register the pretensions of his source manuscript. For example, he also allotted to the *Testament* a full-page woodblock-framed title (f. 324r, with the verso left blank; the text of the *Testament* begins on f. 325r). This same title-frame is used in only six other places in Thynne's edition: at the head of

How good a reader was Thynne? Not good enough to have read the acrostic for what it was (rather than simply as a sign of the care and value invested in the making of the manuscript book), or to have read Usk's "philosophy" at all. But more than good enough to have offered plentiful and eloquent testimony—almost all of it largely inadvertent—about Usk's book: not only about its physical form, but about the "intente" and discursive horizon within which it was designed and produced. Thynne's edition bespeaks professional assurance, not only about its own means and bibliographical "language" and conventions, but also about its counterparts in late fourteenth-century book culture. It is therefore a highly competent professional "reading," legible precisely because of, and through, its own historically situated terms of trade and art.[56]

The testimony it offers must give us second thoughts about the character

---

Troilus, Romaunt of the Rose, Boece, and as the title-page of the book itself; in each of these places it begins a new quire, as it does at the beginning of the *Testament.* The other two full-page titles using this same woodcut as frame occur in mid-quire, marking a significant spacing between shorter verse works (at f. 285r, the third leaf of quire 3D, with the verso blank, it frames the title Thynne gives to the "Complaint unto Pity": *Howe pite is ded and beried in a gentyll hert*), or to mark a division between a sequence of shorter verse works and a longer prose work (at f. 298v, the fourth leaf of quire 3F, it occupies the verso of the last page of the *Assembly of Ladies,* framing the title *The conclusions of the Astrolabie,* and allows the prose text to begin on the facing recto page). Since the *Testament* in Thynne fills six folio quires of 6 (3L-3Q, ff. 324r–359v), plus both sides of one more leaf and col. 1 of the next (3R: ff. 360r–361r, col. 1), it must have been obvious in the marking-off of copy that without the full-leaf framed title the work would fit into exactly six quires with only one column left over—yet the printer accorded it the rare honor of its own title page. While other considerations may also have entered into the printer's disposition of his material, it seems likely from this combination of visual codes that the decorated capitals in his source—or the generous provision of space for them there—together with general signs of comprehensive and skillful planning of the manuscript's text space signalled to Thynne that this was a text with some pretensions as a work of bookmaking art, to be taken at its word—or letters. Blodgett notes that this frame was printed from a woodcut lent to Thomas Godfrey, Thynne's printer, by its owner Thomas Berthelet, the king's printer from 1530 to 1547, whose edition of Gower's *Confessio Amantis* was published in 1532, the same year as Thynne's massive Chaucer; see his chapter "William Thynne" (cited in n. 6 above), p. 51; for discussion of the relations between Thynne and Berthelet see also Fisher, *John Gower,* pp. 12–18, esp, his note 32 (see n. 4 above). If, as both suggest, there was at least a professional friendship between Thynne and Berthelet, then their combined efforts in assembling materials for their respective editions probably cast a rather wide net in gathering literary remains from the era of both Chaucer and Gower. If the lost manuscript of the *Testament* came to light during these efforts by either editor, its preservation in these associations would have led to its identification as a valued piece of Chauceriana, and its elegant presentation format as a book could only have encouraged Thynne's inference that it was esteemed in those circles.

56. The account of the work that I propose here owes much to the methods and approach of Michael Baxandall, in addressing the relations between historically specific professional and craft-skills and the similarly situated terms of aesthetic description, appreciation, and evaluation of the exercise of these skills, and their products. See, for example, his *Painting and Experience in Fifteenth-Century Italy* (Oxford: Oxford Univ. Press, 1972), and *Giotto and the Orators* (Oxford: Clarendon, 1971); on some of the implications of this approach in relation to those of both social and intellectual history and philology, see also Svetlana Alpers, "Is Art History?" *Daedalus* (Summer 1977), 1–13.

portrait of Usk thus far extrapolated from his political misfortune, and inferred from his verbal style and eagerly emulative use of form and genre. In the world in which Usk had a continuous professional identity, he was, on this evidence, far from the headlong, "erratic, overardent" political player he has seemed to most modern scholarship. He spoke with assurance and eloquence the material language of books, and it appears his more respected contemporaries recognized it. And within the terms of his own trade, so did Thynne: paradoxically, the lost manuscript speaks with uncanny clarity through Thynne's professional appreciation of a common language, and perhaps even more clearly through his error than it might done without it. One way or another, "poor Usk" received, it seems, both the "sleigh inseers" and the "good bookamender" he wished for.

Appendix A

Charter-Lengths and Page-Dispositions of the Lost Manuscript

The following chart displays both the quiring and the chapter-divisions of Thynne's source manuscript as I reconstruct it in the essay. Line-counts (labelled "# of lines in chapter") represent the number of Th-lines (lines of type one column wide on a two-column page) per chapter of Thynne's printing of the *Testament*. Page-counts, however, represent the number of manuscript pages per chapter (defining the two sides of a leaf each as a manuscript page) in my reconstruction of Thynne's manuscript source. (Appendix B provides further details on the reconstructed quiring, and remarks on alternative arrangements considered in arriving at the description offered here. Appendix C provides amplified description of Thynne's treatment of chapter-initials and chapter-divisions.)

Chapters are not numbered in Thynne's printing, but indicated (sometimes incorrectly) only by their featured initial letters. I have retained the roman chapter numbers of Skeat (Sk) for ease of reference, substituting arabic numbers only at those places in Book III where my reconstruction differs from his: chapter 4 below is a redivision of Skeat's iv; 5 and 6 designate the reconstructed and re-ordered fifth and sixth chapters (corresponding only in part to Skeat's vi and v respectively, since their boundaries as well as sequence differ in my reconstruction). Under "Comments" I correlate my chapter divisions, explained in the essay, with Skeat's division and sequence, and with the six displaced segments of text (DS 1, DS 2, etc.) he posits; I also indicate Thynne's misdivisions of chapters in Book II where they occur, in chapters x and xi. Preceding the reconstructed chapter-numbers in the chart are the corrected chapter-initials; the signatory acrostic may be read vertically; initials falling on the hair-side of a manuscript leaf in this reconstructed quiring are italicized.

To achieve line-counts usable in reconstructing chapter-lengths in the lost manuscript, I have silently added fractional printed lines to create whole lines, and expressed the total to the nearest .5 of a Th-line, at those few chapter-endings that Thynne set in double hanging-indent format (chapters ending in this way are indicated with an asterisk; see Appendix C for details.) I have not, however, similarly adjusted the line-counts of each chapter to allow for the volume of text-space occupied by Thynne's decorative chapter initials, because their manuscript counterparts also consumed an indeterminable proportion of text-block space. Thynne's printed initials at their most ornate (Prologue, II.i) occupy a little less than 3 full lines of text-space; the next largest (at I.i) consumes 1.25 lines; the next (at III.i) one line. Of the remainder, the 3-line-high letters (or the space for them), four in all, occupy about .7 of a line, the 2-line-high initials about .3 of a line (21 are of this size); the rest of the acrostic-initials are represented simply by textface capitals. These encroachments into text-space are so negligible and infrequent that they have simply been excluded from my specifications of chapter lengths: accuracy to three lines or less is unattainable in reconstructing from printed text the volume of prose text spanning several scribal pages, and unnecessary for the present purposes of schematic comparison. (The Notes in Appendix B discuss the effects on Thynne's printed presentation of the size and placement of chapter-initials in the manuscript.)

In the sixth and seventh columns of the chart I indicate the number of pages each chapter occupied in the manuscript, as I reconstruct it, and the way in which the chapter was divided between quires wherever it continued past the end of one. For the latter situation I specify the leaves of the next quire occupied by the chapter-continuation before noting the occurrence of the next chapter-initial.

MS quire	Chapter begins at:	Chapter initial	Chapter	# of lines in chapter	# of pages in chapter	# of pages of chapter in quire	Comments
Book 1:							
a⁸	1r	M	Prol.	170	8	8	
	5r	A	i	191	8	8	
b⁸	1r	R	ii	267	11	11	
	6v	G	iii	220	9	5	
c⁸			(iii cont'd, 1r–2v)			4	
	3r	A	iv	105	4	4	
	5r	R	v	178	8	8	
d⁸	1r	E	vi	282	12	12	
	7r	T	vii	160.5	7	4	
e⁸			(vii cont'd, 1r–2r)			3	
	2v	E	viii	194	8	8	
	6v	O	ix	179	8	5	
f⁴			(ix cont'd, 1r–2r)			3	
	2v	F	x	167.5	7	5	
χ²			(x concluded, 1r–1v)			2	
Total:				2114	90	(5x16)+8+2	
Book II:							
g⁸	1r	V	i	185	8	8	
	5r	I	ii	196	8	8	
h⁸	1r	R	iii	183	8	8	
	5r	T	iv	198	8	8	
j⁸	1r	W	v	177	7	7	
	4v	H	vi*	211	9	9	
k⁸	1r	A	vii	189.5	8	8	
	5r	V	viii*	172	7	7	
	8v	E	ix	262	11	1	
l⁸			(ix cont'd, 1r–5v)			10	
	6r	M	x	216.5	9	6	

MS quire	Chapter begins at:	Chapter initial	Chapter	# of lines in chapter	# of pages in chapter	# of pages of chapter in quire	Comments
m[8]			(x cont'd, 1r–2r)			3	176.5 lines from *M* to Th's C, in m at *1v*; 40 lines from Th's C to xi (E).
	2v	E	xi	175	8	8	
	6v	R	xii*	163	7	5	103.5 lines from E to Th's T, in m at 4v; 71.5 lines from T to xii (R).
n[8]			(xii cont'd, 1r–1v)			2	
	2r	C	xiii	181	8	8	
	6r	I	xiv	139	6	6	
Total:				2648	112	(7x16)	
Book III:							
p[8]	1r	O	i	248	11	11	
	6v	N	ii*	196	8	5	
q[8]			(ii cont'd, 1r–2r)			3	
	2v	T	iii*	252	10	10	
	7v	H	4	314	12	3	76.5 lines beginning Sk's iv;
r[8]			(4 cont'd, 1r–5r)			9	237.5 lines of Sk's iv (beginning DS 5).
	5v	I	5	265	10	7	39.5 lines ending Sk's iv (in DS 5); 8.5 lines beginning Sk's v (in DS 5); 129 lines beginning Sk's vi (DS 6);
s[8]			(5 cont'd, 1r–2r)			3	88 lines ending Sk's vi (DS 2).†
	2v	N	6	197	8	8	197 lines (rest of Sk's v) (DS 3).
	6v	V	vii	212	8	5	121 lines (DS 4);
t[8]			(vii cont'd 1r–2r)			3	91 lines (beginning DS 1).†
	2v	S	viii	265.5	10	10	265.5 lines (DS 1).
	7v	K	ix	144.5	6	3	64 lines (ending DS 1);
w[2]			(ix concluded, 1r–2r)			3	80.5 remaining lines of ix.
Total:				2094	83	(5x16)+3	

†See Note on Book III in Appendix B for irregularities in chapter-division here.

APPENDIX B

INFERRED QUIRING OF *Testament* MANUSCRIPT

Listed with the contents of each quire are the leaves on which chapter-initials occur in this reconstruction (those falling on the hair-side of a leaf are italicized). All occur in page-initial position, with the possible exception of those in the last two quires of eight in the manuscript; these are discussed below in the Note to Book III. The number of lines per quire is extrapolated from the number of lines and of pages per chapter (in Appendix A) throughout, and from the additional information on quire divisions inferable from the displacements in Book III. Notes on variations and inferences from the patterns follow the quiring of each Book.

Book I: a–e⁸ f⁴ χ1

a: Prologue (1r), 1 (5r)	(361 lines)
b: ii (1r), iii (6v)	(389 lines)
c: iv (3r), v (5r)	(381 lines)
d: vi (1r), vii (7r)	(374 lines)
e: viii (2v), ix (6v)	(375 lines)
f: x (2v)	(187 lines)
χ:	(48 lines)

Note: To assure that the decorated initial page of Book II would be in direct contact with a flesh-side of a leaf, χ1 was probably reversed, placing the text-page 4v of quire f in direct contact with the hair-side of χ1 (neither side had an ornamented initial).

An alternative quiring, avoiding the use of a concluding single leaf, could have been achieved by encompassing chapter vii in 6 pages instead of 7, and chapter ix in 7 pages instead of 8. The result would have placed the last three chapter initials at *2r* and *6r* of quire e, and on *1v* of quire f, all of them hair-side pages by normal folding—an unsuitable arrangement if all initials in Book I were to receive painted embellishment, though (another possible desideratum in the general design) it would place all chapter initials but the last in Book I on a recto page (for a programmatic opposite of this arrangement, see Note to Book III).

In this arrangement, a reversed folding of both quires e and f could have made all three initials fall on the flesh side, but only at the cost of putting a hair-side text-page at the conclusion of the Book, in direct contact with the first decorated initial of Book II. Since this alternative quiring seems to offer as many liabilities as advantages to the overall decorative scheme I infer, and requires a greater compacting of text than anywhere else in the first two Books, it seems to me the less likely hypothesis, but neither alternative materially affects the rest of the reconstruction. The exercise supports the hypothesis, supported further below, that the quiring of each book was separately planned to achieve Usk's general design.

Book II: g–n[8]

g: i (1r), ii (5r)   (381 lines)
h: iii (1r), iv (5r)   (381 lines)
j: v (1r), vi (4v)   (388 lines)
k: vii (1r), viii (5r), ix (8v)   (385.5 lines)
l: x (*6r*)   (382.5 lines)
m: xi (2v), xii (6v)   (366 lines)
       [Thynne's erroneous chapter-divisions made at m1v, m4v]
n: xiii (2r), xiv (*6r*)   (367 lines)

Note: In the last three quires of Book II, the three chapter initials that Thynne correctly identified as such (M, C, I) all fell on hair-sides of the leaf, though on a recto page, while the two he failed to recognize as chapter-initials (E, R) occurred on the flesh-side of the leaf but on verso pages—a pattern inviting two inferences.

The first gains some corroboration from the printer's disordering of quires as well as misidentification of chapter-boundaries in Book III: mid-quire chapter-divisions or those occurring on verso pages (as all but the first did in Book III) more readily escaped his notice than those in positions the printer expected and himself favored for elaborate textual ornament. Whatever prompted the printer's uncertainties, his behavior at such points shows his assimilation of the manuscript's decorative scheme to the canons of his own printerly aesthetic: here Thynne resolved his doubts by choosing to divide his text with two initials beginning sentences that started at the heads of columns in his own printed page-layout. It also shows that he perceived these initials only as ornaments of textual segmentation, not as elements of an acrostic.

The signals (or lack of them) in his source text that caused his uncertainty at these points also prompt conjecture about the ornamental program of the manuscript, and its state of completion. If the painting or rubrications of some or all of the chapter-initials (tasks that would have followed the scribal completion of the text) were lacking or incomplete in Thynne's manuscript source, his mistakes in identifying chapter-divisions where his own canons of ornament did not lead him to expect or favor them would be more readily explicable. His substitution of O for presumptive E in his source text at I.viii, producing "Oft," ("often") for "Eft" ("again," required by the sense as well as the acrostic), warrants such an inference; for additional support for this hypothesis, see the Note on the quiring of Book III.

The greater frequency of Thynne's errors in negotiating chapter-divisions in the latter half of the work might, however, reflect a change in the source manuscript, around the middle of Book II, in the manner of distinguishing chapter-initials from other paragraph head-letters—by a reduction in size, or subduing of other decorative markers, or both. If, after spelling out "Margarete of virtw," chapter initials from this point were no longer adorned by "colors riche" (painting in colors which would have been abraded by contact with hair-side pages), but merely pointed (or planned for pointing) with "red inke," they might have become less immediately distinguishable to the printer as the acrostic began to spell out "merci". In Book III, chapter i, an explicatory prologue expounding for the "slye inseer" the significance of the *ordinatio* of his three-book work, Usk himself identifies red-ink coloration as a middle level of embellishment, midway between paint and pen-flourishing in the hierarchy of textual ornament; he specifically associates this second level with the age of "merciable grace," the second (between "deviation" and "joye") in his scheme of the three ages of human history, which he correlates with the dominant themes and modes of the three books of the *Testament* (see essay).

I have omitted the letter o from the quiring sequence in my reconstruction in order to reserve it to designate a second extra quire (χ in Book I above being the first) in an alternative quiring that could have averted all hair-side chapter initials in Book II. If quire 1 were a quire of four instead of eight leaves, then another quire of four, which I designate o, following it and reverse-folded, would have placed the M of "merci" on a flesh-side page; by a similar reversed folding, the last quire (n) of eight in Book II could have had its two chapter-initials, C and I, on flesh-side pages. Since this arrangement, like the one discussed above for Book I, would not only have created additional sites (here three) of hair-flesh contact of text pages, but placed the hair-side final text-page of Book II in direct contact with the head-initial of Book III, I consider it less likely than the one described above. The plausibility of this alternative quiring of the end of the book, like the similar alternative available for Book I, and the problems of textual ordinatio and spatial planning they address, implies that the manuscript volume was planned and executed as three distinct stints of scribal endeavor, with each book distinguished and unified visually by its own ornamental program, as well as thematically and rhetorically by the modes and principles expounded in the third prologue.

Book III: p–t⁸ w²

p: i (1r), ii (6v)	(368.5 lines)	
q: iii (2v), 4 (7*v*)	(404 lines)	
r: 5 (5*v*)	(414.5 lines)	[Skeat's DS 5 + 6]
s: 6 (2v), vii (6v)	(406 lines)	[Sk's DS 2 + 3 + 4]
t: viii (2v), ix (7*v*)	(420.5 lines)	[Sk's DS 1]
w: ix, remainder	(80.5 lines)	3 pages; last page blank

Note: In three respects the inferable textual disposition of Book III differs from the norms of the two preceding ones. First, its textual density (the number of characters per quire, and on average per page) is slightly higher (25.23 lines per page in Book III), as against a fairly consistent density (23.6 for I, and 23.64 for II) maintained through the first quire of Book III (23.03 lines per page on average in quire p). Second, in this reconstruction all acrostic chapter initials in Book II except the first fall on a verso page—a factor which may have exacerbated the printer's confusion in setting the last three quires of eight (see Note to Book II above). Third, the divisions of chapters in the last two quires suggest the occurrence of mid-page chapter-initials only at the end of the work, where the acrostic reached the point of authorial self-naming.

The simplest explanation for the greater textual density of the final four quires may be the greater average length of the chapters in Book III: 232.67 lines per chapter (and hence on average 9 or 10 pages of text between ornamental initials), as against 192.18 for Book I (including the general Prologue), and 189.14 for Book II, or eight pages per chapter in both of the first two books. In other words, the greater number of Thynne-lines per quire may simply be an artefact of description rather than an indication of different ruling or more compacted hand in the source manuscript.

A second possibility is that these three features of Book III are related and significant aspects of Usk's design for the final book of the work. The greater textual density of the final four quires, and Thynne's disorientation in dividing chapters, suggests that the chapter-initials of this last signatory phrase of the work were marked throughout in simpler fashion, by what Usk calls "coles and chalke" (the black-and-white of pen-flourished initials rather than the coloring of either paint or ink), and were still smaller in scale than those of Book II, and hence difficult to distinguish from paragraph-heads as marks of segmentation; the reduced size of the text-block allocated to these initials could also help to explain the greater textual density of the last quires. Moreover, by situating every letter but the first of the acrostic phrase spelling out the petitioner's name ("on thin Usk") on the verso of the leaf, Usk may have represented through his complex textual semantics a posture of petitionary humility in relation to the more luxuriously ornamented "Margarete of virtw" honored as symbolic addressee, chiefly on recto pages, in the first half of the work.

The possible mid-page placement of the final four chapter-initials—those spelling the author's surname and the N of "thin" preceding it—may also have figured in this visually realized profession of humble service. The N of "thin," immediately preceding the name, occurs at 88 lines rather than the expected 76 lines into quire s; the initial V of chapter vii occurs at 121 lines from the end of the quire, rather than the 132.5 predicted by the general quiring scheme; the S of chapter viii occurs at 91 rather than the expected 106 lines into the next quire, and K of chapter ix is 64 rather than the expected 77–78 lines from the end of its quire. All represent an offset of 11–14 lines from the head of their respective pages, or about mid-page in a format of approximately 26 lines otherwise displaying remarkably consistent inferable amplitude across the length of the work. The quantity of text in the concluding bifolium tends to corroborate the hypothesis that by the end of the work each manuscript page contained 26–27 Th-lines of text: there, I conjecture, the final 80.5 lines occupied three of the four pages of this quire, the last remaining blank as a cover.

A third hypothesis that would account for all of the small anomalies of Book III is more speculative, but also rich in implications about Usk's working methods and the state of Thynne's source manuscript. I posit below, as a heuristic exercise, a simple and regular alternative quiring option that corrects all of the source manuscript's inferred divergences from the general patterns established in the first two books, and achieves a far more elegant disposition of chapter-heads. Using the line-counts and divisions of chapters reconstructed here (see chart in Appendix A), and working back from the end of the Book, one may easily derive a regular quiring layout that satisfies Usk's apparent book-design objectives more simply than the quiring that accounts for Thynne's errors in setting Book III in print. In this arrangement, *all* the chapter initials of Book III appear in page-initial position, and all on a recto page; only three (H and I of chapters 4 and 5, K of chapter ix) fall on the hair-side of the leaf. In its disposition of chapters it differs from the one inferred above only in assigning 10 pages rather than 11 to chapter i. I use capital letters to describe this hypothetical quiring, which I shall call the "corrective" version:

Book III: P1 Q–W⁸

P1: i (1r–1v, cont'd in next quire)	(50 lines)
Q⁸: (1r–4v completes chap. 1), ii (5r–8v)	(394 lines)
R⁸: iii (1r–5v), 4 (*6r*–8v, cont'd in next quire)	(409 lines)
S⁸: (1r–3v completes chap. 4), 5 (*4r*–8v)	(422 lines)
T⁸: 6 (1r–4v), vii (5r–8v)	(409 lines)
W⁸: viii (1r–5v), ix (*6r*–8v)	(410 lines)

Elegant as this arrangement is, however, and easily achievable *in preparing to copy in a presentation manuscript book an already composed text,* this cannot have been the quiring of Book III in the manuscript used by Thynne, as the essay demonstrates. As a heuristic exercise, it points to one further inference, both about how Usk achieved his shapely book-design, and what kind of manuscript text of the *Testament* Thynne used.

As noted in the essay, Usk's overall design for his work as finished manuscript book necessarily required constant mutual accommodation of expository amplitude to the overall formal program of his book-design, by a disposition of his prose into modules of chapter-length that would allow chapter-heads supporting the acrostic to fall in page-initial position. In practice, Usk had to realize his expository intent, and simultaneously *draft* his book design, from the front of the book onward, but would presumably *achieve* the latter in the form of a finished book, only backwards, as it were, in a retrospective act of planning the quiring to accommodate the intended ornament and complete the book, repeating (or directing another to repeat, to his detailed specifications) his scribal labors again to produce the *durchkomponiert* finished and ornamented book. Here, by planning the quiring of the completed text of Book III backward from its end (as he had presumably done for Books I and II), he would have placed the anomalous single leaf at the head of the book, allowing it to be put out for ornamentation while the rest of Book III was being scribally produced as finished copy, with all chapter-initials heading recto pages.

The several anomalies and awkwardnesses in the chapter-division and quire-disposition of Book III, inferred in Thynne's manuscript to account for his displacements of text, tends to suggest that the printer's source manuscript was not finished text as yet unrubricated and unpainted, but rather represented a completed draft copy from which a finished quiring design such as the "corrective" one proposed here could have been planned. Thynne's treatment of chapter-initials in Book III lends support to this hypothesis: all chapter-initials but the first in Book III are either simple textface capitals (chapters ii–iv, and the erroneously identified I of 5), undifferentiated from those used to head any paragraph, or (6–x) Thynne's plainest form of chapter-initial (see Appendix C). In effect, Thynne lost the trail of ornamental initials as a guide to textual disposition not simply because embellishment was **not** complete, but because his manuscript source for Book III represented a completed prose composition not yet recopied into the quiring layout that would have placed the chapter-initials in the quires and page-positions Usk's overall design required, and Thynne by this point expected.

Whether Thynne's manuscript was Usk's holograph draft text, awaiting his or another's finished recopying of Book III into a more elegant quiring layout, or a copy at one or more removes from such a text, it is impossible to guess. It is, however, easy to imagine the circumstances in the later 1380s that might have left Usk suddenly without the material and institutional resources to bring his *Testament* to its finished state throughout as an intricately planned venture into fine book-production, matching in material elegance the rhetorical and literary ambition of the composition, as his one margarete-pearl on offer.

Appendix C

Thynne's Initials at Chapter-Divisions

Chapter	Initial	Description (* indicates occurrence at head of column)
Prologue	M	*Ornamented dark-ground woodblock initial, 7 lines high, width ca. 45% of column
Book I:		
i	A	*Ornamented dark-ground woodblock initial, 5 lines high
ii	R	*Bold undecorated initial, 2 lines high
iii	G	Bold undecorated initial, 2 lines high, after 2-line-high vertical spacing
iv	A	Textface cap, indented 1 space, after 1-line vertical space
v	R	Bold undecorated initial, 2 lines high, after 1-line vertical space
vi	E	Bold undecorated initial, 2 lines high, after 1-line vertical space
vii	T	Bold undecorated initial, 3 lines high, no added vertical space between chapters
viii	O	[Thynne "Oft" for "Eft"] Bold undecorated initial, 2 lines high; no added vertical space between chapters
ix	O	Bold undecorated initial, 2 lines high, after 2-line vertical space
x	F	Textface cap, indented 2 spaces, after 1-line vertical space
Book II:		
i	V	*Ornamented dark-ground woodblock initials, 7 lines high, width ca. 45% of column
ii	I	Bold undecorated initial, 2 lines high, after 1-line vertical space
iii	R	Block of space 3 lines high and equally wide allocated for feature initial, but occupied only by textfont cap in middle of space
iv	T	Bold undecorated initial, 2 lines high, after 1-line vertical space
v	W	Block of space 3 lines high and equally wide allocated for feature initial, but occupied only by textfont cap in middle of space
vi	H	Bold undecorated initial, 2 lines high, after 1-line vertical space
vii	A	Ornamented dark-ground woodblock initial, 3 lines

		high, after 1-line space, following 3-line double hanging-indent ending preceding chapter
viii	V	Bold undecorated initial, 2 lines high, after 1-line vertical space
ix	E	Bold undecorated initial, 2-lines high, after 1-line vertical space, following 6-line double hanging-indent ending preceding chapter
x	M	Block of space 3 lines high and equally wide allocated for feature initial, but occupied only by text font cap in middle of space
Thynne	C	*Bold undecorated initial, 2 lines high
xi	[E]	[chapter-division not indicated in Thynne]
Thynne	T	*Bold undecorated initial, 2 lines high
xii	R	*Bold undecorated initial 2 lines high, after 1-line vertical space, following 3-line double hanging-indent ending preceding chapter
xiii	C	*Bold undecorated initial, 2 lines high, after 1-line vertical space
xiv	I	Bold undecorated initial, 2 lines high, after 1-line vertical space, following 6-line double hanging-indent ending preceding chapter

Book III:

i	O	*Ornamented woodblock framed initial, 4 lines high, $\frac{1}{4}$ width of column
ii	N	Textface cap, merely indented 1 sp, after vertical space of 1 line
iii	T	Textface cap, merely indented 1 sp, after vertical space of 1 line, following 5-line double hanging-indent ending preceding chapter
4	H	Textface cap, merely indented 1 sp, no vertical space separating chapter, following 2-line double hanging-indent after vertical space of 1 line
5	I	In displaced quire r; correct chapter-division unidentified in Thynne and Skeat: midline textface cap only
	[I]	In displaced quire r; incorrectly identified chapter-initial (which heads Skeat's vi): bold undecorated initial, 2 lines high, after 1-line vertical space
6	N	In displaced quire s; bold undecorated initial, 2 lines high, after 1-line vertical space (not identified by Skeat as chapter-initial; occurs 8.5 Th-lines into Skeat's chapter v)
vii	V	*In displaced quire s; bold undecorated initial, 2 lines high
viii	S	In displaced quire t; bold undecorated initial, 2 lines high, after 2-line-high vertical spacing
xi	K	In displaced quire t; bold undecorated initial, 2 lines high, after 1-line vertical space

PETRUCCIO AND THE BARBER'S SHOP

by

Laurie E. Maguire

IN Act 4 of *The Taming of the Shrew* Petruccio orders a tailor and a haber-dasher to present their commissioned clothing designs—designs which Petruccio will ultimately deny Katherine. The haberdasher displays his cap, is insulted by Petruccio, and departs (TLN 2045–70; 4.3.62–85).[1] The tailor then presents his gown, a "loose bodied gowne" with trunk sleeves "curiously cut" (TLN 2117, 2126) which Petruccio also criticises and rejects. Petruccio's sartorial criticisms include a perplexing simile:

> Whats this? a sleeue? 'tis like demi cannon,
> What, vp and downe caru'd like an apple Tart?
> Heers snip, and nip, and cut, and slish and slash,
> Like to a Censor in a barbers shoppe: (TLN 2073–76)

Editors from Rowe on have accepted the orthographic alteration of "Censor" to "censer," a noun which "is usually explained as 'fumigator.' . . . though *OED* gives no examples of this, quoting this line from *Shr.* under Censer, *sb.*[1] 1.b and stating 'commentators are not agreed as to what exactly is re-referred to.' "[2] Despite the uncertainty, "censer" appears to gain additional weight from Doll Tearsheet's insult to the beadle in *2 Henry 4*, "thou thin man in a Censor" (TLN 3190); this line also requires the sense of "censer," although, as Brian Morris points out, "neither [use] sheds light on the other."[3] Ann Thompson admits that "[t]he use of such objects in barbers' shops is not supported by any other contemporary reference," but concludes plausibly that it was "presumably important to sweeten the air" since barbers' shops "were used for minor surgery as well as hairdressing."[4] Most editors concur. Thus, "censer" has made its way into almost all modern-spelling editions of *The Taming of the Shrew.*

The Oxford *Complete Works* is the first edition to tackle the problem by emendation rather than rationalisation. The editors offer *scissor* for *Censor*, an attractive emendation which can be defended on grounds of logic, at least initially. On closer scrutiny however, the Oxford emendation cannot

---

1. TLN quotations are taken from the Norton Facsimile of the First Folio prepared by Charlton Hinman (New York: W. W. Norton & Co., 1968). All modern-spelling quotations are taken from *The Complete Works of Shakespeare*, ed. Stanley Wells and Gary Taylor with John Jowett and William Montgomery (Oxford: Clarendon Press, 1986); references are cited parenthetically in my text.

2. *The Taming of the Shrew*, ed. Brian Morris (London: Methuen, 1981), 4.3.91n.

3. *Ibid.*, 4.3.91n.

4. *The Taming of the Shrew*, ed. Ann Thompson (Cambridge: Cambridge Univ. Press, 1984), 4.3.91n.

be right, because it offers the wrong kind of noun. The sleeve is like a demi-
cannon, like a tart, like a specific object that is big, carved, and cut and
slashed; my reading would therefore disallow the meaning "cut and slashed
as if by scissors" to favour the meaning "like an object which has itself been
cut and slashed."[5]

I suggest that the original reading was *cittern* (or a spelling variant of
that noun). *Cittern* (a musical instrument with a grotesquely carved neck)
makes good sense in the context, is used elsewhere by Shakespeare and at least
ten of his contemporaries in similarly derogatory contexts, and can be amply
documented as a standard item in barbers' shops. I begin by considering the
cittern, its association with barbers' shops, and the metaphoric insults which
arise from the instrument's engraved neck: having established the appropri-
ateness of the cittern metaphor to Petruccio's sartorial criticism, I defend the
need for emendation by considering the nature and rate of compositor B's
typesetting errors in F *Shrew*.

I

The musical instrument familiar to us as the cittern is a member of the
lute family. This pear-shaped, shallow-bodied instrument enjoyed great favour during the sixteenth century, particularly among amateurs who "must
at all times have formed the majority of cittern players."[6] There are several
reasons for the instrument's popularity: the wire strings (plucked by a
plectrum) stayed in tune much longer than the cat-gut strings of the sibling
lute; the right-hand playing technique was easy to learn; and the instrument
was relatively inexpensive. Perhaps for these reasons, the cittern quickly
became a standard item in barbers' shops, where it was provided for the pre-
tonsorial enjoyment of waiting customers (a Renaissance equivalent of magazines or newspapers).

The presence of citterns in barbers' shops is widely referred to by Elizabethan and Jacobean dramatists, so much so that the association can be considered part of the stock dramatic parlance of the period. In Jonson's *The
Staple of News* Pennyboy Junior recounts how his "barber Tom, . . . one
Christmas, . . . got into a masque at Court, by his wit, / And the good means

5. While it is true that the singular noun "scissor" is recorded as an obsolete usage in
the *OED*, it is noteworthy that the noun appears in the plural in all barbers' references I
have come across. See, for instance, Randle Holme, *The Academy of Armoury* (Chester,
1688), III.iii.127: "a pair of Cisers" and "A Set of Cisers"; Stubbes, *Anatomie of Abuses*,
ed. F. J. Furnivall (London, 1877–82), II.i.50: "what snipping & snapping of the cysers is
there"; Ben Jonson, *Epicoene*, ed. R. V. Holdsworth (London: Ernest Benn Ltd., 1979)
3.5.79: "his scissors rust"; J. A. Comenius, *Orbis Pictus* (facsimile of first English edition of
1659, intro. John E. Sadler; London: Oxford Univ. Press, 1968), p. 263: "a *pair of Sizzars*";
John Ford, *The Fancies* in *Works*, ed. W. Gifford, rev. Alexander Dyce, vol. II (London,
1869), 5.2., p. 310): "scissors." The only Shakespearean usage occurs in the plural at *The
Comedy of Errors* 5.1.176: "His man with scissors nicks him like a fool."

6. John M. Ward, *Sprightly & Cheerful Musick. Notes on the Cittern, Gittern and
Guitar in 16th- & 17th-Century England, Lute Society Journal* 21 (1979–81): 40.

of his cittern, holding up thus / For one o' the music."[7] In Lyly's *Midas* (3.2.35) Motto, the barber, reminds his man that he has taught him several skills of the trade, including "the tuning of a cittern" ("tune" has the dual meaning "play" and "put in tune"; see *OED tune* 3a).[8] Oliver the weaver, in Middleton's *The Mayor of Queenborough*, tells how he helped a poor barber who, it seems, was forced to pawn his cittern: "I gave that barber a fustian-suit, and twice redeemed his cittern: he may remember me."[9] In Jonson's *Epicoene* Morose chooses his silent [*sic*] bride on the advice of Cutbeard the barber. When his bride proves talkative, Morose exclaims "That cursed barber! . . . I have married his cittern, that's common to all men."[10] The equation of silence with chastity and speech with promiscuity was a Renaissance commonplace; Morose's cittern analogy subtly links his wife's noise-making capacity with her presumed general availability. Dekker and Middleton similarly suggest sexual availability in *2 Honest Whore* when Matheo denounces Bellafront as a whore, "A Barbers Citterne for euery Seruingman to play vpon."[11]

The above references show that cittern playing in barbers' shops was a firmly entrenched custom.[12] But what relevance do citterns have in the context of Petruccio's criticism of sartorial slashing? It is here that the engravings on citterns are of relevance.

Besides being known for its presence in barbers' shops, the cittern was

7. Ben Jonson, *The Staple of News*, ed. Anthony Parr (Manchester: Manchester Univ. Press, 1988) 1.5.127–130.

8. John Lyly, *Gallathea* and *Midas*, ed. Anne B. Lancashire (Lincoln: Univ. of Nebraska Press, 1969) 3.2.35.

9. *The Mayor of Queenborough* in *The Works of Thomas Middleton*, ed. A. H. Bullen, vol. II (New York: AMS Press, 1964), 3.3.166–167.

10. *Epicoene*, ed. Holdsworth, 3.5.58, 60.

11. *2 Honest Whore* in *The Dramatic Works of Thomas Dekker*, ed. Fredson Bowers, vol. II (Cambridge: Cambridge Univ. Press, 1964), 5.2.151. The association of barbers' shops with music continued for many years. See *The Diary of Samuel Pepys*, ed. John Warrington (London: Dent, 1906; repr. 1966), vol. I, 5 June 1660, p. 70; *The Complete Works of Thomas Shadwell*, ed. Montague Summers, vol. I (1927; reissued New York: Benjamin Blom, 1968), 4.1, p. 71; Middleton, *More Dissemblers Besides Women* in *The Works*, vol. VI, 5.1.70–84; Ben Jonson, *Vision of Delight* line 93, in *Ben Jonson* vol. VII, ed. C. H. Herford and P. and E. Simpson (Oxford: Clarendon Press, 1941).

12. In a nice economy, the teeth extracted by the barber-surgeons were hung up for display on discarded cittern strings. See anon., *Wit's Triumvirate*, ed. Cathryn Anne Nelson (Salzburg: Institut für Englische Sprache und Literatur, 1975), 5.1.288–290; *The Knight of the Burning Pestle* 3.338; *The Woman Hater* in *The Dramatic Works in the Beaumont and Fletcher Canon*, gen. ed. Fredson Bowers, vol. I (Cambridge: Cambridge Univ. Press, 1966) 3.3.109–110; and *Epicoene* 3.5.87–88. This last reference is to a lute string. This may be a careless reference to a cittern; but lutes were apparently available for music making as well. See Margaret Pelling, "Occupational Diversity: Barbersurgeons and the Trades of Norwich, 1550–1640," *Bulletin of the History of Medicine*, 56 (1982): 484–511 (esp. p. 504), and cf. Roger Sharpe, *More Fooles Yet* (1610): "Here comes old *Spunge* the *Barbor* with his Lute" (sig. D2r). An engraving of the interior of a sixteenth-century Dutch barber's shop shows a recorder as well as a stringed instrument hanging on the wall (see Ward, Plate X, between pp. 40 and 41).

renowned for its exaggerated decorative carvings, usually of heads or gargoyle-like figures, situated on the instrument's neck at the top of the peg-box. It is these carvings which, I suggest, Petruccio has in mind when he condemns Katherine's dress for the elaborate slashing and pinking on the sleeves: "Here's snip and nip and cut and slish and slash, / Like to a [cittern] in a barber's shop."

The cittern differs from the lute in being a carved instrument made from one piece of wood—a skilled, but also a practical method of creation in days of unstable glue, damp interior storage conditions, and plentiful trees. (The less hardy lute is a constructed instrument.)[13] Although the precise development of the English cittern is unclear,[14] there is no doubt that, in terms of decoration, in England and on the continent, from medieval times onward, the instrument was characterised by "a crude figure-head on its narrow end."[15] So standard was it that books of cittern music included carvings of gargoyles, animals, and clowns in their illustrations of fretting: see the illustration, reproduced from Thomas Robinson, *New Citharen Lessons* (London, 1609), sigs H4v and I1r.

The earliest recorded dramatic reference to a cittern-head comes from Shakespeare. In *Love's Labour's Lost* Holofernes (as Judas Maccabaeus) is interrupted and taunted by the on-stage audience:

Holofernes	I will not be put out of countenance.
Biron	Because thou hast no face.
Holofernes	What is this?
Boyet	A cittern-head.
Dumaine	The head of a bodkin.
Biron	A death's face in a ring.
Longueville	The face of an old Roman coin, scarce seen. (5.2.602–608)

When Clara beats Bobadilla in Fletcher's *Love's Cure*, "Cittern-head" is included in her terms of abuse.[16] Ford twice uses cittern-head as an insult. In *The Fancies* Secco, the barber, is denounced as "a cittern-headed gewgaw,"[17] and when Cuculus in *The Lover's Melancholy* hopes to be a "head-piece" in

---

13. Robert Hadaway, "The Cittern," *Early Music* 1 (1973): 77–81. See also Francis W. Galpin, *Old English Instruments of Music* (London: Methuen, 1910, rev. and repr. 1965), pp. 15–27.

14. For a discussion of the development of the cittern, see "The Survival of the Kithara and the Evolution of the English Cittern: a Study in Morphology," in Emanuel Winternitz, *Musical Instruments and their Symbolism in Western Art* (London: Faber and Faber, 1967), pp. 57–65, and Ward, *passim*. The cittern's history is complicated by the existence of the semantically and musically similar gittern (which may or may not be the forerunner of the modern guitar; for differing views on this subject see David Munrow, *Instruments of the Middle Ages and Renaissance* [London: Oxford Univ. Press, 1976], p. 26 and Ward, *passim*).

15. Henry H. Carter, *A Dictionary of Middle English Musical Terms* (Bloomington: Indiana Univ. Press, 1961), p. 77.

16. *Love's Cure*, ed. George Walton Williams, in *The Dramatic Works in the Beaumont and Fletcher Canon*, gen. ed. Fredson Bowers, vol. III (Cambridge: Cambridge Univ. Press, 1976), 2.2.108.

17. *The Fancies*, in *The Works of John Ford*, ed. W. Gifford, rev. A. Dyce, vol. II (London, 1869), 1.2, p. 234.

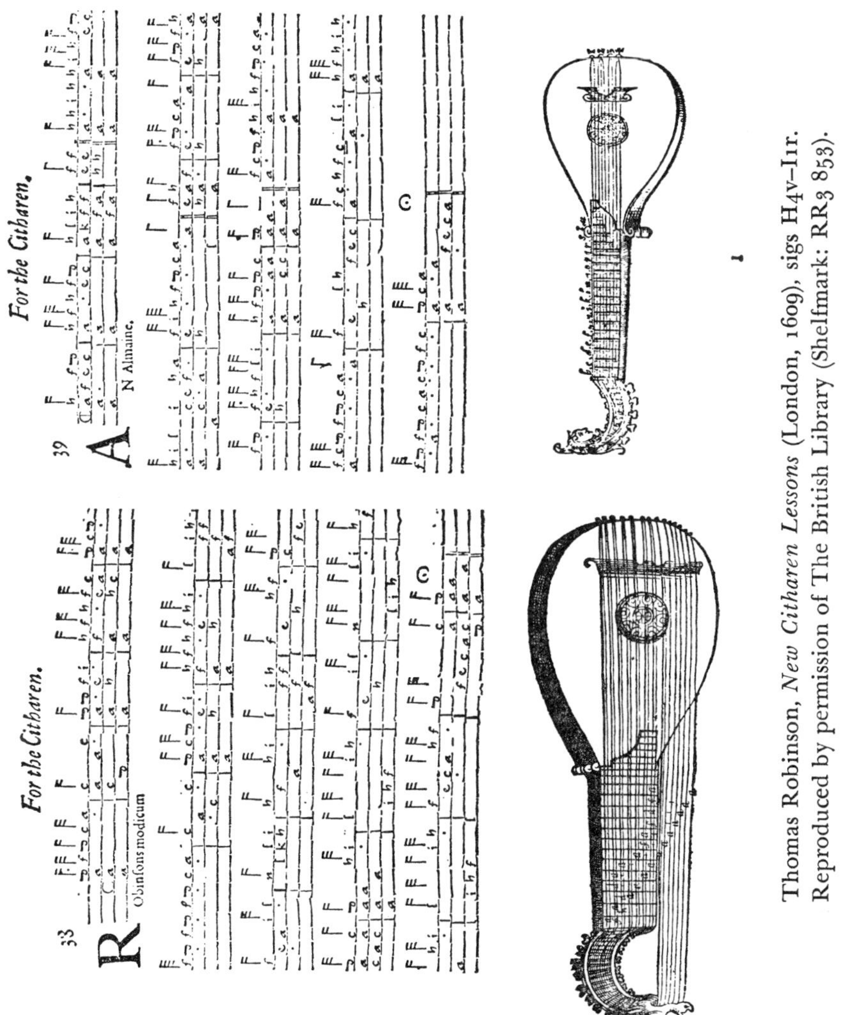

Thomas Robinson, *New Citharen Lessons* (London, 1609), sigs H4v–I1r. Reproduced by permission of The British Library (Shelfmark: RR3 853).

the Chronicles, Rhetias retorts that his head-piece shall be "Of woodcock without brains in't. Barbers shall wear thee on their citterns."[18] Marston talks of fools as "brainless cittern-heads" in *The Scourge of Villainy*,[19] while an extended discussion of citterns and their heads in Massinger's *The Old Law* concludes with a derogatory equation of cittern-heads with fools. Gnotho, having asked if the tavern boasts music, is answered in the affirmative: "here

18. John Ford, *The Lover's Melancholy*, ed. R. F. Hill (Manchester: Manchester Univ. Press, 1985), 2.1.36–39.

19. John Marston, *The Scourge of Villainy*, ed. A. H. Bullen, vol. III (London, 1887), p. 301.

are sweet wire-drawers in the house" (the reference to wires clearly identifies the instruments as citterns or gitterns). A conversation begins concerning the similarities between cittern playing and wine drawing (for example, both require pegs). But, says the butler, "the heads of your instruments differ; yours are hogs-heads, theirs cittern and gittern-heads." The bailiff concludes the discussion with "All wooden heads; there they meet again."[20] It is clear that English Renaissance dramatists did not intend comparison to a cittern or a cittern-head to be flattering. All the above references occur in sequences of abuse. Petruccio's sartorial railing is, I believe, part of the traditional derogatory association. And given other Renaissance dramatists' regular specification of the carved cittern head as the area of ridicule, Petruccio's insult is surely the comparison of the tailor's elaborate pinking with the cittern's grotesque wooden carvings.

II

F1 sig. T4v was set by compositor B. Knowledge of the First Folio's compositors and their characteristics has advanced considerably since Fredson Bowers, following Alice Walker's lead, wrote that "B was . . . slapdash, . . . prone to omit words, and also to alter his text both through memorial failure and his attempts to improve it."[21] Paul Werstine's two major studies[22] have shown that B's error-ridden work on *1 Henry 4* is untypical: in the six Folio plays which B set from largely uncorrected printed copy the errors are neither as many nor as serious as Walker's study, based only on B's performance in *1 Henry 4*, supposed.[23] In the 2360 lines which he set in the six plays studied by Werstine (*Ado, LLL, MND, MV, TA, R&J,*) B made 169 errors (this figure, and the following, are Werstine's). Of the forty-seven literal changes, thirteen are probably "legitimate corrections of error," thus reducing the total of literal changes to thirty-four (literal errors are, as Werstine explains, the least serious, because they are often easily corrected: for example, "nine of those listed result in obvious nonsense in the context"[24]). Of the fifty-nine substitutions, six have been generally accepted by editors and two are probably the result of censorship, thus reducing the total to fifty-one (of which eight are clearly nonsense). There are eleven omissions, ten interpolations, six transpositions, twenty semi-substantive changes, and twenty-three alterations in stage directions.

<hr>

20. *The Works of Massinger*, ed. W. Gifford, vol. IV (London, 1813; reprinted New York: AMS Press, 1966), 4.1., pp. 533–534. In *1 Henry 4* Hal relies on the association between tavern drawers and citterns when he boasts that, by fraternising with "loggerheads" and "hogsheads," he has "sounded the very bass-string of humility" (2.4.4–6).

21. Fredson Bowers, *On Editing Shakespeare* (Charlottesville: University Press of Virginia, 1966), p. 56.

22. Paul Werstine, "Compositor B of the Shakespeare First Folio," *AEB* 2 (1978): 241–63, and "Folio Editors, Folio Compositors, and the Folio Text of *King Lear*," in *The Division of the Kingdoms*, ed. Gary Taylor and Michael Warren (Oxford: Clarendon Press, 1983), pp. 247–312.

23. See especially Werstine, "Compositor B."

24. Werstine, "Compositor B," p. 246.

No comparable study can be made of B's levels of accuracy in *The Taming of the Shrew*, since, unlike the six plays studied by Werstine, the Folio provides our only text of *The Shrew*. Thus, only manifestly obvious errors can be detected, as when the Folio stage direction at S3v (TLN 348) introduces *"Hortensio sister to Bianca"* for *"Hortensio suitor to Bianca."* The error is probably the result of graphic confusion in Elizabethan secretary hand (*suter/sister*); compositors, like typists, tend to take in the overall shape of a word rather than sound out a letter-by-letter correlation. Nonetheless one must conclude that compositor B was not paying much attention to the sense of the line he was setting.

Compositor B set thirteen pages of the Folio *Shrew*—sigs S2v–S6v, T3r–T4v, and sig. V1r—a total of 1723 lines of type. Of these 1723 lines editors have introduced over fifty substantive emendations.[25] Ten of B's perceived errors are the result of simple misreading:[26] F "Brach" for "Breathe" (Ind. 1.15/TLN 20); F *"sister"* for *"suitor"* (1.1.123/TLN 348); F "Conlord" for "coloured" (1.1.207/TLN 513); F "Hath promist me to helpe one to another" for "Hath promised me to help me to another" (mee/one; 1.2.171/TLN 738); F *"Butonios"* for *"Antonio's"* (1.2.189/TLN 756); F "do this seeke" for "do this feat" (feete/seeke; 1.2.267/TLN 839); F "we may contriue" for "we may convive" (1.2.276/TLN 849; this suggestion by Theobald has not been adopted in any edition, even Theobald's: see *Textual Companion* 1.2.276/ 802/p. 171); F "flatter'd them" for "flattered her" (4.2.31/TLN 1879); F "Take me your loue" for "Take in your loue" (inne/mee; 4.2.72/TLN 1924). Theobald's emendation of F "goods" to "gauds" at 2.1.3/TLN 858, although attractive and often accepted by editors, is not necessary: it is rejected by the two recent Oxford editions with a convincing defence of F's reading by H. J. Oliver.[27] As mentioned above, all editors alter F "Censor" to "censer" (4.3.91/ TLN 2076), with the exception of the Oxford *Complete Works* which emends to "scissor."

One apparent error is plausibly explained by eyeskip: F *"Vincentio's* come" for *"Vincentio* come" (1.1.13/TLN 312) is probably the result of the compositor seeing *"Vincentio's* sonne" at the beginning of the next line.

Five probable and three possible errors are the result of omission (I bracket the omitted word or phrase): "with-holds from me. [and] Other more" (1.2.119/TLN 686); "I charge [thee] tel" (2.1.8/TLN 863); "I . . . giue

25. In calculating this total I exclude corrections to the Italian and Latin in the text, and modernisations (e.g. the Oxford *Complete Works*' "pip" for F "peepe" at 1.2.33/TLN 600). Where an emendation is universally rejected by editors, I identify the proposer and/or the sole edition in which the emendation appears; I omit this information when an emendation is generally accepted. Where an emendation seems gratuitous I indicate as much.

26. An obvious *caveat* is necessary: the alleged misreadings may be those of a scribe making a transcript, with B faithfully reproducing the errors in his MS copy. The nature of the underlying copy for F *The Shrew* is not clear, but "scribal copy, or some combination of scribal and autograph copy, cannot be ruled out" (Gary Taylor and Stanley Wells with William Montgomery and John Jowett, *William Shakespeare, A Textual Companion* [Oxford: Clarendon Press, 1987], p. 169).

27. *The Taming of the Shrew*, ed. H. J. Oliver (Oxford: Oxford Univ. Press, 1982); *The Taming of the Shrew* in *The Complete Works*, ed. Wells *et al.*

vnto [you] this yong Scholler" (2.1.76, 79/TLN 939, 942); "it is [a] paltrie cap" (4.3.81/TLN 2066); "'tis like [a] demi cannon" (4.3.88/TLN 2073). F2 regularised the metre at 1.2.251/TLN 823 by adding an auxiliary to the infinitive: "let me be so bold as [to] aske you," although this addition seems unnecessary (the short line is neither unusual nor ineffective). At 1.2.223/TLN 792 the Oxford *Complete Works* conjectures (but does not emend) "Even he *Biancas* father *Biondello*" for F "Euen he *Biondello*," arguing that "Mention of Bianca's name seems necessary to account for Gremio's 'her', and the compositor's eye could easily have skipped from *Bianca* to *Biondello*" (1.2.223/749/p. 171). At 1.1.209/TLN 517 the Oxford editors conjecture (but do not emend) that F "sith it" should be "sith yt it" (p. 171); Malone had earlier emended this metrically short line by postulating an omitted adjective: "In breefe [good] Sir, sith it your pleasure is."

Compositor B seems to insert an otiose word on one occasion (I bracket the insertion): "Were she [is] as rough" (1.2.72/TLN 639). On one occasion he presents "mistris" for "master" (1.2.18/TLN 585), presumably an incorrect expansion of the manuscript's "M.." Incorrect expansion also explains F "Lord" at Ind.2.2/TLN 154 where the metre requires "Lordship." B makes five errors in speech prefixes, possibly the result of authorial error or unclear revision in the MS copy: see *Gru.*[mio] for *Cur.*[tis] at 4.1.23/TLN 1664, *Gre.*[mio] for *Gru.*[mio] at 4.1.104/TLN 1744, *Luc.* for *Hor.* at 4.2.4/TLN 1850, *Hort.* for *Luc.* at 4.2.6/TLN 1853 and 4.2.8/TLN 1855, and *Par.* (for ?) at 4.2.72/TLN 1924.

Apparent errors in pronouns, verb mood and number, and adverb appear on ten occasions: F "could" for "would" (1.1.237/TLN 547); F "you" for "your" (1.1.242/TLN 552); F "at least" for "at last" (1.2.133/TLN 700; this emendation appears only in Hosley's edition[28]); F "my" for "his" (1.2.190/TLN 757; this emendation appears only in the Oxford *Complete Works*); F "yours" for "ours" (1.2.213/TLN 781); F "wooing neighbors" for "wooing. Neighbour" (2.1.75–76/TLN 938; F "me" for "none" (4.2.13/TLN 1861); F "brough" for "brought" (1.1.14/TLN 313); and F "them" for "her" (4.2.31/TLN 1879). F2 changed F1 "shakes" (2.1.141/TLN 1006) to "shake" to avoid false concord, although plural subjects with singular verbs are not uncommon in the Elizabethan period.

Several miscellaneous emendations are not strictly necessary. F2 "corrected" F1's "Christopher" to "Christophero" (Ind.2.72/TLN 225)—a metrical improvement if one elides "tinker" in the same line to "tink'r," but not essential. Editors sometimes expand F *"Alce"* to "Alice" (Ind.2.107/TLN 264), again an unnecessary expansion. Pope's "thirdborough" for F "Headborough" (Ind.1.10/TLN 13–14) seems unhappily literal; his "it is" for F's perceived transposition "is it" (Ind.2.26/TLN 179) is likewise unnecessary, as is F2's alteration of F1's perceived transposition "wilt thou" to "thou wilt" (4.1.37/TLN 1678). The Arden edition's "you mean not her too" for F "you meane not her to—" (1.2.224/TLN 793) is not a significant improvement: F's strained sense reads logically if one accepts the problem as being in the previ-

---

28. *The Taming of the Shrew*, ed. Richard Hosley (Harmondsworth: Pelican, 1964).

ous line, where Gary Taylor's suggested expansion ("Even he, Bianca's father, Biondello"; see above: 1.2.223) smoothes any apparent difficulty. More difficult to explain is F "Soud, soud, soud, soud" at 4.1.128/TLN 1769. Oliver conjectures that this sequence of nonce words is an indication of Petruccio's humming or singing.[29] Some editors (Dover Wilson,[30] Brian Morris) emend to "food" but acknowledge that a problem remains "as to what the compositor who misread 'food' in his copy thought he was setting up";[31] however, the compositor seems untroubled by the problem of "Censor" or of "*sister*" for "suitor." F "heere's none will holde you: Their loue is not so great" (1.1.106/ TLN 411–412) has occasioned a variety of emendations from the Q of 1631 ("there loue") and F3 ("Our loue") to Malone ("Your love")[32] and Sisson ("you there. Love"),[33] but the reading is satisfactory as it stands. Sisson emended F1 "rope trickes" to "rhetricks" (1.2.111/TLN 677–678), making Grumio's corruption of "rhetoric" more obvious, although F's malapropism seems clear as it is.

It is evident that there may be many more possible or actual errors in F *The Shrew* not detectable to us; and it is equally clear that several of the above "errors" are indicative more of editors' need for logic and metrical smoothness than of B's carelessness. What is of particular relevance to us is the sequence of error and difficulty on sig. T4v. Compositorial errors "tend to come in batches," notes Gary Taylor, citing the four errors in three lines of compositor A in F *Macbeth,* and the three errors in eight lines of compositor C in F *Love's Labour's Lost.*[34] The problematic reading "Censor" occurs in a passage where B's accuracy levels had dropped noticeably: he omitted indefinite articles before "demi cannon" 3 lines above (TLN 2073) and before "paltrie" 10 lines above (TLN 2066). Editors have good reason to suspect that "Censor," which has at best only strained relevance, is a mistake.

Censor is a plausible graphical confusion of *Cittern,* particularly if the latter were spelled *Cither.*[35] In *LLL,* the only other play in which the word appears in Shakespeare, the compositor of Q1 set "Cytterne" (sig. I2r), which may indicate the spelling he found in his manuscript copy. Like all Renaissance words, the spelling of Cittern was fluid; furthermore, almost any word ending in -er/ern was likely to be abbreviated (*Cith/Cytt*) with a superior anticlockwise loop for -er/ern. In setting F *The Shrew,* compositor B's hasty, tired, or careless eye would see a four-letter word commencing with *C.* He

29. *The Shrew,* ed. Oliver, p. 183.

30. *The Taming of the Shrew,* ed. John Dover Wilson (Cambridge: Cambridge Univ. Press, 1928; rev. 1953).

31. *The Shrew,* ed. Morris, p. 247.

32. *The Plays and Poems of William Shakespeare,* ed. Edmond Malone, 10 vols (London, 1790).

33. C. J. Sisson, *New Readings in Shakespeare,* vol. I (Cambridge: Cambridge Univ. Press, 1956).

34. Gary Taylor, "Textual and Sexual Criticism," *Renaissance Drama* 19 (1988): 195–225 (p. 217).

35. The modern instrument known as the zither derives from the cittern only in etymology, not morphology. Confusion arises because modern German has only the one word to designate two separate instruments.

may have taken the concluding abbreviation loop to be a tilde indicating omission of a medial *n*, with the descender of secretary *h* or *y* (or possibly a hastily executed *t*) being mistaken for a medial long *s*. Even without a letter-by-letter correlation it is clear that the overall shape of the word, which is what compositors take in, could result graphically in the misreading *Censor*. Whether B made sense of what he saw and subsequently set, or whether he paid no attention to sense whatsoever, as in the *sister/suitor* error, cannot be known. *Censor* is the reading enshrined in F, a word which, as editors have been at pains to point out, yields no graspable meaning at all.

*

W. W. Greg wrote that "To be critically acceptable an emendation must satisfy two criteria: it must afford an absolutely satisfactory text, and it must explain the corruption."[36] Misreading explains the corruption in *The Shrew*: Cittern/Censor is a likely graphic confusion; and, as we have seen from the many references linking citterns with barbers' shops, "Cittern" provides "an absolutely satisfactory text."[37]

36. W. W. Greg, "More Massinger Corrections," *Library* 4th ser. 5(1924): 59–91 (p. 91).

37. I am grateful to Thomas L. Berger, Lynn Hulse, Richard Proudfoot, and George Walton Williams for helpful comments on earlier versions of this essay.

PATTERNS OF PAPER USE IN THE
WORKES OF BENIAMIN JONSON (WILLIAM STANSBY, 1616)

by

David L. Gants

WHILE the numerous textual variants found in the Jonson Folio of 1616 have drawn a good deal of critical attention, the equally intriguing assortment of paper stocks used by William Stansby during the volume's printing has been largely ignored.[1] When the question of paper does arise, comment is usually restricted to the observation that the Folio exists on both "regular paper" and "large paper" stocks, although the basis for distinguishing between those forms is not always clear. The bookseller H. L. Ford is typical in differentiating them according to their current dimensions rather than original size or other characteristics. Ford suggested a more productive line of inquiry when he observed that "An examination of the sheets used in the copies under review discloses over forty differing water-marks, many of them appearing on identical leaves in each volume."[2] He went on, however, only to note that the paper is overwhelmingly watermarked with pots and that paper featuring a "bunch of grapes . . . is often found in the engraved title, but not in evidence in any other portion" (3).

The main challenge to booksellers like Ford and to scholars interested in paper has been a practical one: how to obtain precise images and measurements of watermarked paper easily, inexpensively, and in sufficient quantities so that they can be conveniently studied. The first of a series of important technical breakthroughs occurred in the late 1950s, when Soviet researchers began using beta radiography to obtain sharp images of the physical features of paper. A sheet of paper was placed between x-ray film and a beta source; the rays passed through in proportion to the thickness of the intervening paper, producing a negative image of the sheet when the film was developed. In the 1970s Robin Alston developed the "Ilkley Method," similar in basic procedures except that it substituted incandescent light and common photographic film for beta rays and x-ray film.[3] Also in the 1970s, Thomas Gravell

---

1. For a discussion of the Folio's textual variants, see in particular: *Ben Jonson*, ed. C. H. Herford, Percy Simpson, and Evelyn Simpson, 11 vols. (Oxford: Clarendon, 1925–52); Johan Gerritsen, Review of *Ben Jonson*, *English Studies* 38 (1957), 120–126; Gerritsen, "Stansby and Jonson Produce a Folio," *English Studies* 40 (1959), 52–55; James Riddell, "The Printing of the Plays in the Jonson Folio of 1616," *Studies in Bibliography* 49 (1996), 149–168.

2. Herbert L. Ford, *Collation of the Ben Jonson Folios 1616–31—1640* (Oxford: Oxford Univ. Press, 1932), 4.

3. For a survey of watermark reproduction procedures, see David Schoonover, "Techniques of Reproducing Watermarks: A Practical Introduction" in *Essays in Paper Analysis*, ed. Stephen Spector (Washington, D.C.: Folger Books, 1987), 154–167.

began experimenting with bibliographical applications of Dylux, a pH neutral, photosensitive paper developed by DuPont for proofing photographic negatives.[4] Like beta radiography and the Ilkley Method, a contact print is created by placing the Dylux beneath a sheet of paper; here, however, the energy source is fluorescent light, whose spectrum includes the visible but not the ultraviolet. Each method has its own peculiar advantages, although beta radiography and the Ilkley Method must be used under laboratory or darkroom conditions.

My own study of paper in Jonson's 1616 Folio has relied on beta radiography, because of the unparalleled clarity of images it produces, and Dylux, on account of its speed, convenience, and low cost. Through the offices of the Huntington Library, and from James Riddell's large private holdings, I acquired beta radiograph images of watermarks found in most of the paper groups used in the Folio.[5] For those watermarks not present in Huntington or Riddell copies, and for the numerous variant states that occurred in many of the paper groups, I used Dylux to capture examples from the holdings in the Folger Shakespeare Library, the Special Collections Department at the University of Virginia Library, and from my own copies. To exploit fully the information held in the Dylux images I needed to develop an image enhancement procedure that would highlight the watermarks, chain lines, and wire lines while minimizing the distraction caused by the ink of the text. This I accomplished using computer technology, converting the Dylux exposures to digital form and then manipulating them with inexpensive and readily available software.

Dylux has three technical features that make it extremely useful for such digital analysis: a sensitivity to small changes in the amount of light exposure, thereby giving it the ability to reveal not only watermarks but also chain and wire lines; a broad palette of color within the blue spectrum, allowing one to isolate a detail or group of details in part through color differentiation; and a chemical coating of fine grain which produces images that do not break down under repeated enlargement. These features make Dylux exposures particularly apt subjects for digital image enhancement. The software I employed can also reduce to manageable background haze the type clutter that frequently obscures a watermark. By applying various digital enhancement routines one can easily increase the clarity of a watermark image.

In the observations that follow, I suggest kinds of insights that can be gleaned from this scrutiny of paper. The study is based on a close examination

<hr>

4. See Thomas Gravell, *A Catalogue of American Watermarks, 1690–1835* (New York: Garland, 1979) and *A Catalogue of Foreign Watermarks Found on Paper Used in America, 1700–1835* (New York: Garland, 1983). See also *The Thomas L. Gravell Watermark Archive,* <http://ebbs.english.vt.edu/gravell/gravell.html>, and the *Archive of Papers and Watermarks in Greek Manuscripts,* <http://abacus.bates.edu/Faculty/wmarchive/>.

5. I must express my deep gratitude to Robert Schlosser of the Huntington Library's Photographic Services for his help, and in particular to James Riddell, who shared with me beta images he had made of pot watermarks. Dr. Riddell also showed uncommon generosity by allowing me to use data from his charts of paper distribution in his personal copies of the Jonson Folio.

of 60 copies of the Jonson Folio and is further informed by a survey of paper stocks used in the 74 titles known to have been printed by Stansby from 1615 through 1617. The evidence provides insights into overall patterns in manufacturing the Folio, and it also confirms and expands earlier insights about the production of several problematic sections of the book, including about possible authorial intervention while the volume was at press. While serving as a methodological study, then, it also provides a keener understanding of the forces acting upon the Jonsonian text, and it offers new insights into the workings of one of the busiest printing houses in early modern London.

I

Allan Stevenson has observed that, when planning the various components of a proposed book, the printer or publisher "generally arranged for paper sufficient for that book only and paper homogeneous in size and quality."[6] Economic circumstances fostered such practices, for "Paper was too expensive a commodity, too space consuming, to make any other system really practicable" (21–22). As a consequence of this practice, books from the common press period are often partially or completely printed on paper bearing a common watermark or watermark pair. One also frequently finds the other extreme, that is, a book with "a considerable diversity of papers, mixtures arising from certain practices of gathering and distribution within the paper trade" (21). These groups of papers usually consist of leftover sheets from another project that a printer "would save for later use, or else return to his publisher or patron or paper merchant"[7]—who would then, presumably, pass them on to another customer.

These phenomena are commonly referred to as "runs" and "remnants," and evidence of both occurs with regularity in Jonson's *Workes*. Six groups of paper stocks make up the main supply used in printing 225 of the 257 sheets in the Folio, each group contributing most or all of the paper for a significant portion of production. The book is a folio-in-sixes and collates ¶[6] A–4P[6] 4Q[4]; the runs of paper occur as follows:

Paper Stocks[8]	*Gatherings*
1	G–P
6 & 7 (combined)	3X–4I
6 & 15 (combined)	4K–4Q
10	3G–3N
12	A–E, R–2A, 2Z–3D, 3N–3T
10, 12, & 13 (combined)	2G–2X

6. Stevenson, *Observations on Paper as Evidence* (Lawrence: Univ. of Kansas Libraries, 1961), 20.

7. Stevenson, *The Problem of the Missale Speciale* (London: Bibliographical Society, 1967), 93.

8. I have adopted the numbering system used by James Riddell to identify paper stocks in the Folio, an arbitrary but useful model in which the groups are numbered roughly by the order in which they appear in the book. A breakdown of paper stock usage on a sheet-by-sheet basis is located at the end of this essay.

The distribution of like groups of paper into these recognizable and dominant patterns indicates that Stansby used large agglomerations of mostly homogenous paper stock in his printing work.

In addition, three other smaller groups dominate the production for short spans of time:

Paper Stocks	Gatherings
3	Q, 2C–2F
5	2B–2D, 3E–3F
11	F, 3P–3R

Stansby regularly used remnants he had stored or had acquired from others; they often fill small, temporary gaps or pad the dominant stocks to make them last longer. Occasionally these remnants will provide the major paper source for a short period, as in P3.4, Q1.6, R3.4, 2L, 2O–2P, 2V2.5, 2Y (reset), 3D3.4, 3E, 3F1.6, 3S, 3V, 3X3.4, and 4B.

When one of the groupings gives way to the next, the transitional sections show a blending of the outgoing and incoming stocks over one or more formes. The manner in which runs and remnants appear, disappear, and then reappear can reveal clues about the day-to-day activity in a printing house. For example, at certain points in the Folio's printing, Stansby's use of two distinct paper groups alternates back and forth with strict regularity, as in gatherings L–O, where Group 10 appears briefly in six of twelve sheets, then fades out again. The same phenomenon surfaces in gatherings 3P–3S between Groups 11 and 12, and in a more complicated dance among Groups 10, 12, and 13 in gatherings 2H–2M. These patterns may indicate that, at least for a short time, Stansby used two presses to print the *Workes*; as one press crew used up their supply of paper he allocated more paper from a new supply while the second crew continued working with the original allotment.[9] Stansby's business was quite active during this period, averaging at one point 840 edition sheets per year, and the printing house's busy production schedule must have at times required the shifting of different jobs between presses.

An examination of paper use over time can also shed light on the sometimes muddy relationship among the owners of various of Jonson's texts. Stansby had to negotiate with a number of booksellers in order to secure the rights to print Jonson's *Workes*. Walter Burre owned complete or partial rights to seven of the nine plays, John Smethwicke owned *Every Man out of His Humour*, Matthew Lownes owned *Poetaster*, and various parts of the poetry, entertainments and masques were owned by Stansby, Edward Blount, Richard Bonion, Thomas Thorpe and Henry Walley. In addition, Stansby sold part of the edition to Richard Meighen, a Stationer for whom he had done some work the previous year.[10] Given that the bargaining for rights may

9. In 1615 the Stationers' Company moved to limit the number of presses operated by each master printer, with fourteen stationers (including Stansby) allowed two presses apiece. This does not mean, of course, that those named owned only two devices. As D. F. McKenzie notes, "such a rule can only mean that many of [the printers] had retained . . . far *more* presses than the numbers set down" ("Printers of the Mind: Some Notes on Bibliographical Theories and Printing-House Practices," *Studies in Bibliography* 22 [1969], 55).

10. Mark Bland reckons that Meighen bought a 20% interest in the *Workes*, using as

also have included some solicitation of funding from the original copyright holders, and recognizing that paper constituted a significant expense in a book's production, it would not be surprising if Stansby arranged part or all of his paper supply individually with the different interested parties.[11] In fact, this is what we see in the printing of the plays. *Every Man Out*, owned by Smethwicke, is printed almost exclusively on Group 1 paper, with some remnants in the final quires. This selection of paper changes abruptly to Group 12 with the commencement of printing on *Cynthia's Revels*, owned by Burre. One gathering into *Poetaster*, owned by Lownes, the type of paper used switches again, this time to a mixture of Groups 3 and 5. Finally, with the printing of *Sejanus* and the remaining plays, all owned by Burre, the sheets are again from Group 12, a type that continues with only a few interruptions through *Volpone, Epicoene*, and parts of the *Alchemist* and *Catiline*. Interestingly, the remainder of the Folio (the poems, entertainments, and masques) shows a similar consistency of paper use, with the early sections of *Epigrams* printed on the leftover Burre stock, the section from the middle of *Epigrams* through *Hymenaei* printed primarily on Groups 6 and 7, and the *Haddington Masque* through the end on Groups 6 and 15. The homogeneity of paper use in the final 20 quires indicates that the various owners of the smaller works likely collaborated to purchase the necessary paper, or that by the time of printing the remaining gatherings Stansby had reached agreement with the rightsholders to purchase the titles outright.

II

Throughout most of the Folio, one group or set of groups will give way gradually to the next with evidence of mixing at the transition points. Occasionally the change among types of paper used will be abrupt, as is the case when production shifted from material owned by one investor to another. However, such a sudden change may also indicate a possible disruption or delay in printing. When these abrupt shifts correlate with similar evidence of interruption such as changes in headlines or typography, then we can begin to develop confidence in the probability of these suppositions. In particular, this type of evidence can shed further light on three problematic sections in the Folio: the order of the settings of gathering 2Y, the timing of the resetting and printing of the initial gatherings of *Every Man out of His Humour*, and the delay in printing the first play of the collection, *Every Man in His Humour*.

When Percy Simpson edited *Epicoene* for the Oxford *Ben Jonson*, he as-

---

his evidence a census of over 250 copies of the extant Folios that shows 20% of the main title pages bear Meighen's name. See *Jonson, Stansby and English Typography 1579–1623* (Diss. Oxford Univ., 1995), 217.

11. Peter Blayney has estimated that a play quarto during this period would have cost a printer just under £9, with the paper portion costing just over £2 7s., or approximately 30% of the total production expenses. See "The Publication of Playbooks," in *A New History of Early English Drama*, ed John D. Cox and David Scott Kastan (New York: Columbia Univ. Press, 1997), 396–410.

sumed that Jonson would have insisted his large presentation copies contain as few flaws as possible; consequently, Simpson adopted the dictum that the large paper copies always reflected the latest most-corrected state of a forme (5:148–149). Because gathering 2Y exists in two settings, one on regular paper and one on large paper, Simpson identified the large-paper setting as the later one. In his review of the Oxford edition in 1957, Johan Gerritsen used arguments based on evidence from recrurring headlines to reverse the order of settings (121). The paper evidence supports Gerritsen's version, for the sheets in the large paper copies all show a nearly unbroken string of marks from the Groups D1 and D2 running from gatherings 2S and 3F. On the other hand, the regular paper copies show a disruption in paper usage between gathering 2X and 2Z, with most of 2Y printed on stock not found in the current sequence. Gerritsen also posited that the printing of the second setting took place between gatherings 3E and 3F ("Stansby," 54). Again, the paper evidence bears out and expands somewhat Gerritsen's conclusions. Reset sheet 2Y3.4 bears mostly marks from Group 12, with a few from Group 8, placing it sometime during abrupt changes in paper stocks used for gathering 3C and sheet 3D1.6—the prior contains mostly Group 12, while the latter bears almost exclusively Group 8 watermarks. Reset 2Y1.6 shows mostly Group 8 with a few sheets from Group 13, a mixture that appears elsewhere only at 3D3.4. Finally, reset 2Y2.5 exhibits paper from Groups 5 and 10, with a few rare appearances from groups 12 and 19. This closely matches the mixture of paper groups used in sheets 3E3.4 and 3F1.6. It appears, then, that the printing of reset 2Y was concurrent with the printing of gatherings 3C–3F, and that the reset gathering was printed inner sheet first, followed by the outer and then the middle:

Sheet:	3C3.4	2Y3.4	3D1.6	3D2.5	3D3.4	2Y1.6	3E1.6	3E2.5	3E3.4	2Y2.5	3F1.6
Paper Group											
5	X			X	X			X	X	X	X
8		X	X		X	X	X	X			
10										X	X
12	X	X		X	X					X	X
13					X	X					

While the completion of reset gathering 2Y apparently took place fairly quickly, the resetting and printing of the initial pages of *Every Man Out* seems to have been a much more complicated affair. Kevin Donovan's work on headlines indicates that Stansby printed reset sheets G1.6 and G2.5 first after finishing *Every Man Out* gathering P, and printed reset G3.4, H, and I3.4 at a later time.[12] Riddell subsequently examined the paper use patterns based on a smaller sample of Folios and found that his evidence supported Donovan's conclusions regarding sheets G1.6 and G2.5 ("Printing," 156). Because the stocks upon which the reset G3.4, H, and I3.4 were printed were either too common (Group 11) or unique in the Folio (Group 37), he could not identify

---

12. Donovan, *Studies in the Text of Ben Jonson's Folio* (Diss. Univ. of Wisconsin, 1987; Ann Arbor: UMI, 1987), 120–128.

when those remaining five sheets were printed. Nor does headline evidence reveal anything about these sheets, for their resetting and printing did not occur while the Folio was at press but rather were put off until later. In this case an examination of the paper stocks used in volumes printed immediately after the completion of the Folio is most helpful..

The clearest evidence for dating is found in gathering H; as Ridell noted, the watermarks on these sheets appear nowhere else in the Folio. This paper Group 37 surfaces in a number of other works printed by Stansby with imprint dates of 1617, constituting the first two quires of Joseph Hall's *A Recollection of such Treatises* (STC 12707), the first half of Richard Hooker's *Lawes of Ecclesiastical Politie* (STC 13716), and the middle section of Samuel Purchas's immensely popular *Purchas his Pilgrimage* (third edition; STC 20507). In each of these works, as in the Folio's gathering H, the paper group appears as a distinct, intact run rather than as remnants spread out over a long period. If this paper group came into Stansby's shop as a well-defined bale, as seems to have been the usual practice during production of the Folio, then we can surmise that Stansby paused in the middle of the massive Purchas folio to print the reset sheet from *Every Man Out*, then began the Hooker and Hall volumes.

Sheets G3.4 and I3.4 are more problematic as they are both printed on paper from Group 11, a fairly common type of paper in the Folio. Looking only at paper used in the Folio, Riddell surmised that G3.4 "was set at about the same time that the last two plays, *The Alchemist* and *Catiline*, were going through the press." He also supposed that the other four reset sheets "were run off more or less together, probably at the same time as G3.4" ("Printing," 156). However, an examination of the paper used in other titles Stansby printed during and immediately after the Folio was at press helps us align the reset sheets within the larger production schedule. Headline evidence shows that these Folio sheets were probably printed together but not imposed in a skeleton forme used to print the rest of Jonson's *Workes*; the paper use sequence shows this same Group 11 was the dominant stock used to print the first part of the Purchas volume. In addition, in 1617 Stansby printed the first two-thirds of *Davids Learning* (STC 23827), a commentary by Thomas Taylor on Psalm 32, on Group 11 stock, while the remaining third plus preliminaries are on Group 37. Judging from the sequence of paper use in these works, Stansby printed sheets G and I3.4 first, followed by gathering H, and did so while he also was printing the Taylor and Purchas volumes, and just before he began those of Hooker and Hall.

In the two cases just discussed, evidence drawn from the use of distinct stocks of paper further illuminates earlier insights into how the resetting of pages was handled in Stansby's printing house. However, the case of *Every Man In* involved not a resetting but rather a delay in printing. Headline evidence indicates that printing of the play took place in two phases, with its first gathering A printed between the middle of *Epicoene* (2X5-3D6), and the remaining gatherings B–F between *Catiline* (3L4-3S4) and *Epigrams* (3S5–3Z1). The outer and middle sheets of gathering A consist of paper from Group 12, while the inner sheet is a mix of Groups 5 and 12, distribution that matches paper used during gatherings 2Z through 3C of *Epicoene*, as expected. Riddell's examination of paper use supports the headline evidence here as well.

The remainder of *Every Man In* was printed on a mixture of paper groups, in particular a number of rare types, allowing us to expand upon the outline derived from the headlines. When setting and imposing this play, Stansby's men employed the rules from the skeleton formes used in the printing of *Catiline* to print the final five gatherings B–F, allowing us to place the production of this section after the completion of gathering 3R. However, a closer analysis of the complicated distribution of paper in these gatherings reveals that printing may not have advanced in a straightforward fashion, with B–E printed concurrently with the *Epigrams* and F not printed until early in the *Masques* (4F3 ff.).

The dominance of Group 12 paper in most of gatherings C, D, and sheet E3.4 correlates with paper distribution in 3R, and supports the supposition that they were printed at the end of *Catiline*. Sheet C1.6, however, contains sheets from Groups 16, 25, and 33 in a mixture that does not come into the Folio until 3V3.4, well into the printing of the *Epigrams*. Likewise, sheet B1.6 shows the presence of Group 25, placing it at the same time as 3V3.4. Next, sheets B3.4, B2.5, and E2.5 have a mixture of Groups 6, 7, 11, and 12 that place them at the same spot in the production sequence as sheet 3X3.4, also in the *Epigrams*. Closing out this middle section of *Every Man In*, sheet E1.6 has a number of marks from Group 15, a lot of paper that does not come into use until 3Z, late in the *Epigrams*. The last gathering in this play, F, comprises paper from Groups 6, 7, and 11 in a ratio that matches the paper use only in 4I, the end of *Hymenaei* (4G6–4I5).

For most of the Folio, paper and headline evidence indicates that printing proceeded in a relatively orderly fashion, with gatherings usually printed in the order they were to be bound. With the printing of *Every Man In*, however, paper use patterns point to a rather more jumbled sequence. Stansby began by printing gathering A concurrently with *Epicoene*. He then seems to have printed concurrently with the *Epigrams* all of D, the inner and middle sheets of C, and the inner sheet of E. He then printed the outer sheets of B and C, followed by the remainder of B along with E2.5, and completed this section with E1.6. He then put off the final gathering until he was well into printing the *Masques*. That Stansby chose to print these sheets out of sequence indicates that something may have occurred to force him into this more complicated procedure.

Critics have for more than 100 years discussed the dating of the revisions Jonson made to *Every Man In*, citing internal and external evidence to support proposed dates ranging from 1604 to 1613.[13] James Riddell has argued that Stansby was forced to put off the printing of *Every Man In* until late in the Folio because Jonson had not yet completed his final alterations.[14] While not conclusive, the sequence of printing that I have constructed from the

<hr>

13. See *Every Man in His Humour*, ed. Gabriele Bernhard Jackson (New Haven: Yale Univ. Press, 1969), 221–239.

14. Riddell, "Jonson and Stansby and the Revisions of Every Man in His Humour," *Medieval & Renaissance Drama in England* 9 (1997), 81–91.

paper evidence supports Riddell's dating of the revision concurrently at least in part with the Folio's production. The breaking up of the play's printing into three separate pieces, one in the middle of *Epicoene*, one during the early gathering of the poems, and one in the middle of the masques, as well as the general postponement of the play's printing despite its initial place in the Folio, indicates that Stansby may not have had the completed manuscript when work began. Furthermore, the jumbled order in which gatherings B–E went through the press signifies that Jonson may have been sending pieces of the manuscript to Stansby when he completed the revision, irrespective of overall order. With completion of the Folio looming, one can easily imagine Jonson scrambling to finish the promised revisions before Stansby sent the manuscript to the compositors. There is also contemporary evidence that Stansby sent pages to his authors for correction, so the idea that Jonson both corrected and revised during the printing of his *Workes* is not unreasonable.[15]

Overall, the picture that emerges from the preceding observations shows a printing house bustling with activity, and Stansby himself appears as a master at organizing work. The methods and procedures behind these observations also demonstrate the potential of blending traditional bibliographical scholarship with the tools of digital technology and point to new ways that scholars may build upon the work of their predecessors.

III

The following chart illustrates the distribution of paper stocks throughout the Jonson Folio based on an examination of sixty copies.[16] I have listed individually the fourteen most prevalent stocks of regular paper (1, 3–13, 15–16, and 33) along with the six most prevalent stocks of large paper (M1–4 and D1–2). When a sheet contains reset text, and when a gathering contains two distinct settings, the number of sheets bearing the first setting will be followed (in parentheses) by the number of resettings. Those stocks that occur rarely or sporadically I have combined under the headings "Misc. Regular" and "Misc. Large." The total occurrences are displayed in columns labeled by gathering and sheet (outer, middle, inner). Finally, I have indicated at the top of the chart where a new title commences (including the page in parentheses), and hence where ownership may change.

15. As noted above, Stansby printed the third edition of *Purchas His Pilgrimage* soon after the completion of Jonson's *Workes*. The final leaf of that volume contains an apology from the author in which Purchas comments "There hath been scarsly any sheet (if any) which I haue not perused and corrected my selfe" (5D4ᵛ).

16. For a complete bibliographical description of the paper stocks used in the Jonson Folio, see David Gants, *A Descriptive Bibliography of the "Workes of Beniamin Jonson" London: William Stansby, 1616* (Diss. Univ. of Virginia, 1997; Ann Arbor: UMI, 1997), 198–287.

| Text: | Prelims | | | Every Man In (A1r) | | | | | | | | | | | |
| Gathering: | ¶ | | | A | | | B | | | C | | | D | | |
Sheet:	o	m	i	o	m	i	o	m	i	o	m	i	o	m	i
Paper Group															
1	—	—	—	—	—	—	—	—	—	—	—	—	—	—	—
3	—	—	—	—	—	—	—	—	—	—	—	—	—	—	—
4	—	—	—	—	—	—	—	—	—	—	—	—	—	—	—
5	—	—	—	—	3	31	—	—	—	1	—	—	—	—	—
6	—	—	—	—	—	—	—	15	12	1	—	—	—	—	—
7	—	—	—	—	—	—	—	23	7	1	—	—	—	—	—
8	—	—	—	—	—	—	—	—	—	1	—	—	—	—	—
10	—	—	—	—	—	—	—	—	—	—	—	—	—	—	—
11	—	—	—	—	—	—	1	15	32	—	—	—	—	1	1
12	—	—	—	53	51	23	51	—	2	38	53	53	53	52	52
13	—	—	—	—	—	—	—	—	—	—	—	—	—	—	—
15	—	—	—	—	—	—	—	—	—	—	—	—	—	—	—
16	—	—	—	—	—	—	—	—	—	1	—	—	—	—	—
33	—	—	—	—	—	—	—	—	—	3	—	—	—	—	—
Misc. Regular	36	49	50	—	—	—	1	—	—	9	—	—	—	—	—
M1	1	2	3	1	—	—	4	1	3	2	3	3	3	2	5
M2	—	3	1	—	—	—	1	3	2	4	3	3	3	4	1
M3	—	—	—	1	3	—	—	1	—	—	—	—	—	—	—
M4	—	—	—	1	—	—	—	—	—	—	—	—	—	—	—
D1	—	—	—	—	—	2	—	—	—	—	—	—	—	—	—
D2	—	—	—	1	2	2	—	—	—	—	—	—	—	—	—
Misc. Large	—	—	—	—	—	1	—	—	—	—	—	—	—	—	—

Text:	Every Man In (cont.)						Every Man Out ($G_1{}^r$)								
Gathering:	E			F			G			H			I		
Sheet:	o	m	i	o	m	i	o	m	i	o	m	i	o	m	i
Paper Group															
1	—	—	—	—	—	—	4^2	39(12)	39	33	4^2	4^2	5^2	5^2	4^2
3	—	—	—	—	—	—	(12)	—	—	—	1	—	—	1	—
4	—	2	—	—	—	—	—	—	—	8	—	—	1	—	—
5	—	—	1	—	2	—	—	—	—	—	—	—	—	—	—
6	23	8	—	8	11	6	—	—	—	—	—	—	—	—	—
7	3	6	—	7	12	12	—	—	—	—	—	—	—	—	—
8	—	—	—	—	—	—	—	—	—	—	—	—	—	—	—
10	—	—	—	—	—	—	—	1	—	—	—	—	—	—	—
11	8	30	1	38	27	34	—	—	(13)	—	—	—	—	—	(11)
12	—	50	7	3	1	—	—	—	—	—	—	—	—	—	—
13	—	—	—	—	—	—	—	—	—	—	—	—	—	—	—
15	14	—	—	—	—	—	—	—	—	—	—	—	—	—	—
16	—	—	—	—	—	—	—	—	—	—	—	—	—	—	—
33	1	—	—	—	—	—	—	—	—	—	—	—	—	—	—
Misc. Regular	1	—	—	—	—	—	—	—	—	12(1)	(11)	(11)	—	—	—
M1	—	4	4	5	2	3	—	—	—	—	—	—	—	—	—
M2	4	2	2	1	3	3	—	—	—	—	—	—	—	—	—
M3	—	—	—	—	—	—	(2)	(4)	3	4	3	5	4	4	4
M4	1	—	—	—	—	—	(4)	(2)	3	2	3	1	2	2	2
D1	—	—	—	—	—	—	—	—	—	—	—	—	—	—	—
D2	—	—	—	—	—	—	—	—	—	—	—	—	—	—	—
Misc. Large	1	—	—	—	1	—	—	—	—	—	—	—	—	—	—

Text: *Every Man Out* (cont.)

Gathering:	K			L			M			N			O		
Sheet:	o	m	i	o	m	i	o	m	i	o	m	i	o	m	i
Paper Group															
1	53	52	38	36	53	18	53	40	52	41	2	53	16	4	42
3	—	—	—	—	—	—	—	—	—	—	—	—	3	—	—
4	—	1	14	—	—	—	—	—	—	—	—	—	33	—	11
5	—	—	—	—	—	—	—	1	1	—	—	—	—	15	—
6	—	—	—	—	—	—	—	—	—	—	—	—	—	—	—
7	—	—	—	—	—	—	—	—	—	—	—	—	—	—	—
8	—	—	—	—	—	—	—	—	—	—	—	—	—	—	—
10	—	—	—	17	—	35	—	12	—	12	50	—	—	34	—
11	—	—	1	—	—	—	—	—	—	—	—	—	—	—	—
12	—	—	—	—	—	—	—	—	—	—	—	—	—	—	—
13	—	—	—	—	—	—	—	—	—	—	—	—	—	—	—
15	—	—	—	—	—	—	—	—	—	—	—	—	—	—	—
16	—	—	—	—	—	—	—	—	—	—	—	—	—	—	—
33	—	—	—	—	—	—	—	—	—	—	—	—	—	—	—
Misc. Regular	—	—	—	—	—	—	—	—	—	—	—	—	1	—	—
M1	—	—	—	—	—	—	—	—	—	—	—	—	—	—	—
M2	—	—	—	—	—	—	—	—	—	—	—	—	—	—	—
M3	4	3	4	4	5	2	4	5	4	3	2	3	3	4	3
M4	2	3	2	2	1	4	2	1	2	3	2	3	3	2	3
D1	—	—	—	—	—	—	—	—	—	—	—	—	—	—	—
D2	—	—	—	—	—	—	—	—	—	—	—	—	—	—	—
Misc. Large	—	—	—	—	—	—	—	—	—	—	—	—	—	—	—

Text: *Cynthia's Revels* (P5r)

	P			Q			R			S			T		
Gathering: / Sheet: / Paper Group	o	m	i	o	m	i	o	m	i	o	m	i	o	m	i
1	1	37	45	—	1	—	—	2	—	—	—	—	—	—	—
3	50	—	1	1	51	42	4	—	2	1	2	—	—	—	—
4	2	14	1	—	—	—	—	—	—	—	—	—	—	—	—
5	—	—	—	—	—	—	—	—	1	—	—	—	—	—	—
6	—	—	—	—	—	—	—	—	—	—	—	—	—	—	—
7	—	—	—	—	—	—	—	—	—	—	—	—	—	—	—
8	—	—	—	—	—	—	—	—	—	1	—	20	—	10	—
10	—	1	5	—	—	—	—	—	—	—	—	—	—	—	—
11	—	—	—	—	—	—	—	—	—	—	—	—	—	—	—
12	—	—	1	—	—	—	47	50	—	51	51	33	54	43	53
13	—	—	—	—	—	—	—	—	—	—	—	—	—	—	—
15	—	—	—	—	—	—	—	—	—	—	—	—	—	—	—
16	—	—	—	—	—	—	—	—	—	—	—	—	—	—	—
33	—	—	—	—	—	—	—	—	—	—	—	—	—	—	—
Misc. Regular	—	1	—	52	1	11	2	2	50	—	—	—	—	—	—
M1	—	—	—	—	—	—	—	—	—	—	—	—	—	—	—
M2	—	—	—	—	—	—	—	—	—	—	—	—	—	—	—
M3	3	2	2	3	4	4	—	—	4	—	—	—	3	—	—
M4	3	4	4	3	2	2	—	—	2	—	—	—	3	—	—
D1	—	—	—	—	—	—	—	—	—	—	—	—	—	—	—
D2	—	—	—	—	—	—	—	—	—	—	—	—	—	—	—
Misc. Large	—	—	—	—	—	—	6	6	—	5	6	6	—	6	6

Text:	Cynthia's Revels (cont.)												Poetaster Z4r)		
Gathering:	V			X			Y			Z			2A		
Sheet:	o	m	i	o	m	i	o	m	i	o	m	i	o	m	i
Paper Group															
1	—	—	—	—	—	1	2	—	—	—	—	—	—	—	—
3	—	—	1	—	—	—	—	—	—	—	1	5	—	—	—
4	—	—	—	—	—	—	—	—	—	—	—	—	—	—	—
5	—	—	—	—	—	—	—	—	—	—	—	—	—	—	—
6	—	—	—	—	—	—	—	—	—	—	—	—	—	—	—
7	—	—	—	—	—	—	—	—	—	—	—	—	—	—	—
8	—	—	—	—	—	—	—	—	1	—	—	—	—	—	—
10	—	—	—	—	—	—	—	—	—	—	—	—	—	—	—
11	—	—	—	—	—	—	—	—	—	—	—	—	—	—	—
12	54	53	52	53	38	39	50	53	53	53	52	49	53	53	53
13	—	—	—	—	1	—	—	—	—	—	—	—	—	—	—
15	—	—	—	—	—	—	—	—	—	—	—	—	—	—	—
16	—	—	—	—	—	—	—	—	—	—	—	—	—	—	—
33	—	—	—	—	—	—	—	—	—	—	—	—	—	—	—
Misc. Regular	—	—	—	—	13	12	1	—	—	—	—	—	—	—	—
M1	—	—	—	—	—	—	—	—	—	—	—	—	—	—	—
M2	—	—	—	—	—	—	—	—	—	—	—	—	—	—	—
M3	—	4	3	—	3	—	—	1	—	—	—	—	—	—	—
M4	—	2	3	—	3	—	—	—	—	—	—	—	—	—	—
D1	3	—	—	—	—	—	4	3	1	4	3	3	5	3	2
D2	3	—	—	—	—	—	4	3	2	4	3	3	1	3	4
Misc. Large	—	—	—	6	—	—	—	—	2	—	—	—	—	—	—

Text:	Poetaster (cont.)														
Gathering:	2B			2C			2D			2E			2F		
Sheet:	o	m	i	o	m	i	o	m	i	o	m	i	o	m	i
Paper Group															
1	—	—	1	—	1	1	1	1	1	1	—	—	1	—	—
3	—	20	—	—	1	31	20	14	3	35	36	53	24	47	38
4	—	—	—	—	—	—	—	—	—	—	—	—	—	—	—
5	34	13	51	48	48	18	32	37	48	15	17	—	1	4	13
6	—	—	—	—	—	—	—	—	—	—	—	—	—	—	—
7	—	—	—	—	—	—	—	—	—	—	—	—	—	—	—
8	—	—	—	—	—	1	—	—	—	—	—	—	—	—	—
10	18	18	—	—	1	1	—	—	—	—	—	—	26	2	—
11	—	—	—	—	—	—	—	—	—	—	—	—	—	—	—
12	—	2	1	5	2	—	—	1	—	—	—	—	—	—	—
13	—	—	—	—	—	—	—	—	—	—	—	—	—	—	—
15	—	—	—	—	—	—	—	—	—	—	—	—	—	—	—
16	—	—	—	—	—	—	—	—	—	—	—	—	—	—	—
33	—	—	—	—	—	—	—	—	—	—	—	—	—	—	—
Misc. Regular	—	—	—	—	—	—	—	—	1	2	—	—	1	—	1
M1	—	—	—	—	—	—	—	—	—	—	—	—	2	—	—
M2	—	—	—	—	—	—	—	—	—	—	—	—	—	—	—
M3	2	3	3	4	3	2	—	3	2	—	—	—	2	3	1
M4	4	3	3	2	3	4	—	3	4	1	—	—	—	3	2
D1	—	—	—	—	—	—	3	—	—	3	2	6	—	—	3
D2	—	—	—	—	—	—	3	—	—	2	4	—	2	—	—
Misc. Large	—	—	—	—	—	—	—	—	—	—	—	—	2	—	—

Text: *Sejanus* (2G4ʳ)

Paper Group	2G — o	2G — m	2G — i	2H — o	2H — m	2H — i	2I — o	2I — m	2I — i	2K — o	2K — m	2K — i	2L — o	2L — m	2L — i
1	—	—	—	—	—	—	—	—	—	—	—	—	—	—	—
3	—	—	—	—	—	1	1	—	—	—	4	3	—	5	2
4	—	—	—	—	—	—	—	—	—	—	—	—	—	—	—
5	1	—	—	1	—	—	—	—	—	1	4	—	—	—	—
6	—	—	—	—	—	—	—	—	—	—	—	—	—	—	—
7	—	—	—	—	—	—	—	—	—	—	—	—	—	—	—
8	—	—	—	—	—	—	—	1	—	—	—	—	—	—	—
10	—	—	—	10	52	—	47	—	49	—	—	—	—	33	—
11	—	—	—	—	—	15	—	—	1	—	—	—	—	—	—
12	49	51	52	31	—	17	—	31	—	11	22	49	48	2	29
13	—	—	—	10	—	18	—	19	—	40	19	—	—	—	—
15	—	—	—	—	—	—	—	—	—	—	—	—	—	—	—
16	—	—	—	—	—	—	—	—	—	—	—	—	—	—	—
33	—	—	—	—	—	—	—	—	—	—	—	—	—	—	—
Misc. Regular	2	1	—	—	—	1	5	—	2	—	2	—	4	12	20
M1	—	—	—	—	—	—	—	—	—	—	—	—	—	—	—
M2	—	—	—	—	—	—	—	—	—	—	—	—	—	—	—
M3	—	—	—	—	—	—	—	—	—	—	—	—	—	—	—
M4	—	—	—	—	—	—	—	—	—	—	—	—	—	—	—
D1	2	3	2	3	4	2	3	5	3	4	2	4	2	3	4
D2	4	4	4	3	2	4	3	1	3	2	4	2	4	3	2
Misc. Large	—	—	—	—	—	—	—	—	—	—	—	—	—	—	—

Text:	*Sejanus* (cont.)									*Volpone* (204r)					
Gathering:	2M			2N			2O			2P			2Q		
Sheet:	o	m	i	o	m	i	o	m	i	o	m	i	o	m	i
Paper Group															
1	—	—	—	—	—	—	—	—	—	12	—	—	—	—	—
3	1	3	—	19	—	12	16	—	—	—	—	1	—	—	—
4	—	—	—	—	—	—	—	—	—	—	—	—	—	—	—
5	3	—	1	22	—	—	17	—	—	—	—	—	—	—	—
6	—	—	—	—	—	—	—	—	—	—	—	—	—	—	—
7	—	—	—	—	—	—	—	—	—	—	—	—	—	—	—
8	—	—	—	—	—	—	—	—	—	—	—	—	—	—	—
10	46	—	48	9	1	37	16	—	1	1	—	1	3	1	1
11	—	—	—	—	—	—	—	—	—	—	—	—	—	—	—
12	—	49	—	—	52	3	5	22	20	4	36	31	46	53	32
13	—	—	—	1	—	1	—	32	22	19	18	21	3	—	21
15	—	—	—	—	—	—	—	—	—	—	—	—	—	—	—
16	—	—	—	—	—	—	—	—	—	—	—	—	—	—	—
33	—	—	—	—	—	—	—	—	—	—	—	—	—	—	—
Misc. Regular	4	—	3	2	—	—	—	—	11	17	—	—	1	—	—
M1	—	—	—	—	—	—	—	—	—	—	—	—	—	—	—
M2	—	—	—	—	—	—	—	—	—	—	—	—	—	—	—
M3	—	—	—	—	—	—	—	—	—	—	—	—	—	—	—
M4	—	—	—	—	—	—	—	—	—	—	—	—	—	—	—
D1	2	2	5	3	4	2	3	4	3	—	2	2	—	—	—
D2	4	4	1	3	2	3	3	2	3	—	2	4	—	—	—
Misc. Large	—	—	—	—	—	—	—	—	—	6	2	—	6	6	6

Text:	Volpone (cont.)												Epicoene (2X5[r])		
Gathering:	2R			2S			2T			2V			2X		
Sheet:	o	m	i	o	m	i	o	m	i	o	m	i	o	m	i
Paper Group															
1	—	—	—	—	—	—	1	—	—	3	—	—	—	—	—
3	—	—	13	—	14	—	—	—	—	—	2	—	1	13	—
4	—	—	—	—	—	—	—	—	—	—	—	—	—	—	—
5	—	—	—	—	—	—	1	5	3	—	3	—	—	—	—
6	—	—	—	—	—	—	—	—	—	—	—	—	—	—	—
7	—	—	—	—	—	—	—	—	—	—	—	—	—	—	—
8	—	—	—	—	—	—	—	—	—	—	—	—	—	—	—
10	52	1	24	51	38	50	1	22	48	—	1	14	18	39	50
11	—	—	—	—	—	—	—	—	—	—	—	—	—	—	—
12	—	24	16	1	1	3	34	31	—	36	34	36	32	1	2
13	2	28	—	1	—	—	16	—	—	1	2	—	—	—	—
15	—	—	—	—	—	—	—	—	—	—	—	—	—	—	—
16	—	—	—	—	—	—	—	—	—	—	1	—	—	—	—
33	—	—	—	—	—	—	—	—	—	—	—	—	—	—	—
Misc. Regular	—	—	—	—	—	—	—	—	—	10	13	—	—	2	1
M1	—	—	—	—	—	—	—	—	—	—	—	—	—	—	—
M2	—	—	—	—	—	—	—	—	—	—	—	—	—	—	—
M3	—	—	—	—	—	—	—	—	—	—	—	—	—	—	—
M4	—	—	—	—	—	—	—	—	—	—	—	—	—	—	—
D1	5	—	—	2	4	—	3	4	2	2	2	4	2	2	2
D2	1	—	—	4	1	—	3	2	4	4	4	2	4	4	4
Misc. Large	—	6	6	—	1	6	—	—	—	—	—	—	—	—	—

Text: Epicoene (cont.)

Gathering:	2Y			2Z			3A			3B			3C		
Sheet:	o	m	i	o	m	i	o	m	i	o	m	i	o	m	i
Paper Group															
1	—	—	—	—	1	—	—	—	—	—	—	—	—	—	—
3	—	—	—	—	—	3	—	—	—	—	—	—	—	—	—
4	—	—	—	—	—	—	—	—	—	—	—	—	—	—	—
5	—	(33)	—	—	29	19	14	—	—	17	—	20	—	25	7
6	(1)	—	—	—	—	—	—	—	—	—	—	—	—	—	—
7	—	—	—	—	—	—	—	—	—	—	—	—	—	—	—
8	(46)	—	(6)	—	—	—	—	—	—	—	—	—	—	—	—
10	—	(16)	—	—	—	1	—	—	—	—	—	—	—	—	—
11	—	—	—	—	—	—	—	—	—	—	—	—	—	—	—
12	—	(2)	(47)	53	23	30	35	53	53	29	54	33	54	28	47
13	(7)	—	—	—	—	—	—	—	—	17	—	—	—	1	—
15	—	—	—	—	—	—	—	—	—	—	—	—	—	—	—
16	—	—	—	—	—	—	—	—	—	—	—	—	—	—	—
33	—	—	—	—	—	—	—	—	—	—	—	—	—	—	—
Misc. Regular	—	(2)	—	—	—	—	2	—	—	—	1	—	—	—	—
M1	—	—	—	—	—	—	—	—	—	—	—	—	—	—	—
M2	—	—	—	—	—	—	—	—	—	—	—	—	—	—	—
M3	—	—	—	—	—	—	—	—	—	1	—	—	—	—	—
M4	—	—	—	—	—	—	—	—	—	—	—	—	—	—	—
D1	1	4	2	3	5	—	5	4	3	4	2	4	4	4	4
D2	4	2	4	3	1	6	1	2	3	1	4	2	2	2	2
Misc. Large	—	—	—	—	—	—	—	—	—	—	—	—	—	—	—

Text: *Epicoene* (cont.) = Gathering 3D; *Alchemist* (3E1r) = Gatherings 3E, 3F, 3G, 3H.

Paper Group	3D o	3D m	3D i	3E o	3E m	3E i	3F o	3F m	3F i	3G o	3G m	3G i	3H o	3H m	3H i
1	—	—	—	—	—	—	—	—	—	—	—	—	1	—	—
3	—	—	—	—	—	—	—	—	—	—	—	—	—	—	—
4	—	—	—	—	—	—	2	—	—	—	—	—	—	—	—
5	—	9	14	1	37	46	10	52	52	—	—	—	1	2	2
6	1	—	—	1	—	1	—	—	—	—	—	—	—	—	—
7	—	—	—	—	—	—	—	—	—	—	—	—	—	—	—
8	52	—	16	10	14	2	—	—	—	—	—	—	—	—	—
10	—	—	1	1	1	1	4	—	—	50	37	52	45	27	50
11	—	—	—	—	—	1	—	—	—	—	12	—	—	23	—
12	—	46	8	3	—	—	17	—	—	1	—	—	—	—	—
13	—	—	16	—	1	—	—	—	—	1	—	—	—	—	—
15	—	—	—	—	—	—	—	—	—	—	—	—	—	—	—
16	1	—	—	—	—	—	—	—	—	—	—	—	—	—	—
33	—	—	—	—	—	—	—	—	—	—	—	—	—	—	—
Misc. Regular	—	—	—	37	—	2	19	—	—	—	3	—	5	—	—
M1	—	—	—	—	—	—	—	—	—	—	—	—	—	—	—
M2	—	—	—	—	—	—	—	—	—	—	—	—	—	—	—
M3	—	—	—	—	—	—	—	—	—	1	6	3	—	4	4
M4	—	—	—	—	—	—	—	—	—	3	—	3	—	2	2
D1	1	4	4	3	2	2	4	5	3	1	—	—	3	—	—
D2	—	2	2	3	1	4	2	1	3	1	—	—	—	—	—
Misc. Large	5	—	—	—	3	—	—	—	—	—	—	—	3	—	—

Text:	Alchemist (cont.)									Catiline (3L4r)					
Gathering:	3I			3K			3L			3M			3N		
Sheet:	o	m	i	o	m	i	o	m	i	o	m	i	o	m	i
Paper Group															
1	—	—	—	—	—	—	—	—	—	—	—	—	—	—	—
3	—	—	—	—	—	—	—	—	—	—	—	—	—	—	—
4	—	—	—	—	—	—	—	—	—	—	—	—	—	—	—
5	1	1	1	1	1	—	1	1	—	1	1	1	—	—	1
6	—	—	—	—	—	—	—	—	—	—	—	—	—	—	—
7	—	—	—	—	—	—	—	—	—	—	—	—	—	—	—
8	—	—	—	—	—	—	—	—	—	—	—	—	—	—	—
10	50	47	28	51	19	24	52	30	35	53	51	53	—	12	52
11	1	3	14	—	32	27	1	20	13	—	1	—	—	1	—
12	—	—	6	—	—	—	—	—	—	—	—	—	53	41	—
13	—	—	—	—	—	—	—	—	—	—	—	—	—	—	—
15	—	—	—	—	—	—	—	—	—	—	—	—	—	—	—
16	—	—	—	—	—	—	—	—	—	—	—	—	—	—	—
33	—	—	—	—	—	—	—	—	—	—	—	—	—	—	—
Misc. Regular	—	1	2	—	—	1	—	1	5	—	—	—	1	—	—
M1	—	—	—	—	—	—	—	—	—	—	—	—	—	—	—
M2	—	—	—	—	—	—	—	—	—	—	—	—	—	—	—
M3	3	—	—	4	4	1	3	1	1	3	4	5	—	2	3
M4	—	—	—	2	2	5	2	4	3	3	2	1	—	4	3
D1	3	6	3	—	—	—	—	—	—	—	—	—	2	—	—
D2	—	1	3	—	—	—	—	—	—	—	—	—	4	—	—
Misc. Large	—	—	—	—	—	—	—	—	1	—	—	—	—	—	—

Text:	Catiline (cont.)												Epigrams (3S5r)		
Gathering:	3O			3P			3Q			3R			3S		
Sheet:	o	m	i	o	m	i	o	m	i	o	m	i	o	m	i
Paper Group															
1	—	—	—	—	—	—	—	1	—	—	—	—	—	—	—
3	—	—	—	—	—	—	—	—	—	—	—	—	—	—	—
4	—	—	—	—	—	—	—	—	—	—	—	—	—	—	—
5	—	—	—	—	—	—	—	—	—	—	—	—	—	—	—
6	—	—	—	—	—	—	—	—	—	—	—	—	—	—	2
7	—	—	—	—	—	—	—	—	—	—	—	—	—	—	—
8	—	—	—	—	—	—	—	—	—	—	—	—	—	—	1
10	—	—	—	—	—	—	—	1	1	—	—	—	—	1	—
11	—	—	—	5[2]	5[1]	—	1	5[2]	5[2]	4	—	53	—	—	1
12	54	54	54	1	2	53	53	—	—	49	53	—	53	3[2]	2[5]
13	—	—	—	—	—	—	—	—	—	—	—	—	—	—	1[7]
15	—	—	—	—	—	—	—	—	—	—	—	—	—	—	—
16	—	—	—	—	—	—	—	—	—	—	—	—	1	16	6
33	—	—	—	—	—	—	—	—	—	—	—	—	—	5	2
Misc. Regular	—	—	—	—	—	—	—	—	1	—	—	—	—	—	—
M1	—	—	—	—	—	—	—	—	—	—	—	—	3	3	3
M2	—	—	—	—	—	—	—	—	—	—	—	—	3	3	3
M3	—	3	3	—	—	—	—	—	2	—	—	—	—	—	—
M4	—	3	3	—	—	—	—	—	2	—	—	—	—	—	—
D1	5	—	—	3	2	2	5	4	—	5	2	3	—	—	—
D2	1	—	—	3	4	4	1	2	—	1	4	3	—	—	—
Misc. Large	—	—	—	—	—	—	—	—	2	—	—	—	—	—	—

Text:	Epigrams (cont.)												Forrest (3Z2r)		
Gathering:	3T			3V			3X			3Y			3Z		
Sheet:	o	m	i	o	m	i	o	m	i	o	m	i	o	m	i
Paper Group															
1	—	—	—	—	—	—	—	—	—	—	—	—	—	—	1
3	—	—	—	—	—	—	—	—	—	—	—	—	—	—	—
4	—	—	—	—	—	—	—	—	12	—	—	—	—	—	—
5	—	—	—	—	—	—	—	—	—	—	—	—	—	—	—
6	—	—	—	—	2	1	26	20	4	10	20	25	28	34	20
7	—	—	—	—	1	1	26	32	3	17	32	26	19	11	30
8	—	1	1	2	—	—	—	—	2	—	—	—	—	—	—
10	—	—	—	—	—	—	—	—	—	—	—	—	—	—	—
11	—	—	—	—	—	1	—	—	4	—	—	—	—	—	—
12	48	36	35	8	31	13	—	—	1	—	—	—	—	—	—
13	—	—	—	—	—	—	—	—	—	—	—	—	—	—	—
15	—	—	—	—	—	—	—	—	—	—	—	—	5	7	—
16	2	9	9	28	10	16	—	—	20	—	—	1	—	—	1
33	—	6	7	14	6	10	—	—	5	—	—	—	—	—	—
Misc. Regular	2	—	—	—	2	10	—	—	1	25	—	—	—	—	—
M1	1	2	4	3	5	3	4	2	2	3	6	4	3	4	2
M2	5	4	2	3	1	3	2	4	4	3	—	2	3	2	4
M3	—	—	—	—	—	—	—	—	—	—	—	—	—	—	—
M4	—	—	—	—	—	—	—	—	—	—	—	—	—	—	—
D1	—	—	—	—	—	—	—	—	—	—	—	—	—	—	—
D2	—	—	—	—	—	—	—	—	—	—	—	—	—	—	—
Misc. Large	—	—	—	—	—	—	—	—	—	—	—	—	—	—	—

Text:	*Forrest* (cont.)			*Entertainments* (4B1r)											
Gathering:	4A			4B			4C			4D			4E		
Sheet:	o	m	i	o	m	i	o	m	i	o	m	i	o	m	i
Paper Group															
1	—	—	—	—	—	—	—	—	—	—	—	—	—	—	—
3	—	—	—	—	—	—	—	—	—	—	—	—	—	—	—
4	—	—	—	—	—	—	—	—	—	—	—	—	—	—	—
5	—	—	—	—	—	—	—	—	—	—	—	—	—	—	—
6	—	—	30	2	16	27	20	22	26	25	25	21	23	23	28
7	—	1	21	1	23	25	15	30	17	25	18	21	29	29	24
8	1	—	—	2	—	—	—	—	—	—	—	—	—	—	—
10	—	—	—	—	—	—	—	—	—	—	—	—	—	—	—
11	—	—	—	—	—	—	—	—	—	—	—	—	—	—	—
12	38	51	—	31	2	—	17	—	—	—	—	—	—	—	—
13	—	—	—	—	—	—	—	—	—	—	—	—	—	—	—
15	—	—	—	—	—	—	—	—	9	1	8	8	—	—	—
16	9	—	1	8	7	—	—	—	—	1	—	—	—	—	—
33	4	—	—	8	3	—	—	—	—	—	—	—	—	—	—
Misc. Regular	—	—	—	—	1	—	—	—	—	—	1	1	—	—	—
M1	3	4	4	1	3	4	5	2	4	6	5	3	3	5	3
M2	3	2	3	5	3	2	1	4	2	—	1	3	3	1	3
M3	—	—	—	—	—	—	—	—	—	—	—	—	—	—	—
M4	—	—	—	—	—	—	—	—	—	—	—	—	—	—	—
D1	—	—	—	—	—	—	—	—	—	—	—	—	—	—	—
D2	—	—	—	—	—	—	—	—	—	—	—	—	—	—	—
Misc. Large	—	—	—	—	—	—	—	—	—	—	—	—	—	—	—

Text:	Masques ($4F3^r$)														
Gathering:	4F			4G			4H			4I			4K		
Sheet:	o	m	i	o	m	i	o	m	i	o	m	i	o	m	i
Paper Group															
1	—	—	—	—	—	—	—	—	—	—	—	—	—	—	—
3	—	—	—	—	—	—	—	—	—	—	—	—	—	—	—
4	—	—	—	—	—	—	—	—	—	—	—	—	—	—	—
5	—	—	—	—	—	—	—	—	—	—	—	—	—	—	—
6	23	26	22	32	23	26	25	26	24	16	17	—	22	27	—
7	23	26	29	12	28	26	27	26	28	17	33	—	—	—	—
8	—	—	—	—	—	—	—	—	—	—	—	—	—	—	—
10	—	—	—	—	—	—	—	—	—	—	—	—	—	—	—
11	—	—	—	—	—	—	—	—	—	17	—	51	2	—	—
12	—	—	—	—	—	—	—	—	—	—	—	—	—	—	—
13	—	—	—	—	—	—	—	—	—	—	—	—	—	—	—
15	6	—	—	7	—	—	—	—	—	—	—	—	26	25	52
16	—	—	—	—	—	—	—	—	—	—	—	—	—	—	—
33	—	—	—	—	—	—	—	—	—	—	—	—	—	—	—
Misc. Regular	—	—	1	—	—	—	—	—	—	—	1	—	—	—	—
M1	3	3	—	2	5	3	4	3	5	6	5	4	4	5	2
M2	3	3	6	4	1	3	2	3	1	1	2	3	2	1	4
M3	—	—	—	—	—	—	—	—	—	—	—	—	—	—	—
M4	—	—	—	—	—	—	—	—	—	—	—	—	—	—	—
D1	—	—	—	—	—	—	—	—	—	—	—	—	—	—	—
D2	—	—	—	—	—	—	—	—	—	—	—	—	—	—	—
Misc. Large	—	—	—	—	—	—	—	—	—	—	—	—	—	—	—

Text:	Masques (cont.)														
Gathering:	4L			4M			4N			4O			4P		
Sheet:	o	m	i	o	m	i	o	m	i	o	m	i	o	m	i
Paper Group															
1	—	—	—	—	—	—	—	—	—	—	—	—	—	—	—
3	—	—	—	—	—	—	—	—	—	—	—	—	—	—	—
4	—	—	—	—	—	—	—	—	—	—	—	—	—	—	—
5	—	—	—	—	—	—	—	—	—	—	—	—	—	—	—
6	24	27	—	15	10	19	26	28	27	28	29	25	18	32	24
7	—	—	—	—	—	—	—	—	—	—	—	—	—	—	—
8	—	—	—	—	—	—	—	—	—	—	—	—	—	—	—
10	—	—	—	—	—	—	—	—	—	—	—	—	—	—	—
11	—	2	52	26	24	22	1	—	—	—	—	1	4	—	—
12	—	—	—	—	—	—	—	—	—	—	—	—	—	—	—
13	—	—	—	—	—	—	—	—	—	—	—	—	—	—	—
15	28	23	—	10	16	11	19	23	23	24	23	26	30	20	27
16	—	—	—	—	—	—	—	—	—	—	—	—	—	—	—
33	—	—	—	—	—	—	—	—	—	—	—	—	—	—	—
Misc. Regular	—	—	—	—	1	—	6	—	—	—	—	—	—	—	—
M1	3	2	2	3	3	6	1	4	2	5	6	4	3	3	3
M2	3	3	4	3	3	—	5	2	4	1	—	2	3	3	3
M3	—	—	—	—	—	—	—	—	—	—	—	—	—	—	—
M4	—	—	—	—	—	—	—	—	—	—	—	—	—	—	—
D1	—	—	—	—	—	—	—	—	—	—	—	—	—	—	—
D2	—	—	—	—	—	—	—	—	—	—	—	—	—	—	—
Misc. Large	—	—	—	—	—	—	—	—	—	—	—	—	—	—	—

Text:	4Q	
Gathering:	*Masques* (cont.)	
Sheet:	o	i
Paper Group		
1	—	—
3	—	—
4	—	—
5	—	—
6	23	24
7	—	—
8	—	—
10	—	—
11	—	—
12	—	—
13	—	—
15	20	25
16	—	—
33	—	—
Misc. Regular	1	1
M1	3	3
M2	2	3
M3	—	—
M4	—	—
D1	—	—
D2	—	—
Misc. Large	—	—

JONSON, *BIATHANATOS* AND THE INTERPRETATION OF MANUSCRIPT EVIDENCE

by

Mark Bland

It has increasingly been recognised that the forms of literary evidence are more complex than previous textual theories emphasised. Indeed, it is now a commonplace to suggest that the processes of production and reception involve forms of collaboration that are also part of the meaning of the book as a historical document.[1] It is, perhaps, less widely appreciated that every discussion of a literary work (even the most theoretical) is based on inferences about the physical history of the documents that are a testament to its existence. The point is crucial. Almost everything we claim to know about the biographies of Jonson and Donne, for instance, derives from early manuscript or printed evidence. If we make an error in the dating, or in the attribution, of this material, then the narratives we construct, from the context of the meaning of the documents to the social and intellectual history of the people involved, will be mistaken in their assumptions. Despite an impression that has sometimes been given to the contrary, then, the study of the associations and contexts involved in the production, transmission and reception of texts has not obviated the need for analytical bibliography; rather, it has modified the range of physical reference that may be drawn upon from manuscript and print, for a more complex appreciation of the history of the book requires that we now investigate traditional sources of physical information from a fresh perspective, and examine again the assumptions upon which our narratives are based. As Ernest Sullivan observes: 'Textual scholars need to ponder why as well as how a text and its versions were created'.[2]

Donne and Jonson have often been discussed as rival poets working through different social networks and media of publication, but such a view has ignored both their deep and enduring friendship and the manuscript evidence where their work is often found in the same volumes.[3] Though in some ways convenient, the wish to place them in antithesis with one another is not entirely appropriate, for the differences between manuscript and print

---

1. The standard points of departure are: D. F. McKenzie, *Bibliography and the Sociology of Texts* (London, 1986); J. J. McGann, *A Critique of Modern Textual Criticism* (Chicago, 1983). For problems associated with manuscripts, see: W. S. Hill, 'Editing Nondramatic Texts of the English Renaissance: A Field Guide with Illustrations', *New Ways of Looking at Old Texts: Papers of the Renaissance English Text Society, 1985–1991*, ed. W. S. Hill (Binghamton, 1993), 1–24.

2. E. W. Sullivan II, 'The Renaissance Verse Miscellany: Private Party, Private Text', *New Ways of Looking at Old Texts*, 297.

3. The most important exception is: H. Kelliher, 'Donne, Jonson, Richard Andrews and The Newcastle Manuscript', *English Manuscript Studies 1100–1700*, 4 (1993), 134–173,

are not necessarily as obvious as superficially we might suppose: the distinction being primarily technical and only incidentally sociological or intellectual. All documents are a record of something more than the text, something antecedent and only imperfectly recoverable: they are a witness to the circumstances of, and the use of the intellect in, the history of their creation.[4]

We need, therefore, to understand the bibliographical and textual history of Donne's and Jonson's manuscripts and printed books as involving more than an analysis of a collection of words, or items connected by the elegant and simplifying lines of textual stemmata. Donne and Jonson are linked by more than a few poems that could have been written by either of them.[5] They are linked not only by their association with certain printers, publishers and scribal copyists, but by their shared interest in the dissemination of their work. For Jonson, in particular, the association between manuscript and print, and the way in which they influence one another, was an issue that he repeatedly explored. Yet Jonson has been treated as an author who circulated material primarily through print.[6] Consequently, the concentration on Jonson and the printed book-trade, reinforced by the authority of (and assumptions informing) the Herford and Simpson edition,[7] has meant that Jonson's surviving manuscript material has not been interrogated for the physical, social and intellectual histories to which it bears witness.

Perhaps we know less about Jonson than we have assumed, mistaking the evidence that survives from the past for the larger history to which it belongs, and discounting other information that might be more significant than we supposed. In the first decade of the seventeenth century, we find Jonson writing three epigrams to, or about, Donne, Donne writing a Latin poem on *Volpone*, Jonson's gift of Nicholas Hill's *Philosophia Epicurea, Democratiana, Theophrastica* (Paris, 1601) to Donne, Francis Davison acquiring Donne's poems from Jonson, Donne's close friend George Gerrard sending his 'man' to Jonson for an epitaph on Cecilia Bulstrode, and the gift to Jonson by Edward Herbert of the 1598 edition of Tertullian's *Opera*.[8] Two other

---

4. See, S. A. Morison, *Politics and Script: Aspects of Authority and Freedom in the Development of Graeco-Latin Script from the Sixth Century B.C. to the Twentieth Century A.D.*, ed. N. J. Barker (Oxford, 1972), 1.

5. See, E. M. Simpson, 'Jonson and Donne: A Problem in Authorship', *Review of English Studies*, 15 (1939), 274–282; D. Heyward Brock, 'Jonson and Donne: Structural Fingerprinting and the Attribution of Elegies XXXVIII–XLI', *Papers of the Bibliographical Society of America*, 72 (1978), 519–527.

6. For instance, R. C. Newton, 'Jonson and the (Re-)Invention of the Book', *Classic and Cavalier*, ed. C. J. Summers and T–L. Pebworth (Pittsburgh, 1984), 30–65; M. de Grazia, *Shakespeare Verbatim* (Oxford, 1991), 22–37; A. F. Marotti, *Manuscript, Print and the English Renaissance Lyric* (Ithaca, 1995), 238–247.

7. C. Herford, P. Simpson & E. Simpson, *Ben Jonson*, 11 vols. (Oxford, 1925–52); hereafter H&S. Herford wrote Jonson's biography and the literary assessment, Evelyn Simpson collated the late plays (Volume VI) and assisted with Volumes VII and VIII, and Percy Simpson edited the remainder of the material (including the 'Conversations with Drummond') and wrote the commentary and stage history. For an account of the more familiar problems associated with the Herford and Simpson edition, see C. I. E. Donaldson, 'A New Edition of Ben Jonson?', *Ben Jonson Journal*, 2 (1995), 223–231.

8. B. Jonson, *Workes*, STC 14751–2 (1616), *Epigrams XXIII, XCIIII, XCVI*; B. Jonson,

close friends of Donne's can also be connected to Jonson. Thus, Jonson (together with George Chapman and William Browne) was one of the contributors of preliminary verse to Christopher Brooke's *The Ghost of Richard the Third,* and late in his life Rowland Woodward gave Jonson a copy of *De Agerribus et Pontibus Hactenus ad Mare Extructis Digestum Nouum* (Paris, 1629) by Petrus Bertius.[9] Jonson and Donne are linked not only through their own testimony, their patrons, the book-trade and scribal copying, but also through mutual friends, and it is not surprising that at some point they worked together on a manuscript. The document in question is the Bodleian Manuscript of *Biathanatos,* given by Donne to Edward Herbert, and prepared initially by Jonson. What follows is the evidence for this statement and an explanation as to how Percy and Evelyn Simpson made an error of judgment that has misled scholars (not least Greg) for much of this century.

I

There is an important group of autograph Jonson manuscripts that were all written in 1609 and which are connected to one another through the physical evidence of handwriting and paper.[10] These are *The Masque of Queenes,* the epitaph on Cecilia Bulstrode, the epigram to Sir Horace Vere, and the *Herbert* Manuscript of *Biathanatos.* Another manuscript, a letter to Sir Robert Cotton, will also be discussed in connection with this material, as the letter was redated by Simpson without comment. The manuscript of *Biathanatos* (hereafter *Herbert*) was not included by Simpson in the record of Jonson's manuscript activities, though it was discussed by Evelyn Simpson in her study of *The Prose Works of John Donne.* The reasons for questioning the Simpsons' treatment of this manuscript material will be developed in the following pages. Before Jonson's manuscript activities in 1609 are discussed, however, it will also be necessary to make some preliminary comments about the corroborative information offered by handwriting and the stocks of paper that Jonson was using at the time the manuscripts were written.

Volpone, STC 14783 (1607), A1r [*Workes* (1616), ¶6r]; Hill's *Philosophia Epicurea* is in the library of the Middle Temple, London; for Davison, British Library Harleian MS 298, item 60; for Gerrard, Houghton Library Lowell MS. 1455; the Tertullian is in the library at Charlecote House, Warwickshire, shelfmark L6–22. I would like to thank Jim Riddell and Henry Woudhuysen for this last reference, and the National Trust for permission to mention the volume. Jonson also wrote an epigram to Herbert.

9. C. Brooke, *The Ghost of Richard the Third,* STC 3830-0.3 (1614), A4v; the Bertius is British Library, shelfmark 568.b.22, with Jonson's note 'Ex dono Amicissim. Row: Woodward'. Not listed in D. McPherson, 'Ben Jonson's Library and Marginalia', *Studies in Philology,* 71 (1974), suppl., 1–106. Recorded by T. A. Birrell, *The Library of John Morris* (London, 1976), item 170. There are more than ninety surviving books from Jonson's library not recorded by McPherson.

10. The exception is the newly identified manuscript of *Britains Burse, or The Key Keeper* (Public Record Office PR 14/144, ff. 144–147), which is partly written in Jonson's hand (ff. 144r–145r, 146r lines 1–10) and partly by two other amanuenses. It was written on two sheets of pot. These hastily written sheets were not, however, meant for public circulation and it may be that Jonson distinguished between good paper for formal use and cheaper paper for his own purposes.

Handwriting and paper are two quite independent and impartial witnesses to the history of the preparation of a document, for neither is dependent on the other. While one might legitimately hesitate about the variations in the hand of an author, or about the dates between which paper with a certain watermark was used, in combination the evidence of handwriting and paper is stronger than either alone in establishing the origins of a document. When two independent manuscripts yield exactly the same result from both variables, the evidence of their common origin is strongly persuasive. In fact, it was according to these criteria that the holograph manuscript of Donne's Verse Letter to Lady Carew was dated. The poem shared the same watermark as a letter by Donne, probably to Sir Robert More, written on 7 February 1612 from Amiens.[11] Evidence such as this would obviously be further reinforced if further manuscripts could be shown to share the common elements (handwriting and paper) and particularly if a longer text than a single sheet could be shown to share the same idiosyncratic use of paper—for instance, that it had been gathered in folio and cropped, rather than folded in quarto. Such distinctions are the bibliographic equivalent of a fingerprint.

It is precisely the combination of handwriting, paper, and the idiosyncratic choice of format that links the Jonson manuscripts. In 1609, Jonson acquired a stock of Italian paper. It was most probably manufactured in Venice and is of a very fine quality.[12] The watermark consists of a double pennant flag wth the initials 'G₃'. Paper of this kind, with dozens of variant but broadly similar watermarks, can be traced over a period of about fifty years. As with all watermarks, however, the evidence from a specific mould can be dated more accurately because the weight of the pulp eventually led to distortions in, and the replacement of, both the wire used for the watermark and eventually the mould within a period of six to twelve months.[13] As Stevenson observed, 'the reams made in one week were seldom precisely the same in their markings as those made in another week'.[14]

Compared to paper from northern France, Italian paper was relatively

11. Bodleian Library MS. Eng. Poet d. 197 and Folger Shakespeare Library, MS. L.b.535. See also, H. Gardner, *John Donne's holograph of 'A Letter to the Lady Carey and Mrs Essex Riche'* (London, 1972); N. J. Barker, 'Donne's "Letter to the Lady Carey and Mrs. Essex Riche": Text and Facsimile', *The Book Collector*, 22 (1973), 487–493; P. J. Croft, *Autograph Poetry in the English Language*, 2 vols. (London, 1973), I, 24–27. L. Yeandle, 'Watermarks as Evidence for Dating and Authenticity in John Donne and Benjamin Franklin', from *The First International Conference on the History, Function & Study of Watermarks* (1996), publication forthcoming.

12. E. A. Heawood, 'Paper Used in England After 1600', *The Library*, IV, 11 (1931), 274.

13. A. H. Stevenson, 'Paper as Bibliographical Evidence', *The Library*, V, 17 (1962), 197–212. See also, J. Bidwell, 'The Study of Paper as Evidence, Artefact, and Commodity', *The Book Encompassed: Studies in Twentieth-Century Bibliography*, ed. P. Davison (Cambridge, 1992), 69–82; P. Gaskell, *A New Introduction to Bibliography* (Oxford, 1972), 57–77 (especially 60–66); G. Pollard, 'Notes on the Size of the Sheet', *The Library*, IV, 22 (1941), 105–137; A. H. Stevenson, *The Problem of the Missale Speciale* (London, 1967), 26–99; A. H. Stevenson (ed.), *Briquet's Opuscula: The Complete Works of Dr. C. M. Briquet without Les Filigranes* (Hilversum, 1955), xxxiv–xliii; G. T. Tanselle, 'The Bibliographical Description of Paper', *Studies in Bibliography*, 24 (1972), 27–67.

14. Stevenson, *Briquet's Opuscula*, xxxviii.

uncommon in England during the early seventeenth century as it was of a
better quality and, therefore, more expensive.[15] For present purposes a suggestive outline of the variant watermarks will be given, but the results of
comparing Jonson's paper with other similar stocks have proved to be consistent. There are four moulds to be found in the paper-stocks that Jonson
used in 1609. As watermarks are usually twins, these four moulds represent
two pairs.[16] The most obvious difference between the two pairs is that the first
has flagpoles 43 and 44mm high, while the other pair has flagpoles 54mm
high. All four watermarks are found in *Herbert* and are reproduced from
beta-radiographs (figure 1). As the beta-radiographs show, each mark is distinctive in its detail, with differing widths between the wires as well as in the
sizes and shapes for the letters, flagpoles and pennants; each is also different
in the way the various elements are sewn on the wires and chains of the underlying mould. Each watermark was also cumulatively affected by pulp movement, cleaning of the tray with a scrubbing brush and minor repair, with one
mark (figure 1b) subject to a distinctive process of deterioration in which the
lower curve of the 'G' became flattened and the pennant shifted: this paper
can also be traced in a letter written by Charles Howard, Earl of Nottingham,
on 8 August 1609.[17]

The paper that Jonson used can be shown to differ from other paper with
similar characteristics from the period. For instance, the letters and receipt
written by Donne between 2 February and 6 July 1602, following his elope-
ment with Anne More, were all on paper with a watermark of a draped flag
with a 'G3' countermark.[18] None of Donne's other manuscripts shares exactly
the same watermark, nor does the letter that Christopher Brooke wrote on
25 February 1602, on Donne's behalf (it was written on a sheet of pot). This
material, like that used by Jonson seven years later, is linked by a common
date, handwriting and paper, and forms a self-contained set within the larger
group of Donne's manuscripts. Francis Bacon also used Italian paper: his
letters from 1597–98 have a crossbow and 'G3' mark, while another from 1605
has a flag and 'G3' initials within a circle. A similar circled flag and initials
is to be found in a letter signed by the Privy Council on 21 November 1602.
The paper used for other letters by Bacon includes watermarks with a 43mm
flagpole and a circled lamb and flag countermark on 7 February 1611, a 56mm
high flagpole on 2 July 1613, a 50mm flagpole on 23 July 1619, and a 58mm

15. See, D. C. Coleman, *The British Paper Industry 1495–1860: A Study in Industrial
Growth* (Oxford, 1958), 18–21. Indicatively, in 1621 61,684 reams of French paper were imported into England and only 1,156 reams of Italian. The figures for later in the century are
proportionally similar: in 1662–63, 116,698 reams of French were imported and 1523 reams
of Italian; in 1672, 114,740 reams of French were imported and 2,255 of Italian.

16. A. H. Stevenson, 'Watermarks are Twins', *Studies in Bibliography*, 4 (1951), 57–91.

17. Public Record Office, PR14/145, f. 119.

18. Almost all of the early correspondence is kept together with other letters by Donne
as Folger Shakespeare Library MS. L.b.526–543. The letters and receipt concerned are numbers 526–530, 531–534 and 543. Brooke's letter is f. 530. The other letter from the period is
British Library Cotton MS. Julius C. III, f. 153. E. A. Heawood, *Watermarks: Mainly of the
17th and 18th Centuries* (Hilversum, 1950), plate 202 (1368), gives a close comparison of the
watermark.

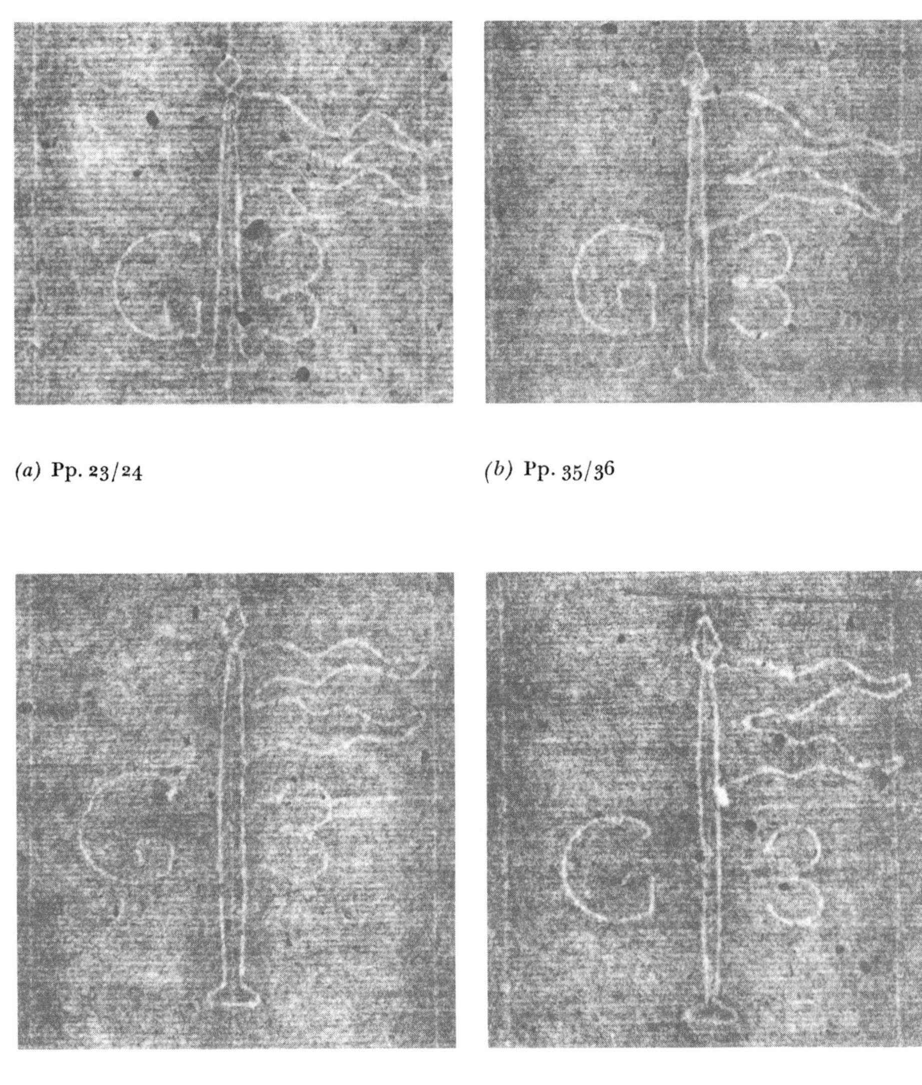

(a) Pp. 23/24

(b) Pp. 35/36

(c) Pp. 253/254

(d) Pp. 257/258

FIGURE 1. Four beta-radiographs: John Donne, *Biathanatos*. MS. e Musaeo 131. With the permission of the Bodleian Library, Oxford.

flagpole with large 18mm initials on 18 September 1623. Yet another variant of the watermark occurs in Donne's letter to Sir Robert More on 10 August 1614, which has a flagpole only 38mm high with the '3' joined to the pennant, while the Dobell Manuscript of Donne's sermons and poems, which may have been prepared around 1620, has a flagpole 54mm high, but in every other respect the watermark differs from that found in *Herbert*. Another undated miscellany, prepared c.1630, has a flagpole 48mm high, and the letters written by the Earl of Pembroke in 1628 and 1629 (used by Sullivan to date *Herbert*) have flagpoles 51 and 55mm high within initials 16mm high. Yet another flag watermark is to be found on a scribal copy of Jonson's epigrams on Inigo Jones from the early 1630s with a flagpole 62mm high, a shorter, dropped flag and a countermark on the outer edge of the other side of the sheet.[19] In dating Jonson's manuscripts by the paper, then, we might be wrong by a few months or a year, but not (with care) by decades. Jonson simply used too much paper and is known to have lived and travelled in too many places for him to be consistently using the same stock of paper in 1603, 1609 and, say, 1635.

The first example of the paper Jonson used is taken from the autograph manuscript of *The Masque of Queenes* (figure 2).[20] It is the most famous and elegant of Jonson's manuscripts and it is probable that Jonson prepared it for Prince Henry within a few months of when the masque was performed in February 1609, as at that time the manuscript would still have had the most resonance as a gift. The paper is Italian and is consistent throughout: the watermarks are of a double pennant flag with the initials 'G3' that conform in every respect (and not otherwise) to the four marks illustrated in figure 1. Physically, perhaps the most distinctive and obvious fact about the manuscript, after the carefulness of the script (it is a work of very fine penmanship), is that despite its size, *The Masque of Queenes* is not a quarto but a cropped folio gathered in single sheets (the page area is 210 x 170mm). Rebinding in the eighteenth century probably reduced the overall size of the page, but the point is that Jonson both used more paper than was necessary and provided generous margins, surrounding the text with a much larger area of space than was required and emphasising the luxurious nature of the manuscript. It is an important and impressive document that reveals how clearly Jonson thought about the structure of the page down to its finest details. With its carefully positioned sidenotes, it is clearly influenced by the scholarly printed books

19. The manuscripts are respectively: Huntington Library MS. HM 2861, 2864 and 128; Folger Shakespeare Library, MS. X.d.30 (40), X.d.158 (1–4), L.b.535; Houghton Library, Harvard, MS. Eng. 966.4; Folger Shakespeare Library MS. V.a.125; Magdalen College, Oxford, MS. 281 items 17 and 18, and Folger Shakespeare Library, MS. X.d.245. See also, J. Donne, *Biathanatos*, ed. E. W. Sullivan II (Newark, Delaware, 1984), xxxviii. Some other Folger manuscripts with flag watermarks, and/or G3 countermarks include: L.a.138 (1 March 1612), L.a.351 (1 February 1607[/8?] = 1c), L.a.401 (11 July 1620), L.a.403 (18 September 1621), L.a.850 (30 September 1620), L.a.853 (17 April, no year), L.a.899 (no date), X.c.29 (3 January 1639), X.d.134 (12 February 1623), X.d.223 (10 January 1601), X.d. 428(2) (27 June 1607 = 1c) X.d.428(50) (no date), X.d.428(56) (11 August 1597, crossbow with G3), X.d.428(172) (13 August 1633), X.d.428(179) (26 July 1613), X.d.438 (no date, c. 1601, earlier state of X.d.223), X.d.490(18–19) (undated), X.d.502(II.10) (1 August 1607 = damaged state of 1b).

20. British Library MS. Royal.18.A.xlv, f. 2ʳ.

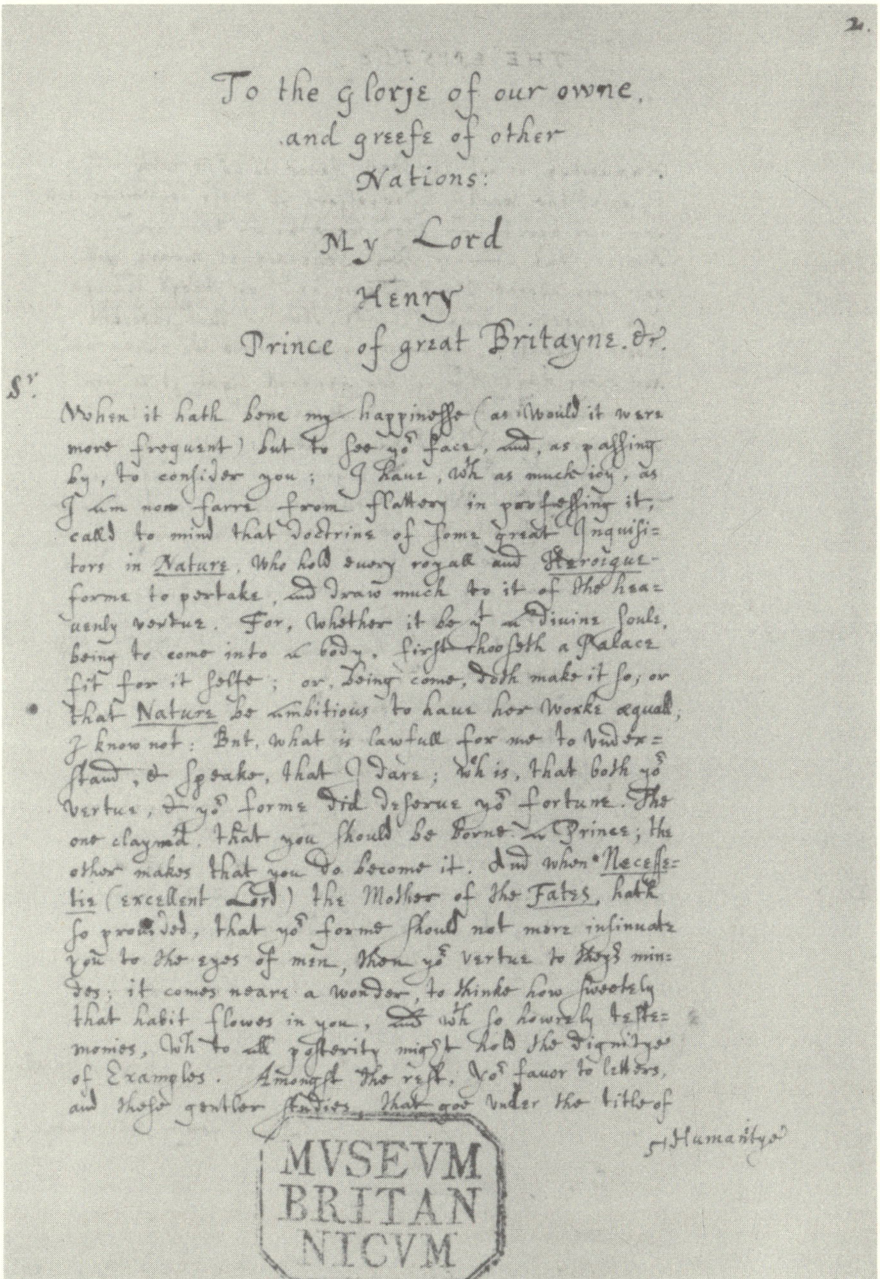
2.

To the glorie of our owne,
and greefe of other
Nations:

My Lord
Henry
Prince of great Britayne. &c.

Sr.

When it hath bene my happinesse (as would it were more frequent) but to see yor face, and, as passing by, to consider you; I haue, wth as much ioy, as I am now farre from flattery in professing it, calld to mind that Doctrine of some great Inquisitors in Nature, who hold euery royall and Heroique forme to partake, and draw much to it of the heauenly vertue. For, whether it be that a diuine soule, being to come into a body, first chooseth a Palace fit for it selfe; or, being come, doth make it so; or that Nature be ambitious to haue her worke equall; I know not: But, what is lawfull for me to vnderstand, & speake, that I dare; wch is, that both yor vertue, & yor forme did deserue yor fortune. The one claymd, that you should be borne a Prince; the other makes that you do become it. And when Necessitie (excellent Lord) the Mother of the Fates, hath so prouided, that yor forme should not more insinuate you to the eyes of men, then yor vertue to theyr minds; it comes neare a wonder, to thinke how sweetly that habit flowes in you, and wth so howrely testimonies, wch to all posterity might hold the dignity of Examples. Amongst the rest, yor fauor to letters, and these gentler studies, that goe vnder the title of

Humanitye

MVSEVM
BRITAN
NICVM

FIGURE 2. Ben Jonson, *The Masque of Queenes.* Royal MS. 18.A.xlv, f. 2r. With the permission of the British Library, London.

with which Jonson was familiar. *The Masque of Queenes* is also, in every sense, a manuscript that has been shaped from Jonson's memory, papers and library. From Jonson's reference to such books as Philipp Ludwig Elich's *Dæmonomagia* (Frankfurt, 1607) and his knowledge of others, such as Balthasar de Beaujoyeulx's *Le Balet Comique* (Paris, 1582), to his record of the performance and the immaculate layout of the textual elements, the manuscript of *The Masque of Queenes* is more than a record of an entertainment. As Stephen Orgel observes, it anatomises 'in a way that is all but unique in English, the relation of a Renaissance poet to the sources of his invention'.[21]

The date of the manuscript can also be confirmed by reference to another of Jonson's manuscripts. The Lowell Manuscript of the Epitaph on Cecilia Bulstrode, now in the Houghton Library, can also be shown to share exactly one of the same watermarks as the *Masque* (1b).[22] This manuscript was written in August 1609 while the servant of one of Donne's closest friends, George Gerrard, was apparently waiting for Jonson to finish writing the poem and the letter that follows it—Jonson excused himself as 'staightned wth time (as yor Man knowes)'. The letter makes quite clear that Jonson was responding to an unexpected request and that he 'was not so much as acquainted' with the matter before the request arrived. Cecilia Bulstrode died on 4 August 1609.

Another manuscript, the epigram to Sir Horace Vere, also suggests that the manuscript for Prince Henry of the *Masque* was written no later than 1609. The manuscript shares the third watermark to be found in *Herbert* and *The Masque of Queenes* (1c).[23] Vere returned to England in 1607, after many years in the Low Countries, before leaving for Europe again as Governor of Brill in October 1609.[24] Jonson would have had less reason to write the poem after Vere's return to Europe when he would have not been able to present it to him, than while Vere was in England and could be approached. On literary and historical grounds, then, a date for the manuscript of between 1607 and 1609 would also seem to be right. The point, however, is that if we accept the dating of the Vere epigram to no later than 1609, we must also admit other evidence that corresponds to such findings. Three autograph manuscripts, all sharing paper with common associations, written by Jonson within a short period of time from one another, are compelling evidence that he was using a

21. S. K. Orgel, 'Jonson and the Amazons', *Soliciting Interpretation: Literary Theory and Seventeenth-Century English Poetry*, ed. E. D. Harvey and K. E. Maus (Chicago, 1990), 134.

22. Houghton Library, Harvard University, Lowell MS. 1455.

23. British Library Add. MS. 29,293, f. 87. If anything, the *c* and *d* variants in *Herbert* lend themselves to a dating earlier than 1609, rather than later. Another Francis Bacon letter (Huntington Library, MS. FBL7) written on 4 August 1606 shares an earlier state of the *d* variant, without the dent at the top of the pennant, the loosened bottom joint (the white spot) or other signs of wear: the two manuscripts represent the extremes of the life of the mould and the circulation of the paper. Similarly, Folger MS. L.a.351 and X.d.428(2) from 1607–8 both share the *c* variant of the watermark. The poem written by Jonson to the Earl of Somerset (pasted in the front of a copy of the 1640 *Workes*: British Library, C.28 m.11) is a single half-sheet without a watermark.

24. *DNB*, XX, 236 (235–239).

common supply of paper, or consistently acquiring paper from the same source at that time.

II

Before showing the relationship between these three manuscripts and *Herbert*, it is appropriate to give another example, both of Jonson's use of Italian paper and, more importantly, of Simpson's mis-description of manuscript material. The example is Jonson's letter to Sir Robert Cotton in British Library Cotton MS. Julius C. III, reproduced by Greg as Jonson's last surviving manuscript in *English Literary Autographs*.[25] The manuscript is in a collection of letters to Sir Robert Cotton, with no letter written later than 1629. The volume was at one time arranged in approximate chronological order with Jonson's letter bound in at f. 62.[26] It was subsequently broken up and re-arranged in alphabetical order with Jonson's letter placed at f. 222. Because the original binding has been destroyed, it is impossible to tell whether the letter was inserted at a later date, or indeed to determine when the volume was originally bound—which is why it is dangerous to modify the physical structure of historical documents. There are, in fact, errors in the original placement of undated letters—one from Donne to Cotton was, for instance, written in 1610, not 1614—but someone had made a fairly serious attempt to get the order approximately right. The confusion that the British Library introduced, however, by re-ordering the letters allowed Simpson to redate the letter without further comment.

When the Cotton Catalogue was first prepared, Joseph Planta (the librarian concerned) did not recognise Jonson's hand and thought the letter had been written by someone called 'Bell'. This is significant because it shows that there was no reason for Planta to have placed the letter out of order on the basis of a mistaken inference. The overwhelming probability must, therefore, remain that the Cotton Catalogue records the placement of the letter at an earlier date by someone with a sense of its position in the chronological sequence. It was Simpson who discovered that 'Bell' was 'Ben'. The letter is slightly cryptic.

S^r, as seriously, as a man but fayntly returning to his despayr'd health,
    can; I salute you. And by these few lines request you,
      that you would by this bearer, lend me some booke, that would
        determinately satisfy mee, of the true site [of *canceled*] & distance
          betwixt Bauli, [and *canceled; next word interlined with caret*] or portus Baiarū,
        and Villa Augusta into w^{c}h (if I erre not) runnes Lacus lucrinus.
They are neare by my historicall ayme to Cumæ Chalcidensium
      Misenū, Auernus. in Campania./
Good S^r adde this to many other Courtesies you haue done mee
      that though I chance to suruiue now, I may herafter dye
      more in yor Debt./

25. W. W. Greg. *English Literary Autographs 1550–1650*, 4 parts (Oxford, 1925–32), I, plate XXIII.

26. J. Planta, *A Catalogue of the Manuscripts in the Cottonian Library Deposited in the British Museum* (London, 1802), 9–10.

164 STUDIES IN BIBLIOGRAPHY

The Booke shall be returned this night   You^r infirm
    w^{t}hout excuse.   BEN. now./

In and of itself, all this undated letter reveals is that Jonson had been
seriously ill, that he wished to borrow a book, and that he was concerned
about the geography of Campania and 'the true site & distance betwixt Bauli,
. . . and Villa Augusta'. In the Catalogue, the letter was placed with other undated material after the letters written in 1609 and thus 'c.1609?' is the pen-
cilled note on the stub in the binding. More generally, this group of material
might represent letters that were thought by whoever gathered them to have
been written during the first decade of the seventeenth century. Simpson, however, concluded that the letter must have been slipped in later and that it
was written towards the end of Jonson's life. He assumed that as Jonson was
'a man but fayntly returning to his despayred health' and signed himself
'You^r infirme BEN. now.', these were the rather desperate laments of an aged
sick man who might 'herafter dye more in yor Debt'. In the Oxford edition,
he placed the letter after the one to Newcastle on 20 December 1631 and
described the letter as 'written in [Jonson's] latest years after the attack of
palsy'.[27] He did not mention that there might be a problem with date or infer
doubt as to its place in the historical sequence. The next step was taken by
Greg, who realised that Cotton's library had been closed by royal order in
1629 and that Cotton had died in May 1631.[28] Access was not permitted to the
Cottonian library again till after Sir Robert's death. Greg therefore redated
the manuscript c.1635 and assumed that rather than being written to Sir
Robert, it had been written to his son, Sir Thomas Cotton.

Yet if Sir Thomas Cotton had inserted the letter in the volume, the
chances are that (like the Desmond Ode in the Christ Church Salusbury
Manuscript) it would have been gathered with other papers that had been
inserted out of order in the same place.[29] The surrounding letters were written
by Sir Anthony Mildmay (who died in 1617), Sir Humphrey Winch (d. 1625),
John Holles, later Earl of Clare (d. 1637) and Sir John Harington (d. 1612).
The likelihood of Jonson's letter being inserted randomly in the wrong place
with this other material at a later date must be viewed as improbable. Instead
of Simpson's interpretation, what seems more likely is that Jonson meant,
with wry humour, that he was recovering—he was 'infirme', no longer seriously ill.

The codicological evidence that this letter was written earlier rather than
later in Jonson's life is corroborated by the paper and handwriting. The
strongly cursive hand (which shows no sign of palsy) is also to be found in
Jonson's copy of Selden's *De Diis Syris* (London, 1617: figure 3), but it is unlike the marginalia found in books from his library printed towards the end

27. H&S, I, 215.
28. K. Sharpe, *Sir Robert Cotton 1586–1631: History and Politics in Early Modern England* (Oxford, 1979), 80–81. Also, C. G. C. Tite, *The Manuscript Library of Sir Robert Cotton*
(London, 1994); C. E. Wright (ed.), *Sir Robert Cotton as Collector* (London, 1997).
29. The Desmond Ode is Christ Church MS. 184, f. 40. For further details: ' "As far
from all Reuolt": Sir John Salusbury, Christ Church MS. 184 and Jonson's First Ode', *English
Manuscript Studies*, 8, forthcoming.

FIGURE 3. John Selden, *De Dijs Syris*, London, 1617. Shelfmark STC 22167.2, front flyleaf. With the permission of the Folger Shakespeare Library, Washington D.C.

of his life (i.e. those in which the evidence for his later hand is unquestionable), or his inscription in one of the Folger copies of Camden's *Annales*, written after 1627, but almost certainly in the 1630s (figure 4). Similarly, the watermark (though cropped) is clearly the double pennant flag with the initials 'G3' (figure 5). The principal difference between the watermarks found in the 1609 manuscripts and this one is that the bottom of the flagpole of the Cotton Manuscript has a double base and the initials are more distant from the flag. As has been shown, this is not surprising as there were literally dozens of variant marks and moulds. In fact, it is exactly the same watermark as that in Robert Cecil's letter to Sir John Peyton in March 1603 about Queen Elizabeth's final sickness.[30]

The disparity of thirty years between the date assigned by Simpson and Greg and the watermark evidence is certainly sufficient to make one pause. It would therefore help if what may seem to be an obscure letter could be connected to a passage in either a Jonson play, poem or masque. The places that Jonson mentions are all to be found on the coast to the north of Naples, and were fashionable resorts for Roman aristocrats. Cumae was the town furthest north, an ancient Greek settlement famous for the sibylline oracles. While none of the places mentioned in the letter occurs in Jonson's texts, the general area, 'Campania', was referred to twice, the first time in *Poetaster* and the second time in *Sejanus*. The passage in *Sejanus* indicates that the watermark

30. Folger Shakespeare Library, MS. X.c.43.

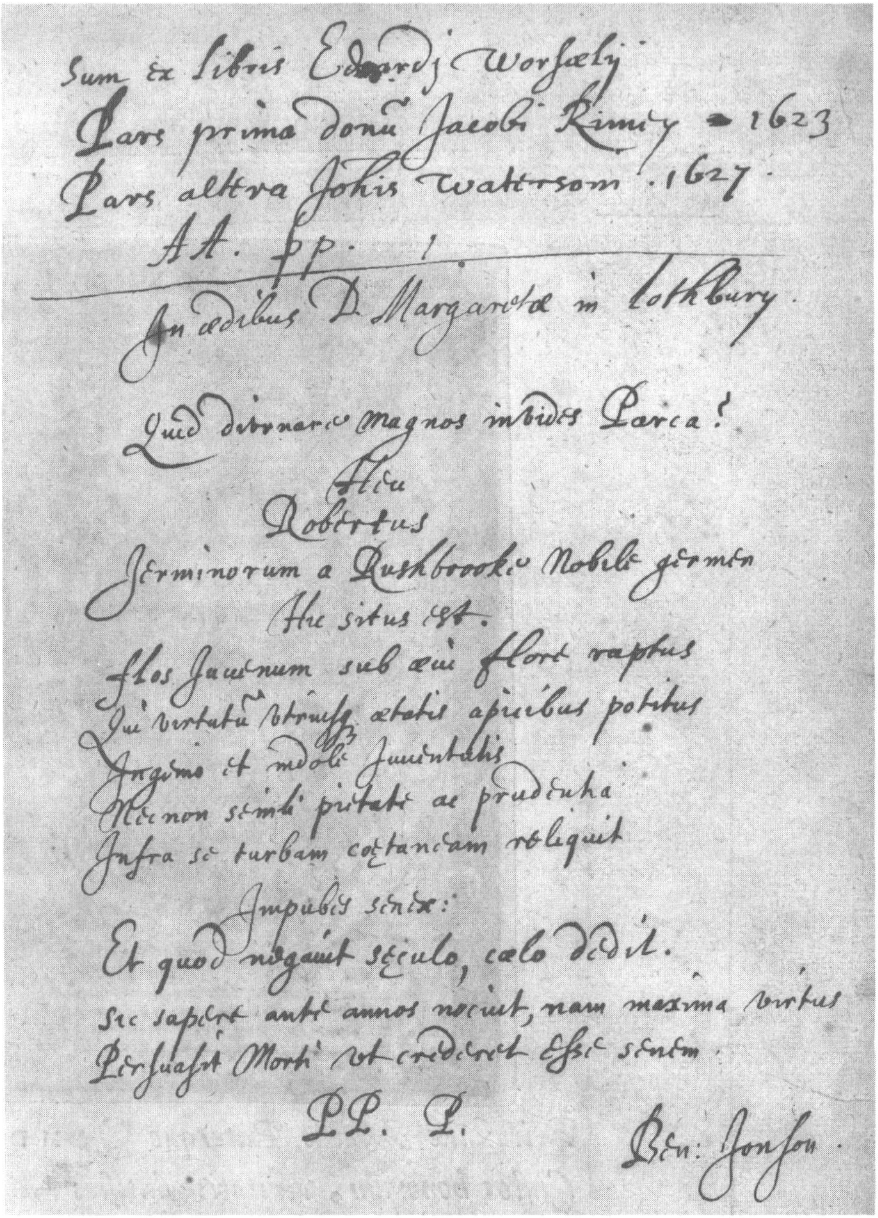

Sum ex libris Edwardi Worsley
Pars prima donu Jacobi Rimey 1623
Pars altera Johis Watersom . 1627 .
AA. pp. 1
In aedibus D. Margaretae in Lothbury.

Quid diurnare magnos invides Parca?
Heu
Robertus
Jerminorum a Rushbrooke Nobile germen
Hic situs est.
Flos Juvenum sub aevi flore raptus
Qui virtutu utrinque aetatis apicibus potitus
Ingenio et indole Juventutis
Necnon senili pietate ac prudentia
Infra se turbam coetaneam reliquit
Impubis senex:
Et quod negavit seculo, caelo dedit.
Sic sapere ante annos nocuit, nam maxima virtus
Persuasit Morti ut crederet esse senem.
PP. P.
Ben: Jonson.

FIGURE 4. William Camden, *Annales*, London 1615, 27. Shelfmark STC 4496 copy 1, recto of engraved portrait. With the permission of the Folger Shakespeare Library, Washington D. C.

FIGURE 5. Photograph. Ben Jonson to Sir Robert Cotton, [1603]. Cotton MS. Julius C. III, f. 222. With the permission of the British Library, London.

evidence is correct and that Simpson and Greg were wrong. At the end of Act Three, Tiberius informs Macro that he is leaving Rome:

> We are in purpose, *Macro*, to depart
> The Citty for a time, and see *Campania*;
> Not for our pleasures, but to dedicate
> A paire of Temples, one, to *Iupiter*
> At *Capua*; Th'other at *Nola*, to *Augustus*.[31]

While the towns Jonson mentions are different, reference to a classical dictionary quickly confirms that the places he writes of in both *Sejanus* and the letter are in close proximity to one another. Jonson was clearly establishing the geography of the area as background to the play.

To summarise: the original order in which the letter was bound indicates a general date in the first decade of the seventeenth century, the cursiveness of the hand indicates that it was written earlier rather than later in Jonson's life, the watermark dates the letter to 1603, and the passage from *Sejanus* dates the letter to 1603. We also know that in 1603 Jonson was staying with Cotton in Conington when he had the dream of his son as the burning babe and news the following morning that he had died. The redating of the letter now means that it is possible that Jonson did not so much abandon his family in London, but rather that he retired to the country in order to protect his wife and son from an illness that had almost killed him. Perhaps Camden thought Jonson's dream was a hallucination from the fever. Perhaps the unstated reason for the emotional force of Jonson's famous epigram is the sense that (however unwittingly) he was directly responsible for his son's death.

The misdating of the letter has created two problems. First, this letter was apparently only one of two manuscripts that could be dated after Jonson's illness in 1628–29. We now know that dating to be wrong. As a consequence, the Cotton Manuscript cannot be securely reproduced as evidence for Jonson's handwriting in his final years. The other putative witness to Jonson's hand towards the end of his life, the Ellesmere Manuscript of the 'Expostu-

---

31. B. Jonson, *Sejanus his Fall*, STC 14782 (1605), G4v–H1r; H&S, IV, 415.

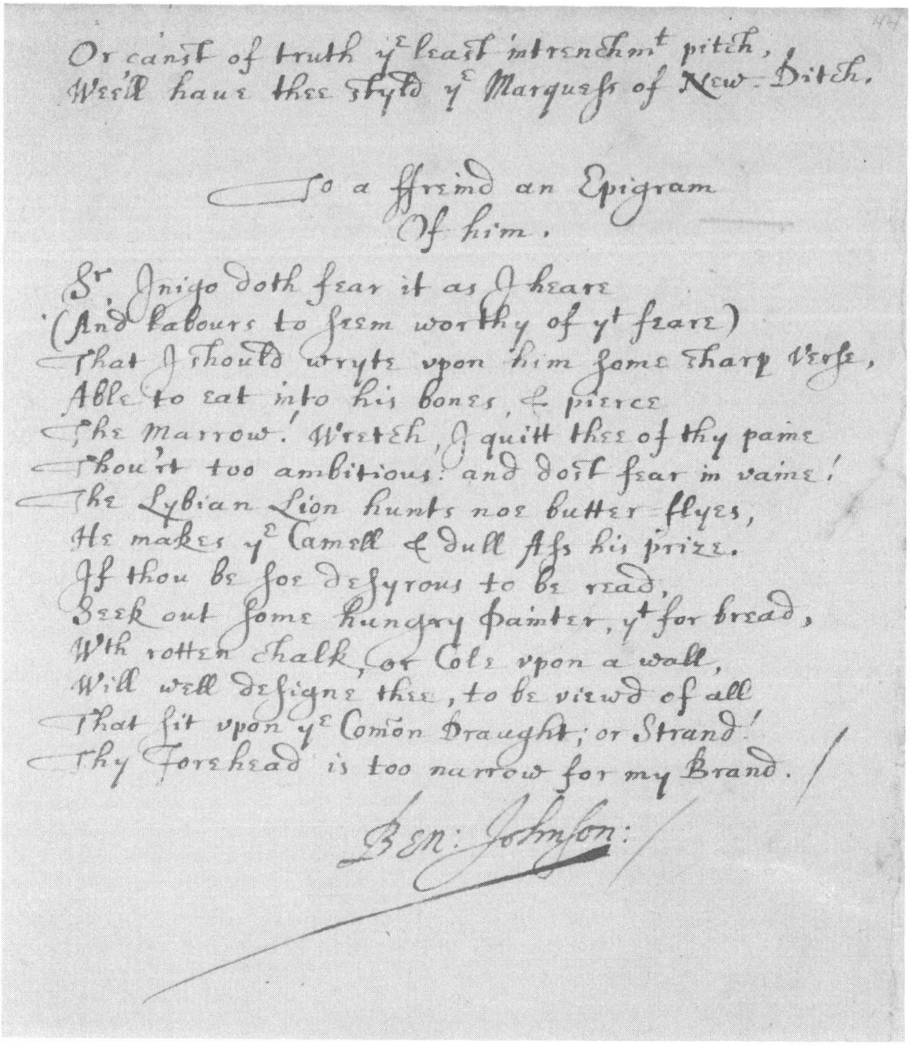

Or canst of truth ye least intrenchmt pitch,
Wee'll haue thee styld ye Marquess of New-Ditch.

To a ffreind an Epigram
Of him.

Sr. Inigo doth fear it as I heare
(And labours to seem worthy of yt feare)
That I should wryte vpon him some sharp verse,
Able to eat into his bones, & pierce
The Marrow. Wretch, I quitt thee of thy paine
Thou'rt too ambitious: and dost fear in vaine!
The Lybian Lion hunts noe butter flyes,
He makes ye Camell & dull Ass his prize.
If thou be soe desyrous to be read,
Seek out some hungry painter, yt for bread,
Wth rotten chalk, or Cole vpon a wall,
Will well designe thee, to be view'd of all
That sit vpon ye Comon Draught; or Strand!
Thy Forehead is too narrow for my Brand.
Ben: Johnson:/

FIGURE 6. Ben Jonson, 'An Expostulation with Inigo Jones' (scribal copy). MS. EL8729, f. 44r. With the permission of the Henry E. Huntington Library, San Marino.

lation with Inigo Jones', has also never been reproduced, nor has any of Jonson's late marginalia. What can be stated for certain is that the Ellesmere Manuscript is not holograph (figure 6). It is a scribal copy.[32] The two other

32. Henry E. Huntington Library, MS. EL8729. Indicatively, the manuscript is signed 'Ben: Johnson:/'. In the same hand, on the verso of the final leaf, is also written 'Mr Ben: Johnsons Expostulatiõ wth Inigo Jones'. Apart from the significant differences in the hand, Jonson would not have spelt his name with an 'h', 'with' would have been contracted 'wth', and he would not have recorded himself in the third person.

late examples of Jonson's hand are the inscription on the front fly-leaf of *Marmora Arundelliana* in pencil and ink (the pencil inscription showing no sign of illness), and the inscription in Camden's *Annales*. Of these two examples, that in the copy of Camden's *Annales* is almost certainly later.

Second, restoring the original date to the letter alters what is known about Jonson's biography. It is not only that Jonson nearly died in 1603 and that both *Sejanus* and the epitaph on his son must now be read with that knowledge. He would also appear to have been far more active in the 1630s than we have assumed. Simpson believed that the illness referred to as 'palsy' was the after-effect of a stroke and this has become the standard story. His partner, Charles Herford, had asserted that Jonson was 'struck down with paralysis in 1628', while David Riggs suggested that Jonson suffered a second stroke in 1626, adding that the stroke in 1628 rendered Jonson 'a paralytic invalid' and 'confined to his house for the rest of his life'.[33] It is possible, of course, that 'palsy' might equally refer to a condition such as Parkinson's Disease. More importantly, what neither Herford nor Riggs knew was that, on 3 May 1632, Jonson in his capacity as city chronologer was amongst the esquires who walked in the funeral procession of Sir John Lemmon, Lord Mayor, 'from Grocers hall to St Michaells church in Crooke Lane'.[34] It is possible that he may have been helped, but there is no indication of this in the document, and unless further evidence can be produced it must be concluded that Jonson's physical disability late in his life has been substantially mis-represented.

Jonson may have left his house only rarely and occasionally spent some days in bed, though we do not know this for certain, but it would appear he could walk and it is quite possible that he attended the opening (and only) night of *The New Inne* on 19 January 1629 as his prefatory comments suggest.[35] It is, in fact, extremely unlikely that if Jonson had been seriously paralysed by two strokes within a short period, he would have lived for another eight years (particularly given the limitations of early modern medical care).[36] Perhaps the only other piece of information that now need be added is that another circumstantial witness adduced to substantiate the severity of Jonson's ill health in his later years is less than reliable. John Pory certainly knew both Cotton and Jonson and in his letters of 15 and 20 September 1632 reported that *The Magnetic Lady* had been advertised for performance. In the second letter, he also mentioned that he had thought Jonson to be dead. On another occasion, in June 1632, Pory had also reported the death of Hugh

33. H&S, I, 91; D. Riggs, *Ben Jonson: A Life* (Cambridge, Mass., 1989), 298, 307–308.

34. British Library Add. MS. 71,131 F. Jonson was in a group of City dignitaries with the Town Clerk, the Auditor, the Beadle and the Chamberlain. Although his pension had been suspended the previous year, the context of this group confirms the identification as genuine. He was probably participating to ensure his pension was paid. The manuscript is amongst recent acquisitions.

35. Jonson, *The New Inne*, STC 14780 (1631), (*)8ᵛ. H&S, VI, 402. Jonson remarked that the Host was 'playd well' and that Lovel was 'acted well too'—comments that would only have any meaning if he had witnessed the performance.

36. A medicinal recipe dated 16 April 1637 and signed by '[Robert] Fludde' is to be found in Jonson's copy of Bede (Cologne, 1612). It was sold by Quaritch (Reference EB 138, 1985). At the time of writing I have not had the opportunity to examine this document.

Holland, thirteen months before Holland's demise.[37] Though used uncritically by Jonson scholars, Pory's reliability as a witness has been viewed rather differently by historians: the letters were once described as concerned with 'the last new rumour' and 'unescapably trivial'.[38] Though they certainly knew each other, one must also wonder how much Pory really knew of Jonson's circumstances at all.

More generally, the point about the Cotton letter and Simpson's treatment of manuscript material is that our understanding of the literary evidence is predicated on the inferences we make about the origins of the material and the conditions of its production. D. F. McKenzie made this observation in these pages almost thirty years ago and it is worth repeating the passage he recalled (via Popper's *Logic of Scientific Discovery*) from Black's *Lectures on the Elements of Chemistry*: 'A nice adaption of conditions will make almost any hypothesis agree with the phenomena. This will please our imagination, but does not advance our knowledge'.[39]

III

It is now time to return to the *Herbert* manuscript of *Biathanatos*. During 1609, Jonson wrote and had staged *Epicœne*, *The Masque of Queenes* and *Britains Burse*, and he wrote several short poems. He also prepared the manuscript of *Herbert*.[40] Although photographs of the hand have been published very recently by Peter Beal, neither the Simpsons, Greg, nor Sullivan, who edited the manuscript of *Biathanatos*, illustrated the hand of the 'scribe', or the error of not connecting it with Jonson would have been noticed long ago (figure 7).[41]

The only book to acknowledge that Jonson may have been responsible for the manuscript was Evelyn Simpson's *The Prose Works of John Donne*, which first appeared in 1924. Percy and Evelyn Simpson had married three years earlier. Perhaps because Evelyn was the Donne scholar, the manuscript was discussed in her book rather than in the first volumes of the Oxford edition of Jonson, which appeared in 1925. In the first edition of *The Prose Works*, Evelyn Simpson indicated there might be a problem:

The Bodleian manuscript raises some difficult problems. The hand in which it is written bears an extraordinary likeness to that of Ben Jonson. But in the absence of any clear external evidence—such as an allusion in Donne's introductory letter—it is

<hr>

37. *DNB*, XVI, 201–202. W. S. Powell, *John Pory/1572–1636: The Life and Letters of a Man of Many Parts* (Chapel Hill, 1979), microfiche 294 and 284–286 (transcriptions of British Library Harley MS. 7000, pp. 336–337 and Public Record Office, C.115/8408). Pory certainly knew Jonson and they had co-operated together as late as 1630 on *The Summe and Substance of a Disputation* (part 2 of STC 10773).

38. D. Mathew, *The Social Structure in Caroline England* (Oxford, 1948), 15.

39. D. F. McKenzie, 'Printers of the Mind: Some Notes on Bibliographical Theories and Printing-House Practices', *Studies in Bibliography*, 22 (1969), 2.

40. Bodleian Library, Oxford, MS. e Musaeo 131.

41. P. Beal, *In Praise of Scribes: Manuscripts and their Makers in Seventeenth-Century England* (Oxford, 1998), 31–57. I would like to thank Peter Beal and Oxford University Press for allowing me access to advance uncorrected page proofs.

impossible to suppose that Jonson had undertaken the arduous task of copying out a treatise of this length. Further there are palaeographical difficulties when a detailed comparison is made with the holograph manuscript of Jonson's *Masque of Queens*, preserved among the Royal Manuscripts in the British Museum. The numerous marginal notes are in Donne's own hand. . . .[42]

We must respect Evelyn Simpson's genuine scholarly caution, for her hesitation is understandable: identifying another person's handwriting accurately can prove deeply embarrassing, as (theatrically) Malvolio discovered in *Twelfth Night*. With no further evidence, she prudently decided to regard the manuscript as a problem. The following year, Greg was supportive of her doubts:

It should be added that other hands occur liable to be confused with Jonson's. A manuscript of *Biathanatos* is preserved in the Bodleian Library (MS. e Musaeo 131) which shows an extremely close general resemblance, though certain technical distinctions make identity improbable.[43]

By 1948, Evelyn Simpson altered the passage concerned:

The hand in which the Bodleian manuscript is written has a resemblance to that of Ben Jonson, though it is certainly not his. The numerous marginal notes are in Donne's own hand. . . .[44]

This opinion has been accepted without question. In 1972, Robert Pirie referred to the manuscript as 'in a scribal hand'; while in 1984, Sullivan observed that it was the work of 'a single professional copyist' and this was also assumed by Speed Hill.[45] Although these are accurate, though partial, statements, the other manuscripts of this 'professional copyist' (unlike, for instance, the Feathery scribe) have not been identified. In 1925, it might have been adequate for Greg to write that 'other hands are liable to be confused with Jonson's: seventy years later, the work of this supposed scrivener has remained limited to a single manuscript.

The real problem with the 'certain technical distinctions' that Greg and the Simpsons made is that they were comparing, as it were, apples with oranges. *The Masque of Queenes* is a very special manuscript that Jonson prepared for Prince Henry. The manuscript shows Jonson's hand at its most stylised and contrived. A similar example can be found in a copy of Martial that he gave to Richard Briggs in 1619.[46] Comparison with *The Masque of*

42. E. M. Simpson, *The Prose Works of John Donne* (Oxford, 1924), 147.

43. Greg, *English Literary Autographs 1550–1650*, I, section XXIII, second page.

44. E. M. Simpson, *The Prose Works of John Donne*, 2nd ed. (Oxford, 1948), 162.

45. R. S. Pirie, *John Donne: A Catalogue of the Anniversary Exhibition of First and Early Editions his Works Held at the Grolier Club* (New York, 1972), 5 (item 10). Sullivan, *Biathanatos,* xxxvii. Sullivan had earlier published three articles, the first of which also referred to 'a single professional copyist' (54): 'The Genesis and Transmission of Donne's *Biathanatos*', *The Library*, V, 31 (1976), 52–72; 'Manuscript Materials in the First Edition of Donne's *Biathanatos*', *Studies in Bibliography*, 31 (1978), 210–221; "Bibliographical Evidence in Presentation Copies: An Example from Donne', *Analytical and Enumerative Bibliography*, 6 (1982), 17–22. See also, W. S. Hill, 'John Donne's *Biathanatos*: Authenticity, Authority and Context in Three Editions', *John Donne Journal*, 6 (1987), 109–133.

46. Folger Shakespeare Library, STC 17492, Copy 1, A1ᵛ.

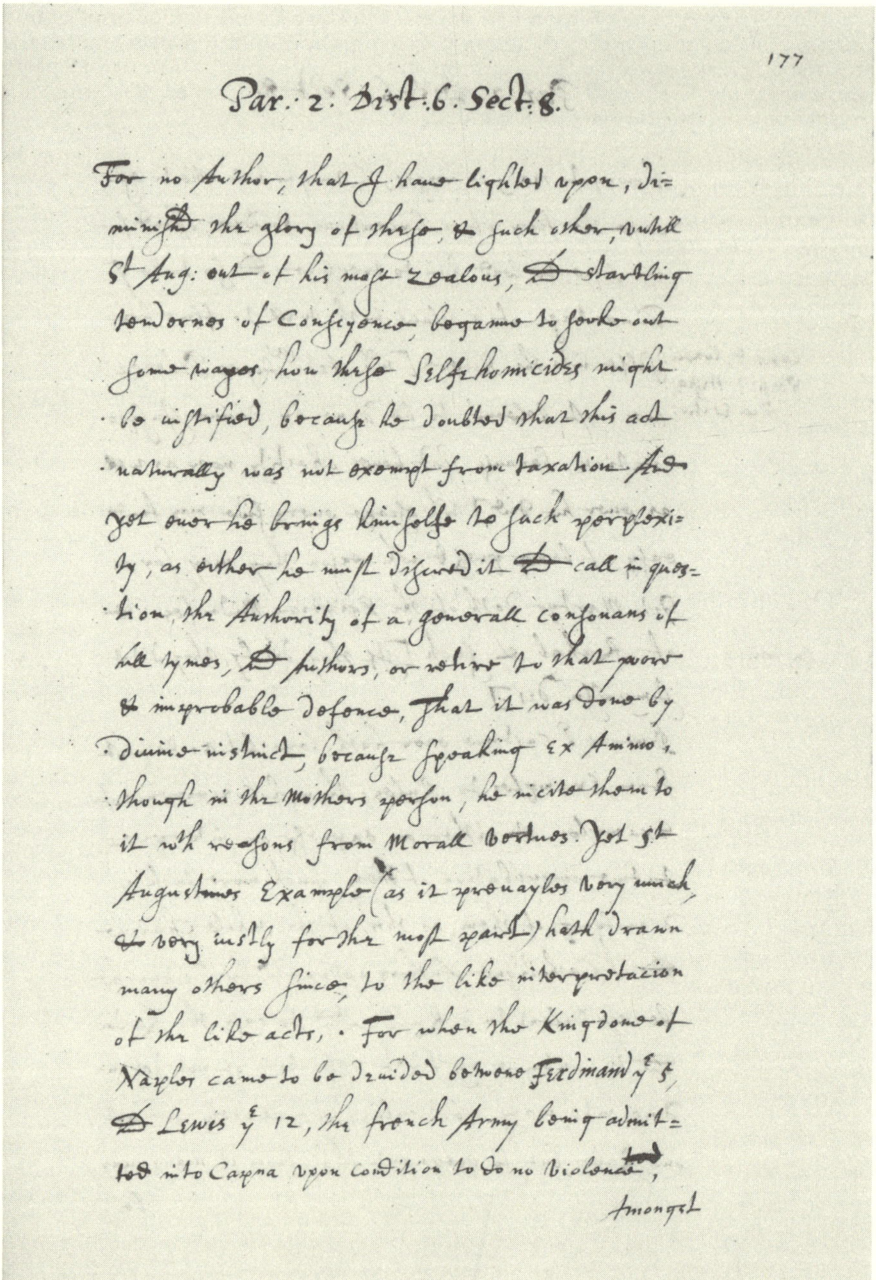

177

Par. 2. Dist. 6. Sect. 8.

For no Author, that J haue lighted vpon, di=
minisht the glory of these, & such other, vntill
St Aug: out of his most zealous, & startling
tendernes of Conscyence, beganne to seeke out
some wayes how these Selfhomicides might
be iustified, because he doubted that this act
naturally was not exempt from taxation. And
yet euer he brings himselfe to such perplexi=
ty, as either he must disaued it & call in ques=
tion, the Authority of a generall consonans if
all tymes, & Authors, or where to that poore
& improbable defence, that it was done by
diuine instinct, because speaking Ex Animo,
though in the Mothers person, he incites them to
it wth reasons from Morall bonnes. Yet St
Augustines Example (as it preuayles very much,
& very iustly for the most part) hath drawn
many others since, to the like interpretacion
of the like acts. For when the Kingdome of
Naples came to be diuided betwene Ferdinand ye 5,
& Lewis ye 12, the french Army being admit=
ted into Capua vpon condition to do no violence,

amongst

FIGURE 7. John Donne, *Biathanatos*. MS. e Musaeo 131, p. 177. With the permission of the
Bodleian Library, Oxford.

Epitaph.

Stay, view this stone: And, if thou beest not such,
Read here a little, that thou mayst know much.
It covers, first, a Virgin; and then, one
That durst be that in Court: a vertu' alone
To fill an Epitaph. But she had more.
She might have claym'd t'have made the Graces foure;
Taught Pallas language; Cynthia modesty;
As fit to have encreas'd the harmony
Of Spheares, as light of starres; She was earthes Eye:
The sole Religious house, and Votary,
Wth Rites not bound, but conscience. Wouldst thou All?
She was 'Sell Boulstred. In wch name, I call
it Vp so much truth, as could I here pursue
Might make the Fable of Good Women true.

See what the obedience of friendship is, and the hazard it runnes. This I have done, streightned wth time (as yor man knowes) to let you know yor power in mee. If it be well, as I thinke it is, for my invention hath not cooled so much to iudge, show it, though the greater witts have gone before. It hath somwhat in it moris antiqui, and suggesting the sodaynesse of it may passe. for till yor Letter came, I was not so much as acquainted wth the sad argument, wch doth strooke me and keepes me a heavy man, (would God, I had seene her before that some of live might have corrected some preiudices they have had iniuriously of mee. By yor next commodity, write me yor liking of it, and some newes; I will answere it wth yor other request if I can for any businesse, wch is now very waighty to mee, by reason of some embarquings.

Yor true Lover
Ben: Jonson

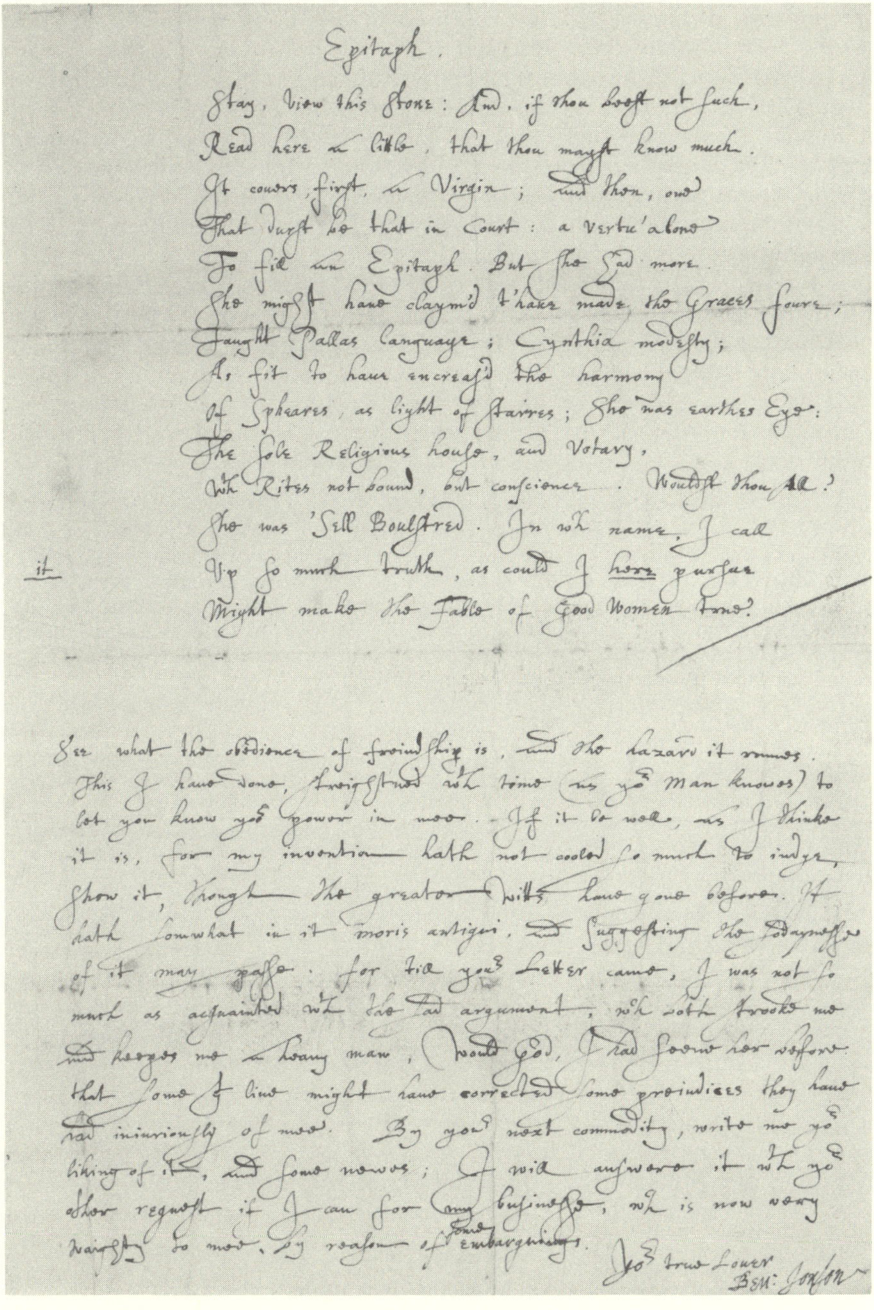

FIGURE 8. Ben Jonson, 'An Epitaph on Cecilia Bulstrode'. Lowell MS. 1455. With the permission of the Houghton Library, Harvard University.

Queenes was, of course, the test Simpson always applied against any other possible Jonson manuscript, but that is scarcely reassuring, for the variety of the evidence concerning Jonson's handwriting found in his manuscripts and marginalia is far more complicated. The moment *Herbert* is compared with the Lowell Manuscript (figure 8), the fallacy is obvious. The Lowell Manuscript is a fine example of Jonson's typical hand in 1609, carefully written but far more fluent than *The Masque of Queenes.*

Another document, however, shows that Evelyn Simpson decided to suppress material originally intended for her book before the first edition of *The Prose Works of John Donne* appeared. These alterations involve more significant matters than merely an adjustment of tone. At the bottom of an uncatalogued cardboard box titled 'Printed Pieces, Notes and Proofs' among her papers, now in the Osborn Collection at the Beinecke Library, Yale University is an envelope which contains part of the original typescript for the *Prose Works.* The passage that has been quoted, before it was altered for publication, first read:

The Bodleian manuscript raises some difficult problems. The hand in which it is written bears an extraordinary likeness to that of Ben Jonson. Mr. Percy Simpson, who as an editor of Jonson is thoroughly familiar with the latter's hand, has examined the manuscript of *Biathanatos* and declares that the general resemblance is so striking, as well as the agreement of individual letters and groups of letters, that he is disposed to believe the manuscript is in Jonson's autograph. If this can be substantiated it will furnish an additional proof of Jonson's admiration for Donne. The numerous marginal notes are in Donne's own hand. . . .[47]

There was also a further passage that was removed:

But if the Bodleian manuscript is really in Jonson's hand, we cannot date it as late as 1619, and a date between 1602 and 1608 would seem probable. Mr. Simpson believes that it shows a slightly earlier form of Jonson's handwriting than that exhibited in the *Masque of Queens* (1609), of which the holograph manuscript is to be found among the Royal MSS. in the British Museum.

It is quite clear from this that Percy Simpson *believed* the manuscript to be in Jonson's hand. If he changed his mind, he left no statement as to why he did so. It would be possible to speculate why the Simpsons decided not to address the manuscript in the context of the Jonson edition (including the problems it could have created for the first two volumes of the edition while it was already at the press), but that is not the main issue. Put simply, the scholarly opinions of Percy and Evelyn Simpson on Jonson's manuscript material cannot be accepted without question. In the case of both the Cotton manuscript and *Herbert*, Percy Simpson began with an assumption about Jonson's biography and then made a judgment about the nature of the evidence before him based on those opinions. In both instances, he was wrong.

47. Beinecke Library, Yale University, E. M. Simpson MSS, Uncatalogued Box containing Printed Pieces, Notes and Proofs of material primarily relating to Evelyn Simpson, in an envelope with the following note in Evelyn Simpson's hand: 'Part of the typescript for the 1st edition (1924) of *A Study of the Prose Works of John Donne.* Much of the typescript was cut up and used for other works."

Of course, we do not have a letter or similar document by Jonson that explicitly states that he copied *Biathanatos*—therefore, another form of corroborative evidence would help 'determinately satisfy' the question of his involvement. Paper, as a neutral record of such associations, is the best witness we could have, and that is why it is such an important control when discussing these issues.

Simpson, though considered a perfectionist, never took records of watermarks or other forms of evidence provided by paper. Sullivan, however, did— though he dated the manuscript on inferences about when it might have been copied, and did not record the distinctive evidence that could be derived from the characteristics of the mark or differences in the mould. The account that Sullivan provided of the paper to be found in the manuscript therefore needs to be modified.[48] The manuscript consists of 142 leaves, not all of which are conjugate, folded as folio but cut down to quarto size.[49] The paper has four variant watermarks of a double pennant flag with the initials 'G3' (figure 1). The volume is quired in a combination of single sheets and in fours.

As well as the paper used for the manuscript, there is a group of front and rear endpapers. A pair of front and the rear flyleaves are folded as quarto, the rear without watermark and the front with a small bunch of grapes with a stalk. The front flyleaves are quired with a folio sheet of which the first leaf is a stub (which has been numbered) and on the verso of the second is the record of Herbert's gift of the volume to the Bodleian: the watermark was on the cropped leaf. Following the leaf with the record of Herbert's gift is another single folio leaf with a stub bound in before the manuscript. This leaf, on which Donne wrote his letter to Sir Edward Herbert, is without a watermark. These pages have been recorded by the Bodleian as i–x—in order to avoid confusion, the Bodleian method of numbering the preliminary leaves of the manuscript has been retained here. There is also a single folio leaf after the manuscript (but before the rear flyleaves) with a crown and grape watermark—whether this was originally conjugate with Donne's letter is uncertain, but it is probable as the distance between the chainlines (which are much wider than the other paper) is the same. The structure is suggestive of the way in which the manuscript was put together and then turned into the book that was given to Sir Edward Herbert. The volume was bound in gilt-ruled reverse calf with a central ornament of five crossed arrows and a bow, quartered with brown morocco and secured with blue silk ties, of which the stubs remain.

Excluding the endpapers that have been described, the remainder of the volume was initially prepared by Jonson before Donne added the sidenotes. This section entirely consists of paper with flag watermarks, and indicates

48. Sullivan, *Biathanatos*, xxxvii–xxxviii. Sullivan identified only a single generic watermark (the flag). He stated that the text and the preliminaries may have been written at different times and that the watermarks between the two parts are different, the text having a flag with G3 and the preliminaries and endpapers a grape and table watermark.

49. For instance, the leaf pp. xxi–ii is a cancel. In both the final section of the manuscript and the second part of the preliminaries Jonson used the half of the sheet with the watermark for the extra leaf the two halves are not common to each other.

something of the history of its preparation as a document. The watermarks are twins, and these twins change approximately halfway through the manuscript when the sheets begin to be mixed together. The second pair of watermarks first occurs at pages 135–138 and 175–178, where the new paper is bound as the inner sheet of the quire (in fours). The first group of papers is indicated by roman type and the second group by italic. The division between them is as follows:

c.250 x 165mm 2°, pp. 284: *xi–xiv* xv–xxxvi, 1–134 *135–138* 139–174 *175–178* 179–184 *185–212* 213–228 *229–258*

There are two parts to the preliminaries and the differences in paper are suggestive. Pages xi–xiv include the title and a list of authors cited. Pages xv–xxxvi is a descriptive list of contents.[50] It would appear that this second section was prepared while the manuscript was being written, as it is on the first group of paper. The first two leaves were then written after the rest of the manuscript had been finished: they are on the second group of paper. The way in which the second group of papers gradually replaces the first suggests that Jonson was steadily working through a single supply of paper that had been mixed together when the sheets were first placed in a heap at the papermill. The conclusion is corroborated by the presence of all four watermarks in the much shorter manuscript of *The Masque of Queenes.*

As *Herbert* is also a Donne manuscript, with Donne's marginal notes added to the text, most of Donne's manuscripts have also been examined for their watermark characteristics, to discover whether any of them share the same paper. There are thirty-eight surviving letters and one poem in Donne's hand and six other documents written by him. Like Jonson, Donne appears to have liked fine papers and, as has been shown, he used paper of this kind. While it has not proved possible to examine every holograph Donne manuscript for this study, none so far seen shares exactly the same watermarks as those used by Jonson. The only holograph letter written by Donne that has been dated to 1609 is on a sheet of pot.[51]

Paper and handwriting are two quite independent and impartial witnesses to the history of the preparation of a document. Three acknowledged manuscripts in Jonson's hand written in close proximity to one another are also associated by common watermark evidence. When the paper is also used in the same unusual manner (folded as folio, rather than quarto, and cropped) as another manuscript to which it is in other ways related, it is a piece of evidence that is particularly compelling. In the one manuscript that was

---

50. Indicatively, Jonson signed p. xi 'A' and p. xv 'B'. Any other signatures were cropped.

51. Of the other most immediately pertinent material, there are ten letters, the Verse letter written to Sir Robert More on 28 July 1614, for instance, has a crowned eagle water- *Index of English Literary Manuscripts 1450–1625*, 2 vols. (London, 1980), I, 243–245; R. C. Bald, *Donne and the Drurys* (Cambridge, 1959), Appendix, 159–165, items 65, 69 and 71. The letter written to Sir Robert More on 28 July 1614, for instance, has a crowned eagle watermark with a crozier on its breast; that to William Trumbull on 10 September and to either Sir George or Sir Robert More on 3 December has a pot watermark with a half crescent and the initials 'PO'.

prepared as a presentation text, *The Masque of Queenes,* the paper was prepared in exactly the same manner. The conclusion is unavoidable. Jonson was responsible for preparing and copying the *Herbert* manuscript of *Biathanatos.* When *Herbert* is compared with all the available evidence, the euphemism of 'certain technical considerations' dissolves in its imprecision.

What we know of Donne and Jonson's biographies also reinforces the likelihood that Jonson prepared *Herbert* about the same time as he was working on the manuscript of *The Masque of Queenes.* Donne was on the Continent between November 1611 and August 1612, while Jonson travelled with Ralegh's son between the spring of 1612 and early 1613. They are unlikely, therefore, to have collaborated on *Herbert* while either was absent or when they were both in Europe. This suggests that the possible dates between which *Herbert* must have been prepared can not have been before late 1608 (when *Biathanatos* was first written by Donne) or after November 1611 (when Donne travelled overseas).[52] For other reasons, an undated letter to Sir Henry Goodyere, that is accepted as having been written in 1609, would also seem to confirm that *Herbert* was being prepared at that time.[53] The contextual evidence increases the certainty with which *Herbert* can be dated and, once again, the date that seems most plausible in 1609: paper, biography and correspondence coincide.

The most important issue, however, remains the cumulative evidence that Jonson prepared *Herbert*: the problem is not *if* he did so, it is *why*, and what his involvement might imply. In 1619, Donne famously commented to Sir Robert Ker that 'I have always gone so near supressing it [*Biathanatos*], as that it is onely not burnt: no hand hath passed upon it to copy it, nor many eyes to read it: onely to some particular friends in both Universities, then when I writ it, I did communicate it'.[54] In fact, as Peter Beal has recently shown, a second manuscript of *Biathanatos* survives.[55] Known as *Canterbury*, the manuscript is textually variant from both *Herbert* and the 1644 Quarto prepared by Donne's son. At best, then, Donne's comment to Ker is a little disingenuous.

Canterbury is also important for present purposes, because it contains a textual variant that casts some light on Jonson's involvement with *Herbert.* As Beal has shown, Jonson mis-read the name 'Hillel' and wrote 'stilled'; the same error was made in the 1644 Quarto. The scribe of *Canterbury*, however, understood the reference and copied Donne correctly.[56] The implication is that Jonson was copying from Donne's papers, and that Donne did not notice the error when adding his sidenotes and making corrections. It is clear that

<hr>

52. R. C. Bald, *John Donne: A Life* (Oxford, 1970), 201; J. Carey, *John Donne: Life, Mind and Art* (London, 1980), 204–209; Sullivan, *Biathanatos,* ix, xxxiii; Hill, 'John Donne's *Biathanatos*', 110.

53. Donne refers to Hugh Broughton's conversion to Rome. The letter is reproduced in E. M. Simpson et al. (eds.), *John Donne: Selected Prose* (Oxford, 1967), 130–133. See also, Sullivan, 'Genesis and Transmission', 53.

54. Simpson, *John Donne: Selected Prose,* 152.

55. Beal, *In Praise of Scribes,* 31–57.

56. Beal, *In Praise of Scribes,* 45–46.

they must have worked closely together. This is not, of course, to claim Jonson as an author, but rather as a collaborative participant in the creation of the text. It is not impossible that two friends would have discussed the issues as they worked together.

There are many reasons why Jonson might have helped Donne, from a wish to collaborate and a genuine interest on his part in the issues involved, to being paid in cash or kind (and the two are not mutually exclusive). The reason he prepared the manuscript is, of course, an ultimately insoluble problem, but it does indicate a serious ellipsis in our knowledge about Jonson and Donne. Rather than suppressing the connection, we need to recognise their close association with one another. It is not satisfactory to elide the space and construct a narrative that ignores the problem as has happened in the past. For, as Jeffrey Masten's work on textual collaboration makes clear, such co-operation between authors was habitual in the early modern period.[57] Evelyn Simpson's hesitations are understandable, but they also derived from a view of authorship that we now recognise to be too narrowly focused.

IV

That Jonson was involved in the preparation of *Biathanatos* indicates that we need to adjust our understanding of textual production in two ways. First, *Biathanatos* is deeply instructive as to how the preparation of a manuscript might be influenced by the culture of print, for the layout of the page indicates a consciousness about structure and design down to the use of running-titles and the creation of the preliminary matter. In this, Jonson departs from the traditional manuscript practices of the medieval period— he had been influenced by the printed books with which he was familiar. Similarly, the depth of the script on the page and the width of the line is typical of a quarto printed in great primer on large paper. The care with which the manuscript was produced, then, suggests that Jonson wished to create a document with the physical elegance of a private manuscript and the formal structure of a printed book. It is a visual essay on the way in which the variety of textual forms affect each other, and it reinforces the point that is implicit in both *The Masque of Queenes* and the 1616 *Workes* about the importance that Jonson attached to the visual structure of the page. Given that this is so, the cumulative evidence of *Biathanatos* and *The Masque of Queenes* must also oblige us to reconsider the typographic and literary authority of the 1616 *Workes* from a perspective that is deeply influenced by the social and personal networks of manuscript culture. For Jonson to have recorded on the title-page of his *Workes* that he was 'Contentus paucis lectoribus' is only the most obvious manifestation of these connections.

Second, we need to adjust our understanding about the circulation of manuscripts in the early modern period away from the author and back to the scribe, for one of the problems behind editing Jonson and Donne is identify-

---

57. J. Masten, *Textual Intercourse: Collaboration, Authorship, and Sexualities in Renaissance Drama* (Cambridge, 1997).

ing the person responsible for the scribal transcriptions, and their relationship with the author or patron involved. Equally, we need to understand, as
the first point also suggests, the complex social network behind the preparation of manuscripts and printed books. Sir Henry Spelman, for instance, was
closely associated with Camden, Selden and Cotton, and the fact that a manuscript that belonged to him, now in Cape Town, contains poems by Jonson,
Donne, Carew, Herrick and others, written in that part of the miscellany by
a single hand, is a matter that must receive closer attention than it has in the
past.[58]

The larger problem that the association with Donne and the redating of
the letter present is biographical. As the approximately three hundred surviving books from his library also testify, Jonson was not quite the person that
legend would have him be. It is not just his learning, friendships and character that have been mis-represented, or simply that his late plays are more
thoughtful and finer works of literature than their reputation might have
us believe. The fact that Simpson and Greg got Jonson's late handwriting
wrong, for instance, means that it is quite possible that there are yet other
autograph manuscripts by Jonson, written in the 1630s, that have not been
identified. Equally, Jonson's intellectual biography needs to be rewritten
from a perspective that also includes such associative manuscript activity as
his marginalia. If a copy of Martial had been owned and as heavily annotated
by Shakespeare as the 1615 and 1619 editions once owned by Jonson are, they
would have long ago been photographically reproduced, edited and inten-
sively studied.[59] Similarly, Jonson's marginalia in his copy of Francisco
Modio's *Pandectae Triumphales* have only ever been briefly discussed, and it

58. L. F. Casson, 'The Manuscripts of the Grey Collection in Cape Town', *The Book
Collector*, 10 (1961) 154–155; Beal, *Index of English Literary Manuscripts 1475–1625*, I, 257
(Δ60), MS Grey 7 a 29. See also, M. Hobbs, 'Early Seventeenth-Century Verse Miscellanies and
Their Value for Textual Editors', *English Manuscript Studies 1100–1700*, 1 (1989), 182–210;
S. W. May, 'Manuscript Circulation at the Elizabethan Court', *New Ways of Looking at Old
Texts*, 273–280; E. Doughtie, 'John Ramsey's Manuscript as a Personal and Family Docu-
ment', *New Ways of Looking at Old Texts*, 281–288; Sullivan, 'The Renaissance Manuscript
Verse Miscellany', *New Ways of Looking at Old Texts*, 289–297. Although he is not present
in the Dalhousie Manuscript, discussed by Sullivan, Jonson is closely associated with all the
other participants: perhaps this is the reason for Sullivan's slip when he suggests that it was
Jonson who altered line 8 of Wotton's poem (written c. 1638) in deference to the religious
sensibilities of Digby and others (297). See also, M. H. Butler, 'Sir Francis Stewart: Jonson's
Overlooked Patron', *Ben Jonson Journal*, 2 (1995), 101–127. As well as the dedication of
Farnaby's Lucan to Stuart (107), Farnaby also gave copies to Jonson (Bodleian Arch. H.f.27)
and John Wilson (St. Paul's School, London). This links Wilson, who was headmaster of
Westminster, into this circle: Jonson's large-paper gift copy of his *Workes* to Wilson is now
in the Pierpont Morgan Library, shelfmark 16254/W4D, his large-paper gift copy to Farnaby
is now in Japan.

59. Both are now at the Folger Shakespeare Library: STC 17492 Copy 1, and PA 6501
A2 1619 Cage. Three studies of Jonson's marginalia have recently appeared: R. C. Evans,
Habits of Mind: Evidence and Effects of Ben Jonson's Reading (Lewisburg, Penn., 1995); J. A.
Riddell and S. Stewart, *Jonson's Spenser: Evidence and Historical Criticism* (Pittsburgh,
1995); A. L. Prescott, 'Jonson's Rabelais', *New Perspectives on Ben Jonson*, ed. J. Hirsh
(Madison, N.J., 1997), 35–54.

remains generally unknown as a witness to his work as a writer of masques.[60] The point could be expanded by further reference to the marginalia (both verbal and non-verbal markings) in such unrecorded books from Jonson's library as Viperano's *De Obtenta Portugalia*, Brisson's *De Formulis et Sollemnibus* (an important source for *Sejanus*) or the *De Re Culinaria* of Apicius.[61] The importance of this material is not confined to the ways in which it might be incorporated into any future edition of Jonson but, also, the way in which it documents the history of Jonson's reading practices and the development of his ideas.[62]

This awareness of the connections between people and manuscripts, books and readers, must also, in the end, be the point behind the creation of an archive of digital images intended to complement the literary texts that we are now creating in electronic form. Editing in this way is both a fashionable and inevitable consequence of computerisation, and the implications that it will have for textual scholarship are only beginning to be appreciated.[63] As Jerome McGann has observed, the problems associated with the physical form of the codex 'grow more acute when readers want or need something beyond the semantic content of the primary textual materials'.[64] Indeed, as McGann recognised, the most primary images 'beyond' the semantic field of words are the historical documents, not only because 'the book's (heretofore distributed) semantic and visual features can be made present to each other' but also 'since all [the] separate books and documents can also be made simultaneously present to each other, as well as all the parts of the documents'.[65]

The dates and attributions that have been made in this study for the letter to Sir Robert Cotton, *Herbert* and the Ellesmere Manuscript illustrate in their respective ways the care that must be taken both in preserving access to the primary materials (in order to ensure that such research is possible) and in

60. Clare College, Cambridge, H.4.5. See also, D. C. McPherson, 'Ben Jonson's Library and Marginalia', 71–72.

61. Respectively: Cambridge University Library, M*.10.28[2] (noticed in passing by McPherson as bound with another book of Jonson's, but not recorded by him despite the evidence of the contemporary vellum binding typical of Jonson's books, his writing on the spine and his marginalia in the text), Emmanuel College, Cambridge, S5.2.41, and British Library, 453 d.26.

62. Also, N. J. Barker, 'Manuscript into Print', *Crisis in Editing: Texts of the English Renaissance*, ed. R. McLeod (New York, 1994), 1–19; A. F. Marotti, 'Malleable and Fixed Texts: Manuscript and Printed Miscellanies and the Transmission of Lyric Poetry in the English Renaissance', *New Ways of Looking at Old Texts*, 159–173; B. M. Rosenthal, *The Rosenthal Collection of Printed Books with Manuscript Annotations* (New Haven, 1997).

63. For instance: McKenzie, *Bibliography and the Sociology of Texts*, 60–61; J. J. McGann, 'The Rationale of HyperText', *Text*, 9 (1996), 11–32; W. Chernaik, C. Davis and M. Deegan (eds.), *The Politics of the Electronic Text* (Oxford: Office for Humanities Communication, 1993); W. Chernaik, M. Deegan and A. Gibson (eds.), *Beyond the Book: Theory, Culture, and the Politics of Cyberspace* (Oxford: OHC, 1996). On the implications of electronic archives as a form of non-reading: D. F. McKenzie, 'Computers and the Humanities: A Personal Synthesis of Conference Issues', *Scholarship and Technology in the Humanities: Proceedings of a Conference Held at Elvetham Hall, Hampshire, UK., 9th–12th May 1990*, ed. M. Katzen (London, 1991), 157–169.

64. McGann, 'The Rationale of HyperText', 13.

65. McGann, 'The Rationale of HyperText', 14.

considering all the evidence before representing early modern texts in a visual medium. The real issue, however, is that any archive that is too narrowly conceived around a single author (particularly in the early modern period where the evidence is usually more diffuse) will, finally, be merely illustrative. This is not to deny the author, but to suggest that a sociology of texts requires that we recover, in far greater complexity, the communities of interest that link these documents together.

To some, this may seem deeply unfair, but the simple truth is that the textual problems created by collaboration and association will not go away. Whether it be in the association of writers, the typographic or calligraphic design of the page, the physical materials that are used, the activities of those involved in the production of textual material, or the history of the preliminary documents (personal papers, printer's copy, typescript) prior to a completed version, the composition of the elements, the choices involved, the adaptions and alterations made, will all reveal the history of the use of the intellect. To read the surface of a text without recognising its historical significance as a document is to reduce language to a historical abstraction that is separated from the socio-cultural and physical constructions of its meaning.

Indeed, simply to assume that the reproduction of an original document in codex or digital form is satisfactory as a representation of historical understanding and that it absolves an editor from further responsibility in that regard is a fallacy that the work of McKenzie, McGann and others long ago exposed. As Hugh Amory observed: 'The issues are not merely theoretical: every question about the author's intention involves a question about the intentions of the editors, correctors, compositors and printers, who are also his or her earliest readers' and, one must also add, the same is true of scribal copyists.[66] The facsimile serves a useful purpose, but its representation is not the same as an appreciation of the processes that create such a document, the compromises that may have been involved, or the uses to which it was put. The facsimile (at one remove) makes rare documents accessible. The editorial problem, however, is not only to understand what those documents represent and what they mean, but what they do not record. This is, ultimately, the justification for historically edited texts. It is not only that modern spelling is a historically constructed concept that is both anachronistic and under pressure from popular culture, though that is undoubtedly true. Old spelling registers, in all and in the most simple of ways, the difference (*difference* and *différance*) of early modern texts, and the fact that they are not of this historical moment—with all that implies about marriage, gender, cultural materialism, power, privilege and the other multitudinous interests that we wish to explore. 'The claim . . . is no longer for their truth, as one might seek to define that by authorial intention, but for their testimony, as defined by their historical use'.[67]

Further, we need to appreciate that the study of the associations and contexts involved in the production, transmission and reception of texts does not,

---

66. H. Amory, Review of 'The Life and Work of Fredson Bowers', *Text*, 9 (1996), 471.
67. McKenzie, *Bibliography and the Sociology of Texts*, 20.

in the end, lead to greater confusion of information but to a greater clarity
as connections are made and historical issues resolved. It may be, for instance,
a laborious and difficult task to recognise the same hand and common sources
of paper in the documents of different authors, but the results of such work
have profoundly enriched our understanding of the social and personal networks that link the circulation of texts in early modern England. As contemporaries, as friends, as the finest verse poets of their generation, Jonson
and Donne are linked in manuscript after manuscript, and it is only by drawing the thread through this material that we will ever supersede the Herford
and Simpson edition. Just as Donne and Jonson collaborated on a manuscript
of *Biathanatos,* so too must Jonson and Donne scholars collaborate both in
the creation of new scholarly resources and in the resolution of common
textual problems. Rare poems ask rare friends.[68]

68. I would like to thank Lois Potter, Kristen Poole, Julian Yates and the English seminar at the University of Delaware to whom I presented an earlier version of this paper, and
also Jim Riddell, Robert Pirie, Stephen Orgel, Barbara Mowat, David Vander Meulen, Don
McKenzie, Jeff Masten, Nicolas Kiessling, David Kastan, Speed Hill, David Gants, Arthur
Freeman, Ian Donaldson, David Bevington and Peter Beal for their interest and their
comments. I would also particularly like to thank Ian Gadd for consulting material on my
behalf in Oxford and London.

'OF WHICH BEING PUBLICK THE PUBLICK JUDGE': POPE AND THE PUBLICATION OF *VERSES ADDRESS'D TO THE IMITATOR OF HORACE*

by

James McLaverty

ONE of the unsolved riddles of Pope's literary career is the appearance on the same day, 8 March 1733, of two different versions of an attack on his writing, family, person, and morals: *Verses Address'd to the Imitator of the First Satire of the Second Book of Horace* and *To the Imitator of the Satire of the Second Book of Horace*. Both the authorship of the poem and the sources of the dual publication are shrouded in mystery. While one version advertised itself as 'By a Lady' (generally identified as Lady Mary Wortley Montagu), the other version did not, and it is known to have been revised subsequently by a gentleman (Lord Hervey). Advertisements for the two versions appeared on the very same day; the imprints carried the names only of a publisher (James Roberts) or a mercury (Anne Dodd); the versions differed widely in accidentals, though not in substantives; and both at subsequent points in their advertising campaigns criticized the other as a piracy. Paradoxically, publication of this most vicious of personal attacks suited Pope. His chief concern at the time was with the poem's manuscript publication, particularly at Court, and the damage it might do to his standing there; he had already been under pressure to withdraw his criticism of Lady Mary in the imitation of the *First Satire* as a sign of his loyalty to the King and Queen. Print publication of the attack on the imitator let him off the hook and gave him the chance to reply. The consequent controversy not only excused him from moderating his attacks on Lady Mary; it provided a justification for publishing the *Epistle to Arbuthnot*, focusing an anti-court, oppositional stance, and it gave an impetus to the publication of his *Works* and *Letters* in 1735. Immediately, it had the benefit of distracting attention from his relation to the simultaneously published *Essay on Man*. In an excellent account of the controversy surrounding the satire on the imitator of Horace, Professor Isobel Grundy wrote, 'The versions which were printed may have been authorized by him [Lord Hervey], by Lady Mary, by both, or by neither.'[1] My aim in this paper is to examine the variant editions of the

---

1. Grundy, '*Verses Address'd to the Imitator of Horace*: A Skirmish between Pope and Some Persons of Rank and Fortune', *Studies in Bibliography*, 30 (1977), 96–119. Further valuable material is to be found in Robert Halsband and Isobel Grundy's edition of Lady Mary's *Essays and Poems and Simplicity, A Comedy* (1979); in Professor Grundy's thesis, 'The Verse of Lady Mary Wortley Montagu: A Critical Edition', (D. Phil., University of Oxford, 1971); in Rosemary Cowler's edition of *The Prose Works of Alexander Pope*, II (1986), pp. 431–498; in Maynard Mack, *Alexander Pope: A Life* (1985), pp. 554–562; and in J. V. Gueri-

attack and their context, and to venture a new hypothesis: that the instigator of publication was the imitator, Alexander Pope himself. It was probably in 1733 that Pope had a four-volume collection of pamphlet attacks bound, introducing them with a quotation from Job 31.35: 'Behold it is my desire, that mine Adversary had written a Book. Surely I would take it on my shoulder, and bind it as a crown unto me.' By publishing *Verses Address'd to the Imitator* and replying in the *Epistle to Dr. Arbuthnot*, he would have realized this desire.[2]

There are three figures involved in discussions of the authorship of the poem, Lady Mary Wortley Montagu, Lord Hervey, and William Wyndham, and the current consensus is that all three probably had a hand in it, with the major role being played by Lady Mary and Lord Hervey. The occasion for the attacks, as the titles for the different versions imply, came in Pope's *Imitation of the First Satire of the Second Book of Horace*, published on 15 February. Lord Hervey was given a glancing blow in the first paragraph:

> The Lines are weak, another's pleas'd to say,
> Lord *Fanny* spins a thousand such a day. (lines 5–6)

Lady Mary was more plainly insulted later on:

> Slander or Poyson, dread from *Delia's* Rage,
> Hard Words or Hanging, if your Judge be *Page*.
> From furious *Sappho* scarce a milder Fate,
> P—x'd by her Love, or libell'd by her Hate. (lines 81–84)[3]

Sappho was readily identified by contemporaries as Lady Mary, while Delia was taken as a reference to Lady Deloraine, later to become William Wyndham's wife. Two of the four contemporary manuscript copies of the consequent attack on Pope, at Oxford and in the Portland papers, assigned the poem to Lady Mary, but in the British Library there is a scribal copy which Lord Hervey has revised, and at Ickworth a copy of *To the Imitator of the Second Satire of Horace* which Hervey has prepared for a second edition, with a draft preface and a draft title-page including the words 'Publish'd by the Author'.[4] The evidence for William Wyndham's involvement comes from

<hr>

not, *Pamphlet Attacks on Alexander Pope* (1969), pp. 224–226. David Foxon provides a characteristically thorough account of the editions in *English Verse 1701–1750*, 2 vols (1975), V39–41, V44, V46.

2. The octavo volumes, which once belonged to J. W. Croker, are now BL C.116.b.1–4; they do not include either of the attacks on the imitator of Horace. Pope's fly-leaf inscription is quoted by Maynard Mack in *Collected in Himself* (1982), pp. 395–396, and by Guerinot, p. li. The attacks range in date from 1711 to May 1733, and some provided material for *The Dunciad*. It is unclear why the collection stops in 1733. It is certainly possible that the publication of *Verses* crystallized and realized a long-term project.

3. Quotations are from the *Twickenham Edition of the Poems of Alexander Pope*, IV, ed. John Butt, 2nd edn (1953).

4. An account of the four manuscripts and of Hervey's papers is to be found in Professor Grundy's thesis, pp. 513–514. The four manuscripts are BL Add. MS 35335, ff. 53–54 (annotated by Hervey), BL Add. MS 31152, ff. 25–26, Bodley MS Eng. Misc. 399, ff. 76–77, Longleat, Portland MS xix, ff. 149–150. Of these, the first and last generally agree with *To*

an annotation by the second Earl of Oxford on his copy, 'The Authors of this poem are Lady Mary Wortley Lord Harvey & Mr Windham under tutor to the Duke of Cumberland and married to my Lady Deloraine', while Maynard Mack has identified a likely reference to Wyndham's involvement in a couplet in *To Arbuthnot*:

> To please a *Mistress*, One aspers'd his life;
> He lash'd him not, but let her be his Wife. (lines 376–377)[5]

The most important statement about authorship—the only statement by a principal, other than by Pope himself—comes from Lady Mary Wortley Montagu. Lady Mary denied writing the poem in a letter to Dr. Arbuthnot concerning the references to Sappho in *To Arbuthnot*. Sherburn assigns the letter to the day after the poem's publication on 2 January 1735:

> I cannot help taking Notice of the terrible malice he bears against the Lady signify'd by that name, which appears to be irritated by supposing her writer of the verses to the Imitator of Horace, now I can assure him they were wrote (without my knowledge) by a Gentleman of great merit, whom I very much esteem, who he will never guess, & who, if he did know he durst not attack; but I own the design was so well meant, & so excellently executed that I cannot be sorry they were written ... I desire Sir as a favour that you would shew this Letter to Pope...[6]

The letter is unlikely to be an instance of plain lying; there is no motive for a lie. Lady Mary shows no anxiety to appease Pope—she sharply criticizes him for attacking the dead James Moore Smythe and claims that Congreve ridiculed his wit and conversation—her aim is to damage his position, not to escape censure. The disclaimer of authorship is either truthful or equivocal, alluding to the truth with sufficient disguise to mislead Pope.[7] It follows that

---

the Imitator, the third agrees with the *Verses* but lacks the couplet added in the revised edition, and the second is intermediate. But none of these manuscripts is an autograph and their authority is uncertain.

5. See, for a general account of Lady Mary and Lord Hervey in this context, Grundy, '*Verses Address'd to the Imitator of Horace*'; for Oxford's note, my 'Pope in the Private and Public Spheres: Annotations in the Second Earl of Oxford's Volume of Folio Poems, 1731–1735', *SB*, 48 (1995), 33–59 (49–50 and 55); and, for the Wyndham couplet, Mack, 'A Couplet in the *Epistle to Dr. Arbuthnot*', *TLS*, 2 September 1939, p. 515. Wyndham is probably referred to as 'W——m' in 'Letter to a Noble Lord', *Prose Works*, II, 452.

6. *The Correspondence of Alexander Pope*, ed. George Sherburn, 5 vols (1956), III, 448–449.

7. Habits of equivocation, at least as practised by Pope, seem not generally understood. For example, when Pope says, 'I can truly affirm, that, ever since I lost the happiness of your conversation I have not published or written, one syllable of, or to either of you; never hitch'd your *names* in a *Verse*, or trifled with your *good names* in *company*' ('Letter to a Noble Lord', *Prose Works*, II, 445), he is exploiting the gap between reference and naming. An attack that does not name its victim but refers to him or her only by a nickname or an attribute is open to various interpretation; it can be denied, and Pope often offers such a denial. Hervey focuses on this issue in his draft preface to *To the Imitator*. The play is not always on the indeterminacy of reference. When the Advertisement to the *Dunciad Variorum* says the commentary 'was sent me from several hands, and consequently must be unequally written' (1729, 4°, p. 3), I suspect Pope is equivocating on a basis Lady Mary may be using in her letter.

the 'Gentleman of great merit' is either Lord Hervey or William Wyndham. Wyndham might be said to have written the verses in the sense that he physically wrote them down or transcribed them; he may, for example, have pieced together fragments from others while adding ideas of his own. But as under-tutor to the Duke of Cumberland, Wyndham was hardly an important figure who was likely to intimidate Pope. Hervey, on the other hand, came from a powerful family and had influence at court, especially with the Queen. The papers in the British Library and at Ickworth show him taking a proprietorial interest in the poem. He alone could be the sole author of the attack on the imitator; the others could only have been co-authors or amanuenses. Lady Mary's claim that Pope 'durst not attack' him reads oddly in the light of the violent denunciation of Sporus in *To Arbuthnot*, but perhaps she failed to recognise Hervey under this name or was challenging Pope to a more open encounter. This paper does not claim to dispel the mystery surrounding the authorship of the attack on Pope as the imitator of Horace, but it is sympathetic to the simplicity of believing Lord Hervey when he says he wrote the attack ('Publish'd by the Author') and believing Lady Mary when she says she did not. Discussion of the authorship and publication of the poem should proceed by subjecting the statement on the title page of the *Verses,* 'By a Lady', to a sharp and salutary scepticism.[8]

Both versions of the poem were strongly advertised. The version I shall refer to as *Verses* was advertised in both the *London Evening-Post* and the *Daily Post* for 8 March:

> *This Day is publish'd, Price* 6d.
> *(Being the same Size with the Dialogue)*
> Verses address'd to the Imitator of the first Satire of the Second Book of Horace.
> By a LADY of QUALITY.
> Printed for A. Dodd without Temple-Bar, and sold at all the Pamphlet-shops in Town.
> *(London Evening-Post)*

The *Whitehall Evening-Post* for the same day advertised its rival, which I shall call *To the Imitator*:

> To the IMITATOR of the SATIRE of the Second Book of Horace.
> Printed for J. Roberts near the Oxford Arms in Warwick Lane.

On the following day, 9 March, the advertisement for the *Verses* appeared in slightly different form in the *Daily Post,* saying more explicitly, '*(Being very proper to be bound up with Mr. Pope's* Dialogue with his Council)', while the advertisement for *To the Imitator* appeared there for the first time. 9 March is the date assigned for publication of the *Verses* by the *Grub-Street Journal* in its list of 'Books and Pamphlets published since Mar. 8' on 29 March. Interestingly, it has the *Verses* right next to 'An essay on man:

---

8. Discussions of authorship based on style are inconclusive. In his *The Life of Lady Mary Wortley Montagu* (1956), pp. 141–144, Robert Halsband gives the major role to Lady Mary, but Isobel Grundy's subtle and sophisticated discussion in her thesis, unfortunately unpublished, finds important elements of Hervey's style present ("The Verse of Lady Mary Wortley Montagu', p. 512).

Part I. a poem'. Advertisements for the *Essay on Man*, Part I appeared as early as 20 February, but there was fresh advertising for it on 9 March, which coincided with Pope's first mentioning it slyly in his correspondence. The *Essay* was entered in the Stationers' Register on 10 March, and, as entry was not efficacious if the work was already published, it seems likely that was the intended day of official publication. The contiguity of the *Essay* and the *Verses* in the *Grubstreet Journal* may be significant: two Popeian campaigns marching in step, the Horatian controversy leaving the *Essay on Man* free to enjoy the impartial reception its anonymity invited.[9] On 10 March, two days after the first advertisement, a publisher's war was declared in the *London Evening-Post*. After an advertisement for the *Verses* on the same lines as the previous day's in the *Daily Post*, the notice continued:

N.B. The publick are desired to observe the VERSES has the ABOVE TITLE; and the Words, *By a Lady*, and printed for A. Dodd, be in the Title Page; for there is a *spurious* and *piratical Edition* of these VERSES abroad, printed from a very bad Copy.

An advertisement for *To the Imitator* appears in the same paper. The publishers of *To the Imitator* retaliated the following day in the *Whitehall Evening Post*, adding to the customary advertisement, 'This being the Genuine and Correct Edition, is in Three Sheets'.

The next stage in the advertising campaign came with a new edition of the *Verses*. The advertisement in the *London Evening-Post* for 20 March turns technical on the matter of compatibility with Pope's *Dialogue*, saying the *Verses* are proper to be 'stitch'd up' with it; it adds the motto, '*Si Natura negat, facit Indignatio Versus*. JUV.'; and it adds a new paragraph:

In that *spurious* Edition in three sheets (one of which is only the Title) the MOTTO, and one whole COUPLET in Page 5, are omitted; besides many notorious Blunders, and literal Errors.

The claim is cheeky, for the *Verses* had not itself included this material in its previous existence. The *London Evening-Post* of 27 March completes this stage of the campaign by changing the grammar of the 'N.B.' section of the advertisement for the *Verses*. They now 'have' the above title, and the subjunctive disappears: the words 'By a Lady' 'are' in the title page. There was also a coda. After the publication of *To Arbuthnot* early in 1735, advertisements for a fifth edition of the *Verses* appeared in the *London Evening-Post* from 16 to 23 January, quoting Pope's Advertisement to that poem and recommending the poems for binding together.

A general view of the advertising campaign highlights several features. The leading role was played by the *Verses*: there were more advertisements for this version, and they went on longer; the *Verses* advertisements initiated

9. Lawton Gilliver, who played a leading role in the *Grubstreet Journal*, had inside knowledge of Pope's intrigues in this period, including his authorship of the *Essay on Man*. John Huggonson, who printed Part I of the *Essay*, started printing the *Journal* in October 1733, taking over from Sam Aris, who printed Part III. See my 'Lawton Gilliver: Pope's Bookseller', *SB*, 32 (1979), 101–124.

the quarrel over authenticity and counter-attacked when those for *To the Imitator* replied; the *Verses* were advertised again in 1735.[10] Whereas the advertisements for *To the Imitator* are neutral, those for the *Verses* have their preoccupations, and even a sense of humour. There is an insistence on the Lady's authorship, with the first advertisement particularly emphatic about her status ('By a LADY of QUALITY') and a later advertisement insisting that the words 'By a Lady' are a sign of the legitimate edition. There is a recurrent concern with the binding of the poem with Pope's works, the *First Epistle of the Second Book of Horace* and then *To Arbuthnot*. The *Verses'* advertisements give the title of Pope's imitation in full and in brackets as the sub-title, a 'Dialogue'. There is also an unusually detailed interest in the text: in the additional couplet in the second edition and in Pope's advertisement to *To Arbuthnot*. Finally, it should be emphasized that such campaigns are rare. There is nothing else at all like it in the newspapers of this immediate period, but we do find advertising controversy again later in the year when Hervey published his further attack on Pope, *An Epistle from a Nobleman*, and Pope's advertisements for his *Letters* in 1735 are very lively in their denunciations of Curll.[11]

There are three established explanations for the double publication of this poem: that one is a piracy of the other; that one is published by Lady Mary and one by Lord Hervey; that one or both are simply the consequence of a bookseller's illicitly obtaining copy. To these I wish to add a fourth: that Pope himself was responsible for the *Verses* edition.

The idea that one of the versions was a piracy of the other is a common explanation of the double publication, but it does not gain support from examination of the editions themselves. *To the Imitator* has been branded a piracy, perhaps because its advertisement appeared in the *Daily Post* on 9 March rather than 8 March like that for the *Verses*, though it was itself advertised in the *Whitehall Evening-Post* on the 8 March.[12] A good reply to this charge, however, is to be found in *To the Imitator*'s advertised response, 'This being the Genuine and Correct Edition, is in Three Sheets'. The scornful reply from the *Verses*, that one sheet is taken up with the title, deliberately misses the point. The *Verses* takes two sheets only: it is unlikely that anyone copying it would waste money on an extra sheet of paper; the cost of paper was around half the expense of printing a book. A pirate would generally

10. Professor Grundy made an admirable survey of the advertisements. Without making an exhaustive search, I have noted the following advertisements. *Verses: London Evening-Post* 8, 10, 13, 15, 20, 22, 27, 29 March 1733, 16, 18, 21, 23 January 1735; *Daily Post* 8, 9 March 1733; *Daily Post-Boy* 9 March 1733; *St. James's Evening-Post* 10, 13 March 1733. *To the Imitator: Whitehall Evening-Post* 8, 13 March; *Daily Post* 9, 12 March; *London Evening-Post* 10, 13 March; *Daily Post-Boy* 9 March; *Daily Journal* 9, 12 March.

11. See Reginald Harvey Griffith, *Alexander Pope: A Bibliography*, 2 vols (1922–27), II, 300.

12. R. W. Rogers seems the first modern writer to say it is a piracy, in *The Major Satires of Alexander Pope* (1955), p. 143; J. V. Guerinot agrees, pp. 224–226; and so does Rosemary Cowler, *Prose Works*, II, 465.

aim to print more cheaply than the original.[13] The argument applies only slightly less powerfully in the case where a bookseller has got hold of a manuscript without any right to the copy: half-titles and pages with a small number of lines are usually for demanding authors or booksellers supplying the smart end of the trade; they are not for pirates. *To the Imitator* is attractively printed, on good paper, in sum, a quality product. There is also the evidence that Lord Hervey revised *To the Imitator* for a second edition, which implicates him in the original publication. Hervey prepared a copy of this Roberts version for a second edition, with a preface and a draft title-page reading 'the second Edition corrected by the Author'. His papers also contain revisions to the printed copy of *An Epistle from a Nobleman*, his attack on Pope later that year, and a copy of *An Elegy to a Young Lady . . . With an Answer* (1733). These are all the work of Roberts and a printer I shall refer to as the 'fruit basket' printer, and this is as strong evidence as one is likely to find that these publications were authorized by Hervey himself.[14]

The *Verses*, which is crammed into two sheets, cannot mount so straightforward a defence against a charge of piracy, but examination of the printer's changes shows an equivalent care for presentation. As David Foxon points out in *English Verse 1701–1750*, there are three interestingly different versions of *Verses* in 1733. V39 is the first edition; in the second edition or variant state, V40, 'Apparently sheet A and outer forme of B are reset', while V41 is 'Largely reset and corrected'. V41 is used as copy text in the Halsband and Grundy edition; it has the motto and the additional couplet referred to in the *Verses* advertisements. The reason for the revision to produce V41 is, therefore, clear, but why the revisions for V40? I suspect the purpose of V40 was to correct incompetent setting, quite possibly by an apprentice. The main problem is spacing between words, which is inadequate, though there are other mistakes, like the full-stop in the dropped head which does not sit correctly on the line and the failure to capitalize 'Distinction' on page 4, a feature noted by Mr. Foxon. The eccentricity of spacing is pervasive, but striking examples are to be found on page 3, line 4 'modernScandal', line 5, 'oneside', 'how*Horace*', line 10 '*Greek*hedid', and page 4, line 7 'rail,or'. Close

---

13. A good example of such costs is James Watson's piracy of Pope's letters. Maynard Mack includes much information in his transcription of documents from the legal case, but the clearest figures are the 9d. that Watson thinks represents his cost per book, and the cost of paper for 1600 copies, £30 12 0, which amounts to 4.59d. per book (*Collected in Himself* [1982], pp. 498 [letter 17] and 497 [letter 13]). In a survey of unauthorized printings of the *Dunciad*, David L. Vander Meulen demonstrates a general concern to publish cheaply, often in smaller formats, but some willingness to spend money on paper and illustrations in order to produce competitive products; see 'Unauthorized Editions of Pope's *Dunciad*, 1728–1751', in *Writers, Books, and Trade*, ed. O M Brack (1994), pp. 221–242.

14. Though Halsband, who records the information about Hervey's copy of the *Epistle*, would disagree (*Lord Hervey* [1973], p. 163). Professor Grundy gives transcriptions of Hervey's preface and title-page in her thesis, "The Verse of Lady Mary Wortley Montagu", pp. 514–516.

examination of damaged types shows resetting to have followed the pattern suggested by Mr. Foxon. V40 may well be a consequence of stop-press correction: someone noticed what the incompetent compositor was doing and tried to put it right.[15] Both formes of sheet A were corrected, but only page 8, the last, of the outer forme of B. Subsequently, when the addition of the extra couplet for V41 necessitated the moving round of text, complementary changes were made: the inner forme of A, which began the text, was again reset, but page 4 of the outer forme, which had been corrected, retained much of its old type; page 5 of the outer forme of B, which had not been reset, now was, but pages 6 and 7, the inner forme of B, remained largely the same, in spite of the shift in type to accommodate the new couplet on page 5. Ironically, the apprentice seems to have been at work again on page 5, with bad spacing and a turned elision mark in 'belov'd' in line 18.[16] The impression given by this examination of the three 1733 versions of the *Verses*, therefore, is of care for correct and elegant printing, even though the original execution may have been inadequate. Of course, the new material for V41 is evidence of some form of authoritative intervention, but, even without it, the concern for correctness is at odds with a piratical job.

That neither version is a direct copy of the other is also evident from collation. Dr. Grundy notes in her edition that there are only four verbal variants in the text and one in the title. This represents a strong correspondence between them, but it obscures the large degree of accidental variation. I have recorded 103 variants in all. Spelling and elision variations are probably most interesting (*Verses'* reading first): stripe'd/strip'd, Copist/Copyst, shou'd/should [consistently], heav'n/Heaven, drawst/draw'st, Carcass/Carcase, rancorous/rancrous, Dullness/Dulness, Out-cast/Outcast, hate'st/hat'st. There are many variations in punctuation and some in typography. An interesting example of the latter is the inclination to greater italic in *To the Imitator*, including '*Human Kind*' (line 33) and '*beware your Head*' (line 59), where the italic seems to have rhetorical purpose. These variations are not likely to have been made by a compositor working from printed copy. The necessary conclusion is that these editions were prepared from different, good quality, manuscript transcriptions.

The second possible explanation for the two versions is one put forward briefly and tentatively by David Foxon: that Lady Mary was responsible for one version, the *Verses*, and Lord Hervey for another. This is a plausible explanation and the difficulties for it arise only from the identification of the author of the *Verses* as 'a Lady' and its relation to Lady Mary's usual publishing practice—or non-practice. As we have seen, she denied 'writing'

---

15. His name may have been John Bateman. See *Stationers' Company Apprentices 1701–1800*, ed. D. F. McKenzie, Oxford Bibliographical Society, n.s. 19 (1978), p. 387, for his binding on 5 December 1732. In representing his work I have exaggerated the deficiencies by completely closing spaces that are inadequate in the printed text.

16. The examination of the type would have been facilitated by use of a Hinman collator, but the Bodleian Library's Hinman collator is no longer available and my eyesight is inadequate to the British Library collator.

the *Verses* in a letter to Arbuthnot, and she would have been affronted by the charge that she had published them. Isobel Grundy explains, 'As a woman and an aristocrat, Lady Mary frequently expressed horror at the idea of writing for print' (*Essays and Poems*, p. 172). The nub of the question is not whether she could have published them but whether in doing so she would have identified herself by putting 'By a Lady' on the title page. The vital role of these words in identifying her should not be overlooked: the lady could have been no one else, and it is questionable whether without this title-page Lady Mary would have been identified as the author at all. Advertisements for the *Verses* consistently emphasize that they are 'By a LADY of QUALITY' or 'By a LADY'; the public are advised that they should look for these words as a sign of authenticity. But in relation to the poem, with its often crude attack, this generic identification of the author can ring ironically:

> If none with Vengeance yet thy Crimes pursue,
> Or give thy manifold Affronts their due;
> If Limbs unbroken, Skin without a Stain,
> Unwhipt, unblanketed, unkick'd, unslain;
> That wretched little Carcass you retain:
> The Reason is, not that the World wants Eyes;
> But thou'rt so mean, they see, and they despise. (lines 66–72)

This is not a ladylike stance (whether it is characteristic of actual eighteenth-century ladies is beside the point), as contemporary responses, like that in *A Proper Reply to a Lady* by 'a Gentleman', point out:

> *Sappho* alone cou'd take the base Pretence
> To frame this vulgar virulent Defence,
> And vent rank Wit at Modesty's Expence. (lines 5–7)

Pope himself in the 'Letter to a Noble Lord' of November 1733 picks up the contrast between status and stance, saying, 'I am no man of Quality', and adding that Curll is capable of the same insults as one of Hervey's 'rank and quality' (*Prose Works*, II, 449). Later, in the advertisement of *To Arbuthnot*, he suggests that the reflections on the imitator of Horace are unworthy of persons of 'Rank and Fortune'. In this context 'By a Lady' is hardly a neutral designation; it exposes the writer to ridicule.

The best evidence for Lady Mary's involvement in publication of the *Verses* lies in the changes made for V41, which suggest something like authorial involvement. There are two major alterations. The first is the motto added to the title-page: 'Si Natura negat, facit Indignatio versus. JUVENAL'. This, however, has an immediate business consequence, and, I suspect, purpose, because 'versus' seems to confirm that this edition, the *Verses*, rather than *To the Imitator*, is the authentic one. The tag is famous, except that Juvenal writes 'versum'. 'If nature fails, then indignation generates verse', Niall Rudd translates, adding the following line, 'doing the best it can, like mine or like Cluvenius' '.[17] Swift remarks on the *Verses*' use of the motto in

___

17. *Juvenal: The Satires*, trans. Niall Rudd, intro. William Bar (1991), p. 5.

a letter to Pope, who has drawn the controversy to his attention, saying that
it is inappropriate to resentment of personal injury (*Correspondence*, III,
368). The line is self-deprecating. The implication—that the writer is not
gifted enough to compose ordinarily—is modestly amusing in the mouth of
Juvenal or Swift or Pope; but in the mouths of Lord Hervey and Lady Mary
it comes uncomfortably close to the truth. The second major change is the
additional couplet:

> Nor Dignity nor Innocence is spar'd,
> Nor Age, nor Sex, nor Thrones, nor Graves rever'd. (lines 38–39)

The reference to 'Thrones' introduces the political dimension that so worried
Pope and helped prepare his reply in *To Arbuthnot*. Lord Hervey adds the
couplet to his copy of *To the Imitator* in preparing a new edition of the
poem; it is present in three of the four surviving manuscripts. This could be
a later thought by Lady Mary, or it might simply have been omitted from
some manuscript copies. Some further small changes may be due to the
compositor: two semi-colons for colons (though another seems to have fallen
off in the rearrangement), and even 'Copi'st', the best either edition has
managed in negotiating the historical change from 'copist' to 'copyist'. Two
other developments, however, seem purposive. The porcupine compared
with Pope is made singular and its back now 'shoots' (ll. 73–74), while in the
penultimate line of the poem a semi-colon is restored. The first version
ended:

> And with the Emblem of thy crooked Mind,
> Mark'd on thy Back, like *Cain*, by God's own Hand;
> Wander like him, accursed through the Land.

V40 changed this, for good grammatical reasons no doubt, to 'Hand,', but
V41 restores the powerful rhetorical pause before the final line. These alterations are the most perplexing in the history of the *Verses*. Someone was taking care of the text. Lord Hervey can be ruled out, for his draft title-page
contains a quite different motto:

> ———omnes
> Vicini oderunt, noti, Pueri atque Puellae.
> Miraris?———Hor;

'Everyone hates you'—a motto much more appropriate to the spirit of the
Verses. The changes provide the best evidence for Lady Mary's involvement,
but if 'By a Lady' and the ambiguous nature of the 'Si natura negat' motto
rule her out, we are left with a conscientious bookseller who corrected his
text (either from the original manuscript, or, more likely, from a variant
one), or some other interested party. The curious nature of the motto, suggesting the authors' lack of talent and directly supporting the authenticity
of the *Verses* version, admits the candidature of Pope or one of his friends,
and they would be more likely to encounter copies of the poem than a bookseller would.

The publication arrangements are evidence against Lady Mary's involvement. The *Verses* were published by Mrs. Dodd and, on strong ornament evidence, they were printed by Henry Woodfall.[18] There is no real evidence to link Lady Mary with Dodd and none at all to link her with Woodfall; on the contrary, most of the links are between Dodd, Woodfall, and Pope. *A Genuine Letter Written from Constantinople* was published by Dodd and Roberts in 1719, but it was sent to the press by Abbé Conti, not by Lady Mary. The appearance of Dodd's or Roberts's name on a title-page is in itself of only minor interest—they handled a huge volume of newspapers, pamphlets, and books, and their names appeared on many title-pages—but patterns of association are worth remarking. The appearance of their names regularly on an author's publications or on a group of publications, or the information that the author dealt with them directly, or the association of their names with a particular printer may be significant. Mrs. Dodd tended to be associated with opposition literature. James Sutherland points out that in 1731 she had been in trouble with the authorities for publishing *The Craftsman*, a journal with a particular antipathy towards Hervey, as a Pope-Hervey conflict at the end of 1733, discussed later, will illustrate.[19] Roberts, on the other hand, was associated with the pro-government party, to which both Hervey and Lady Mary belonged. The appearance among Hervey's papers of three pamphlets published by Roberts and printed by the 'fruit basket' printer sets up something of a pattern. The printer's ornaments used in *To the Imitator* provide links with the two other publications. The large and distinctive fruit basket tailpiece also appears in Hervey's further attack on Pope, *An Epistle to a Nobleman to a Doctor of Divinity*. And it is used once more in a piece that may be Lady Mary's or Lord Hervey's, *An Elegy to a Young Lady, In the Manner of Ovid. By* ———— [James Hammond] *With an Answer: By a Lady, Author of the Verses to the Imitator of Horace*, printed for Roberts in 1733. The complexity of cross-reference in this title page is rather dizzying. By using the title, *Verses*, the Roberts/fruit-basket team are now referring to the rival publication in order to identify the author of one of their own. Halsband and Grundy attribute the *Answer* to Lady Mary, but Dodsley, who in compiling his *Collection* first identified James Hammond as the author of the *Elegy*, identified Lord Hervey as the author of the *Answer* to the elegy, and, presumably, the lady in question.[20] The most amusing way of reading this evidence from Hervey's papers is to assume that Hervey wrote and approved the publication of *To the Imitator* (his revisions and publication plans suggest that) and that 'By a Lady, Author of the

18. In 'Pope in the Private and Public Spheres', p. 41, I mistakenly identified the printer as John Huggonson, a printer who was, like Henry Woodfall, closely associated with Pope in the 1730s. The ornaments identified by Richard J. Goulden, *The Ornament Stock of Henry Woodfall 1719–1747*, Occasional Papers of the Bibliographical Society No. 3 (1988) are, in the order they appear in the *Verses*: Foxon V39: 229, 5, 379 [the tailpiece on p. 8 not in Goulden]; V40: 229, 5, 381(1), 218; V41: 229, 5, 381(1), 218; V44: 298, 5, 379, 219.

19. See his edition of *The Dunciad* in *The Twickenham Edition of the Poems of Alexander Pope*, V, 438.

20. *A Collection of Poems*, 4 vols (1755), IV, 75–78. Professor Grundy takes the view that the poem is another collaboration ('The Verse of Lady Mary Wortley Montagu', pp. 528–531).

Verses to the Imitator of Horace' is a neat joke at the expense of the publishers of the *Verses*, with their mistaken attribution. Associated ornaments are also found in *The False Patriot: An Epistle to Mr. Pope*, a poem attacking Pope's friendship with Bolingbroke, printed for James Roberts in 1734.[21] Lady Mary's publications (with or without *To the Imitator* and the *Answer*) also point in a Roberts, if not a fruit-basket, direction. As Robert Halsband shows in his biography and edition of Lady Mary's letters, her chief contact with the book trade was Roberts. When in 1737 she published her own pro-Walpole newspaper, *The Nonsense of Commonsense*, she dealt with Roberts and gave him instructions about printing. More strikingly, when she advertised for news of her runaway son in 1727, the reward for recovery was to be paid by Roberts.[22] Given Lady Mary's earlier association with Roberts, and this pattern of anti-Pope publication, it is difficult to see why she should have used Dodd and Woodfall for this poem.

The third explanation of the two separate publications of the attack on the imitator of Horace was that either or both were simply the work of rival members of the book trade who had come upon the poems illicitly. The evidence of the care taken in printing—the three sheets of *To the Imitator* and the correction and revision of the *Verses*—makes this unlikely, and Hervey's subsequent revision of *To the Imitator* and involvement with Roberts and the same printer mean that for this version we can rule it out altogether. The *Verses* could, however, be the output of some particularly scrupulous bookseller who obtained a copy of the manuscript and later corrected it from another manuscript in order to emphasize the merits of his edition. The imprints are not much help. Mrs. Dodd, a mercury, and simply a distributor, can be ruled out. The name that appears with hers in the 1735 edition, 'J. Fisher, against Tom's Coffee-house in Cornhill', is not much more helpful. His name appears with Dodd's in two of the four books with his name on the imprint listed by *ESTC*: *Miscellaneous Poems on Several Occasions*, by Mr. Dawson (1735) and *The Remembrancer* (1735). All four works belong, like the 'fifth' edition of the *Verses*, to 1735–6. His name may have appeared because he was an associate of Dodd's. A bookseller who would have enjoyed publishing the *Verses*, and might have taken trouble over it, is Bernard Lintot, at odds with Pope since the publication of the Odyssey in 1725. His opinion of Pope would not have differed greatly from that of

21. I have not been able to identify the 'fruit basket' printer. He also printed George Lyttelton's *Blenheim* (a tribute to the house) in 1728, *The Freeholder's Alarm to His Brethren* in 1734, and some of both the eighth and tenth edition of L. Desprez's edition of Horace. This is a quality printer, and I have wondered whether he might be Roberts himself. The five publications contain ornaments: 7 headpieces; 4 tailpieces; 4 factotums; and one initial. They are well-cut ornaments, many of them designed by Francis Hoffman.

22. See Halsband, *The Life of Lady Mary Wortley Montagu*, p. 142, and *The Complete Letters of Lady Mary Wortley Montagu*, 3 vols (1965–67), II, 114. The *Nonsense of Common Sense* was printed by Charles Ackers on the evidence of the factotum, no. 165 in J. C. Ross, *Charles Ackers' Ornament Usage*, Oxford Bibliographical Society Occasional Publication 21 (1990). Ackers or, more probably, Samuel Palmer helped print the Desprez Horace, eighth edition, but I do not think Ackers is the fruit-basket printer.

the authors of the *Verses* and he would not have been sorry to see him ridiculed in print. Lintot used Woodfall for printing in the 1730s (for Pope's *Works* I, for example), and he might have playfully mimicked Pope's concern with collections of his works by styling advertisements in a Popeian manner. But when a bookseller's candidature can be advanced because he might imitate Pope and because he used the same printer to print Pope's *Works*, it seems worth turning to the case for Pope's own involvement in the publication of the *Verses* instead.[23]

The suspicion that Pope was involved in publication of the *Verses* arises for three reasons. He had a motive, both a specific and a general one. He had the means, through his contacts with the book trade. And he had something of a criminal record of clandestine publication: within a few months he seems to have been entangled in another offence. Pope's motives are clearest in his 'Letter to a Noble Lord', which, with his correspondence, constitutes the best guide to the whole affair.

Late in 1733 Hervey attacked Pope again, largely repeating a number of stale charges in *Epistle from a Nobleman to a Doctor of Divinity*, published on 10 November, and Pope drafted a reply, 'A Letter to a Noble Lord. On occasion of some Libels written and propagated at Court, in the Year 1732–3', which he dated 30 November, though it was not immediately published and first appeared in Warburton's edition of Pope's *Works* in 1751. This 'Letter' seems an example, like Pope's own *Letters* and Bolingbroke's *The Idea of a Patriot King*, of Pope's using his close relationship with the printer John Wright to have a work printed in readiness for publication should an opportunity arise. But the immediate use of the printed 'Letter' was for private circulation to friends and to Hervey's patron, the Queen. Warburton says, 'It was for this reason [the original propagation of the libel] that this Letter, as soon as it was printed, was communicated to the Q.'[24] The 'Letter' is concerned with the *Verses* as well as with Hervey's *Epistle*, and they are referred to as '*Verses* on the *Imitator* of *Horace*', not *To the Imitator of the Satire of the Second Book of Horace*; the same title is used in the notes of *To Arbuthnot*. From the 'Letter' we learn that publication in print was of secondary importance to Pope. What mattered most was the initial, manuscript publication, which was at Court and, particularly, before the Queen:

Your Lordship so well knows (and the whole Court and town thro' your means so well know) how far the resentment was carried upon that imagination [that Lord Hervey

23. Another bookseller who used Woodfall for his printing was R. Montagu at the General Post Office in Great Queen's Street. I have not been able to relate him to Lady Mary's Montagus, and I suspect bookselling (even of curious books from a warehouse) by a member of the family would not have been regarded as respectable or worthy of encouragement.

24. *Works*, ed. by Warburton (1751), VIII, 258; the 'Letter' does not figure in the Contents of Warburton's edition and seems to be an afterthought. Hervey claimed, 'Pope has not written one word but a manuscript in prose never printed, which he has shown to several of his friends, but which I have never seen', Earl of Ilchester, *Lord Hervey and His Friends 1726–38* (1950), p. 189 (cited by Cowler, p. 440). What Hervey had not seen was probably the printed 'Letter'. For Pope's relations with Wright, see my *John Wright, Pope's Printer*, Oxford Bibliographical Society Occasional Publication 11 (1977).

had been attacked in the imitation of Horace], not only in the *Nature* of the *Libel* you propagated against me, but in the extraordinary *manner, place,* and *presence* in which it was propagated; that I shall only say, it seem'd to me to exceed the bounds of justice, common sense, and decency. (*Prose Works,* II, 444)

Later in the 'Letter', when Pope, pointing to his position as a Catholic under penal laws, is reminding Hervey of his vulnerability to the disapproval of those in power, he says, 'you inadvertently went a little *too far* when you recommended to THEIR perusal and strengthened by the weight of your Approbation, a *Libel*' (*Prose Works,* II, 455). The first of these passages occasioned Warburton's original note about the printed letter being sent to the Queen. A major concern in the 'Letter' is with this first manuscript publication of the *Verses* and the damage it might have done Pope with the King and particularly the Queen. The attack on Hervey in *To Arbuthnot* as an evil counsellor,

> Or at the Ear of *Eve*, familiar Toad,
> Half Froth, half Venom, spits himself abroad . . . (lines 319–320)

is a general one, but it is also particular and a reference to the propagation of the *Verses.*

One of Pope's informants about these events at Court was an unlikely one—Sir Robert Walpole. Walpole was drawn into Pope's quarrel with Lady Mary as early as 1729. Pope wrote to Fortescue on 13 September, 'I have seen Sir R. W. but once since you left. I made him then my confidant in a complaint against a lady, of his, and once of my, acquaintance, who is libelling me, as she certainly one day will him, if she has not already. You'll easily guess I am speaking of Lady Mary.'[25] This warning seems to have had no consequences, but it may have led Walpole to intercede between Pope and Lady Mary after the publication of the *First Satire of the Second Book of Horace* on 15 February 1733. The clues to what he might have said are in two letters from Pope to Fortescue. The second of these two letters, endorsed by Fortescue 18 March, provides the broader picture:

I wish you would take an opportunity to represent to the Person who spoke to you about that Lady, that Her Conduct no way deserves *Encouragement* from him, or any other Great persons: & that the Good name of a Private Subject ought to be as sacred even to the Highest, as His Behavior toward them is irreproachable, loyal, & respectfull.—What you writ of his Intimation on that head shall never pass my lips. (*Correspondence,* III, 357)

The letter is deliberately mysterious, but it invites interpretation. The 'Person' is surely Fortescue's friend Walpole, and the 'Great persons' are the King and Queen. The intimation seems closely related to Pope's fear for his personal position expressed in the 'Letter to a Noble Lord'. Walpole seems to have warned him that his loyalty as a subject had to be beyond question, and possibly that the attack on Lady Mary had led to that loyalty's coming into question. Issues of personal relationships and political power

25. The year is supplied by Sherburn (*Correspondence,* III, 52–53), but there is little doubt that Pope thought Lady Mary was libelling him and his friends in 1729 and 1730.

were becoming intertwined. The earlier letter, of 8 March, deals explicitly with the attack on Lady Mary in the *First Satire*, an attack we know she resented because of Peterborow's letter to her conveying Pope's denial that she was meant. Pope tells Fortescue,

Your most kind Letter was a Sensible pleasure to me: & the Friendship & Concern shown in it, to suggest what you thought might be agreeable to a Person whom you know I would not disoblige, I take particularly kindly. But the affair in question of any alteration is now at an end, by that Lady's having taken her own Satisfaction in an avowed Libell, so fulfilling the veracity of my prophecy. (*Correspondence*, III, 354)

Walpole ['a Person'] had evidently asked for a particular sign of Pope's loyalty in the form of an agreement to alter the lines on Sappho, an agreement Pope declines to make. The date of this letter is highly significant: it is written on the very day of the first advertisement of the *Verses* and *To the Imitator*, 8 March. Pope was somehow able to seize upon his vindication the instant it became available. The publication of the *Verses* constituted the complete justification of his original attack. Lady Mary, not Pope, was a public libeller; if he was in trouble at Court, it was because of her misrepresentation. I take it that when Pope says the 'Libell' is avowed he does not mean that it calls itself one (it does not) but that it declares its author ('a Lady'), something only the *Verses* does. Pope shows no distress at the newly published attack, either here or in a letter written to John Caryll on the same day; he shows instead some satisfaction that his judgement of Lady Mary has been justified. In short, publication of the *Verses* is to his advantage.

Pope's opinion at the time of writing his letters to Fortescue was that Lady Mary was directly responsible for the 'Libel'. By the time of the 'Letter to a Noble Lord' he adopted the view that Lady Mary had a supporting role in writing the *Verses*, 'I wonder yet more how a *Lady*, of great wit, beauty, and fame for her poetry . . . could be prevail'd upon to take a part in that proceeding' (*Prose Works*, II, 444), but he goes on the express perplexity about the precise allocation of responsibility:

There was another reason why I was silent as to that paper—I took it for a *Lady*'s (on the printer's word in the title page) and thought it too presuming, as well as indecent, to contend with one of that *Sex* in *altercation*; For I never was so mean a creature as to commit my Anger against a *Lady* to *paper*, tho' but in a *private Letter*. But soon after, her denial of it was brought me by a Noble person of *real Honour* and *Truth*. Your Lordship indeed said you had it from a Lady, and the Lady said it was your Lordship's; some thought the beautiful by-blow had *Two Fathers*, or (if one of them will hardly be allow'd a man) Two Mothers; indeed I think *both Sexes* had a share in it, but which was *uppermost*, I know not: I pretend not to determine the exact method of this *Witty Fornication*: and, if I call it *Yours*, my Lord, 'tis only because whoever *got* it, you *brought it forth*.

Here, my Lord, allow me to observe the different proceeding of the *Ignoble poet*, and his *Noble Enemies*. What he has written of *Fanny*, *Adonis*, *Sappho*, or what you will, he own'd he publish'd, he set his name to: What they have *publish'd* of him, they have deny'd to have *written*; and what they have *written* of him, they have denied to have *publish'd*. One of these was the case in the past Libel, and the other in the present. For tho' the parent has own'd it to a few choice friends, it is such as he has been obliged to deny in the most particular terms, to the great Person whose opinion *concern'd him most*. (*Prose Works*, II, 448)

The information in this passage makes the picture a little clearer. Hervey was responsible for putting the poem before the King and Queen (he 'brought it forth'); in doing so, he said it was by a Lady. Lady Mary denied authorship and said it was Hervey's. The innuendo about the sex of the author is very closely related to the subsequent Sporus attack ('now Master up now Miss'). It is possible that some of the material there ('Now trips a Lady') is directly related to the problem of the authorship of the attack. Pope is witty about the collaboration but he seems as baffled by it as twentieth-century scholarship has been. He is clearer about publication, 'what they have *publish'd* of him, they have denied to have *written*' is referred to the present 'libel', *Epistle from a Noble Lord*, which its parent has owned to friends but denied to 'the great Person whose opinion *concern'd him most*', whom I take to be the Queen. 'What they have *written* of him, they have deny'd to have *publish'd*' must, therefore, apply to the *Verses*, and it would suit my argument very well if Lady Mary had denied publishing them. Pope's confidence in Lady Mary's writing of the *Verses* seems to have weakened with the progress of time; perhaps that explains why he treated her so mildly in *To Arbuthnot*. It is possible that he made a mistake by believing the title-page of the *Verses*, as he claims here; alternatively the title page of the *Verses* may have reflected his own mistake, a mistake similar to the ones he had already made in attributing to her *A Pop on Pope* and *One Epistle to Mr. A. Pope*.

In addition to his particular motive for putting the *Verses* in the public sphere, where they could be acknowledged and challenged, Pope had general motives for making them public. This period saw him with a greatly enhanced sense of the potentiality of print. His chief project was the anonymous publication of *An Essay on Man*. He believed that declaring his authorship at first would prejudice him 'both in reputation and profit' (*Correspondence*, III, 350) and his letters show a gleeful pleasure in contrasting the performance of the author of the *Essay* with his own in the *First Satire of the Second Book of Horace*:

The town is now very full of a new poem intitled *an Essay on Man*, attributed, I think with reason, to a divine. It has merit in my opinion but not so much as they give it. . . . I find there is a sort of faction to set up the author and his piece in opposition to me and my little things, which I confess are not of so much importance as to the subject, but I hope they conduce to morality in their way. . . . (*Correspondence*, III, 354)

This letter, written, like that to Fortescue, on the day of publication of the *Verses*, 8 March 1733, shows Pope plotting an increased pleasure in the revelation that the rival authors are one and the same man; if the satirical author had just been attacked as a Cain-like enemy of mankind, so much the better. Later that same month Pope wrote to Curll in the first stage of his campaign to trick him into publishing an edition of his letters. The publication of both the letters and a new volume of works, contracted for the previous December, was central to a complex act of self-definition that preoccupied Pope for the remainder of his career. He publicised the private man, shaping the public's perception of both his works and character. His personal and secret control of printing and publishing processes enabled him to create public monuments like the *Works* and the *Letters* and shape their reception; monuments were the fruits of guile. Combining with the anonymous *Essay on Man*, the manoeuvres surrounding the *Verses* were a preliminary positioning in this campaign. The printing and private circulation of the 'Letter to a Noble Lord', at least as far as sending it to the Queen, began the delicate play on the boundaries of the public and private that characterized Pope's conduct in this period. His first new publication after the attack from Lady Mary and Lord Hervey was *The Impertinent, Or a Visit to the Court*, an adaptation of Donne's attack on courtiers, which he disguised as a shoddy piracy. The aristocrats had provided him with a topic for a new phase in his career.[26]

The second ground for suspicion that Pope was involved in publication of the *Verses* lies in his book-trade contracts. The *Verses* were published by Dodd and printed by Woodfall. Mrs. Dodd's name appears on the title-page of the *Dunciad*, and, although she may have had no direct connection with Pope, her name was consequently associated with his. Henry Woodfall, on the other hand, was personally connected with Pope. According to John Nichols, Pope was responsible for giving him his start in business: 'At the age of 40 he commenced master, at the suggestion, and under the auspices of Mr. Pope, who had distinguished his abilities as a scholar whilst a journeyman in the employment of the then printer to this admired author'.[27] Even if this story is discounted, for there are difficulties in linking Pope with Woodfall's master, John Darby, there is documentary evidence of Woodfall's printing Pope's *Works* I in 1735 (though this may have been arranged by Lintot) and of his printing directly for Pope in 1737.[28] Much of Pope's printing in the late 1730s was done by Woodfall. Although it would be wrong to argue that Pope would never have employed a printer used by his enemies for an important hostile publication, printers were associated with particular groups, and Woodfall was associated with Pope's.

Suspicion sharpens with the republication of the *Verses*, again printed by Henry Woodfall, on 14 February 1735, soon after the publication of the *Epistle to Dr. Arbuthnot* on 2 January 1735. The publications fit like two branches of a campaign. *To Arbuthnot* was preceded by the Pope's Advertisement, which insisted on its links with the *Verses*:

This Paper is a Sort of Bill of Complaint, begun many years since, and drawn up by snatches, as the several Occasions offer'd. I had no thoughts of publishing it, till it pleas'd some Persons of Rank and Fortune [the Authors of Verses to the Imitator of

---

26. The redirection of the satire from Grub Street to the failings of the aristocracy had already begun with the *Epistles* to Burlington and Bathurst. Maynard Mack gives a detailed and telling account of *The Impertinent* in his *Life*, pp. 603–607.

27. *Literary Anecdotes of the Eighteenth Century* (1812–15), I, 300 n.

28. P.T.P., 'Pope and Woodfall', *Notes and Queries*, 11 (1855), 377–378.

Horace, *and of an* Epistle to a Doctor of Divinity from a Nobleman at Hampton Court,] *to attack in a very extraordinary manner, not only my* Writings *(of which being publick the Publick judge) but my* Person, Morals, *and* Family, *where of to those who know me not a truer Information may be requisite.*

The *Verses* are not, therefore, incidental to the publication of the poem, one of many attacks to which the poet responds; they are the cause and justification of publication. Addressing the poem to Arbuthnot is bound in to this relationship:

I have, for the most part spar'd their Names, *and they may escape being laugh'd at, if they please.*
    I would have some of them know, it was owing to the Request of the learned and candid Friend to whom it is inscribed, that I make not as free use of theirs as they have done of mine.

Arbuthnot acted as go-between both before and after the publication of *To Arbuthnot.* Two letters from Lady Mary to Arbuthnot protest her innocence in October 1729, a further letter to him from her denies her authorship of the *Verses* on 3 January 1735, and a letter from Lord Hervey tells Henry Fox that Arbuthnot had asked him why he had been so severe on Pope (*Lord Hervey and His Friends,* p. 189). The strong links of *To Arbuthnot* with the *Verses* are not confined to the title and advertisement. On page 16 Pope adds a note to the line, 'Or at the Ear of *Eve,* familiar Toad': 'In the fourth Book of *Milton,* the Devil is represented in this Posture, It is by justice to own, that the Hint of *Eve* and the *Serpent* was taken from the *Verses on the Imitator of* Horace.' On page 17 a note lists common charges against Pope in relation to Addison, Broome, and the Shakespeare, allegations 'shamelessly repeated' even in '*The Nobleman's Epistle*'. On pages 18–19, in a note beginning with Curll's attacks on his family, he adds,

But, what is stranger, a *Nobleman* (if such a Reflection can be thought to come from a Nobleman) has dropt an Allusion to this pitiful Untruth, in his *Epistle to a Doctor of Divinity:* and the following Line,
    Hard as thy Heart, and as thy Birth Obscure,
had fallen from a like Courtly pen, in the *Verses to the Imitator of Horace.*

Professor Grundy has written well on how Pope reworks the material of the attack on the imitator of Horace, turning it against the attackers. Pope uses the *Verses;* he wants and expects his readers to know them. In response, the new edition of the *Verses* was advertised on 14 February:

This Day is publish'd, Price 6d.
The fifth Edition Corrected.
(Proper to bind with an Epistle from Mr. Pope to Dr. Arbuthnot, and Mr. Pope's other Pieces in Folio.)

Verses address'd to the Imitator of the first Satire of the second Book of Horace, by a Lady.

Si Natura negat, facit indignatio versus. Juvenal

Mr. Pope in his Advertisement to his Epistle to Dr. Arbuthnot, says, 'I had no thought of publishing it, till it pleased some Persons of Rank and Fortune (the

Author of the Verses to the Imitator of Horace) to attack in a very extraordinary Manner, not only my Writings, (of which being Publick, the Publick judge) but my Person, Morals, and Family, whereof, to those who know me not, a truer Information may be requisite.

Printed for A. Dodd, without Temple-Bar; J. Fisher, against Tom's Coffee-house in Cornhill; and sold at most Pamphlet Shops in Town.

The style of advertisement is familiar from those of March 1733: informative, engaged, seeing the *Verses* as an adjunct to Pope's works. The new edition follows the earlier ones very closely. It is printed by the same printer, Woodfall, using the same distinctive ornament on the first page, but reverting to the ornamental initial of the first edition. There are a number of small changes that may or may not be compositorial: four commas removed (including 'Weeds as they are' for 'Weeds, as they are,'); one comma added; one capital missing; one paragraph not indented; 'while' for 'whilst' and 'overmatch'd' for 'over-match'd'; and two changes creating direct links to *To Arbuthnot*. '*Hard as thy Heart, and as thy Birth obscure*' is italicised with an asterisk leading to a note to *To Arbuthnot* and '*Eve*' has a similar asterisk and note. It is inconceivable, I think, that this edition was produced by Lady Mary or Lord Hervey or any of their friends. In drawing attention to Pope's response to and redeployment of this material, it is surely in Pope's camp. The person responsible for the cross-references to *To Arbuthnot* may well have been responsible also for removing the commas around 'as they are', and for the familiar style of advertisement; and the same person may have been responsible for the earlier changes supplying the motto and the additional couplet. The *Epistle from a Nobleman*, which also has close links with *To Arbuthnot*, was not reprinted at this time, possibly because it was published by Hervey, who can have had no desire to freshen up the context of *To Arbuthnot*. The publishers of the *Verses*, on the other hand, were keen to do so.

The concern in the advertisements with compatibility of format connects with a Popeian hobby-horse. David L. Vander Meulen has recently called attention to Pope's role in advertising and the need for greater attention to his advertisements,[29] and at this time Pope's plans for collected works and the need for good relations with his public made him particularly concerned about format. Advertisements of the complete *Essay on Man*, for example, offered separate epistles to make up sets, and those for the *First and Second Satires of the Second Book of Horace* offered copies of sizes compatible with earlier publications, just as the first advertisement of the *Verses* declared it to be 'the same Size with the Dialogue'.[30] There is an over-fussiness in the advertisements for the *Verses* that suggests the amateur's hand and yet falls short of parody. At other points there is humour. I have already suggested the emphasis on 'By a Lady' should be read ironically, and, when we

29. '*The Dunciad in Four Books* and the Bibliography of Pope', *Papers of the Bibliographical Society of America*, 83 (1989), 293–310 (304–306).

30. Griffith, *Alexander Pope: A Bibliography*, books 336 and 342. See David Foxon, *Pope and the Early Eighteenth-Century Book Trade* (1991), pp. 94–95 for an illustration of Pope's advertisement for the *Odyssey*.

remember that Hervey revised a copy of *To the Imitator* for a second edition, the attack on that publication as 'spurious' and 'piratical' seems a case of conscious mockery. The grammatical error in the early attempts to cast *To the Imitator* in the role of piracy (there is a wavering about the subjunctive) is not a serious problem for the Pope-as-publisher hypothesis; there is ample room for confusion in the passing on of instructions.

The third ground for suspicion of Pope's involvement in publication of the *Verses* is connected with the controversy over Hervey's *Epistle from a Nobleman to a Doctor of Divinity* and 'Verses on Dr. Sherwin'. This was in itself a perplexing affair, but enough of it can be understood to throw some light on the *Verses*. Hervey's *Epistle* appears to have been published on 10 November 1733, but the intriguing part of the narrative starts around 20 November, when Hervey was thrown into a panic by what he took to be the threatened publication of a lampoon he had written on Dr. Sherwin, the addressee of the *Epistle*.[31] The supposed threat can be identified in the advertisement in the *London Evening-Post* for 20 November:

Next Week will be publish'd,
LETTERS and EPISTLES in Prose and Verse, between the Right Hon, the Lord
HERVEY, and the Rev. Dr. SHERWIN.
Printed for A. Dodd near Temple-Bar.

Dodd had not published Hervey's *Epistle*, but she was the publisher of the *Verses* and also the distributor of *The Craftsman*, a paper at war with Hervey; he would have feared the worst. A parallel advertisement was found the same day in the *Daily Courant*:

Speedily will be Publish'd
AN Epistle from a NOBLEMAN from HAMPTON-COURT, to the Reverend Dr.
SHERWIN. To which is *added*,
The Reverend Dr. *Sherwin's Latin* Epistle to the Lord *Harvey*; and also,
Verses on the said Dr. by the same Lord.
Printed for J. Roberts in *Warwick-Lane*. Price 1s. 6d.

The publisher of *To the Imitator* was now also implicated. Both advertisements named Hervey and both threatened the publication of additional material (in the Roberts advertisement the lampoon, 'Verses on the said Dr.' is referred to specifically). Hervey took steps to avert danger. He persuaded Sherwin the lampoon was an 'Epitaph on Ford' and he asked the Duke of Newcastle to intervene with the *Daily Courant*. The result was a statement in the issue of 22 November 1733:

An Advertisement having been incautiously inserted in the Paper on Thursday last, as likewise in other Papers, That shortly would be publish'd, *An Epistle from a Nobleman to the Rev. Dr. Sherwin, and Dr. Sherwin's Latin Epistle to the Lord Hervey, &c.* we can now assure the Publick that there was no such Poem wrote by the Lord Harvey, nor *Latin* Epistle sent his Lordship by *Dr. Sherwin*.

This was a mistake, as Hervey told his friend Fox:

---

31. Hervey's own account is in his letter to Henry Fox, *Lord Hervey and His Friends*, pp. 189–191.

The jumble of the advertisements in the *Daily Courier* is too long a story for me to enter into the particulars of it. The first of them was owing to a mistake of the Duke of Newcastle, whom I desired to order the printer to say that nothing promised by a former advertisement to be published should come out; and instead of that they said what was come out was not mine, though I had own'd it to every mortal, and to Arbuthnot, who came to me from Pope about it. (*Lord Hervey and His Friends*, p. 179)

The *Daily Courant* of 10 December got the message right and also apologized for using Hervey's name. I suspect Hervey's letter to Fox is disingenuous, and that the question of his authorship of the *Epistle from a Nobleman* was a live issue. According to Pope, he had not owned the poem to 'the great Person whose opinion *concern'd him most*' and the planned denial in the *Courant* is confusing and equivocal. Certainly Pope's friends were keen Hervey should own the poem in public. *The Craftsman* seized on the dithering in the *Courant* ('pitiful Equivocation', it called it) on 15 December, and on 29 December published a challenge to Hervey at the end of its home news section. Elwin and Courthope printed the challenge as Pope's, and they have been followed in this view by Halsband and Cowler.[32] Having told the story of owning, disowning, and owning again, the paper declares, 'unless the said noble Lord shall next Week in a Manner as *publick as the Injury*, deny the said Poem to be his, or contradict the Aspersions therein contain'd, there will with all Speed be published A MOST PROPER REPLY to the same.' The threatened reply might be Pope's 'Letter to a Noble Lord', just written, printed, but not published, or the anonymous *A Most Proper Reply to the Nobleman's Epistle*, which Professor Cowler has attributed to Pope. Whether we find Pope's hand directly in the challenge and the *Most Proper Reply* or not, it would be difficult to deny his influence on this mini-campaign, which so strongly served his interest.

Hervey was right in seeing the advertisements as dangerous, but most probably they were a form of bluff or trap. If the aim of *The Craftsman* and/ or Pope had been to publish the lampoon on Sherwin, they would simply have done it. Hervey told Henry Fox that the printer of *The Craftsman* (probably Richard Francklin rather than Henry Haines) had sent a copy of the lampoon to Sherwin and asked him to sign a certificate saying that Hervey was the author of the *Epistle from a Nobleman*. Sherwin, secured by Hervey's deceit, declared, 'Let him print if the dares.'[33] This provides the vital clue to the non-publication of the 'Letter to a Noble Lord' and possibly to the double publication of the original attack on the imitator of Horace. If Hervey would not admit publicly to writing the *Epistle*, Pope could not with any dignity or safety publish the 'Letter to a Noble Lord' attacking him for writing it. Dr. Sherwin's certificate would have given him the go-ahead, but Sherwin refused to sign it. *The Craftsman*'s challenge to own up or re-

---

32. *The Works of Alexander Pope*, ed. by W. Elwin and W. J. Courthope, 10 vols (1871–89), V, 263; Halsband, *Lord Hervey*, p. 163; Cowler, *Prose Works*, II, 487–490.

33. *Lord Hervey and His Friends*, p. 191. My account differs from Halsband's because he does not quote the *Daily Courant* advertisement in full or identify the issues of naming and new material (*Lord Hervey*, p. 163).

tract was similarly unsuccessful. Perhaps, and this can be no more than speculation, Hervey was similarly approached over the *Verses*. The aim this time would have been to get an assurance they were by Lady Mary. The threat would have been to publish them if the information was not forthcoming. Hervey's response may have been to cry 'publish and be damned' and to order his own rival edition. Hence the signs of haste—a loosely conceived title, for example—in the Roberts edition. The *Verses* publisher would then have gone ahead as threatened, printing 'By a Lady' on the title page, as the closest he could get to holding Lady Mary responsible. Publication of the two versions on the very same day would still be a coincidence, but one easy to explain: one edition would have motivated the other without having to be published first.

Pope's role in the publication of the *Verses* is not established beyond reasonable doubt, but I think it provides the best available explanation for the known facts: the oddity of the dual publication; the coincidental publication of the *Essay on Man*; Pope's immediate knowledge and use of the fact of publication; the involvement of Dodd and Woodfall; the advertising campaign; the republication with *To Arbuthnot*. The manoeuvres with a manuscript in order to get the authorship of *An Epistle from a Nobleman* declared seem to reveal a parallel case. There can be no doubt that controversy over the Horatian satires benefited Pope by heightening the success of the *Essay on Man* deception. And he was glad to have an 'avowed libel' by Lady Mary that justified his attacks and saved him from the embarrassment of a retraction. It also gave an impetus to *To Arbuthnot* and the major projects of the following years. The *Verses* justified a full act of self-vindication, an explanation of the writer as well as of his works. If Pope was behind publication of the *Verses* the act has a significance to parallel Johnson's famous letter to Chesterfield rejecting the power of patronage. Verses circulating privately represented a narrow circle of power, a circle to which Pope had no direct access. The 'Letter to a Noble Lord', printed but only circulated privately, represents a curious half-solution; but public attack and publick response gave Pope a voice. In the Advertisement to *To Arbuthnot* he noted that the attack on him went beyond his writings 'of which being publick the Publick judge' to his person, morals, and family. His response was to draw them before the public judgement also. In the short term his tactic was a success, but the history of his reputation (like that of the British Royal Family) shows the dangers of such attempts to manipulate the boundaries of the public sphere.

CREATING A GOOD IMPRESSION AT THE OXFORD BIBLE PRESS IN 1743

by

B. J. McMullin

IN writing about the phenomenon of 'signing by the page' (*Studies in Bibliography* 48 (1995), 259–268, esp. pp. 266–267) I referred to the 1743 Oxford quarto Bible, which I was able to record existing in two states: (i) totally innocent of cancellation, represented by one exemplar only, Bodleian Bib. Eng. 1743.d.1; (ii) containing at least 63 (*vere* 62) cancellantia, represented by three exemplars, British Library 3050.ee.8(2), National Library of Wales BS185.d43(4to), and Durham University Bamburgh Castle L.iii.7–10.[1] This edition is the first Bible to be printed by Thomas and Robert Baskett in succession to their father John—the imprint reads '*OXFORD*: Printed by THOMAS BASKETT and ROBERT BASKETT, Printers to the UNIVERSITY. M DCC XLIII.' The volume is gathered in eights, as is usual for English Bibles in quarto, and the gatherings are signed, in conventional fashion, $1–4—i.e. leaves $5–8 are unsigned. In state (ii) 61 of the 62 obvious cancellantia occur in the $5–8 sequence (the other is $3 in a four-leaf gathering) and are stigmatized by being signed by the page—i.e. according to the page within the gathering occupied by their recto; thus cancellans $7 is signed '$13' in such a system, $7^r occupying the thirteenth page in the gathering. The system of signing by the page can therefore be taken to be a guide to replacing unsigned leaves for agents apparently not accustomed to inferring foliation (and it might be noted that, as here, Bibles are customarily not paginated, so that that form of location was not available either). At the time of writing I opined that 'there is no reason to suppose that the cancellation in this volume is confined to the second half of gatherings. Indeed, one would expect that there would be about the same number of cancellantia in the first halves of gatherings, signed in the conventional manner—i.e. as their corresponding cancellanda' (p. 266). In fact, disturbances to the patterns of watermarks, chainlines and tranchefiles in the BL exemplar suggested that there were at least a further 51 cancellantia in the $1–4 sequence, though since that exemplar has been rebacked some leaves may have been repositioned, thus erroneously suggesting cancellation; additionally some cancellantia may in that exemplar agree in the three criteria with their corresponding cancellanda

---

1. There are undoubtedly further exemplars in the United States—*NUC* records maybe three: those at Yale (27½ cm.) and the New York Public Library (4°) presumably represent this edition, though that at the Newberry (no format or measurement) could equally be from the 12° edition of the same year.

and consequently may have escaped identification. Nonetheless the likelihood was that the \$1–4 sequence too would contain 60-odd cancellantia.

What at that stage seemed required was the capacity to bring together the Bodleian exemplar and one of the exemplars in state (ii) in order to carry out a textual comparison. The opportunity for such a comparison was later afforded by the presence—not initially realised—of a second exemplar in the National Library of Wales, BX5145 A4 d43(4to), which is in state (i).[2] NLW BS185 (the exemplar in state (ii)) is defective, lacking nine leaves (3R2 3R8 3S1 4A8 4E7 4E8 4H8 4I1 4I2), none of which, however, are cancellantia in the other exemplars of state (ii); discounting those leaves but taking account of B1 and B2, which in BS185 are from state (i) but in other exemplars of state (ii) are cancellantia, the comparison reveals that, as anticipated, there are 70 identifiable cancellantia in the \$1–4 sequence. Hence the total number of cancellantia in the 1743 Bible is at least 132.

In the process of cancellation the opportunity was taken in a few instances to simplify the binder's task by making changes in conjugacy, though on the evidence of surviving exemplars by no means all opportunities for such simplification were taken (it remains possible, however, that binders have separated cancellantia which were printed as conjugate pairs).

Exemplars in state (i) collate:

πA^2 A–$3P^8$ $3Q^4$ $3R^2$; (NT:) $^x3Q^4$ $^x3R^8$ $3S$–$4H^8$ $4I^2$

State (ii) in its 'ideal' form is probably best represented by the following formula:

πA^2 A^8(±1,2; −5,6 +5.6; ±7) B^8(±1,2; −3,4 +3.4; ±5,7,8) C^8(±1,3) D^8(±6,8) E^8(±3,4,6; −7,8 +7.8) F^8 G^8(−4.5,6,7 +4.7, 5.6; ±8) H^8(±2,4,7) I^8(±1; ±4.5) K^8(±1.8; ±2; −3,4 +3.4) L^8(±1,3) M^8(±2; −6,8 +6.8; ±7) N^8(±2,6) O^8(±5) P^8(±1) Q^8(±1) R^8(±7) S^8(±5) T^8(−3,4 +3.4; ±5,6) U^8 X^8(±6,7,8) Y^8(±1,2,5,7) Z^8(−1,2 +1.2) $2A^8$(±1,2,4,6,8) $2B^8$ $2C^8$(±4,5,8) $2D^8$(±7) $2E$–$2F^8$ $2G^8$(±1.8; ±2,4) $2H^8$(±1.8) $2I^8$(±5,7) $2K^8$(±3,4,8) $2L^8$(±2,3.6,4) $2M^8$(±4,5,6) $2N^8$(±3,8) $2O^8$(±3.6) $2P^8$(±8) $2Q^8$(±1.8; ±4.5) $2R^8$(±5) $2S^8$(±1) $2T^8$ $2U^8$(±4,7) $2X^8$ $2Y^8$(−2,3 +2.3; ±5,8) $2Z^8$(±1) $3A^8$(±6) $3B^8$(±2,6) $3C^8$(±1,4) $3D^8$ $3E^8$(±4) $3F^8$(±4) $3G^8$ $3H^8$(±4,6) $3I$–$3N^8$ $3O^8$(±3) $3P^8$(±1) $3Q^4$ $3R^2$; (NT:) $^x3Q^4$(±3) $^x3R^8$ $3S$–$4A^8$ $4B^8$(±1.8; ±6) $4C^8$(±2,4,7) $4D^8$(±1,3) $4E$–$4F^8$ $4G^8$(±2) $4H^8$(±5) $4I^2$ (Note that the cancels at I8 and R1 have been excluded from the formula; both were corrected at press and so are found with state (ii) readings either as integral leaves or as cancellantia. Similar instances may be awaiting discovery in exemplars as yet unexamined.)

The extent of the cancellation in the 1743 Bible is in itself a matter of surprise: 132 cancellantia among the 622 leaves—i.e. 21.2% of the leaves in state (ii) may be cancellantia. I am not aware of any sizeable publication approaching this level of cancellation, whatever the period or country, the closest that I can come being the quarto issue of Baskerville's edition of

2. On my first visit the relevant section of the card catalogue was away being microfilmed and thus BX5145 escaped my notice; and I had failed to realise that it was already recorded on the Eighteenth Century Short Title Catalogue database. I should like to acknowledge the assistance of Mr. Charles Parry of the National Library of Wales during my visits to that library.

Ariosto's *Orlando Furioso*, 1773, which contains what Philip Gaskell regards as 'the amazing total' of 66 cancellantia—this in a total of 901 leaves, a rate of 7.3%, or not much more than a third of that in the 1743 Bible.[3] But the Baskett brothers and John Baskerville were quite different in their customary approach to their texts, even if Baskerville did not manage to secure the accuracy that he strove for; and while Baskerville was producing, with obvious concern for appearance and textual accuracy, a foreign-language text which might be expected to be available for sale for a number of years, the Baskett brothers were producing, with no obvious concern for appearance, what might be considered a run-of-the-mill text in English in which accuracy was not by any means a customary concern and which in the normal course of events would be exhausted within a couple of years. The cancellation in the 1743 Bible should also, therefore, be seen in the context of a particular tradition of textual transmission and in the context of Bible-publishing at Oxford.

Bibles as a genre show scant regard for textual accuracy, and in the eighteenth century probably only the 1762 Cambridge folio/quarto (DMH 1142/1143)[4] and the 1769 Oxford folio/quarto (DMH1194/1196) were actually edited, as opposed to being set from whatever exemplar was at hand, regardless of the state of its text and apparently without any thought of reproducing it *literatim*. It can confidently be asserted that the textual condition of the Authorised Version (first published in 1611—DMH309) is one of virtually unrelieved progressive deterioration. The deplorable textual condition of the AV was a matter of concern as early as 1659, when William Kilburne—in *Dangerous errors in several late printed Bibles to the great scandal, and corruption of sound and true religion*—could claim to have 'discovered . . . many thousands'. Similar complaints continued to be voiced well into the nineteenth century—for example, Thomas Curtis in 1833 calculated that there were 'upwards of *Eleven Thousand*' intentional departures from the 1611 text, a figure 'not at all including the general alterations of the orthography or minute punctuation'.[5]

One difficulty in assessing the various claims is knowing what standard

3. Philip Gaskell, *John Baskerville; a bibliography* (Cambridge: at the University Press, 1959), no. 48. It might be noted, too, that Sir Walter Scott's *Life of Napoleon Buonaparte* (1827) may contain 130 cancellantia, but this in nine volumes, comprising 2028 leaves—a rate of 6.5%; see William Ruff, 'Cancels in Sir Walter Scott's "Life of Napoleon" ', *Edinburgh Bibliographical Society Transactions* 3 (1948–55), 137–151, and B. J. McMullin, 'Notes on Cancellation in Scott's *Life of Napoleon*', *Studies in Bibliography* 45 (1992), 222–231.

4. DMH = A. S. Herbert, *Historical Catalogue of Printed Editions of the English Bible 1525–1961; revised and expanded from the edition of T. H. Darlow and H. F. Moule, 1903* (London: British and Foreign Bible Society; New York: American Bible Society, 1968).

5. Thomas Curtis, *The Existing Monopoly, an Inadequate Protection, of the Authorised Version of Scripture. Four Letters to the Right Hon. and Right Rev. the Lord Bishop of London; with Specimens of the Intentional, and Other Departures from the Authorised Standard. To which is added, a Postscript, containing the "Complaints" of a London Committee of Ministers on the Subject; the Reply of the Universities; and a Report on the Importance of the Alterations made* (London: Effingham Wilson; Straker; L. J. Higham; and Starling, 1833).

to judge a particular edition against. The 1611 text has obvious general authority, being closest to the translators' manuscript, which is presumed to have served as the immediate copy, but in some eyes it has total authority, even in accidentals—this despite the fact that as a text it is a composite work translated from sources themselves translations of indeterminable authority and that as a publication it is the product of an early-seventeenth-century London printing house. In other words specific substantives may be subject to challenge and the accidentals have no particular warrant.

An exemplar of 1611 cannot have been the source of the corrections made in 1743, since some of those corrections are in the marginal references (which had become more numerous by 1743) and in the marginal dates (which were not included in an English Bible until 1679, at Oxford (DMH744/745)). In both states, by and large, 1743 represents a modernisation of 1611's spellings (of the breake/break, hee/he kind), though, in resetting, state (ii) tends to take that process further; otherwise most of the changes in state (ii) are either corrections of obvious errors in (i) or errors introduced into (ii)—indeed, state (i) is more often in agreement with 1611 than is state (ii). The changes in the marginalia suggest a printed source, while the changes in the text could just as well have been made independently of any such source by a careful reader in the printing house. In other words I have not been able to establish that the corrections made in 1743 were effected in order to bring the text into strict conformity with an identifiable printed source. We must wonder, therefore, what the motive for making the corrections was.

Though the differences between the two states can be isolated it is not a straightforward matter to distinguish needed corrections identified in the process of proof-reading from indifferent variants introduced in the process of resetting. A few random textual comparisons (confined to the early gatherings) show that only very occasionally—when the differences are few—can the reason for the cancellation be established. Thus in the marginal notes at the head of column 2 on A5^r state (i) reads '2281. | 2247. | ^{d} 1 Chr. | l. 19', state (ii) '2281. | ^{d} 1 Chr. | l. 19 | 2247.'; since the only apparent change on A5^v is the introduction of a space in the marginal notes of no significance the reason for the cancellation must have been to effect the reordering on A5^r. Elsewhere, where the differences are more numerous, it is difficult to be categorical in distinguishing the intended from the incidental, as a comparison of the two states of B5, comprehending Genesis 27–29, reveals (asterisks are used to isolate the element of variation):

Changes in punctuation (1, 3, 7, 10, 13, 14, 16) improve the rhetorical effect of the text and bring it into general conformity with the text as a whole (e.g. by having a comma after the frequent 'behold')—but the resulting text is by no means consistent in this respect. The replacement of 'lift' by 'lifted' (2) is part of the process of modernisation, which sees 'borne' replaced (erroneously according to modern usage) by 'born', as in 'I have borne/born him'. The supplying of an apostrophe (5, 6) should be set against an omission (8) and against the fact that on the two pages there are about 20 other possessives—including one proper name (Abrahams)—in which the apostro-

RECTO

Chapter:Verse	State (i)	State (ii)
1. 27:37	and what shall I do now unto *thee‸* my son?	thee,
2. 27:38	And Esau *lift* up his voice	lifted
3. 27:43	Now therefore, my *son‸* obey	son,
4. 28:Chapter head	*Padan-aram,*	Padan-aram.
5. 28:Chapter head	*Jacobs* ladder	Jacob's
6. 28:Chapter head	*Jacobs* vow	Jacob's
7. 28:4	give thee the blessing of *Abraham‸* to thee, and to thy seed	Abraham,
8. 28:5	*Jacob's* and Esau's mother	Jacobs
9. 28:9	Mahalath the *daughter* of Ishmael	daughters
10. 28:12	and *behold‸* a ladder set upon the earth	behold,
11. 28:13	And behold, the *Lord God* stood above it,	Lord
12. 28:13	and said, I *am the* *Lord* of Abraham	Lord God
13. 28:14	and in *thee‸* and in thy *seed‸* shall	thee, / seed,
14. 28:15	And *behold‸* I *am* with thee	behold,
15. 28:15	I have spoken to *thee*	the

VERSO

Chapter:Verse	State (i)	State (ii)
16. 29:10	And it came to *pass‸* when Jacob saw Rachel	pass,
17. 29:24	*handmaid*	hand-maid

phe is not supplied in resetting. The hyphenation of 'handmaid' (17) should be contrasted with its retention as one word in the resetting of B6ʳ. The resetting corrects a final mark of punctuation (4), but it also introduces two errors of its own (9, 15). The remaining changes (11, 12), though in isolation not obviously needed corrections, do in fact bring the text into conformity with the tradition of 1611 and may well be the occasion for the cancellation. Nonetheless, given the general textual state of the Bible in the middle of the eighteenth century, these do not seem to be the kinds of error that would cause even a moment's pause.

The cancels cluster in the early gatherings (63—virtually half—are in the first alphabet), but, as the variations in B5 demonstrate, it is difficult to know why—i.e. it would be impossible to determine with any confidence whether the decline in the scale of cancellation as the volume progresses results from a greater tolerance of error or from improved standards of setting or initial proof-reading, since to modern eyes most of the variations are indifferent in the absence of a known yardstick against which the 1743 text may have been judged.

Another context within which to view the 1743 edition is that of Oxford quarto Bibles. Assuming that no edition has disappeared completely, there were five Oxford quartos in the preceding decade (1733, 1736, 1738, 1739, 1740) and seven in the following (1744, 1746, 1747, 1749, 1752 (two editions), 1753). Thus the 1743 appeared in the middle of a 21-year period in which there are 13 surviving Oxford quarto Bibles, an average of one every 19 months or so. In other words the Baskett brothers can have anticipated printing another edition in the same format within a period not exceeding two or three years. (In the event a new edition in quarto must have been set in train very soon after the completion of the 1743.) In that light the extensive correction in 1743 appears all the more puzzling: Why go to the trouble of inserting so many cancellantia in a volume which they could anticipate disposing of practically straightaway and therefore be starting to set a new edition of almost immediately? In view of the general textual state of the Bible in the eighteenth century and of the nature of the corrections themselves I cannot better my earlier suggestion: that in producing their first Bible Thomas and Robert Baskett were anxious to improve on their father John's standards. John was possibly no worse than Bible-printers of the preceding century, but his 1717 Oxford folio—the so-called 'Vinegar Bible'— had earned the additional sobriquet 'a Baskett-ful of Errors'. If such was their intention, Thomas and Robert were unsuccessful. Or could it be that the brothers were reacting to the resumption of Bible printing at Cambridge? In 1743, after a lapse of sixty years, the Cambridge University Press published a Bible, a duodecimo on two qualities of paper (DMH1063); unlikely as it may seem, could Thomas and Robert have been attempting to demonstrate that their product was textually superior to their competitors'?

Commonly eighteenth-century English Bibles are bound with a *Book of Common Prayer*, a metrical psalter (almost invariably the version of Sternhold and Hopkins) and perhaps—particularly with folios and quartos—an *Index to the Holy Bible* or—particularly with octavos—various devotional works. Surviving exemplars of the 1743 Oxford quarto are therefore unexceptionable in that two (NLW BX5145 and BL) are bound with an Oxford quarto *Book of Common Prayer* with the same imprint and all five with a quarto *Index*, inferentially from Oxford (like most, if not all, eighteenth-century indexes which are bibliographically distinct volumes, this edition has only a caption title and no colophon). There is no corresponding *Sternhold and Hopkins*: at this period when Oxford Bibles have one bound in it is an edition printed by one or other of the London stationers. In both the *Book of Common Prayer* and the *Index* there are also two states, corresponding with those for the Bible; in state (ii) both have cancellantia signed by the page. The binder's volumes are 'pure': state (i) of both is found only with state (i) of the Bible, state (ii) only with state (ii)—thus NLW BX5145 contains all three in state (i), BL all three in state (ii).

The *Book of Common Prayer* collates in state (i) a⁸ A–F⁸ G⁴; in state (ii) there are cancellantia at least at A6 (signed 'A11'), F5 (signed 'F9') and F6 (signed 'F11') and probably at D1, E3 and F3, which have press figures in state (i) but not in state (ii), thus giving the provisional collation a⁸ A⁸ (±6) B–C⁸ D⁸ (±1) E⁸ (±3) F⁸ (±3,5,6). The *Index* collates in state (i) a–d⁴; in state (ii) there are cancellantia at least at a3 (signed 'A5') and a4 (signed 'A7') but no other patent indications of cancellation, so that state (ii) may well be represented as a⁴ (±3,4) b–d⁴. I have not attempted at this stage to establish the full extent of the cancellation in the two works but have confined myself to a comparison of the five leaves identified as cancellantia by their signatures, a comparison which was sufficient to establish the nature of the variations. In the *Book of Common Prayer* the changes are not of the kind that might have been expected and that are regularly found in the first half of the eighteenth century—i.e. those occasioned by deaths, births and marriages within the royal family—but almost exclusively variations in punctuation and capitalisation, with the occasional correction of an erroneous reference. In the *Index* the changes are of a similar character: variations in accidentals, with the odd correction of an apparent error (like 'save' for 'spare'). As with the Bible, in both works it may be that the correction of the odd error was the occasion for the cancellation and that the variations in accidentals are 'indifferent', being a product of the resetting.

Bibliographically speaking, the major point of interest in the 1743 Oxford quarto Bible, *Book of Common Prayer* and *Index* is the method of signing cancellantia in the \$5–8 sequence—i.e. 'by the page'. As I have already suggested, such a method does appear to be designed to facilitate the process of effecting cancellation by people unaccustomed to inferring the signature of an unsigned leaf (note the more customary—though by no means universal—practice of signing cancellantia by the leaf, according to the position of the corresponding cancellanda, whether signed or not, so that cancellans \$7 in the 1743 Bible would be signed '\$7'). Admittedly Bibles are normally not paginated, thereby removing an alternative form of reference for those unfamiliar with signatures; on the other hand, with the practice of dividing the Bible into verses, begun in English in 1560 with the publication of the first edition of the Geneva Bible (DMH107), it contains its own reference system—one need only look at the headline to know where a particular leaf belongs. Hence it is all the more puzzling that signing by the page should be adopted for a Bible. It has been tempting to believe that the method was designed to aid owners of volumes to effect the cancellation themselves; such a supposition was at least attractive in the case of the *Book of Common Prayer*. But here the nature of the corrections renders such a supposition untenable: owners of Bibles can have been no more than indifferent to the changes made on most leaves. Moreover, the cancellation of conjugate pairs and cancellation in which conjugate pairs replace disjunct leaves mean that the process can have taken place only before the sheets were bound—i.e. the practice of signing by the page now appears to have been employed for the benefit of members of the trade, either in the printing house or in the binding shop.

The textual changes in the 1743 Oxford quarto Bible, *Book of Common Prayer* and *Index* are themselves of little consequence: most are such as to cause no more than a momentary stumble in reading (silently or aloud). But their very inconsequentiality confers on them an interest and gives rise to a number of questions which have been raised in the body of this essay: Why bother to make the changes in the first place, particularly given the general textual state of the Bible in the middle of the eighteenth century and the speed with which editions of quarto Bibles published from Oxford were exhausted? What is the temporal relationship between the two issues (noting that they are virtually 'pure', on the evidence of the small number of surviving exemplars examined)? Why were cancellantia in the $5–8 sequence signed by the page? For whose benefit was the system employed, especially given that the privileged printers used the system for bringing the *Book of Common Prayer* up to date? I would be pleased to be enlightened on any of these points.

PROFITS FROM PLAY PUBLICATION: THE EVIDENCE OF *MURPHY v. VAILLANT*

by

JUDITH MILHOUS AND ROBERT D. HUME

RELATIVELY little is known about the terms on which plays were published in the later eighteenth century.[1] So far as we are aware, no source exists that is comparable to British Library Add. MS. 38,728, which contains a large number of publication agreements (including many for plays) dating from the first half of the century. Figures have come to light for scattered plays, but the specifics of publication agreements and the profits made by the playwrights remain a relatively dark subject. Consequently we are pleased to be able to present a substantial amount of information about the early plays of Arthur Murphy from a heretofore unknown Exchequer lawsuit. Our source is Public Record Office E 112/1649, no. 2392, filed by Arthur Murphy against Paul Vaillant in Hillary Term 15 George III (1775).[2]

Arthur Murphy (1727–1805) had his first piece staged in 1756 and ultimately produced more than fifteen plays for the patent theatres in London. He was an industrious professional writer who also published some political and dramatic journalism but eventually devoted himself to a career in the law. He commenced his legal studies in 1757; was called to the bar in 1762; and by 1765 had largely turned his attention away from the theatre, though he had several new plays staged in the 1770s and one as late as 1793. He is probably best known for his "Essay on the Life and Genius of Henry Fielding" (prefaced to the 1762 *Works*), but his two-volume *Life of David Garrick* (1801) has also been extensively cited by later writers.[3]

1. The standard study remains Shirley Strum Kenny's overview, "The Publication of Plays," in *The London Theatre World, 1660–1800*, ed. Robert D. Hume (Carbondale: Southern Illinois Univ. Press, 1980), pp. 309–336.

2. Quotations otherwise unidentified are from this source. We have silently expanded some abbreviations and added a few periods at the ends of sentences for clarity. Exchequer records have rarely been used by literary and musicological scholars, but by the mid-seventeenth century virtually any case that could be brought in Chancery could equally well be filed in Exchequer. See Judith Milhous and Robert D. Hume, "Eighteenth-Century Equity Lawsuits in the Court of Exchequer as a Source for Historical Research," *Historical Research* 70 (1997), 231–246.

3. Much of what is known about Murphy comes from the documents printed in the early biography written by his executor. See Jessé Foot, *The Life of Arthur Murphy, Esq.* (London: Printed for J. Faulder by John Nichols and Son, 1811). Foot has always been regarded as a somewhat treacherous source, and the figures he gives for copyright sales of some of the plays have been almost entirely ignored. Two modern biographies appeared simultaneously more than a generation ago: John Pike Emery, *Arthur Murphy: An Eminent English Dramatist of the Eighteenth Century* (Philadelphia: Univ. of Pennsylvania Press for Temple University

Murphy's principal publisher during his first decade was Paul Vaillant, and the lawsuit gives us financial and other information about nine of his plays, two revisions of them, and one political novella translated from French. The period covered is 1756 to 1767. Murphy brought the suit as a cross action to block execution of a judgment against him in the Court of Common Pleas. Vaillant claimed that he had paid (and loaned) Murphy £186 3s 1d more than he owed him, and he sued to collect. Our concern here, however, is less with the particulars of this case than with what the testimony on both sides tells us about play publication and its profits. How typical Murphy's publication arrangements and remuneration were we cannot be sure. He started by selling his copy outright; quarrelled with Vaillant over whether he should receive additional pay for a revised text; and finally tried having Vaillant print plays at Murphy's own expense and sell them on commission. The financial and legal ramifications are complex.

I. Fourteen Year Sale of Copyright

We must start by addressing a difficulty: Murphy and Vaillant disagree quite drastically about both the dates and contract prices of virtually all their agreements. What are we to conclude when Murphy says he sold a play to Vaillant for £157 10s in March 1759 and Vaillant replies that he bought the play for £105 on 7 February 1760? To complicate this tangle further, the play in question premiered in April 1759 and was published almost immediately (which seems to favor Murphy's story)—but Vaillant offers to produce the signed and witnessed contract, dated as he has specified. We will disclose the result of the case immediately: the Court of Exchequer found for Vaillant.[4] Our reading of the evidence suggests that the court came to the right conclusion. But such contradictions in what ought to have been simple matters of fact are unsettling.

Why would Murphy make the claims he did, knowing (as he told the court himself) that Vaillant kept excellent records? Two quite separate matters are at issue: price and date. So far as we can determine, Vaillant is right about the prices. Both men are correct about the dates. Let us explain. Murphy and Vaillant struck a bargain for each play at roughly the time of premiere (whether before or after cannot be determined), but they sometimes did not "reduce the agreement to writing" and put cash on the barrelhead until a later date.[5] Murphy gives the date at which a bargain was struck; Vaillant gives the date of the formal written agreement and cash payment.

Publications, 1946), and Howard Hunter Dunbar, *The Dramatic Career of Arthur Murphy* (New York: Modern Language Association, 1946).

4. The decree is P.R.O. E 126/31 (Michaelmas 1775), no. 8. "It is thereupon Ordered and Decreed by the Court that the plaintiffs Bill be & the same is hereby dismissed Out of this court with Costs to be Taxed for the said Defendant."

5. If this casualness strains the reader's credulity, let us point out that Oxford University Press did not bother to put together a written contract for Mr Hume's *The Development of English Drama in the Late Seventeenth Century* (1976) until some months after it was published. The terms, however, were precisely as agreed in early 1975.

When the agreement remained oral, they give the same date. Murphy's inflated prices are more troublesome, but we will offer a conjecture. At least five of his figures *must* be false: Vaillant held the signed agreements and offered to produce them to the court. Our best guess is that Murphy was simply stalling. He knew that Common Pleas had found against him, and that Vaillant held £479 13s 10d of receipts and "notes" from him as against only £293 9s 9d that Murphy had been able to document was owed to him by Vaillant. Inflating the alleged prices of seven plays and one revision by £233 (which is what Murphy apparently did) was a means of seeming to show that Vaillant owed Murphy money, not vice-versa. Murphy cannot have expected to bamboozle the Court of Exchequer, but the suit did buy him more than six months of breathing room. He probably hoped for longer: most Exchequer cases dragged on at least two or three years. He owed Vaillant nearly £200, which was a very large sum of money, and time to scrape it up might have been of the essence. At any rate, the discrepancies in testimony need not concern us unduly: Vaillant's prices appear to be correct.[6]

Murphy sold publication rights in seven plays to Vaillant between January 1756 and November 1761. The titles, performance dates, publication agreement dates, contract dates (if different), and prices are specified in Table 1.

Table 1: Plays sold by Murphy to Vaillant

Title	Acts	Premiere date	Agreement date	Contract date	Publication date	Price
Apprentice	2	2 Jan 1756	Jan 1756	17 Jan 1756	8 Jan 1756	£40
Upholsterer	2	30 Mar 1758	Mar 1758	13 Mar 1759	12 Apr 1758	£42
Orphan of China	5	21 Apr 1759	Mar 1759	7 Feb 1760	2 May 1759	£105
Way to Keep Him	3	24 Jan 1760	Jan 1760	7 Feb 1760	5 Feb 1760	£52 10s
Desert Island	3	24 Jan 1760	Jan 1760	7 Feb 1760	29 Jan 1760	£52 10s
All in the Wrong	5	15 Jun 1761	Nov 1761	(oral)	21 Nov 1761	£105
Old Maid	2	2 July 1761	Nov 1761	(oral)	25 Nov 1761	£42

The most obvious fact to be discerned from this list is that a five-act mainpiece brought the author a hundred guineas (£105), whereas a three-act play was worth just half that and a two-act afterpiece fetched £40 or £42. The 1760 version of *The Way to Keep Him* and *The Desert Island* are a pair of three-act entertainments written to be performed together. The former was popular and the latter was not, yet what they brought Murphy from his publisher was fifty guineas each. He got more from Vaillant for the successful show only when he rewrote it as a five-act mainpiece (a subject to be addressed in due course).

6. One of the more curious features of the differing testimony about prices is that Foot gives copyright sale prices for several of Murphy's early plays (p. 308), and the figures he gives are identical with those claimed by Vaillant. This is interesting: Foot almost unquestionably derived his information from Murphy's own papers—a fact that calls the honesty of Murphy's testimony even further into question.

From the start of their business relationship, Vaillant and Murphy operated quite casually about written agreements. When *The Apprentice* premiered on 2 January 1756, Murphy was unknown. The work proved immediately popular, and by 8 January Vaillant had it in print at 1s. Terms may have been agreed on before the premiere, but the formal contract was not signed until more than a week after publication. Vaillant recites it: "London 17th January 1756 I do hereby Assign and make over to Mr Paul Vaillant his Heirs Executors or Assigns for and in Consideration of the Sum of forty pounds to me by him paid this day the full and entire property of a ffarce in two Acts written by me and entitled the Apprentice. Witness my Hand and seal Arthur Murphy." Vaillant adds: "And which said Paper was signed and sealed in the presence of Margaret Chastel and John Edwards and was drawn up in Writing by this Defendant and is now in the possession or power of this Defendant." What exactly was Murphy selling? In the words of the Copyright Act of 1710, he was transferring "the sole Right of Printing or Disposing of Copies" for fourteen years. Murphy is careful to state the period in his testimony; Vaillant consistently leaves it out, and it was not specified in their written contracts. According to the Act, ownership "shall Return to the Authors thereof, if they are then Living, for another Term of Fourteen Years."[7] Accustomed to the longstanding Stationers Company presumption of perpetual right, booksellers tended either to bargain for all assignable rights or to operate as though they had.[8]

Subsequent deals between Murphy and Vaillant were even more casual. *The Upholsterer*—another immediate and longstanding success—was published two weeks after its 30 March 1758 premiere, but not formally contracted for between author and publisher until a year later.[9] Terms for *The Orphan of China*—a *succès d'estime*—were apparently agreed upon in March 1759; again the play was published two weeks after its premiere on 21 April, but the paperwork did not get done until 7 February 1760.[10] Indeed, on the same day Murphy and Vaillant concluded a bargain for the three-act version of *The Way to Keep Him* and *The Desert Island*, which had received their premieres two weeks earlier and were coming up to the last of their eleven joint performances. Vaillant recites the written agreements for all of these plays, and according to his testimony (accepted by the court), he and Murphy

7. The full text of the Act is printed by Harry Ransom, *The First Copyright Statute* (Austin: Univ. of Texas Press, 1956). Quotation from p. 117.

8. For discussion, see David Saunders, *Authorship and Copyright* (London and New York: Routledge, 1992), chapter 2, and John Feather, *Publishing, Piracy and Politics: An Historical Study of Copyright in Britain* (London: Mansell, 1994), chapter 3.

9. An advance notice appeared in the *Public Advertiser* for 1 April 1758, and publication "This Day" was advertised in the same paper on 12 April.

10. Two colleagues had tried to capitalize on the play even before Vaillant announced publication "This Day" in the 2 May 1759 *Public Advertiser*. R. Baldwin had republished an alternative translation, and J. Coote had offered a 6d *Account of the new Tragedy of the Orphan of China, and its Representation* (19 and 24 April *Public Advertiser*). Onstage, *The Orphan of China* had the nine performances that allowed Murphy three benefits, but no more this season.

used their meeting of 7 February 1760 to tidy up their joint affairs: "about the seventh day of ffebruary 1760 . . . All accounts between the Complainant and this Defendant were closed and balanced. And . . . on the twenty sixth day of ffebruary 1760 a new Account was opened." For reasons not clear to us, author and publisher did not bother with written publication agreements under their new "Account."

As of February 1760 Murphy was an exceptionally promising young dramatist. Four of his five plays had been successful, and all of them had been mounted by the Garrick management at Drury Lane—London's best. Murphy was probably satisfied with his publisher, or he would have struck bargains elsewhere. He does not appear, however, to have been content with what he was earning from the theatre itself, for in the summer of 1761 he joined forces with Samuel Foote and rented the Drury Lane theatre to offer a summer season. *All in the Wrong* and *The Old Maid* premiered there in June and July. Both enjoyed numerous performances. No account books survive for this venture, but "Mr. Murphy's Statement of his Case with Messrs. Garrick and Lacy" supplies some important financial details and explanations of the venturers' agreement.[11]

Under this special summer arrangement, Murphy stood to benefit from four separate sources of income. (1) Benefits for his new plays. He was allowed three benefits for *All in the Wrong*, which netted him £77 17s 10½d, £2 8s 2½d, and £6 respectively. Two benefits in which *The Old Maid* served as afterpiece yielded £56 19s 11½d and £13 10s 2d, so Murphy derived a total of £156 16s 2½d from "author's benefits." (2) Murphy and Foote were splitting managerial profits. Their agreement with Garrick and Lacy was that the rent on Drury Lane would be one-fifth of the net profits of the summer season. Murphy mentions in passing in his *Life of Garrick* that "Foote received somewhat above three hundred pounds for his half-share," which implies that Murphy likewise got £300 as comanager and that Garrick and Lacy collected about £150 between them (one-fifth of a presumptive £750 total profit).[12] (3) Another part of the agreement with Garrick and Lacy was that if the benefits for Murphy's new plays did not make him £300 for *All in the Wrong* and £100 for *The Old Maid* (i.e., a total of £400), then they had the right to pay him the difference and take the two plays into the regular Drury Lane repertory. By Murphy's calculations the two plays had earned him only £121 11s 11½d. (Because *The Old Maid* was an afterpiece, he allowed only half of the profits earned on those nights to count as "its" earnings, which explains the discrepancy between this figure and the £156 16s 2½d total benefit earnings.) If we accept this basis of calculation, then Garrick and Lacy ought to have paid Murphy another £278 8s 9½d [*recte* 10½d] to bring the total up to £400. In fact, they paid him only £200, thereby inflaming his temper.[13] (4) Sale of copyright. Vaillant claims to have paid Murphy exactly

---

11. Printed by Foot, pp. 174–176.

12. Arthur Murphy, *The Life of David Garrick, Esq.*, 2 vols. (London: Printed for J. Wright by J. F. Foot, 1801), I, 361.

13. See Foot, pp. 176–180.

the same amounts that had been established as his going rates: one hundred guineas for the mainpiece and fifty guineas for the afterpiece. Granting that the managerial profits are a round figure, Murphy's total earnings from the summer company venture must have been something like £814. The copyright fees of one hundred and fifty guineas were by no means a trivial sum, but they represent far less than could be earned in the theatre and lead us to a broader question.

How much of Murphy's income from playwriting was he deriving from performance and how much from print? Drury Lane accounts are only spottily preserved, but we can get some idea. Murphy received a benefit on the eighth night of *The Apprentice*. Richard Cross, the prompter at Drury Lane, estimated a gross of £200; assuming that Murphy paid the standard £63 house charges, he should have netted roughly £137 or more than three times what Vaillant paid him for publication rights.[14] For *The Upholsterer* he was given an unadvertised benefit on the tenth night. Cross estimated the take at £180, so the net should have been circa £117, or close to triple the publisher's fee. As a mainpiece, *The Orphan of China* entitled its author to benefits on the third, sixth, and ninth nights. Assuming Cross's estimates to be reasonably accurate, Murphy ought to have netted something like £231,[15] which is more than double the payment from Vaillant. No figures survive for *The Way to Keep Him* and *The Desert Island*, but since they ran more than nine nights Murphy ought to have made something on the order of £200 and conceivably a bit more. In sum, publisher's fees added handsomely to the profits of playwriting, but they constituted (so far as this very limited sample permits us to judge) something like 20-35 percent of the total that an author might hope to make from a play with a decent run.

One warning: Murphy would probably not have received any remuneration for the afterpieces from the theatre if they had died after four or five nights. Little evidence exists about theatrical compensation for afterpieces. Authors' benefits were not always advertised, and especially not for afterpieces, as we sometimes learn from Cross's annotations.[16] Management was resigned to giving up the profits of the third, sixth, and ninth nights for a mainpiece (if it lasted that long), but if a benefit was given for an afterpiece, it commonly occurred on the sixth night or later. No benefit was allowed if the piece failed to survive that long. We offer the hypothesis that management had the option of compensating the author of a flop with a flat cash payment, if any remuneration was given at all. Let us underline the obvious: big money

14. Pertinent parts of Cross's diary are printed in *The London Stage, 1660–1800*, Part 4: 1747–1776, 3 vols., ed. George Winchester Stone, Jr (Carbondale: Southern Illinois Univ. Press, 1962). All performance dates and statistics are from this source.

15. Cross was, unfortunately, a rather erratic estimator. See Judith Milhous and Robert D. Hume, "Receipts at Drury Lane: Richard Cross's Diary for 1746–47," *Theatre Notebook*, 49 (1995), 12–26, 69–90, esp. p. 72. In seasons for which treasurer's accounts are preserved Cross can be shown to have overestimated by as much as £81 and underestimated by as much as £29. Overall, he appears to be high by 3 or 4 percent.

16. "Benefit for ye Author, tho' not put so in the Bills" (26 February 1751); "For ye Author of ye Farce tho' not advertis'd" (6 May 1758).

could be made only from success in the first run of a mainpiece, but for a failure, the publication fee might be a very large part of such profits as the author ever got. Indeed, benefits carried no guarantees and sometimes lost money: the copyright money could conceivably be the *only* remuneration the writer would ever receive from his or her play.

II. Revised Versions

In two cases Murphy revised a play of his own. This was not common practice at the time, in part no doubt because the system of remunerating playwrights did not encourage further attention to something already in the public domain so far as performance rights were concerned. The two occasions on which Murphy carried out revisions were quite different, and they raise interesting publication questions.

The first was anomalous. *The Way to Keep Him* had originally been produced as a three-act mainpiece. It was tried a couple of times in the spring of 1760 as an afterpiece, but it was too long. To do the theatre much service it needed to become a five-act mainpiece. In the course of the summer and autumn Murphy duly expanded it, and the play received its premiere as a full-dress mainpiece on 10 January 1761. It enjoyed an immediate run of eight nights (including two command performances) and went on to become a repertory staple. How the Drury Lane management compensated Murphy for his trouble is not clear. No author's benefit was advertised, and no accounts or prompter's diary survive for this season. A flat fee may have been negotiated, or Murphy may have received an unadvertised benefit. What he got from Vaillant for publication rights was fifty guineas. (Author and publisher concur in saying that an oral agreement was struck in January 1761.) The fee seems fair: Murphy had written two additional acts, and he got more than the standard price of a two-act afterpiece.

The second instance concerns "Alterations and Additions" to Murphy's second play, *The Upholsterer*. This afterpiece had been successful at Drury Lane, and in 1763 the new Covent Garden management decided to add it to their repertory. The usual method of doing so would have been simply to buy some printed copies and mount the piece unaltered without compensation of any kind to the author. In this instance, however, the Covent Garden managers decided to shorten and lighten the piece. Comparison of the Vaillant edition of 1763 with that of 1758 shows that the two are substantively identical until page 39, at which point they diverge drastically.[17] Murphy added some material for the low-comedy characters; reduced sentiment, pathos, and jealous love complications; and wound up cutting twelve pages to about eight. The impact of the piece is therefore greatly altered, even though 80 percent of the play is unchanged. The revision should have required little time or effort, so we are not surprised that no author's benefit was advertised. We presume, however, that Murphy got something for his trouble. Though far from new, the piece proved even more popular at Covent

17. We have used Folger PR 1241 E4 (1758) and PR 1241 M65 (1763).

Garden than it had at Drury Lane, enjoying 20 performances there its first season.

Vaillant naturally wanted to issue a revised edition, representing *The Upholsterer* as it was now to be seen at Covent Garden—and toward the end of the year, he did so. Whether he owed Murphy anything on account of this revised edition was sharply disputed between them. Murphy charges that "some Time in the Month of November 1763" (*recte* October), he

made considerable additions to and Alterations in the Theatrical piece Intitled the Upholsterer and the said Paul Vaillant has printed and sold the said additions without any agreement with your Orator for the copy right thereof and the Profits arising by such sale he has converted to his own Use and benefit. . . . And the said Paul [Vaillant] sometimes pretends that the above mentioned ffarce called the Upholsterer has allways been by him Printed and sold in the same form and in the exact words of the Manuscript Copy sold and deliverd to him by your Orator in the Month of March 1758 and that no Additions to or Alterations in the same were ever made by your Orator whereas your Orator charges and so the Truth is that some time in the year 1763 he did make large additions to and considerable Alterations in the said ffarce of the Upholsterer and that the said Paul Vaillant possessed himself of the said Additions and Alterations by applying to the Prompter of Covent Garden Play House for the same without the Knowledge Consent or Privity of your Orator & did in or about the Month of December 1763 print Publish and Vend the same and hath ever since printed published and sold the same acquiring thereby considerable Profit and hath ever since constantly Refused to account with your Orator for the same. And the said Paul Vaillant sometimes Admits that such Additions and Alterations as above stated were made to the said ffarce called the Upholsterer by your Orator but then he pretends that your Orator in the Month of March 1758 when the said ffarce was sold to him the said Paul Vaillant agreed and contracted that all future Alterations and Additions which your Orator should at any Time make should be the Property of him the said Paul Vaillant without any Additional Price or consideration for the same. Whereas your Orator Charges and so the Truth is that he never made any such Agreement as is pretended by the said Paul Vaillant & that he is well Intitled to the mean profits that have accrued from the sale thereof or a compensation for the said Additions and Alterations. But the said Paul Vaillant Refuses to make your Orator any compensation or to Account with your Orator for the Profits of such sale.

Vaillant replied that he had indeed acquired the alterations and published them, but that he had done so with Murphy's permission and cooperation:

he this Defendant did Possess himself of the said Alterations and Additions by Applying to the Prompter of Covent Garden Play House for the same and which application this Defendant made with the Express Authority and Licence of the said Complainant who gave the same to this Defendant and that he this Defendant hath Printed and sold the said piece with such Additions and Alterations but not the Additions and Alterations by themselves without any Agreement with the Complainant for the Copy right thereof otherwise than the Complainants giving the same to this Defendant and thereby made large Profits but he this Defendant doth refuse to set forth what such Profits were he insisting upon his own Property in the said piece with the Additions and Alterations for the reasons herein mentioned and the profits arising by such sale he this Defendant hath converted to his own Use and benefit. And this Defendant humbly insists that he has a right to Convert such profits to his own use and benefit for that the said Complainant did voluntarily and of his own free will give such Additions and Alterations to him this Defendant.

The theory of copyright was very much in its infancy, and eighteenth-century courts consistently had difficulty with alterations and translations (and in the realm of music, rescorings for different instruments). How much difference was required to create a new work?

Not to compensate an author for printing new material that warranted a new edition and improved the saleability of a title seems manifestly unfair. Contrariwise, the publisher would have had grounds for complaint if the author made relatively minor alterations and then proceeded to sell copyright of the "new" work to another publisher. So far as we know, Murphy had not attempted to do the latter, but Vaillant quite definitely did the former. The information that a publisher could, for a consideration, routinely acquire "acting" copy from the prompter as early as 1763 is interesting. Vaillant says that "the Prompter . . . usually has a Gratuity for furnishing a Publisher with a Manuscript Copy of Theatrical Pieces & to whom this Defendant gave a gratuity on that account." (His failure to state the amount of the "gratuity" is frustrating.) Yet apparently the playwright's authorization was necessary if he or she was living, and Murphy had agreed. Exactly what happened will probably never be known. Perhaps Murphy assumed he would be compensated and was disagreeably surprised. Or perhaps he made the charge of theft only long afterwards in the heat of the lawsuits between the two. The fact that Murphy went on publishing with Vaillant for four more years suggests that he was not violently unhappy about his treatment over *The Upholsterer* in late 1763.

III. Publishing at the Author's Risk

On 9 January 1764 Covent Garden mounted a double bill by Murphy. *No One's Enemy but his Own* (3 acts) struggled through four nights, with a single author's benefit on the third (receipts unknown). *What we must all come to* (2 acts) was taken off after the first night. Why these shows failed so dismally is not at all clear, especially given that when Murphy revamped the afterpiece as *Three Weeks After Marriage* (1776), it proved steadily popular throughout the rest of the century. Whether Vaillant declined to pay full price for a pair of flops or Murphy thought he could make more money by having the works printed at his own risk is anyone's guess. Murphy's account of their agreement is as follows.

And your Orator some time in the Month of January 1764 delivered to the said Paul [Vaillant] Two several Copys of Two other Theatrical pieces One of which was intitled No one's Enemy but his own, a Comedy in Three acts and the other of the said Pieces was Intitled What we must all come to a Comedy in Two acts. But your Orator did not sell or Transfer the Copy Right of the said Two last mentioned pieces But delivered the said two Copys to be printed publishd and sold for your Orators Profit and Advantage. And the said Paul Vaillant agreed to print and Publish the Last two pieces for the usual Commission allowed to Booksellers by all authors who do not sell or Transfer their Copy right. And the said Paul Vaillant undertook to sell and dispose of the Printed Copys of the said Two pieces to and for your Orators Profit and

Advantage and also Agreed to sell the said comedy in Three Acts called No one's Enemy but his own at and for the price of One shilling and six pence for each Printed Copy and also to sell the said other piece Intitled What we must all come to at and for the price of one shilling for every Printed Copy. And the said Paul [Vaillant] further promised and agreed to keep a true and just Account of the Copys of the said Two pieces which he should dispose of or sell to Booksellers or others and to carry the several sums which he should receive for the same to the Credit of your Orator and to let and permit your Orator at all seasonable times to have ffree Inspection of the Book or Books in which such Account should be kept.

Murphy charges, however, that Vaillant "sometimes" pretends that he bought copyright for the two plays for £167, and sometimes admits that he agreed to print and sell them "for your Orator's Benefit and Advantage." But in the latter case "he pretends that he printed" only 2500 copies of each title and has sold only 806 of *No One's Enemy but his Own* and 722 of *What we must all come to*, and that he therefore retains unsold 1694 copies of the one and 1778 of the other. Vaillant claims that the total charges and expenses of printing, paper, stamp duty, advertising, and publishing came to £58 5s 9d, and that "from the sale of the said Two pieces the Ballance due to" the author is only £8 1s. Murphy counters that he believes "& doubts not to prove" that Vaillant "did order & cause . . . Archibald Hamilton in the said Month of January 1764 to print ffour thousand of each of the said pieces & that the Number of Printed Copys amounted together to Eight Thousand which were your Orator charges all Sold." This is a mind-boggling number of copies of two flat failures in the theatre, but Murphy goes on to claim that "sometime in the Month of May 1764 the said Paul Vaillant caused the said Archibald Hamilton or some other printer to print two Thousand Copies more & that of the 1st mentioned Number of Printed Copys there are very few Remaining now on hand." Consequently "it will appear from the Books of . . . Paul Vaillant that a Balance of no less than Three hundred pounds remains due to your Orator" for these two plays. These figures are difficult to believe, and the Court of Exchequer did not accept them.

Vaillant admits "that the Complainant did not sell or Transfer the Copyright of the said two last mentioned pieces to this Defendant but delivered him the said two copies to be printed published and sold for the Complainants profit and advantage." He insists, however, that only a single edition of 2500 copies of each play was ever printed by Hamilton or anyone else, and that only 807 and 722 copies respectively were ever sold. "And he this Defendant agreed to print and publish the said two pieces for the usual Commission allowed to Booksellers by all Authors who do not sell or Transfer their Copyright and undertook to sell and dispose of the printed Copies of the said two pieces to and for the Complainants profit." Vaillant denies that he agreed "to keep a true and just account of the Copies of the said pieces which he should dispose of or sell to Booksellers or others . . . tho' he apprehends that such promise was necessarily implied in the Transaction."

Vaillant summarizes the sales and the amounts owed to Murphy in a brief "Schedule" appended to his answer and reproduced in Table 2.[18]

18. We have reformatted slightly for clarity.

Table 2: Sales and Royalties on Plays Published at Murphy's Risk

		Owed to Author
What we must all come to [sold at 1s]		
617	sold	£22 4s
1858	unsold	
25	Mr Murphy Actors and Stamp	
2500		
105	sold since the 1767 accounting	£ 3 15s 9d
No One's Enemy but his Own [sold at 1s 6d]		
761	sold	£38 1s
1714	unsold	
25	Mr Murphy Actors and Stamp	
2500		
46	sold since the 1767 accounting	£ 2 6s
	Total owed to Murphy:	£66 6s 9d
	less cost of publication:	£58 5s 9d
	balance:	£ 8 1s

Whatever number of copies might theoretically have been printed, the chances are good that the number of unsold copies is reported accurately, since Vaillant had turned them over to Thomas Lowndes when he left the business in 1773 and Lowndes could have been called on to testify. We note one oddity: the commission paid to the bookseller was not the same for the two plays. In the case of *No One's Enemy but his Own* (sold at 1s 6d), Vaillant kept 6d (one third of the price) from each copy, and credited the author with a 1s royalty. For *What we must all come to* (sold at 1s) however, the fee was neither 6d nor one-third of the price (4d). The sum Vaillant actually collected was just over 3½ pence per copy, which seems extremely peculiar. This is not just a matter of a copying error in the "Schedule," since neither the main total nor the later sales work out to a rational royalty for the author. We have no explanation.

The figures in Table 2 permit us to calculate a rough economic basis for play publication at this time. Vaillant states (and Murphy does not challenge the figures) that the total manufacturing, advertising, and stamp duty cost of the two plays came to £58 5s 9d (which when subtracted from the author's share of sales left Murphy the depressing sum of £8 1s for the two plays). We might, therefore, assume that publishing 2500 copies of a standard mainpiece cost upwards of £35, while an afterpiece might come to something like £25. Consider the implications of these figures. The mainpiece, if sold at 1s 6d, might generate a gross income of £187 10s. If the author were paid £105 cash down for the copyright (as Murphy had been for *The Orphan of China* and *All in the Wrong*), then the publisher was investing £140 up front in the hope that he might someday recover his investment and make a profit. Ignoring storage and overheads, he would eventually make about £45 *if* all the copies sold. Not until upwards of 1867 copies had been sold would the book start to go into the black. In view of these figures one can readily see why publishers liked to sell fractional interests to a number of friends, getting some cash back immediately and spreading the risk. The figures on after-pieces are similar. If sales were 2500 at a shilling each, the potential gross would be £125. The cost would be about £25 for manufacturing plus £52 10s copyright payment to the author, for a total of £77 10s. The cost recovery figure is marginally better: 1550 copies would pay for the book, and if all copies sold, the printer might hope for roughly £45 in profit (again ignoring overheads).

What is absolutely clear from these particular figures is that Murphy would have been vastly better off if he had received for these plays what he had been paid for his earlier work—£105 plus £52 10s would have totalled £157 10s as opposed to £8 1s. Whether Vaillant offered him those terms the lawsuit does not say. Conceivably, Vaillant offered less—the plays were, after all, failures—and Murphy refused. Whatever happened, the likelihood is that Murphy's total profit from this pair of plays was not much more than a hundred pounds, and far less if his single benefit was poorly attended.

IV. The Dispute over *Belisarius*

The one non-dramatic work by Murphy that Vaillant published is a translation of a French novella by Jean-François Marmontel.[19] We consider it here for the sake of clarifying the grounds of the entire dispute and because it sheds some interesting light on the process of hasty commercial translation and the economics of such publication.

Murphy charges that "in the Month of ffebruary 1767" he delivered to Vaillant "the Manuscript Copy of a Book Intitled Belisaurius which was originally written in ffrench by Monsieur De Marmintal, and which your Orator Translated into the English Language." The translation was "to be by him Published and sold for your Orators profit and Advantage and your Orator did not Transfer or sell nor make any Bargain or Agreement to Transfer or sell the Copy of the said Translation." Murphy alleges that Vaillant has "sold sundry Large Impressions of the said Work amounting to Ten thousand Copies at and for the price of four shillings for each Printed Copy," but that he has paid Murphy nothing and refuses to show him the accounts. Later in his bill of complaint Murphy says that Vaillant "sometimes" claims that Murphy made him a gift of the translation, and sometimes claims that he bought the copyright for £21, giving "colour to this his pretence" by having lent Murphy £21, taking a promissory note for it dated 5 March 1767, and then "falsely & fraudulently" writing "a certain Memorandum at the foot of the above mentioned promisory Note" concerning *Belisarius*. Murphy maintains that "a ballance of ffive hundred pounds" is due to him on sales

19. *Murphy v. Vaillant* proves beyond question that Murphy was the translator of *Belisarius*, by M. Marmontel (London: Printed for and Sold by P. Vaillant . . . and by Robinson and Roberts, 1767). Emery (pp. 97–98 and notes) says that "Murphy's authorship has been generally overlooked by modern critics" but fails to explain the basis of his attribution. *NCBEL* does not credit Murphy with the work and neither does the 1975 Garland facsimile.

of the translation, which would be a very modest profit on sales allegedly totalling £2000 (10,000 copies at 4s each).

On this evidence, Vaillant would certainly seem to be a fraud and a cheat. His answer, however, makes much better sense than Murphy's charges:

in or about the Month of february 1767 he having received Intelligence that a Book intitled Belisarius written in French by Monsieur de Marmontel was then publishing in Paris[20] he this Defendant procured from Paris by the Post the first three or four sheets of the said work as they were printed off with design to have the same Translated into English and to secure to himself the Property in the said Translation and to sell such Translation for his own emolument and being desirous of Employing the said Complainant in that business he this Defendant carried the said first three or four sheets of the said work written in ffrench to the said Complainant who agreed and undertook to Translate the same for and on the Account of him this Defendant and to oblige him and not otherwise and said that as he was then called to the bar he would not put his Name to the Title as he would not choose any longer to be considered as a writer for hire least the Publick should imagine that he attended to such kind of Business more than to the Law.

Murphy had been educated in France at the English Jesuit College at St. Omer. He was not merely boasting when he said in the unsigned Translator's Preface that this was "not journeywork: it was undertaken *con amore*, with a kind of affection for the various graces of M. Marmontel's performance."[21] Vaillant says that Murphy accordingly carried out the translation as Vaillant brought him fresh copy hot from Paris, but that no agreement for sale of the work was ever made.[22] He admits that he loaned Murphy £21 and that without Murphy's knowledge or consent he wrote a memorandum on the promissory note that might be taken to imply that the £21 (which had not been repaid) was payment for *Belisarius*. He admits to having printed five thousand (not ten thousand) copies and having sold 4,200 of them, but at "the Price of three shillings for each Printed Copy of the two first Editions when bound and of three shillings and six pence for the subsequent Editions and not at the Price of four shillings."[23] The gross receipts must have been close to £700,[24] and even allowing lavish costs for printing, paper, copper plates,

---

20. *Bélisaire* received its *approbation* on 20 November 1766, its *privilège du roi* on 16 December, and was listed in the *Catalogue hebdomadaire* of 7 February 1767. See the edition by Robert Granderoute (Paris: Société des Textes Français Modernes, 1994), lix, 212–214.

21. *Belisarius*, p. iv.

22. Later in his reply, Vaillant hedges a bit, denying that he considered the translation a "present," but insisting that it was delivered to him "without bargaining for any Price or Consideration for the same." He "allowed" Murphy credit for £21 on the advice of his attorney, who "thought it was proper to do so to prevent the Complainant from afterwards setting up any claim on this Defendant with respect to the said Translation."

23. What Vaillant may have told Murphy when not under oath is something else again. Murphy charges in his bill of complaint that Vaillant claimed he had printed 1500 copies, sold 1300 at 2s each, and received in toto only £130, "which . . . he pretends is not sufficient to Reimburse him for the Costs & Charges of paper printing Binding publishing & the copper plate Engravings." On the evidence of this suit, however, Murphy must be regarded as a less than reliable source. The initial publication announcement in the *Public Advertiser* of 7 March 1767 described the book as "One Volume 12mo, Price 3s. bound."

24. Vaillant says he sold 1500 at 3s and 2700 at 3/6, which would be a gross of £697 10s.

and so forth, the net profit ought to have been more than £400—a sum Murphy would no doubt have liked to collect.

Neither man's story seems wonderfully plausible: we must believe either that Murphy gave away the translation or that Vaillant was a bare-faced thief who agreed to publish the manuscript at the author's risk and then appropriated all the profits when they proved substantial. Fortunately, there is one further piece of evidence, and it hoists Murphy neatly by his own petard. Vaillant offers to put in evidence

a Letter written by the said Complainant to him this Defendant in the Words and figures following that is to say, Dear Sir, . . . inclosed I send you the Plan of a projected Edition of Murphei Opera Omnia. I have this Affair very much at heart and am eager to see it executed. I wish to do it in conjunction with you in Preference to all others. I beg you will consider of it and let me know your Thoughts. The pieces with this Mark X are your own already but I suppose if you do not choose to be concerned that by Custom the Author may give a Complete Edition of his Works. I am Dear Sir Yours sincerely Arthur Murphy Lincolns Inn 26th November 1770. To Paul Vaillant Esqr. And in the said Letter was inclosed a plan which is referred to by the said Letter and which is of the Complainants Handwriting and Marking as to the said Mark And is now in this Defendants custody or Power. In which plan the said Composition or work [*Belisarius*] is with several others marked with the said Mark X as being the property of this Defendant.

This seems conclusive: as of 1770 Murphy had admitted of his own accord that *Belisarius* was Vaillant's property.

Some comments made in passing by both parties clarify the nature of this project and the relations between author and publisher. Murphy complains that he spent ten weeks on the job, which is not possible, given the French and English publication schedules. He says that Vaillant told him "that if the said Work had been transacted by an unskilful hand or by any of the Persons whom Booksellers occasionally hire & call Hackney writers that the merit of the original ffrench would have suffered & been obscured to such a degree that the Translation would probably have a very indifferent Sale & the profits of course would have been much Diminished." He also says that Vaillant sent him "sundry Notes Cards or Letters recommending to your Orator to persevere in the said Translation & assuring him that the Translation if finished as it began would redound very much to the profit as well as the Reputation of your Orator." These notes were apparently not saved, for Murphy does not offer to put them in evidence.

Vaillant replies that Murphy "was employed in the whole ffive Weekes in making the said Translation and not more," and that "had it not been for the Delay occasioned by not receiving the French Work from Paris regularly the said Complainant could easily have translated the said Work in twelve Days" because "the whole Work when printed amount[ed] to no more than ten sheets and an half" (which is correct if one includes the prelims). Murphy, he says, "performed the Translation with so much facility as not to be obliged even to transcribe his Copy for the press." He says he might have made dismissive remarks about "Hackney Writers" and "believes that he might write to him the Complainant some flattering Letter or Letters in order to induce him the Complainant to take more Pains for this Defendant saith that the Complainant translated it so very fast that he this Defendant was in Fear that it would be done too much in a Hurry." Naturally he denies saying anything that might imply that Murphy would benefit financially beyond the £21 loan that Vaillant did not mean to insist on his repaying.

Why Murphy did what he did we will probably never know. One can, however, understand his ex post facto frustration. He had scribbled off a translation in the course of a few weeks, working part time and doing no revision—with the result that Paul Vaillant had profited to the extent of some £400 or more. Marmontel's radical critique of the French government drew praise from Murphy, along with a statement that helps explain Vaillant's eagerness. The translator asserts that Marmontel "has had the genius and the courage to think with freedom, even in Paris, where we understand, by the last post, that his book is now suppressed" (vi), news that presumably helped sales.[25] Murphy may have done the translation essentially as a favor, but probably had no inkling that it would prove so valuable a property. When Vaillant subsequently took him to court, demanding nearly £200 from him, Murphy had some cause to feel that Vaillant had not only picked his pocket but was trying to strip his carcass clean.

V. The Author's Dilemma

We do not wish to overgeneralize from the particulars made known in this one case. They concern one writer, one publisher, and a period of just over a decade. By the standard of the contracts preserved in British Library Add. MS. 38,728 for the 1730s and 1740s, Vaillant's prices seem decidedly generous. Taking into account Murphy's relatively junior status as a playwright, the prices seem even more lavish, particularly for afterpieces. John Watts (publisher of most of the plays for which contracts are known in the earlier period) rarely paid more than £50 for a mainpiece and often bought afterpieces for 5 guineas or even less. Until more facts have been discovered for the post-1750 period, the representativeness of these prices and the commonness of outright sale of copyright of plays must remain questionable. Likewise we simply do not know how often playwrights chose to have plays published at their own risk in the 1760s, what they were charged by their printers, or what the bottom line looked like. The prices given for copyright do not seem out of line with those given by Dodsley at about the same time.[26]

Surveying the practices described in *Murphy v. Vaillant*, we are struck by two points in particular: the casualness with which author and publisher

25. The Translator's Preface is dated 2 March 1767. Sale of Marmontel's book was forbidden ca. 20/21 February. See John Renwick, *Marmontel, Voltaire and the Bélisaire Affair*, Studies on Voltaire and the Eighteenth Century, 121 (Banbury, Oxfordshire: Voltaire Foundation, 1974), p. 319. Referring to the controversial Chapter XV, Renwick also notes that whereas most of the book was translated literally, "the gain of *c.* 300 words in less than eleven pages is both considerable and illuminating" (p. 139, n. 30).

26. See *The Correspondence of Robert Dodsley 1733–1764*, ed. James E. Tierney (Cambridge: Cambridge Univ. Press, 1988), Appendixes B and E.

did their business, and the extent to which Vaillant was prepared to loan Murphy money without charging him interest. Up to February 1760 Murphy and Vaillant operated a bit sloppily (formalizing contracts long after publication, for example), but they struck bargains, eventually reduced them to writing before witnesses, and paid over the money due. When they balanced their books on 7 February 1760 they were all square with little room for difference of opinion. (Murphy tried to obscure this settlement, but Vaillant was able to prove conclusively that all transactions prior to this date were settled and hence irrelevant to the lawsuit.) After that, they depended on oral agreements not made before witnesses, even when they drastically changed the terms on which they were doing business. They should unquestionably have made a written agreement about *No One's Enemy but his Own* and *All in the Wrong*. Their failure to set clear terms for *Belisarius* is even stranger.

Between 26 February 1760 (when their "new Account was opened") and 23 December 1767 (when Vaillant presented Murphy with a bill for £192 5s 10d) Murphy collected substantial sums from Vaillant. Vaillant held receipts and notes of hand amounting to £405 1s 7d, to which he added £16 6s 6d "Book debt" and £58 5s 9d for printing the two plays at Murphy's risk for a total of £479 12s 10d [*recte* 13s 10d]. He calculated what he owed Murphy for this period as £52 10s for the alteration of *The Way to Keep Him*, £105 for *All in the Wrong*, £42 for *The Old Maid*; £6 13s for 38 copies sold of the *Gray's Inn Journal* at 3/6 each, £25 19s 9d for 722 copies of *What we must all come to*, £40 7s, for 805 copies of *No One's Enemy but his Own*, and £21 allowed for *Belisarius*—"amounting in the whole to the sum of" £293 9s 9d. The difference, £186 3s 1d, reflects loans and cash advances on unsold books. Vaillant says apropos of his obtaining and printing the revised text of *The Upholsterer* that Murphy gave him "the said Additions and Alterations . . . partly moved by this Defendants Civilities to him & not requiring Interest from him for Money advanced to him." We would guess that Vaillant regarded Murphy as a promising writer worth some coddling and concessions, and that he therefore allowed the playwright to draw money he had not yet earned. When Murphy showed clear signs of withdrawing from full-time playwriting, Vaillant not unnaturally totted up his accounts, discovered that he was owed upwards of £200, and tried to collect. Murphy put him off for fully six years before the claim went to the Court of Common Pleas—and then tried to block execution of the judgment of that court by filing a cross-bill in Exchequer.

More significant than the specifics of the case are the larger issues of authorship and remuneration. A playwright could sell his or her text and collect cash up front, but the transaction effectively concluded his interest in his book. In theory he would regain copyright after fourteen years, but relatively few plays had significant sales fifteen years after they came out. The author could choose to have the work printed at his or her own risk, but what was to prevent the printer from cheating the author blind? Costs might be padded. Worse, extra copies might be manufactured and sales concealed.

How would the author know? Murphy demanded access to Vaillant's account books—but businesses have been known to keep more than one set of books. And whatever the accounts might show, a steep price to a printer or a binder or a supplier of goods can conceal a cash kickback to the proprietor of the business.

Consider the playwright's options. Should the publication agreement be negotiated before or after the premiere? Success might raise the price, but failure would probably lower it. Really substantial profits from playwriting required multiple benefits from a mainpiece, but a mainpiece that died in three nights or so would not be easy to sell to a publisher. Conventional wisdom among twentieth-century commentators holds that eighteenth-century playwrights were exploited and bilked by publishers who acquired rights to plays for flat fees and then pocketed all the profits. There are certainly cases on record in which the publisher sold enormous numbers of copies of a text he had acquired for a relative pittance. Bernard Lintot, for example, bought Farquhar's *The Recruiting Officer* for £16 2s 6d and *The Beaux Stratagem* for £30.[27] There is another side to this coin, however. The playwright might get a substantial amount of much-needed cash in a lump sum up front, leaving all risk to the publisher. Unquestionably, the only way for a playwright to make a lot of money from publication was to accept risk and have the book printed "for the Author." John Gay did this with *Polly* in 1729, capitalizing on a subscription and the notoriety of the playhouse ban.[28] One of the more interesting implications of *Murphy v. Vaillant*, however, is that for an ordinary play, outright sale of the copy might well have proved a better deal for the author than has generally been supposed.[29]

27. John Nichols, *Literary Anecdotes of the Eighteenth Century*, 9 vols. (London: For the Author, 1812–1816), VIII, 296.

28. See Calhoun Winton, *John Gay and the London Theatre* (Lexington: University Press of Kentucky, 1993), p. 135. From subscriptions and sales Gay may have netted as much as £3000.

29. For a broader consideration of earnings from plays in the eighteenth century and a full list of known payments for copyright, see Judith Milhous and Robert D. Hume, "Playwrights' Remuneration in Eighteenth-Century London," *Harvard Library Bulletin*, forthcoming.

THE FIRST TITLE PAGE OF *LYRICAL BALLADS*, 1798

by

Mark L. Reed

I

As Wordsworth and Coleridge's joint collection *Lyrical Ballads* enters the third century of its age, almost everyone interested agrees that the few extant copies of the 1798 edition having a title-page imprint addressed "BRISTOL" and naming as publisher "T. N. LONGMAN" represent the earliest issued form of this immensely important book, a form succeeded by that of an abundantly surviving issue having an imprint addressed "LONDON" and naming as publisher "J. & A. ARCH." This happy state of agreement quite rightly ignores unsubstantiated nineteenth-century bibliographic reports of an even earlier title-page imprint. Less properly, it neglects carefully reasoned arguments for the existence of such an imprint by a distinguished modern bibliographer, D. F. Foxon. Foxon's proposals are only a part of his indispensable essay "The Printing of *Lyrical Ballads*, 1798,"[1] but overlooked or not, they make uneasy the historical status of the Bristol-Longman issue of the 1798 *Lyrical Ballads,* and hold forth the bemusing possibility that somewhere a copy of this book awaits discovery containing a title page earlier than that of the black-tulip Bristol-Longman issue, as a tulip of unexampled blackness. Absolute certainty about the matter is not possible, but a much firmer ground of probability is available. To reach it some preliminary review is necessary, first, of the little that seems more or less clear about the early history of *Lyrical Ballads* and, second, of Foxon's arguments.

II

Portions of what I offer as a consensus view of the early history of the book may seem almost tediously familiar.[2] In spring of 1798 Wordsworth,

1. *The Library* 5th ser. 9 (1954), 221–241. Foxon notes nineteenth-century reference to an earlier title page in Bohn's edition of Lowndes's *Bibliographer's Manual* (I, 493), repeated by Knight in his edition of Wordsworth's Poems (1882–1889, I, xl). It is also repeated by J. R. Tutin, "The Bibliography of Wordsworth," *Complete Poetical Works of William Wordsworth* (London, 1888), pp. 897–912 (also issued separately).

For assistance in the preparation of this article I am indebted to Drs. H. George Fletcher, David McKitterick, Robert Petre, and Robert Woof, to Professors James A. Butler, Bruce Graver, and Peter Lindenbaum, to Courtney Lehmann, and to the staffs of the libraries named hereafter.

2. I draw especially on Foxon and on Joseph Cottle, *Early Recollections, Chiefly Relating to the Late Samuel Taylor Coleridge* (London, 1837), I, 310–325, II, 23–27; Cottle, *Remi-*

Coleridge, and their friend the Bristol bookseller Joseph Cottle settled on a plan that Cottle publish a joint collection of Wordsworth's and Coleridge's poems, *Lyrical Ballads*. Authorship was to remain anonymous.[3] Printing went forward in Bristol during the summer. The poems printed began with Coleridge's "The Rime of the Ancyent Marinere" and concluded with Wordsworth's "Lines Written a Few Miles above Tintern Abbey," and among them was a poem by Coleridge (based on a juvenile poem by Wordsworth), "Lewti," which had already been published pseudonymously. What resulted bibliographically from the printing was a volume with collation $\pi 1$ $2\pi 1$ $[A]^8$ $B-N^8$ O^4 $(-O_4)$: $\pi 1$ containing the title: $2\pi 1$, the table of contents; $[A]1$ through $O1$, the text; $O2$, a list of errata; and $O3$, an advertisement of books published jointly by Biggs and Cottle, T. N. Longman, and Lee and Hurst. Apparently just as printing concluded, however, someone—most likely Coleridge—recognized that the true authorship of "Lewti" was public knowledge and that the anonymity of the book was compromised; so "Lewti" was cancelled and replaced by another poem of Coleridge's, "The Nightingale." At much that same moment Wordsworth brought forward a short prefatory essay for the book. The products of these two events, for printing and binding, were four new leaves for "The Nightingale," replacing the three leaves occupied by "Lewti;" three new leaves for Wordsworth's prefatory essay, inserted between title leaf and contents leaf; and a new contents leaf, now following the prefatory essay rather than the title and listing "The Nightingale" instead of "Lewti." Accordingly, "The Nightingale" was printed on a half sheet for gathering as a four, and the prefatory essay and new contents page were likewise printed on a half sheet for gathering as a four; and the

---

niscences of Samuel Taylor Coleridge and Robert Southey (London, 1847), pp. 166–185; *Lyrical Ballads by William Wordsworth and S. T. Coleridge*, ed. Thomas Hutchinson (London, 1898), pp. ix–xvi; Thomas J. Wise, *Bibliography of the Writings in Prose and Verse of William Wordsworth* (London, 1916), pp. 14–34; Wise, *Two Lake Poets, A Catalogue of Printed Books, Manuscripts and Autograph Letters by William Wordsworth and Samuel Taylor Coleridge* (London, 1927), pp. 3–6; Wise, *The Ashley Library* (London, 1922–1936), VII, 4–5; Robert W. Daniel, "The Publication of the 'Lyrical Ballads', *MLR* XXXIII (1938), 406–410; *The Letters of Samuel Taylor Coleridge*, ed. E. L. Griggs, (Oxford, 1956), I, 411–413; Mary Moorman, *William Wordsworth, A Biography: The Early Years* (Oxford, 1957; rev. 1968), pp. 370–409; *The Letters of William and Dorothy Wordsworth, The Early Years, 1787–1805*, ed. Ernest de Selincourt, rev. Chester L. Shaver (Oxford, 1967), pp. 217–228; Mark L. Reed, *Wordsworth: The Chronology of the Early Years* (Cambridge, MA, 1967), pp. 238–249; James A. Butler, "Wordsworth, Cottle, and the *Lyrical Ballads*: Five Letters, 1797–1800," *JEGP* 75 (1976), 139–153; James Butler and Karen Green, eds., '*Lyrical Ballads' and Other Poems* (Ithaca, NY, 1992), pp. 11–15, 44; Alan D. Boehm, "The 1798 *Lyrical Ballads* and the Poetics of Late Eighteenth-Century Book Production," *ELH* 63 (1996), 453–487.

3. Coleridge, writing to Cottle probably on 4 June, urges as compelling anonymity the circumstance that "to a large number of persons" his name "*stinks*." (*The Letters of Samuel Taylor Coleridge*, as cited in note 2; Reed, pp. 238–239.) Dr. Robert Woof points out to me that Coleridge's phrasing shows him fully aware of the existence of political hostility of the sort that was from July until September to fuel lampoons of him in the *Anti-Jacobin*, where he was ridiculed in the poem "The New Morality," the poem "The Anarchists," and Gillray's caricature based on the first poem.

collation of the revised volume became $\pi 1$ $2\pi^4$ [A]^8 B—D^8 (—D8) χ^4 E^8 (—E1, 2) F—N^{8}O^4 (—O4): $\pi 1$ containing the title; $2\pi 1$, 2, 3 containing the prefatory essay; $2\pi 4$ containing the new table of contents; D, χ, and E now incorporating "The Nightingale"; and the rest remaining unaltered. The title pages of the earliest-bound copies known, however, indicate that by the time they were printed Cottle had resigned the office of publisher; for their imprint is, in full, "BRISTOL: | PRINTED BY BIGGS AND COTTLE, | FOR T. N. LONG-MAN, PATERNOSTER-ROW, LONDON. | 1798." Cottle's retreat had probably been caused by an intimidating combination of financial ill-health and doubts—possibly induced by Robert Southey—regarding sales; but Longman, although Cottle had undoubtedly approached him, had not yet formally undertaken the publication.

The scene of events widened beyond Bristol in late August when, certainly not before holding the completed *Lyrical Ballads* in their hands, Wordsworth, Dorothy Wordsworth, and Coleridge set off for Germany. By 28 August William and Dorothy, at least, had reached London, where William planned diplomacy of some sort with Longman. On 5 September Southey wrote about the book to William Taylor of Norwich in phrasing that suggests he thought it well distributed; and by the second week of September copies had been received by London literati and by acquaintances of Cottle and the authors. By mid-September Wordsworth had recognized that Longman would not participate in the enterprise, and, without consulting Cottle, had found a willing publisher in Joseph Johnson (who had published Wordsworth's only earlier books *An Evening Walk* and *Descriptive Sketches*). Cottle by then not only knew about Longman but had probably already sold the edition to the Arch brothers and set about printing a new title page and binding copies for them. On 15 September the uninformed Wordsworth wrote to Cottle from Yarmouth asking him to transfer the edition to Johnson. Next day, none the wiser, he, Dorothy, and Coleridge sailed for Germany. The Arches announced *Lyrical Ballads* to the public on 4 October. Cottle was to have paid Wordsworth thirty guineas upon completion of printing, but because of his embarrassed circumstances did not complete payment until July 1799.

Copies representing the ideal first Bristol-Longman collation of the book as just described—$\pi 1$ $2\pi 1$ [A]^8 B—N^{8}O^4 (—O4)—are found at Yale University (Beineke Library) and Princeton University. Copies representing the ideal second Bristol-Longman collation as just described—$\pi 1$ $2\pi^4$ [A]^8 B—D^8 (—D8) χ^4 E^8 (—E1, 2) F—N^8 O^4 (—O4)—are found at Cornell University; Harvard University (Widener Collection); New York Public Library (Berg Collection); Wellington University (Alexander Turnbull Library). On the recto of the front free end paper of the Harvard copy appears an owner's inscription by a friend of Wordsworth's, John Frederick Pinney, dated at Pinney's home, "Great George Street | Bristol, 1798", and on the front pastedown appears a note, apparently in the same hand, "Coleridge's Rime of the Ancyent Marinere", but how Pinney obtained the book remains uncertain.

Copies representing the ideal second Bristol-Longman collation except in lacking leaf O3 are at Indiana University (Lilly Library) and Trinity College, Cambridge (*The Rothschild Library*, Cambridge, 1954, item no. 2603 and plate XLVI); and in a private collection, copy presently on deposit at the Pierpont Morgan Library (*Rothschild Library*, item no. 2602); and another was in a private collection when examined in 1994. The Trinity College copy contains early revision of "The Ancyent Marinere" in the autograph of Coleridge, and one of the leaves containing revision has been rudely folded and torn out—as if used for a memorandum—and later replaced: it is hard to imagine that the rudeness came from anyone but Coleridge, in a copy that he at the time regarded as practically expendable—so, likely to have been in his hands soon after printing. Other Bristol-Longman copies survive incomplete and/or with redundant leaves—one each at the New York Public Library (Berg Collection) and Yale (Beineke Library), and two at the British Library. These four appear to be variously the results of making-do, of bibliophilic preservation, and of jest. This New York Public Library copy evidently once belonged to Coleridge's and Southey's sister-in-law Martha Fricker and was probably presented to her by Coleridge.[4] It is bound in calico-cloth-covered boards in a fashion characteristic of bindings done by members of the Southey family for—although perhaps not exclusively for—what Southey called his "Cottonian Library." It lacks a title leaf but retains the "Lewti" contents leaf, and the body of the book is of the first ideal collation, $[A]^8$ B–$N^8 O^4$ ($-O_4$).[5] Certainly one of the British Library copies, and probably the Yale copy, were bound deliberately to preserve together both the earlier "Lewti" and later "Nightingale." This British Library copy (C 58 c 12 [1]), which once belonged to Southey, includes the Bristol-Longman title leaf, the "Lewti" contents leaf, also $2\pi^4$ (including the "Nightingale" contents leaf), and also a complete D^8 including "Lewti," but lacks O_3.[6] The Yale copy (In W890 798c) is the same except that it lacks also the "Lewti" contents leaf. The other British Library copy is like ideal-collation "Nightingale" copies except that following page 62 (that is, between D_7 and χ_1) is inserted a leaf containing Thomas Beddoes' "Domiciliary Verses," which were intended as a parody of the poetic style of the surrounding volume. The leaf was printed and inserted at Beddoes' direction.[7] I have examined all of these books. The

4. See John D. Gordan, *William Wordsworth, 1770–1850, An Exhibition* (New York, 1950), p. 6; Foxon, p. 236.

5. This copy was reproduced in facsimile in the Noel Douglas Replica Series, London, 1926; and again by the Scolar Press, Menston, in 1971.

6. Stitchholes show that the contents leaf was earlier bound in wrong way around between $[A]_2$ and $[A]_3$, following the leaf containing the Argument for "The Ancyent Marinere." (Foxon, p. 237, notes this placement but not the reversal.) The earlier placement seems too strange to have resulted from mere carelessness. One might conjecture that the original Cottonian binder (a) had no title leaf, (b) wished the book to commence with the next-most-impressive title available, the half title for "The Ancyent Marinere," on the recto of $[A]_1$, (c) doggedly wanted to keep the table of contents near the front, yet was forced to recognize that any such placement of it would one way or another intrude as an irrelevance on "The Ancyent Marinere," and (d) decided that the least of evils would be to insert the leaf after the Argument leaf but reversed so that the blank, less preoccupying, side of the leaf would meet a reader's eye first.

7. Concerning these four copies see especially Foxon, pp. 224–225, 233–237, and Duncan

sheets of at least two of them—that containing Beddoes' verses and that at Cornell—were first gathered by the binder with a "Lewti" contents leaf following the Bristol-Longman title, then altered by substitution of four-leaf 2π for the "Lewti" contents leaf, plainly in a process of conversation of first-collation copies to second-collation: a clear sign that the Longman title was in use, and so almost certainly printed, before $2\pi^4$—and, for reasons to be indicated more distinctly below—before χ as well.[8] The volume as finally published by J. and A. Arch is, apart from the title leaf, identical with the second-ideal-collation Bristol-Longman *Lyrical Ballads* as already described.

III

Foxon's argument concerning the title page of the first issue of *Lyrical Ballads* is an outgrowth of other arguments of his, which must also be reviewed briefly, about the printing of the last gathering of the volume, O, and $2\pi^4$ and χ. Foxon demonstrates from point-hole evidence that $2\pi^4$ (prefatory essay and new table of contents) and χ ("The Nightingale") were probably printed together on a single sheet for binding as fours. He also shows that the placement of the point-hole in half-sheet O differs from that of the point-holes in $2\pi4$ and χ—implying use of a different press—and that the placement indicates half-sheet (that is, work-and-turn) imposition. The weight of this last conclusion, combined with two other facts, pushes over another domino. The other facts are that when the London-Arch title leaf contains a watermark (as it often does) it is the "YD 1795" portion of the regular watermark of *Lyrical Ballads* sheets, "LLOYD 1795"; and that when the first leaf of gathering O contains a watermark, it is the same portion of that same watermark. Thus the "YD 1795" portion of the watermark could not possibly appear in a London-Arch title leaf that had been printed as O4. Since the Bristol-Longman and London-Arch title pages are identical except for publisher's imprint, one might have been tempted to suppose incorrectly that the London-Arch imprint was an alteration made while O4 was in press.

Other evidence drawn by Foxon from paper indicates to him in turn, however, that the Bristol-Longman title was not printed on O4. No example of the title leaf in the eight Bristol-Longman copies investigated by him contained a watermark at all—an unlikely circumstance, by "the laws of chance," if this title had been printed on O4 (p. 227); and the paper in its own right seemed different from that of the printed sheets generally, or "odd"

Wu, *"Lyrical Ballads* (1798): the Beddoes Copy," *The Library* 6th ser. 15 (1993), 332–335. Wu cites John Edmonds Stock, *Memoirs of the Life of Thomas Beddoes, M.D.*, (London [&c.], 1811), p. 114.

8. Foxon, p. 235, notes that the verso of the title leaf of the Beddoes copy reveals offset from a table of contents. Since the "Nightingale" table of contents was printed on the recto of the fourth leaf of its gathering, it—unlike the "Lewti" contents leaf as originally bound—could not have offset on the verso of the title leaf. The verso of the title leaf of the Cornell Bristol-Longman copy retains similar table-of-contents offset.

(p. 238). Having shown that neither the known Bristol-Longman title nor London-Arch title was printed as O4, he concludes—his conclusion is stated both with qualification (in various places) and absolutely (once)—that O4 contained an earlier title page.[9] This title page would have contained an imprint of the sort that Cottle intended for the book when arranging plans for the volume with Wordsworth and Coleridge in the spring: one naming him as publisher. The Bristol-Longman title should accordingly be regarded as an intermediate or "trial" printing used for a small number of advance copies. The London-Arch title was the permanent, or "true," cancel that replaced the Cottle title.

Foxon finds further indication of the probable content of O4 in the visible content of O1, 2, 3—respectively the conclusion of "Tintern Abbey," the errata list, and the publishers' advertisements—reasoning that had the printer not by then expected to receive materials additional to the title and contents, he would scarcely have printed the "quite gratuitous" leaf of publishers' advertisements on O3: he would have printed the title and table of contents on the remaining two leaves and so finished off the book. The presence of the publishers' advertisements shows him killing time and space: not improbably held up in particular by the prospect of the introductory essay or because the need to cancel "Lewti" was realized, he finished off O "as best he could" (p. 237); that is, he printed the Cottle title and postponed printing the contents leaf in hope of combining it with the introductory essay.

Briefer attention is given by Foxon to the printing of the other preliminary leaf, which contained the table of contents that included "Lewti," but he remarks that none of the three examples of the "Lewti" contents leaf known to him contained a watermark, and that the opinions of unprompted independent witnesses confirmed that the paper of these leaves differs from that of the body of the book. The status of this leaf, thus, appears to resemble that of the Bristol-Longman title—basically, that of a stop-gap—and the leaf was printed probably so that a few copies of the first-state printing might be bound up at once for inner-circle distribution.

Foxon summarizes his inferences as being "on the following lines":

The body of the book was printed by mid-August, and Southey warned Cottle that it would be a failure. Cottle offered it to Longman and printed proofs of the Longman title-page. Then "Lewti" was canceled and the preliminaries printed; and copies were made up with the Longman title-page, since the Wordsworths were about to leave Bristol and wished to see the book completed. (pp. 240–241)

This picture has been variously enriched since Foxon wrote, especially by Butler, Butler and Green, and Boehm, but has not been basically altered nor in most respects is likely to be. Our present concern is with the limited subject of a bibliographic presumption that Foxon will have supposed that his reader, having reached this late point in his essay, would regard as implicit

---

9. Possibly unfairly I construe as absolute the conclusion of his remark regarding gathering O, "What is quite impossible is that the [watermark date] should appear on the fourth leaf—that is, the title page" (p. 227).

in the sentences just quoted: that the printing of *Lyrical Ballads* as accomplished by mid-August included a title page antecedent to the "proof" Bristol-Longman title page. This presumption is inextricable, however, from another also implicit: that the "Lewti" contents page did not make part of the original printing and was not intended for publication.

IV

With regard to Foxon's views of the relationship between title and table of contents, one might indeed feel uncomfortable with the pace of a scenario in which, while the original printing of the book perhaps included a Cottle title page on O4, and while no evidence exists that the cancellation of "Lewti" was determined before that title was printed, nonetheless either the cancellation of "Lewti" or the arrival of Wordsworth's prefatory essay occurred at a moment so exactly timed that it caused the printer to pull up short and print the "Lewti" table of contents merely for nonce purposes and on nonstandard paper. And one might also feel, regarding the printer's supposedly "gratuitous" use of space on the half sheet O for advertisements, that Cottle in his weak financial condition would hardly have regarded such advertisements as a matter of little importance. But in any case, at a more concrete level, one must also notice the degree to which Foxon's fundamental logic depends on his assessments of paper.

These assessments are in fact crucial, as Foxon himself helps us see. He points out that the setting of type for both contents pages, except for the line originally listing "Lewti," is the same (p. 224). So if he had found the paper of the "Lewti" contents leaf to be the same as that of the rest of the volume, he would have felt necessary—barring preclusive evidence such as an inappropriate watermark—to consider the possibility that the "Lewti" table of contents rather than a Bristol-Cottle title might have occupied O4. As already indicated, he also points out that the setting of type for the Bristol-Longman title is, apart from imprint, the same as the London-Arch. So if the Bristol-Longman title had been found printed on the same paper as the rest of the book, the leaf on which it is printed would have had to be regarded as physically no worse suited for public issue than the London-Arch title even though, in the event, it was not printed in a full run. Finally, if both the contents leaf and the title leaf had been found printed on the same paper as the rest of the volume, the story (watermarks not contradicting) would be, prima facie, that the "Lewti" contents leaf was printed as O4, that the Bristol-Longman title was printed at practically the same time, and that the binder, when he used the Bristol-Longman title for copies of the book containing "Lewti," was using the only title leaf that had been printed. And no reason would be evident why copies in either of the two ideal Bristol-Longman-imprint collations should not have been thought, at the time they were bound, ready for open-market sale as soon as Longman became the publisher that the title page announced him to be. Probably, in fact, both these leaves were printed on the same paper as the body of the book, and probably the "Lewti" table of contents was printed on O4.

V

To be remarked first and generally is that anyone who examines a number of copies of *Lyrical Ballads* will readily discern variations of color, weight, and texture in the Lloyd sheets. The Bristol-Longman title leaf of the Harvard-Widener copy, for example, is of paper distinctly heavier than that of $2\pi^4$ just following it, but the paper of gathering O in the same volume is also distinctly heavier than that of $2\pi^4$, and much like that of the title leaf. But with regard to the title leaf specifically, if Foxon had been able to examine the copy of the Bristol-Longman *Lyrical Ballads* at the Alexander Turnbull Library, he would have seen that its title leaf contains the watermark "YD 1795," in the same position in which such marks appear in the London-Arch title leaf and elsewhere. While this watermark supplies secure proof of his contention that the Bristol-Longman title was not printed on O4, it contradicts his contention that the paper of the Bristol-Longman title leaf was not as much suited for the market as was the London-Arch. Although in the end not many such leaves can have been printed, Cottle plainly planned that the remainder of the run, when printing it became prudent, be of title leaves identical with the ones already printed.

To show so much, however, does not deductively eliminate the possibility that, nonetheless, a Bristol-Cottle title, at first equally suited for a general public, was printed on O4, and superseded by the Longman title. External evidence of such a Bristol-Cottle title is of course very slight: it consists of little more than the facts that Cottle in the spring of 1798, to his credit, wanted to be publisher, and years afterward, not surprisingly, regretted that he had not been. The only sign of his having held that intention at any time in 1798 after spring is his absurdly disingenuous assertion to that effect in a letter to Joseph Johnson of 2 October 1798, just two days before publication of the book by Arch; and even decades later he did not say that he published the book, merely that "the volume of the 'Lyrical Ballads' was published."[10] Also, if any question existed when printing first concluded as to who the publisher was to be—and plainly such a question did exist—Cottle and all concerned would have appreciated that by printing the table of contents on O4 all the run of the book except for an easily-attached first leaf, the title leaf that would identify the publisher, could be made ready for boarding without further delay. But only internal evidence of a kind not yet found— specifically, a leaf O4 physically intact and conjunct with O1, and printed with title or something else (probably a table of contents)—would settle matters beyond dispute.[11] With all respect to Foxon and his advisors I will

10. Butler, pp. 143–144; *Reminiscences* I, 326. *Early Recollections*, p. 185, states, ". . . the 'Lyrical Ballads' were published."

11. Offset from a "Lewti" contents page on examples of O3v would of course fit the

say that the paper of the four "Lewti" contents leaves known to me is not distinguishable from paper to be found elsewhere in the same and other copies of *Lyrical Ballads*; and if a "Lewti" contents leaf could be found containing a watermark appropriate for O_4—that is, a "Llo"—it would establish a very strong probability that the "Lewti" contents were printed on that leaf. Unfortunately, none of these four surviving leaves contains any watermark; but a copy of the London-Arch issue of *Lyrical Ballads* at the University of Virginia brings us very close to one.

This volume, which is in the McGregor Library of the Special Collections Department of Alderman Library (E 1798.W67), is uncut and unrestored. It measures 17.2 x 10.8 cm., is bound in boards covered with greyish brown laid paper (chain-line intervals 2.9–3.2 cm.), and has a backstrip that was probably once brownish white but has become aged and worn to dark greyish brown. The front and rear covers retain inscriptions, respectively "Wordsworth" and "Southey | poems | Southey," apparently in one hand and reflecting suppositions of the authorship of the anonymous book. Another early inscription possibly in the same hand has been erased at the head of the front pastedown. End papers are of white laid paper (chain-line intervals 2.6–2.7 cm.). Collation of gatherings [A]–O is that of ideal second-Bristol-Longman-collation copies and of London-Arch copies, gathering χ and leaves E7, 8 having been incorporated as usual. But the preliminaries—π and $2\pi^4$—reveal a troubled history. The front free end paper has been slit down the fold to separate it from its conjugate the front pastedown; it has been tightly pasted to the title leaf; the title leaf has been in turn tightly pasted to $2\pi1$; and the whole ungainly assemblage has been stitched in as a single gathering. The gap between pastedown and free end paper allows sight of upper sewing, where one may observe that the stitching-in of this gathering required the binder to stretch and loop thread abnormally. Additionally, following 2π, a stub remains attached to the recto of [A]1. The stub, varying in width from .5 cm. at head to 1.2 cm. at foot, has been torn vertically along its inner and outer edges. The tearing was done neatly, that of the inner edge (which is somewhat roughened by effects of binding) probably with the aid of a straightedge, that of the outer edge certainly so.

Only one explanation seems readily apparent for these contrivances: the preliminary leaves were changed after the original binding had been completed. At least part of the purpose of the change must have been to insert $2\pi^4$; had that gathering already been present, the binder would not have needed to remove and reattach it in order to deal as he wished with the only other leaves that could imaginably have been present, the title leaf and the contents leaf. Whether a Bristol-Longman title was replaced here by the

---

argument but would not be unassailable proof of it: gathered copies could have been stacked lacking title leaves and O_4, with "Lewti" contents that had been printed elsewhere from O_4 facing the last pages (versos of O_3) of copies above. I have observed small smudges of ink on O_3^v in several copies, but never in shapes meaningfully correspondent with the table of contents.

present London-Arch title cannot be told; but inasmuch as the book is elsewhere competently bound, some title leaf and some contents leaf were probably originally present. That the stub now attached to the recto of [A]1
remains from anything except a leaf of the kind that immediately precedes
[A]1 in every complete copy of the 1798 *Lyrical Ballads*—a contents leaf—is
improbable in the extreme. And quite impossible is that this sometime contents leaf can have listed "The Nightingale," for "Nightingale" contents
leaves are part of $2\pi^4$, the gathering here sewn in late and rather painfully.
A last feature to be noted of this stub is that it contains at the fold near the
foot a watermark letter "o." Its height is the same as that of the "o" of "Llo"
elsewhere in the volume, 1.35 cm., and so is its position, 1.9 cm. up from the
deckle edge. This watermark letter makes certain that the paper of the stub
is that of the rest of the book, and its location is where such a mark would be
found on the fourth leaf of a folded half sheet of which the first leaf contained a watermark "YD 1795"—as O1 often does. Alternative explanations
might be devised somehow, but no serious doubt can be possible either that
the stub belonged to a "Lewti" contents leaf or that that leaf was printed as
O4 of a half sheet as illustrated in the following diagram:[12]

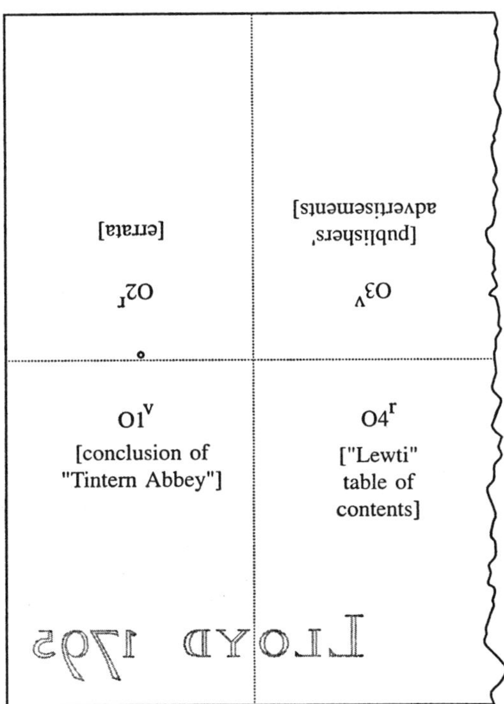

12. One such explanation would be that, even though no copy has been seen lacking a
table of contents, the binder in this one instance omitted the contents leaf and attached a

How a "Lewti" contents leaf came to be bound into a copy containing the cancel "Nightingale" is not hard to imagine. Binding, as Foxon explains, was done from stacked folded sheets and cancels.[13] The somewhat complicated transition from a collation containing "Lewti" and the "Lewti" contents leaf to one containing $2\pi^4$ and χ, and the substitution of one title for another, would have entailed stack rearrangements leading easily to temporary confusion. That the binder afterwards chose to remove the "Lewti" contents leaf by tearing it out on a straightedge, leaving a stub, rather than by pulling the leaf out entirely, can I suspect be attributed to caution, consequent on earlier oversight: when he stitched in folded $2\pi^4$ the "Nightingale" table of contents would have been hidden from view on the recto of $2\pi4$, and most likely the thought did not strike him that a proper-looking table of contents right before his eyes needed removal. Later, when extracting that leaf, he (or whoever did so), conscious of the over-elaboration of the stitching, wished to avoid tugging at the fold.

VI

In sum: both the Bristol-Longman title and the "Lewti" contents leaves of *Lyrical Ballads* were printed in a form physically appropriate for general sale with the sheets of the body of the book, and the "Lewti" table of contents is almost certainly what was printed on the fourth leaf of half sheet O. Equally surely, the first title leaf printed and the Bristol-Longman title leaf were one and the same, and were prepared for copies of the book intended for early distribution while business arrangements were settled that would allow completion of a full print run of the leaf. Joseph Cottle helped originate and produce *Lyrical Ballads*, owned copyright for about a year, distributed Bristol-Longman copies, and, for all we know, may have sold a few such copies. At one time he wished to publish the book. Later, he wished that he had done so. If wishes were imprints, we should not lack copies of *Lyrical Ballads* with a title page announcing Joseph Cottle as publisher.

Bristol-Cottle title directly to [A]1; in which case of course the stub would remain from a Bristol-Cottle title with a watermark appropriate for O4. Among improbabilities that this hypothesis would have to accommodate is that although the binder included the gathering χ—which for reasons noted elsewhere was almost certainly printed after the Bristol-Longman title—in the body of text sheets, he yet employed a title leaf printed earlier than the Bristol-Longman.

13. In this copy, for example, leaves E7 and E8 have the same watermark, a case impossible unless leaves from different sheets had been mixed in stacks. Concerning gathering and binding of leaves E7, 8 in ideal-collation "Nightingale" copies see Foxon, pp. 227–229.

ATTRIBUTIONS OF AUTHORSHIP IN THE *BRITISH CRITIC* DURING THE EDITORIAL REGIME OF ROBERT NARES, 1793–1813

by

EMILY LORRAINE DE MONTLUZIN

UNLIKE John Henry Newman, editor of the *British Critic* during most of its final and turbulent years, the conductors of the early series of the periodical left no extant master list of contributors. Though Archdeacon Robert Nares's authorship of the prefaces to volumes 1–42 is well established[1] and though Derek Roper in *Reviewing before the "Edinburgh," 1788–1802* (London, 1978) notes in passing a handful of reviewers whom he mentions as *British Critic* contributors,[2] no list exists in print of attributions of authorship in the first series of the *British Critic* (1793–1813) comparable to that appearing in Esther Rhoads Houghton's "The *British Critic* and the Oxford Movement," *Studies in Bibliography* 16 (1963): 119–137 (encompassing the years 1836–43). Nevertheless it is possible, using John Nichols's invaluable *Literary Anecdotes of the Eighteenth Century* (9 vols.; London, 1812–15) and *Illustrations of the Literary History of the Eighteenth Century* (8 vols.; London, 1817–58) as well as the *Gentleman's Magazine*'s obituary columns and the rich literary memoirs of the Cornish clergyman and poet Richard Polwhele, among other sources, to unearth the identities of a number of contributors to the *British Critic* during its first series, over which Nares presided as editor. It is the purpose of this article to identify the authors of over 100 reviews that appeared during Nares's editorial regime and integrate them with Nares's prefaces, thus lifting to a degree the curtain of anonymity that has long made the first series of the *British Critic* virtually *terra incognita* among eighteenth- and early-nineteenth-century British literary periodicals.[3]

The *British Critic* in its early years was very much a product of its times, and any attempt to explain the deep sense of commitment of Nares and his fellow contributors to preserve the *status quo* in Church and state falls short

1. [Joseph Jekyll], obituary for Robert Nares, *GM* 99-i (1829): 371.

2. Pp. 23, 265 (n. 53, n. 54, n. 60), 268 (n. 99). Among the contributors to the *British Critic* whom Roper cites (p. 23) are the geologist Jean André Deluc (1727–1817) and the sermon writer Samuel Partridge (1750–1817), though their contributions have not been identified. In addition, Roper notes (*ibid.*), the *British Critic*'s contributors in all probability included Thomas Maurice (1754–1824), the historian of India; and Thomas Rennell (1754–1840), dean of Westminster and master of the Temple.

3. Nathaniel Teich's six-page account of the *British Critic* over the course of its entire run (1793–1843) provides valuable information concerning the review, but his treatment of Nares's first series is of necessity cursory at best. (See Nathaniel Teich, "*The British Critic*," in Alvin Sullivan, ed., *British Literary Magazines: The Romantic Age, 1789–1836* [Westport, Connecticut, 1983], pp. 57–62.)

if it does not take into proper consideration the political climate from which the *British Critic* sprang and which molded its editorial outlook. Quite simply, the two decades during which Nares served as editor constituted one of the most traumatic periods in recent British history, and to Nares and his fellow conservatives the events of those years must have resembled nothing less than a political and social earthquake whose aftershocks never seemed to end. The *British Critic* came into being early in that volatile period as part of a deliberate counterattack launched by a variety of conservative groups (some of them interconnected) to stem the sudden and alarming groundswell of Jacobinism within the British Isles. In January 1793 a coalition of High-Church followers of the Reverend William Jones of Nayland, calling itself the Society for the Reformation of Principles by appropriate Literature, established a new monthly literary review to be published by the old and respected firm of Rivingtons, which under the joint aegis of the devout and ardently Tory brothers Francis and Charles Rivington then stood at the head of the religious book trade in London. According to its prospectus the purpose of the periodical was two-fold: to provide an alternative to the powerful Opposition literary reviews—the *Monthly*, the *Critical*, the *English*, and the *Analytical*—and to defend the Constitution and the Church against all attackers (*BC* 1 [1793]: 1–2). Thus the *British Critic* was ushered into the world, blessed by the imprimatur of the Church and funded in part by William Pitt's secret service money,[4] with "PRO PATRIA" on its frontispiece and the defense of orthodoxy on every page.

Religion was without a doubt the dominant element in the character of the *British Critic*, and to the periodical's original conductors, the Reverend Robert Nares (1753–1829) and the Reverend William Beloe (1758–1817), fell the task of shaping the *British Critic*'s religious policy during its first series. Beloe, classicist, prebendary of Lincoln and St. Paul's, and (briefly) Keeper of Printed Books in the British Museum ("which situation he lost, by an act of treachery and fraud on the part of a person admitted to see and examine the Books and Drawings" [*Lit. Anec.* 9: 94]) was the High-Church force on the editorial board of the periodical. Nares, the author of "several timely pamphlets, well calculated to abate the torrent of revolution and infidelity" (*GM* 99–i [1829]: 370), Keeper of Manuscripts in the British Museum, and archdeacon of Stafford, represented the more moderate wing of the Church. Scholarly opinion for a long time has differed concerning which of the two, Nares or Beloe, should be accorded the title of official editor. Though some earlier press historians have named Beloe as first editor and Nares as his assistant and successor,[5] John Nichols can safely be trusted in calling Nares the

4. Derek Roper believes that two grants of £50 each that Nares received from Pitt's secret service money were in fact start-up funds for the *British Critic* (Roper 23, 180, and 265 [n. 50]).

5. See for example Francis E. Mineka, *The Dissidence of Dissent: The Monthly Repository, 1806–1838, under the Editorship of Robert Aspland, W. J. Fox, R. H. Horne, & Leigh Hunt; with a Chapter on Religious Periodicals, 1700–1825* (Chapel Hill, 1944), p. 51; John O. Hayden, *The Romantic Reviewers, 1802–1824* (London, 1969), p. 44; and Reiman 1: 125.

editor and Beloe the co-proprietor.[6] "Mr. Beloe was joint Proprietor with Mr. Archdeacon Nares, and the respectable house of Rivington," Nichols asserts. "The Editorship was entrusted to the judgment, sagacity, learning, and acuteness, of Mr. Nares . . ." (*Lit. Anec.* 9: 95n). Nichols's evidence is conclusive. Not only was he the most scrupulously accurate press historian of his day, incessantly revising his massive *Literary Anecdotes of the Eighteenth Century* and *Illustrations of the Literary History of the Eighteenth Century* and his meticulously compiled obituary columns in the *Gentleman's Magazine*; in addition he was a personal acquaintance of Nares, the colleague to whom Nares appealed to print in the *Gentleman's Magazine* unpublished installments of several ongoing *British Critic* reviews[7] when Nares was replaced as editor by William Van Mildert, Thomas F. Middleton, and Thomas Rennell. Certainly Nares's correspondence with the *British Critic*'s contributors is testament to his editorial responsibility in assigning review articles to his stable of writers, determining the printing schedule for reviews, offering to send proofs, making editorial emendations, and apologizing for an omission in text.[8]

To a greater degree than any other literary journal of its day, with the possible exception of the *Anti-Jacobin Review*, the *British Critic* was a periodical with a mission. Nares's rather florid preface to the 1800 volume makes clear the sense of ideological commitment that he and his contributors shared. "At a time of gloom and apprehension," he tells his readers, "when Faction and Impiety had grown insolent and menacing, and those principles which our Church and Constitution support . . . had scarcely any public advocates; . . . duty bid us quit our private walk, to do our utmost for the general cause." Nearly a decade of revolution and war abroad and political turmoil at home had brought no security and surely, in Nares's mind, no justification for letting down his guard. "The season of gloom is not yet past! Britain, after exhausting her strength to support the liberties of Europe . . . [is still menaced]. The storm lowers on every side; and the power that wages

---

Walter [James] Graham, *English Literary Periodicals* (New York, 1930), p. 221, takes the path of least resistance in naming Nares and Beloe as joint editors.

6. Roper 23, and Teich, "*The British Critic*," in Sullivan, ed., *British Literary Mazazines: The Romantic Age*, p. 58, concur in considering Nares to have been the *British Critic*'s editor. Nares and Beloe did, however, have an equal interest in the financial fortunes of the *British Critic*, each owning a one-third share in the periodical, with Francis and Charles Rivington holding the third equal share.

7. See for example Nares's letter to Nichols of 17 March 1814 (*Illust.* 7: 621, 621n) concerning the eventual publication of John Hellins's review of Baily's *Doctrine of Life Annuities and Assurances* (GM 84-i [1814]: 261–264, 472–477) and Nares's letter to Nichols of 23 May 1814 (*Illust.* 7: 622, 622n) concerning the eventual publication of George Gleig's review of McCrie's *Life of John Knox* (GM 84-i [1814]: 569–571) and of Gleig's cover letter (GM 84-i [1814]: 545) pertaining to the review. See also Nares's recommendation of Richard Polwhele's services as a reviewer "to my successors," as he phrased it (*Illust.* 7: 618–619).

8. See for example Nares's correspondence with Thomas Percy, Bishop of Dromore (*Illust.* 6: 583; 7: 601, 601n, 604–607, 607n), Samuel Parr (*ibid.*, 7: 609), and Richard Polwhele (*ibid.*, 7: 610; *Biog. Sketches* 3: 176).

war against all duties, human and divine, is daily gaining strength by victories." Consigning the nation's fate to God's hands, Nares reiterates his intention to do his part as a foot soldier for Church and King. "Our office is clearly marked. It is, to wield the arms that we are competent to use, in defence of a pure church and wisely ordered state . . ." (*BC* 16 [1800]: i–iii). The battlefield imagery Nares invokes was no mere rhetorical flourish; and the 1801 preface even more explicitly employs the language of combat, as Nares conjures up a picture of the *British Critic*'s Old Roman contributors, sacrificing their peaceful leisure, like Cincinnatus leaving his plough, to fight the good fight against the Jacobin menace. "[T]here are enemies with whom, for the sake of public happiness and tranquillity, BRITISH CRITICS must not make even a moment's truce," Nares declares. "These are, the assailants of religion, infidelity and impiety; or the disturbers of the state, faction and disloyalty; enemies, whose inroads called us from our voluntary studies, to a state of literary warfare; to wield the pen, and shed the ink, which otherwise would have been quietly consumed, in defense of all that we hold sacred in religion, valuable in law, or useful in society" (*BC* 18 [1801]: i).

Though the *British Critic*'s spirit never faltered, its effectiveness in the fight against radicalism eventually waned. To a large extent the decline was the result of a chain of unsettling shifts in management and recastings in format. The commencement of the second series saw drastic changes in organization and soon the elimination of the entire British Catalogue section, that monthly conglomeration of thumbnail reviews that allowed conservative reviewers such scope in awarding damnation or praise to scores of authors, popular or obscure. With the mid-1820's came the end of the second series, a short-lived third, the change from monthly to quarterly publication, the commencement of a fourth series, and merger with the *Quarterly Theological Review* to form the *British Critic, Quarterly Theological Review and Ecclesiastical Record*. Meanwhile a parade of short-term editors—Archibald Montgomery Campbell,[9] James Shergold Boone, Samuel Roffey Maitland, John Henry Newman, and Thomas Mozley—brought another element of discontinuity to the review's career.

The *British Critic* fell in 1843, the victim not of victorious Jacobins or later British radicals, but of its own extremism. A take-over by the Oxford Movement, in the form of Newman, Mozley, and their adherents, precipitated a drastic decline in circulation and led the Society for the Propagation of the Christian Gospel to sever its 75-year connection with the Rivington publishing house. In 1843 the anti-Oxford-Movement forces, led by William Palmer of Worcester College, prevailed upon Francis Rivington (great-grandson of the founder of the firm) to halt publication of the *British Critic* on the grounds that it was dividing the Church that it had been established to defend.[10] It was an ignominious end for a periodical that had always prided

9. See Esther Rhoads Houghton, "A 'New' Editor of the *British Critic*," *Victorian Periodicals Review* 12 (1979): 102–105.

10. Good surveys of the events leading to the downfall of the *British Critic* are provided in Houghton's "The *British Critic* and the Oxford Movement," *Studies in Bibliography*

itself on the purity of its principles and the sacredness of its mission.

While the fight against political and religious radicalism consumed a disproportionate amount of the *British Critic*'s attention, the review did upon occasion become embroiled in apolitical controversies. One of those was a contentious dispute over the existence and location of ancient Troy, a dispute launched by the publication of *Observations upon a Treatise, entitled A Description of the Plain of Troy, by Monsieur le Chevalier* (1795) and *A Dissertation concerning the War of Troy and the Expedition of the Grecians, as described by Homer, shewing that no such Expedition was ever undertaken and that no such city of Phrygia existed* (1796) by Jacob Bryant (1715–1804), classical scholar and author of theological treatises. The debate was joined with passion by contending armies of Troy skeptics and Troy apologists, two in the latter camp being the *British Critic*'s William Vincent and John Whitaker.

The attribution of the various articles appearing in the *British Critic* concerning the Troy controversy requires an especially careful sifting of evidence. The root of the difficulty lies in William Vincent's categorical claim to have supplied all the reviews printed in the *British Critic* dealing with the *querelle* over Troy. Writing to John Nichols on 1 February 1814 with regard to the *British Critic*'s two-part treatment of J. B. S. Morritt's *A Vindication of Homer, and of the ancient Poets and Historians who have recorded the Siege and Fall of Troy* (BC 12 [1798]: 632–645; 13 [1799]: 116–135), Vincent declares, "[T]he Review which you impute to Gilbert Wakefield, and call *indecent*, was mine, as were all the articles in the 'British Critick,' on the several publications relative to the Controversy about the Troad. . . . Mr. Bryant's answer [to the review] in his '*Expostulation*' was outrageous," Vincent adds. "He called the Writer an Assassin, which in a following article, and by private correspondence I called upon him to retract. This he would not do; and therefore I dropped the controversy . . ." (*Illust.* 3: 772–773). Vincent relied upon a colleague to reply to Bryant on his behalf in the *British Critic*'s critique of Bryant's *Expostulation* (BC 15 [1800]: 55–69), appending several trenchant paragraphs of his own.[11] Vincent himself clearly wrote the joint review of J. B. S. Morritt's *Additional Remarks on the Topography of Troy, &c. in Answer to Mr. Bryant's last Publication* and of William Francklin's *Remarks and Observations on the Plain of Troy, made during an Excursion in June, 1799* (BC 16 [1800]: 418–424). He supplied the review of Richard Chandler's *The History of Ilium or Troy* (BC 22 [1803]: 545–549), an article devoted entirely to the Troy controversy, noting that "we enter with pleasure into every part of the debate . . ." (p. 545). He specifically claimed authorship (in *Illust.* 3: 773) of the review of William Gell's *Topography of Troy* (BC 25 [1805]: 349–361), in which he seized the opportunity to attack Bryant's contention that Troy did not exist, while professing "that

---

16 (1963): 119–137, and Houghton's and Josef L. Altholz's "*The British Critic, 1824–1843,*" *Victorian Periodicals Review* 24 (1991): 111–118.

11. Vincent's concluding paragraphs are to be found on p. 69.

we have always respected . . . [Bryant's] abilities, his learning, and integrity"
(p. 350). Vincent in addition may have written the critique of Bryant's *Observations upon some Passages in Scripture* (*BC* 24 [1804]: 665–679; 25 [1805]:
46–58), a critique that includes a paragraph (p. 666) seeking to refute Bryant's
opinions concerning Troy. He may also have reviewed Edward Daniel
Clarke's *Travels in various Countries of Europe, Asia, and Africa, Part the
First* (*BC* 38 [1811]: 484–497, 603–616), though it contains no reference to the
Troy controversy, since Vincent acknowledged authorship of the review (*BC*
40 [1812]: 97–110, 616–624) of Part the Second of Clarke's *Travels*, which
covers Clarke's visit to the supposed site of Troy. In fact, the first installment
of the *British Critic*'s two-part review of that work is almost entirely devoted
to a recapitulation of the various opinions of Chevalier, Bryant, Morritt,
Francklin, Chandler, Gell, and others with regard to the Troy controversy.
Conversely, in a letter of 3 February 1814 to John Nichols, Vincent noted
that he was not the author of the review of Hobhouse's comments on the Troy
controversy and that in fact his critique of Clarke was his final review for the
British Critic on the subject of Troy, adding, "I have concluded my labours,
with my friend Nares's resignation of his concern in the 'British Critick'"
(*Illust.* 3: 773–774).

Vincent's claims to a virtual monopoly of the *British Critic*'s coverage of
the Troy controversy notwithstanding, Richard Polwhele provides evidence
that Polwhele's friend, John Whitaker—not Vincent—wrote the articles concerning the debate over Troy that appeared in the numbers of the *British
Critic* before December 1798:

> In 1796 [Polwhele writes], the famous controversy began respecting the very
> existence of Troy, and of the Trojan War, which had been opened by the learned
> and excellent Jacob Bryant in two quarto tracts. One of these was entitled "Obser-
> vations upon a Treatise entitled, 'A Description of the Plain of Troy, by M. Le
> Chevalier:'" [*sic*] the other, "A Dissertation concerning the War of Troy and the
> Expedition of the Greeks, as described by Homer; showing that no such Expedition
> was ever undertaken, and that no such City of Phrygia ever existed." . . . Nor was he
> overlooked in the British Critic.
> It was not possible that Dr. Vincent should be inattentive to this contest, or in-
> different to the subject of it; but at the time when it commenced, he was too much
> occupied by his own objects to take up the pen. The Review [*i.e.*, the *British Critic*]
> had then its most learned contributor in Whitaker; who furnished two powerful
> articles on Bryant's first Dissertation [*BC* 9 (1797): 535–547, 591–603]. It was not till
> Mr. Morritt's able *Vindication of Homer* appeared in 1798, that Dr. Vincent began
> to take an active part in the controversy. He then entered the field with spirit against
> the venerable, but paradoxical mythologist; and though assailed by rather unfair
> weapons, never afterwards receded from his ground. He fought with vigour, but with
> a strict regard to the laws of literary chivalry. His first critique, upon the subject of
> Homer and Troy, appeared in the Brit. Crit. Vol. XII. p. 632 [*BC* 12 (1798): 632–645],
> in a Review of *Mr. Morritt's* work. . . . (*Biog. Sketches* 3: 100n–101n)

Polwhele also supplies evidence[12] of an additional Whitaker contribution
concerning the Troy controversy, Whitaker's review of Bryant's *A Disserta-*

---

12. See Whitaker's letter of 26 July 1797 to Polwhele, *Biog. Sketches* 3: 120.

tion concerning the War of Troy, and the Expedition of the Grecians, as described by Homer (BC 9 [1797]: 604–615). The attributions of authorship listed below accept as conclusive Polwhele's intimate knowledge of his friend Whitaker's reviews. Polwhele's information thus provides a useful corrective to Vincent's blanket claim to the authorship of "all the articles in the 'British Critick,' on the several publications relative to the Controversy about the Troad" (*Illust.* 3: 772–773).

The attributions that follow encompass, besides Nares's prefaces and several of his reviews, articles by twelve additional *British Critic* contributors: John Brand, George Ellis, George Gleig (Bishop of Brechin), John Hellins, Samuel Parr, Thomas Percy (Bishop of Dromore), Richard Polwhele, Richard Porson, John Stoddart, William Vincent, John Whitaker, and Joseph White. All attributions of authorship appear first in the "Synopsis by Contributor," which provides a convenient listing of the finds according to author. The "Chronological Listing in the *British Critic*" next sets forth for each item the full citation from the *British Critic*, the author's name, and the source of the attribution. Abbreviated titles used in the "Chronological Listing" as well as in the notes appear as follows:

BC	*British Critic.*
Biog. Sketches	Polwhele, Richard. *Biographical Sketches in Cornwall.* 3 vols. Truro, 1831.
DNB	*Dictionary of National Biography.* 1908–1909 ed.
GM	*Gentleman's Magazine.*
Illust.	Nichols, John. *Illustrations of the Literary History of the Eighteenth Century.* 8 vols. London, 1817–58.
Lit Anec.	————. *Literary Anecdotes of the Eighteenth Century.* 9 vols. London, 1812–15.
Reiman	Reiman, Donald H., ed. *The Romantics Reviewed: Contemporary Reviews of British Romantic Writers.* Part A: *The Lake Poets.* New York, 1972.
Roper	Roper, Derek. *Reviewing before the "Edinburgh," 1788–1802.* London, 1978.
Trad. and Recoll.	Polwhele, R[ichard]. *Traditions and Recollections; Domestic, Clerical, and Literary.* 2 vols. London, 1826.

SYNOPSIS BY CONTRIBUTOR

BRAND, Rev. John [Fitz-John][13] (1743–1808): rector of St. George's, Southwark; brother of the radical feminist Hannah Brand; rabid Tory, bitter opponent of Dissenters, and "profound mathematician" (*GM* 78–ii [1808]: 1134), who published political and financial pamphlets and supplied the *British Critic* as well as the *Anti-Jacobin Review* with articles on finance and political economy.

BC contributions: 9 (1797): 284–295 [?]; 19 (1802): 268–279, 374–381, 580–588; 20 (1802): 329–330.

13. The Reverend John Brand, rector of St. George's, Southwark, is not to be confused with the Reverend John Brand (*ca.* 1743–1806), rector of St. Mary-at-Hill and secretary to the Society of Antiquaries.

ELLIS, George (1753–1815): diplomat, poet, and antiquarian; author of *Specimens of Early English Poets* and *Specimens of Early English Romances in Metre*; contributor to the *Rolliad*; collaborator with George Canning and John Hookham Frere in launching the *Anti-Jacobin; or, Weekly Examiner* and later the *Quarterly Review*, to which Ellis would be a steady contributor.
BC contributions: 19 (1802): 570–576; 20 (1802): 8–13.

GLEIG, George (1753–1840): bishop of Brechin and primus of the Scottish Episcopal Church; successful campaigner for the lifting of the penal laws that restricted Scottish Episcopacy and for a full partnership between the Scottish Episcopal Church and the Church of England; co-editor of the third edition of the *Encyclopaedia Britannica* and contributor to a variety of periodicals.
BC contributions: 42 (1813): 343–359, 448–461, 554–581.

HELLINS, Rev. John (d. 1827): vicar of Potterspury, Northants.; self-taught mathematician; author of a number of papers on mathematics and astronomy published in the Royal Society's *Philosophical Transactions* and contributor of specialized reviews of mathematical works to the *British Critic* between 1795 and 1814 (*GM* 98–i [1828]: 181).
BC contributions: 6 (1795): 413–418; 21 (1803): 272–284; 23 (1804): 143–156, 489–494; 24 (1804): 653–660; 25 (1805): 141–147; 38 (1811): 622–628; 42 (1813): 502–512.

NARES, Rev. Robert (1753–1829): canon residentiary of Lichfield and archdeacon of Stafford; philologist; Keeper of Manuscripts at the British Museum; co-conductor and principal editor of the *British Critic*, 1793–1813, in which capacity he supplied the prefaces to the 42 volumes of the first series and moderated the influence of Beloe and his High-Church friends upon the periodical's religious policy.
BC contributions: 1 (1793): i–xii; 2 (1793): iii–xvii; 3 (1794): iii–xxi; 4 (1794): iii–xxi; 5 (1795): i–xvi; 6 (1795): i–xvi; 7 (1796): i–xx; 8 (1796): i–xx; 9 (1797): i–xix; 10 (1797): i–xxii; 11 (1798): i–xvi; 12 (1798): i–xvi; 13 (1799): i–xix; 14 (1799): i–xviii; 15 (1800): i–xxii; 16 (1800): i–xxii; 17 (1801): i–xix; 18 (1801): i–xx, 529 [concluding sentence of 524–529]; 19 (1802): i–xv; 20 (1802): i–xxi, 295–298; 21 (1803): i–xvi, 406–411; 22 (1803): i–xvii; 23 (1804): iii–xix; 24 (1804): iii–xx, 231–243; 25 (1805): iii–xix, 98 [?]; 26 (1805): iii–xx; 27 (1806): iii–xvi; 28 (1806): iii–xix; 29 (1807): iii–xv; 30 (1807): iii–xix; 31 (1808): iii–xix; 32 (1808): iii–xviii; 33 (1809): iii–xix; 34 (1809): iii–xxiii; 35 (1810): iii–xix; 36 (1810): iii–xx; 37 (1811): iii–xx; 38 (1811): iii–xix; 39 (1812): iii–xvi; 40 (1812): iii–xx; 41 (1813): iii–xx; 42 (1813): iii–xxiii.

PARR, Rev. Samuel (1747–1825): rector of Wadenhoe, Northants.; schoolmaster, preacher, and raconteur; "the Whig Dr. Johnson," whose large girth and bushy wig were caricatured by cartoonists and whose habits of supporting reformist causes, flogging schoolboys, and detesting Evangelicals earned him equal fame; the only known contributor to the *British Critic* who proudly swam against the conservative tide.
BC contributions: 3 (1794): 48–61, 121–139, 302–330, 412–424; 5 (1795): 58–62 [?], 148–156 [?], 344–358 [?].

PERCY, Thomas, bishop of Dromore, County Down (1729–1811): ballad collector chiefly known for his publication in 1765 of *Reliques of Ancient English Poetry*, which exerted a significant influence upon British readers' growing interest in primitive verse and thus upon early Romanticism.

BC contributions: 16 (1800): 345–361; 18 (1801): 286–295, 359–365, 524–529 [with Robert Nares, who wrote the concluding sentence, p. 529]; 25 (1805): 99.

POLWHELE, Rev. Richard (1760–1838): vicar of Manaccan, Cornwall; author of West Country histories, sets of literary memoirs, and the anti-feminist poem *The Unsex'd Females*; contributor to numerous periodicals, particularly the *Anti-Jacobin Review*, in which he used his critic's license to parade his Church-and-king sentiments and denounce radicals who "muttered sedition from their lurking-holes and scattered, in dark corners, the seeds of anarchy."[14]

BC contributions: 34 (1809): 173–177 [?], 616–621; 35 (1810): 1–15, 112–120; 42 (1813): 586–593.

PORSON, Richard (1759–1808): regius professor of Greek at Cambridge; author of critical editions of Euripides; best known in his lifetime for his contentious quarrel with Archdeacon George Travis, whose assertion of the authenticity of 1 John 5: 7 Porson attacked in *Letters to Archdeacon Travis in Answer to Defence of the Three Heavenly Witnesses*.

BC contribution: 17 (1801): 453–460.

STODDART, Sir John (1773–1856): journalist and jurist; writer for *The Times*, 1810–16 (under the signature "J.S."); founder and editor of *The New Times*, in which capacity he was attacked remorselessly by William Hone and Hone's caricaturist George Cruikshank, who satirized Stoddart as "Dr. Slop"; later chief justice and justice of the vice-admiralty court on Malta.

BC contribution: 17 (1801): 125–131.

VINCENT, Rev. William (1739–1815): headmaster of Westminster School, where he gained dubious distinction in 1792 for expelling Robert Southey for daring to write *The Flagellant* as an exposé of Vincent's notorious penchant for flogging; dean of Westminster; widely respected classical scholar, particularly in the study of geography and ancient voyages; the *British Critic*'s leading opponent of Jacob Bryant and Bryant's fellow Troy skeptics.

BC contributions: 2 (1793): 1–6 [?], 146–152 [?], 301–309 [?]; 3 (1794): 510–517, 620–629; 10 (1797): 221–233, 362–374; 12 (1798): 632–645; 13 (1799): 116–135; 15 (1800): 69; 16 (1800): 418–424; 22 (1803): 545–549; 24 (1804): 665–679 [?]; 25 (1805): 46–58 [?], 349–361; 36 (1810): 209–228 [?]; 38 (1811): 484–497 [?], 603–616[?]; 40 (1812): 97–110, 616–624.

WHITAKER, Rev. John (1735–1808): rector of Ruan Lanihorne, Cornwall; antiquary and author of a badly flawed *History of Manchester*; writer for the *Anti-Jacobin Review*, the *English Review*, and the *Gentleman's Magazine* as well as the *British Critic*; fiery opponent of Jacobins and Dissenters,

14. [Richard Polwhele], "*The Lawfulness of Defensive War . . . ,*" *Anti-Jacobin Review* 3 (1799): 185.

though not so fanatical as to deserve Richard Warner's characterization of him as "half-cracked with ultra loyalty."[15]

BC contributions: 1 (1793): 109 [?]; 8 (1796): 81–84; 9 (1797): 241–246, 354–363, 535–547, 591–603, 604–615, 699; 11 (1798): 13–17, 140–148, 345–358; 13 (1799): 97–108, 275–284, 356–362, 410–419; 14 (1799): 639–649 [?]; 15 (1800): 21–31 [?], 260–263; 16 (1800): 530–537.

WHITE, Rev. Joseph (1745–1814): Laudian professor of Arabic and regius professor of Hebrew at Oxford; specialist as well in Syriac and Persian studies; deliverer of the controversial 1784 Bampton Lecture, which gave rise to charges of plagiarism that would seriously damage his reputation; reviewer of various publications in Hebrew and oriental literature for the *British Critic*.[16]

BC contributions: 2 (1793): 43–51 [?]; 4 (1794): 413–416 [?]; 8 (1796): 446–449 [?], 577–587; 9 (1797): 667–669 [?]; 11 (1798): 603–606 [?]; 14 (1799): 38–45 [?], 121–127 [?]; 15 (1800): 354–356 [?]; 17 (1801): 324–325 [?]; 19 (1802): 1–15 [?], 134–154 [?], 283–293 [?], 343–355 [?], 524–530 [?], 623–631 [?]; 20 (1802): 53–61 [?], 165–171 [?], 641–645; 26 (1805): 287–292; 27 (1806): 53–57 [?]; 28 (1806): 465–479 [?], 608–619 [?]; 29 (1807): 134–147 [?], 368–375 [?], 496–508 [?]; 30 (1807): 15–23; 31 (1808): 22–25.

CHRONOLOGICAL LISTING IN THE *BRITISH CRITIC*

1 (1793): i–xii. "Preface." Robert Nares. [*GM* 99–i (1829): 371]

1 (1793): 109. Review: "*A Discourse, preached on Sunday, December 30, 1792, at the Parish Church of Kenton, &c.* By the Rev. R. Polwhele." John Whitaker [?]. [*Trad. and Recoll.* 1: 153n]

2 (1793): iii–xvii. "Preface." Robert Nares. [*GM* 99–i (1829): 371]

2 (1793): 1–6. Review: "*The History, civil and commercial of the British Colonies in the West Indies.* By Bryan Edwards, Esq. of the Island of Jamaica." William Vincent [?]. [Vincent in a letter of 3 February 1814 to John Nichols notes that he has reviewed Bryan Edwards's

---

15. Richard Warner, *Literary Recollections* (2 vols.; London, 1830) 2: 127.

16. White's obituary (*GM* 84-i [1814]: 628) states that he "was the Reviewer of publications in Hebrew and subjects of Oriental literature in 'The British Critic.'" For the purpose of determining which *British Critic* reviews White wrote or may have written, this article makes use of the following guidelines: Scholarly reviews of oriental literature (especially Arabic or Persian literature) are assumed to be White's, particularly if they contain explications of passages quoted in oriental characters. Reviews of oriental literature of which White's authorship is less sure are attributed to him with a cautionary question mark. Scholarly reviews of Hebrew works (particularly those emphasizing textual criticism and containing explications of passages in Hebrew script) are also attributed to White with a question mark, taking into consideration the fact that expertise in Hebrew scholarship was not as specialized an accomplishment as expertise in Arabic and Persian. (In those cases a second strong possibility exists for the author of the reviews in question: Rev. George Bennet [1750–1835], described by the *DNB* [2: 229–230] as a Hebraist and "[o]ne of the principal contributors to the 'British Critic,' . . . [who] reviewed from time to time the works of some of the most celebrated English divines . . . ," though the *DNB* does not identify them.) Reviews of works dealing with the history, theology, jurisprudence, etc., of oriental lands are not assigned to White, even provisionally, as Thomas Maurice (who supplied unidentified contributions to the *British Critic*) or other reviewers could likewise have written them.

Jamaica (*Illust.* 3: 774), a statement that appears to refer to this review]

2 (1793): 43–51. Review: "*An Hebrew and English Lexicon. . . . The Third Edition. . . .* By John Parkhurst." Joseph White [?]. [*GM* 84–i (1814): 628]

2 (1793): 146–152. Review: "Edwards's *History of the West Indies* [cont.]." William Vincent [?]. [See attribution for *BC* 2 (1793): 1–6]

2 (1793): 301–309. Review: "Edwards's *History of the West Indies* [conc.]." William Vincent [?]. [See attribution for *BC* 2 (1793): 1–6]

3 (1794): iii–xxi. "Preface." Robert Nares. [*GM* 99–i (1829): 371]

3 (1794): 48–61. Review: "[Dr. Charles Combe and Henry Homer, eds.,] *Q. Horatii Flacci Opera, cum variis Lectionibus, notis Variorum, et Indice Locupletissimo. Tom. II.*" Samuel Parr. [*Illust.* 7: 609; *Lit. Anec.* 3: 163n; *GM* 95–i (1825): 369, 369n]

3 (1794): 121–139. Review: "*Q. Horatii Flacci Opera* [cont.]." Samuel Parr. [*Illust.* 7: 609; *Lit. Anec.* 3: 163n; *GM* 95–i (1825): 369, 369n]

3 (1794): 302–330. Review: "*Q. Horatii Flacci Opera* [cont.]." Samuel Parr. [*Illust.* 7: 609; *Lit. Anec.* 3: 163n; *GM* 95–i (1825): 369, 369n]

3 (1794): 412–424. Review: "*Q. Horatii Flacci Opera* [conc.]." Samuel Parr. [*Illust.* 7: 609; *Lit. Anec.* 3: 163n; *GM* 95–i (1825): 369, 369n]

3 (1794): 510–517. Review: "*A critical Inquiry into the Life of Alexander the Great, by the Ancient Historians. From the French of the Baron de St. Croix: with Notes and Observations, by Sir Richard Clayton, Bart.*" William Vincent. [*Illust.* 3: 774]

3 (1794): 620–629. Review: "Sir Richard Clayton's Translation of St. Croix's *Inquiry into the Life of Alexander the Great* [conc.]." William Vincent. [*Illust.* 3: 774]

4 (1794): iii–xxi. "Preface." Robert Nares. [*GM* 99–i (1829): 371]

4 (1794): 413–416. Review: "*Specimens of Hindoo Literature. . . .* By N. E. Kindersley." Joseph White [?]. [*GM* 84–i (1814): 628]

5 (1795): i–xvi. "Preface." Robert Nares. [*GM* 99–i (1829): 371]

5 (1795): 58–62. Review: "*Q. Horatii Flacci quae supersunt, recensuit et notis instruxit,* Gilbertus Wakefield. . . ." Samuel Parr [?]. [Similarities in both style and emphasis with Parr's review of *Q. Horatii Flacci Opera* (*BC* 3 [1794]: 48–61, 121–139, 302–330, and 412–424); inclusion in various installments of the review of Wakefield's *Horace* of references to Wakefield's *Silva Critica* (which Parr in *BC* 3 [1794]: 320 had announced his intention to discuss in the *BC*); Nares's comment of 10 April 1794 to Parr that "[w]e now begin to look forward to your remarks on Wakefield, which shall have a place as early as possible, and as distinguished, whenever it may suit you to furnish us with them" (*Illust.* 7: 609)]

5 (1795): 148–156. Review: "Wakefield's *Horace* [cont.]." Samuel Parr [?]. [See 5 (1795): 58–62]

5 (1795): 344–358. Review: "Wakefield's *Horace* [conc.]." Samuel Parr [?]. [See 5 (1795): 58–62]

6 (1795): i–xvi. "Preface." Robert Nares. [*GM* 99–i (1829): 371]

6 (1795): 413–418. Review: "*The Method of finding the Longitude. . . .* By William Wales." John Hellins. [*GM* 98–i (1828): 181]

7 (1796): i–xx. "Preface." Robert Nares. [*GM* 99–i (1829): 371]

8 (1796): i–xx. "Preface." Robert Nares. [*GM* 99–i (1829): 371]

8 (1796): 81–84. Review: "[Richard Polwhele's] *The Influence of local Attachment with respect to Home.*" John Whitaker. [*Biog. Sketches* 3: 105, 108]

8 (1796): 446–449. Review: "[C. F. Volney's] *Simplification des langues Orientales, où Méthode nouvelle et facile d'apprendre les langues Arabe, Persane, et Turque.*" Joseph White [?]. [*GM* 84–i (1814): 628]

8 (1796): 577–587. Review: "*Specimens of Arabian Poetry, from the earliest Time to the Extinction of the Khaliphat. . . . By J. D. Carlyle.*" Joseph White. [*GM* 84–i (1814): 628]

9 (1797): i–xix. "Preface." Robert Nares. [*GM* 99–i (1829): 371]

9 (1797): 241–246. Review: "*Essays, by a Society of Gentlemen at Exeter.*" John Whitaker. ["The Rev. John Whitaker," *Palatine Note-book* 1 (2 May 1881): 80; *Trad. and Recoll.* 2: 463–464, 467]

9 (1797): 284–295. Review: "*Additional Facts, addressed to the serious Attention of the People of Great Britain, respecting the Expences of the War, and the State of the National Debt. By William Morgan, F.R.S. Third Edition.*" John Brand [?]. [*Illust.* 6: 532]

9 (1797): 354–363. Review: "*Essays, by a Society of Gentlemen at Exeter* [cont.]." John Whitaker. ["The Rev. John Whitaker," *Palatine Note-book* 1 (2 May 1881): 80; *Trad. and Recoll.* 2: 463–464, 467]

9 (1797): 535–547. Review: "*Observations upon a Treatise entitled, A Description of the Plain of Troy, by Monsieur Le Chevalier. By Jacob Bryant.*" John Whitaker. ["The Rev. John Whitaker," *Palatine Note-book* 1 (2 May 1881): 80; *Biog. Sketches* 3: 100n–101n, 120]

9 (1797): 591–603. Review: "Mr. Bryant's Observations on the Plain of Troy." John Whitaker. ["The Rev. John Whitaker," *Palatine Notebook* 1 (2 May 1881): 80; *Biog. Sketches* 3: 100n–101n, 120]

9 (1797): 604–615. Review: "*A Dissertation concerning the War of Troy and the Expedition of the Grecians, as described by Homer; shewing that no such Expedition was ever undertaken, and that no such City of Phrygia ever existed. By Jacob Bryant.*" John Whitaker. ["The Rev. John Whitaker," *Palatine Note-book* 1 (2 May 1881): 80; *Biog. Sketches* 3: 120. See also *BC* 9 (1797): 603, which indicates that the same person who wrote the review in *BC* 9 (1797): 591–603 wrote the review in *BC* 9 (1797): 604–615]

9 (1797): 667–669. Review: "[Ouseley's] *Oriental Collections, for January, February, and March, 1797.*" Joseph White [?]. [*GM* 84–i (1814): 628]

9 (1797): 699. Note in "Acknowledgements to Correspondents" re "a long letter [received by the *British Critic*] from a writer in the 'Essays published by a Society of Gentlemen at Exeter.' " John Whitaker. ["The Rev. John Whitaker," *Palatine Note-book* 1 (2 May 1881): 80]

10 (1797): i–xxii. "Preface." Robert Nares. [*GM* 99–i (1829): 371]

10 (1797): 221–233. Review: "*An authentic Account of an Embassy from the King of Great-Britain to the Emperor of China. . . . By Sir George Staunton.*" William Vincent. [*Illust.* 3: 774]

10 (1797): 362–374. Review: *"Authentic Account of the Embassy to China* [conc.]." William Vincent. [*Illust.* 3: 774]

11 (1798): i–xvi. "Preface." Robert Nares. [*GM* 99–i (1829): 371]

11 (1798): 13–17. Review: *"The Sentiments of Philo Judaeus.* . . . By Jacob Bryant." John Whitaker. ["The Rev. John Whitaker," *Palatine Note-book* 1 (2 May 1881): 80; *Trad. and Recoll.* 2: 486]

11 (1798): 140–148. Review: *"The Sentiments of Philo Judaeus.* . . . By Jacob Bryant [cont.]." John Whitaker. ["The Rev. John Whitaker," *Palatine Note-book* 1 (2 May 1881): 80; *Trad. and Recoll.* 2: 486]

11 (1798): 345–358. Review: *"The History of Scotland.* . . . By John Pinkerton." John Whitaker. ["The Rev. John Whitaker," *Palatine Note-book* 1 (2 May 1881): 80; *Trad. and Recoll.* 2: 485]

11 (1798): 603–606. Review: "[Ouseley's] *The Oriental Collections, for April, May, and June, 1797."* Joseph White [?]. [*GM* 84–i (1814): 628]

12 (1798): i–xvi. "Preface." Robert Nares. [*GM* 99–i (1829): 371]

12 (1798): 632–645. Review: *"A Vindication of Homer, and of the ancient Poets and Historians who have recorded the Siege and Fall of Troy. In Answer to Two late Publications of Mr. Bryant.* . . . By J. B. S. Morritt." William Vincent. [*Illust.* 3: 772–773]

13 (1799): i–xix. "Preface." Robert Nares. [*GM* 99–i (1829): 371]

13 (1799): 97–108. Review: *"Archaeologia, or Miscellaneous Tracts relating to Antiquity."* John Whitaker. ["The Rev. John Whitaker," *Palatine Note-book* 1 (2 May 1881): 80; *Trad. and Recoll.* 2: 499]

13 (1799): 116–135. Review: "Morritt's *Vindication of Homer* [conc.]." William Vincent. [*Illust.* 3: 772–773]

13 (1799): 275–284. Review: *"Archaeologia, or Miscellaneous Tracts relating to Antiquity."* John Whitaker. ["The Rev. John Whitaker," *Palatine Note-book* 1 (2 May 1881): 80; *Trad. and Recoll.* 2: 499]

13 (1799): 356–362. Review: *"Archaeologia, or Miscellaneous Tracts relating to Antiquity."* John Whitaker. ["The Rev. John Whitaker," *Palatine Note-book* 1 (2 May 1881): 80; *Trad. and Recoll.* 2: 499]

13 (1799): 410–419. Review: *"The History of Devonshire.* . . . By the Reverend Richard Polwhele." John Whitaker. [*Trad. and Recoll.* 2: 497]

14 (1799): i–xviii. "Preface." Robert Nares. [*GM* 99–i (1829): 371]

14 (1799): 38–45. Review: "[Ouseley's] *The Oriental Collections, for July, August, September, October, November, December, 1797."* Joseph White [?]. [*GM* 84–i (1814): 628]

14 (1799): 121–127. Review: "[Ouseley's] *The Oriental Collections, for 1797* [conc.]." Joseph White [?]. [*GM* 84–i (1814): 628]

14 (1799): 639–649. Review: *"Iter Britanniarum; or, that Part of the Itinerary of Antoninus which relates to Britain; with a new Comment.* By the Rev. Thomas Reynolds." John Whitaker [?]. [*GM* 100–i (1830): 373]

15 (1800): i–xxii. "Preface." Robert Nares. [*GM* 99–i (1829): 371]

15 (1800): 21–31. Review: "Reynolds's *Iter Britanniarum* [conc.]." John Whitaker [?]. [*GM* 100–i (1830): 373]

15 (1800): 69. Concluding paragraphs (p. 69) of review: *"An Expostulation, addressed to the British Critic.* By Jacob Bryant [pp. 55–69]." William Vincent. [*Illust.* 3: 772–773]

15 (1800): 260–263. Review: *"Grecian Prospects: a Poem. . . . By Mr. Pol-whele."* John Whitaker. [*Biog. Sketches* 3: 143–144]

15 (1800): 354–356. Review: *"Epitome of the Ancient History of Persia, ex-tracted and translated from the Jehan Ara, a Persian Manuscript. By William Ouseley. . . ."* Joseph White [?]. [*GM* 84–i (1814): 628]

16 (1800): i–xxii. "Preface." Robert Nares. [*GM* 99–i (1829): 371]

16 (1800): 345–361. Review: *"The History and Antiquities of the County of Leicester. By John Nichols. . . . Volume III. Part I."* Thomas Percy, Bishop of Dromore. [*Illust.* 7: 589n; 8: 88n]

16 (1800): 418–424. Review: *"Additional Remarks on the Topography of Troy, &c. in Answer to Mr. Bryant's last Publication. By J. B. S. Morritt [;] Remarks and Observations on the Plain of Troy, made during an Excursion in June, 1799. By William Francklin."* William Vincent. [*Illust.* 3: 772–773]

16 (1800): 530–537. Review: *"Specimens and Parts; containing a History of the County of Kent. . . . By Samuel Henshall [;] The Saxon and English Languages reciprocally illustrative of each other. . . . By Samuel Henshall."* John Whitaker. [*Trad. and Recoll.* 2: 500]

17 (1801): i–xix. "Preface." Robert Nares. [*GM* 99–i (1829): 371]

17 (1801): 125–131. Review: *"Lyrical Ballads, with other Poems: in Two Vols. By W. Wordsworth. Second Edition."* John Stoddart. [Rei-man 1: 131, citing Chester L. Shaver, ed., *The Letters of William and Dorothy Wordsworth*, vol. 1: *The Early Years 1787–1805* (2d ed., rev.; Oxford, 1967), p. 320, n. 3]

17 (1801): 324–325. Review: *"A Hebrew Grammar, for the Use of the Stu-dents of the University of Dublin. By the Rev. Gerald Fitz-gerald. . . ."* Joseph White [?]. [*GM* 84–i (1814): 628]

17 (1801): 453–460. Review: *"[Gilbert Wakefield's] T. Lucretii Cari de Rerum Natura Libros Sex."* Richard Porson. [*DNB* 20: 455]

18 (1801): i–xx. "Preface." Robert Nares. [*GM* 99–i (1829): 371]

18 (1801): 286–295. Review: *"Letters addressed to a young Man. . . . By Mrs. West."* Thomas Percy, Bishop of Dromore. [*Illust.* 7: 592n]

18 (1801): 359–365. Review: *"Mrs. West's Letters to a Young Man* [cont.]." Thomas Percy, Bishop of Dromore. [*Illust.* 7: 592n]

18 (1801): 524–529. Review: *"Letters addressed to a young Man* [cont.]." Thomas Percy, Bishop of Dromore, and Robert Nares (who wrote the concluding sentence, p. 529). [*Illust.* 7: 592n; 593–594, 594n]

19 (1802): i–xv. "Preface." Robert Nares. [*GM* 99–i (1829): 371]

19 (1802): 1–15. Review: *"Critical Remarks on the Hebrew Scriptures: corre-sponding with a new Translation of the Bible. By the Rev. Alex-ander Geddes. . . . Vol. I. . . ."* Joseph White [?]. [*GM* 84–i (1814): 628]

19 (1802): 134–154. Review: *"[Geddes's] Critical Remarks on the Hebrew Scriptures, &c.* [cont.]." Joseph White [?]. [*GM* 84–i (1814): 628]

19 (1802): 268–279. Review: *"A Comparative View of the Public Finances, from the Beginning to the Close of the late Administration. By William Morgan."* John Brand. [*Illust.* 6: 532]

19 (1802): 283–293. Review: *"[Geddes's] Critical Remarks on the Hebrew Scriptures, &c.* [cont.]." Joseph White [?]. [*GM* 84–i (1814): 628]

19 (1802): 343–355. Review: "[Geddes's] *Critical Remarks on the Hebrew Scriptures*, &c. [cont.]." Joseph White [?]. [*GM* 84–i (1814): 628]

19 (1802): 374–381. Review: "*A Comparative View of the Public Finances*, &c. [cont.]." John Brand. [*Illust.* 6: 532]

19 (1802): 524–530. Review: "[Geddes's] *Critical Remarks on the Hebrew Scriptures*, &c. [cont.]." Joseph White [?]. [*GM* 84–i (1814): 628]

19 (1802): 570–576. Review: "[Walter Scott's] *Minstrelsy of the Scottish Borders. . . .*" George Ellis. [Roper 33, 57, and 277 (n. 12) citing H. J. C. Grierson, ed., *The Letters of Sir Walter Scott* (12 vols.; London, 1932–37), 1: 185n]

19 (1802): 580–588. Review: "*A Comparative View of the Public Finances*, &c. [conc.]." John Brand. [*Illust.* 6: 532]

19 (1802): 623–631. Review: "[Geddes's] *Critical Remarks on the Hebrew Scriptures*, &c. [cont.]." Joseph White [?]. [*GM* 84–i (1814): 628]

20 (1802): i–xxi. "Preface." Robert Nares. [*GM* 99–i (1829): 371]

20 (1802): 8–13. Review: "*The Complaynt of Scotland, written in 1548; with a Preliminary Dissertation and Glossary. By John Leyden. . . .*" George Ellis. [Roper 33, 57, and 277 (n. 12) citing H. J. C. Grierson, ed., *The Letters of Sir Walter Scott* (12 vols.; London, 1932–37) 1: 185n]

20 (1802): 53–61. Review: "[Geddes's] *Critical Remarks on the Hebrew Scriptures*, &c. [cont.]." Joseph White [?]. [*GM* 84–i (1814): 628]

20 (1802): 165–171. Review: "[Geddes's] *Critical Remarks on the Hebrew Scriptures*, &c. [conc.]." Joseph White [?]. [*GM* 84–i (1814): 628]

20 (1802): 295–298. Review: "*The Miscellaneous Works of Oliver Goldsmith.*" Robert Nares. [*Illust.* 7: 598, 601–602; 8: 671]

20 (1802): 329–330. Review: "*Remarks on Mr. Morgan's Comparative View of the Public Finances, from the Beginning to the Close of the late Administration.*" John Brand. [*Illust.* 6: 532]

20 (1802): 641–645. Review: "*A Specimen of the Conformity of the European Languages, particularly the English, with the Oriental Languages, especially the Persian. . . . By Stephen Weston. . . .*" Joseph White. [*GM* 84–i (1814): 628]

21 (1803): i–xvi. "Preface." Robert Nares. [*GM* 99–i (1829): 371]

21 (1803): 272–284. Review: "*Elementary Treatises on the fundamental Principles of practical Mathematics. . . . By Samuel Lord Bishop of* Rochester (now of St. Asaph)." John Hellins. [*GM* 98–i (1828): 181]

21 (1803): 406–411. Review: "*The Infidel Father. By . . . [Mrs. West].*" Robert Nares. [*Illust.* 7: 601, 601n]

22 (1803): i–xvii. "Preface." Robert Nares. [*GM* 99–i (1829): 371]

22 (1803): 545–549. Review: "*The History of Ilium or Troy. . . . By the Author of 'Travels in Asia Minor and Greece'* [Dr. Richard Chandler]." William Vincent. [*Illust.* 3: 772–773]

23 (1804): iii–xix. "Preface." Robert Nares. [*GM* 99–i (1829): 371]

23 (1804): 143–156. Review: "*Analytical Institutions, in Four Books: originally written in Italian, by Donna Maria Gaetana Agnesi. . . . Translated into English, by the late Rev. John Colson. . . . Now first printed . . . under the Inspection of the Rev. John Hellins.*" John Hellins. [*GM* 98–i (1828): 181]

23 (1804): 489–494. Review: "*An Introduction to the Theory and Practice of plane and spherical Trigonometry.* . . . By Thomas Keith." John Hellins. [*GM* 98–i (1828): 181]

24 (1804): iii–xx. "Preface." Robert Nares. [*GM* 99–i (1829): 371]

24 (1804): 231–243. Review: "*English Metrical Romances, selected and published by Joseph Ritson* . . .; [*Ritson's*] *Bibliographica Poetica: a Catalogue of English Poets, of the twelfth, thirteenth, fourteenth, fifteenth, and sixteenth Centuries.*" Robert Nares. [*Illust.* 7: 601, 603–606]

24 (1804): 653–660. Review: "*Analytical Institutions, in Four Books,* &c. [cont]." John Hellins. [*GM* 98–i (1828): 181]

24 (1804): 665–679. Review: "*Observations upon some Passages in Scripture.* . . . By Jacob Bryant." William Vincent [?]. [*Illust.* 3: 772–773; internal evidence]

25 (1805): iii–xix. "Preface." Robert Nares. [*GM* 99–i (1829): 371]

25 (1805): 46–58. Review: "[*Bryant's*] *Observations upon some Passages in Scripture* [conc.]." William Vincent [?]. [*Illust.* 3: 772–773]

25 (1805): 98–99. Staff note: "In Addition to Art. II. of the *British Critic*, for September, 1804. On Ritson's *Metrical Romances*." Robert Nares [?] (p. 98) and Thomas Percy, Bishop of Dromore (p. 99). [*Illust.* 7: 606–607, 607n]

25 (1805): 141–147. Review: "*Analytical Institutions, in Four Books,* &c. [cont.]." John Hellins. [*GM* 98–i (1828): 181]

25 (1805): 349–361. Review: "*The Topography of Troy.* . . . By William Gell." William Vincent. [*Illust.* 3: 773]

26 (1805): iii–xx. "Preface." Robert Nares. [*GM* 99–i (1829): 371]

26 (1805): 287–292. Review: "*Tentamen Palaeographiae Assyrio-Persicae.* . . . *An Essay on the Ancient Writing of the Assyrio-Persians; or an Attempt to illustrate the Monuments of those Nations, who in the earliest Ages inhabited Middle Asia: especially Inscriptions in the Wedge-like (or Arrow-headed) Character. By M. Ant. Aug. Hen. Lichtenstein.*" Joseph White. [*GM* 84–i (1814): 628]

27 (1806): iii–xvi. "Preface." Robert Nares. [*GM* 99–i (1829): 371]

27 (1806): 53–57. Review: "*Three Tracts on the Syntax and Pronunciation of the Hebrew Tongue; with an Appendix, addressed to the Hebrew Nation. By Granville Sharp.* . . ." Joseph White [?]. [*GM* 84–i (1814): 628]

28 (1806): iii–xix. "Preface." Robert Nares. [*GM* 99–i (1829): 371]

28 (1806): 465–479. Review: "*The Book of the Prophet Isaiah: in Hebrew and English. The Hebrew Text metrically arranged: the Translation altered from that of Bishop Lowth.* . . . By Joseph Stock. . . ." Joseph White [?]. [*GM* 84–i (1814): 628]

28 (1806): 608–619. Review: "*The Book of the Prophet Isaiah, in Hebrew and English* . . . [cont.]." Joseph White [?]. [*GM* 84–i (1814): 628]

29 (1807): iii–xv. "Preface." Robert Nares. [*GM* 99–i (1829): 371]

29 (1807): 134–147. Review: "*The Book of the Prophet Isaiah, in Hebrew and English* . . . [conc.]." Joseph White [?]. [*GM* 84–i (1814): 628]

29 (1807): 368–375. Review: "*The Book of Job, metrically arranged according to the Masora, and newly translated into English, with Notes Critical and Explanatory.* . . . By the Right Rev. Joseph Stock, DD.*

Bishop of Killalla. . . .” Joseph White [?]. [*GM* 84–i (1814): 628]

29 (1807): 496–508. Review: *“The Book of Job . . .* [conc.].” Joseph White [?]. [*GM* 84–i (1814): 628]

30 (1807): iii–xix. “Preface.” Robert Nares. [*GM* 99–i (1829): 371]

30 (1807): 15–23. Review: *“Ancient Alphabets and Hieroglyphic Characters explained: With an Account of the Egyptian Priests, their Classes, Initiation, and Sacrifices. In the Arabic Language by Ahmad Bin Abubekr Bin Washih, and in English by Joseph Hammer. . . .”* Joseph White. [*GM* 84–i (1814): 628]

31 (1808): iii–xix. “Preface.” Robert Nares. [*GM* 99–i (1829): 371]

31 (1808): 22–25. Review: *“Fragments of Oriental Literature. . . .* By Stephen Weston. . . .” Joseph White. [*GM* 84–i (1814): 628]

32 (1808): iii–xviii. “Preface.” Robert Nares. [*GM* 99–i (1829): 371]

33 (1809): iii–xix. “Preface.” Robert Nares. [*GM* 99–i (1829): 371]

34 (1809): iii–xxiii. “Preface.” Robert Nares. [*GM* 99–i (1829): 371]

34 (1809): 173–177. Review: *“General View of the Agriculture of the County of Devon. . . .* By Charles Vancouver.” Richard Polwhele [?]. [*Biog. Sketches* 3: 176]

34 (1809): 616–621. Review: *“A Tour through Cornwall. . . .* By the Rev. Richard Warner of Bath.” Richard Polwhele. [*Illust.* 7: 610]

35 (1810): iii–xix. “Preface.” Robert Nares. [*GM* 99–i (1829): 371]

35 (1810): 1–15. Review: *“The Life of St. Neot. . . .* By the Rev. John Whitaker.” Richard Polwhele. [*Illust.* 7: 610; *Biog. Sketches* 3: 176]

35 (1810): 112–120. Review: *“An Essay on the Identity and general Resurrection of the human Body. . . .* By Samuel Drew.” Richard Polwhele. [*Illust.* 7: 610]

36 (1810): iii–xx. “Preface.” Robert Nares. [*GM* 99–i (1829): 371]

36 (September 1810): 209–228. Review: *“Ta-Tsing-Leu-Lee, being the fundamental Laws, and a Selection from the supplementary Statutes of the penal Code of China. . . .* By Sir George Thomas Staunton.” William Vincent [?]. [As Vincent reviewed Staunton’s *Authentic Account of an Embassy from the King of Great-Britain to the Emperor of China* for *BC* 10 (1797): 221–233, 362–374, it is possible that he reviewed Staunton’s *Fundamental Laws of China* as well]

37 (1811): iii–xx. “Preface.” Robert Nares. [*GM* 99–i (1829): 371]

38 (1811): iii–xix. “Preface.” Robert Nares. [*GM* 99–i (1829): 371]

38 (1811): 484–497. Review: *“Travels in various Countries of Europe, Asia, and Africa. By Edward Daniel Clarke, LL.D. Part the First*[.] *Russia, Tartary, and Turkey. Vol. I.”* William Vincent [?]. [Vincent reviewed Clarke’s Part the Second in *BC* 40 (1812): 97–110; see below]

38 (1811): 603–616. Review: “Clarke’s *Travels.* [Part the First; conc.].” William Vincent [?]. [See *BC* 38 (1811): 484–497]

38 (1811): 622–628. Review: *“The Doctrine of Interest and Annuities analytically investigated and explained. . . .* By Francis Baily.” John Hellins. [*GM* 98–i (1828): 181]

39 (1812): iii–xvi. “Preface.” Robert Nares. [*GM* 99–i (1829): 371]

40 (1812): iii–xx. “Preface.” Robert Nares. [*GM* 99–i (1829): 371]

40 (1812): 97–110. Review: *“Travels in various Countries of Europe, Asia,*

and Africa. By Edward Daniel Clarke, L.L.D. Part the Second." William Vincent. [*Illust.* 3: 772–773]

40 (1812): 616–624. Review: "Clarke's *Travels* [conc.]." William Vincent. [Vincent wrote the first part of the review; see *BC* 40 (1812): 97–110]

41 (1813): iii–xx. "Preface." Robert Nares. [*GM* 99–i (1829): 371]

42 (1813): iii–xxiii. "Preface." Robert Nares. [*GM* 99–i (1829): 371]

42 (1813): 343–359. Review: "*The Life of John Knox. . . . By Thomas Mc-Crie."* George Gleig, Bishop of Brechin. [Gleig's letter (signed "G—— B——") in *GM* 84–i (1814): 545; *Illust.* 7: 622, 622n]

42 (1813): 448–461. Review: "*The Life of John Knox, &c.* [cont.]." George Gleig, Bishop of Brechin. [Gleig's letter (signed "G—— B——") in *GM* 84–i (1814): 545; *Illust.* 7: 622, 622n]

42 (1813): 502–512. Review: "*The Doctrine of Life Annuities and Assurances. . . . By Francis Baily* [cont.]." John Hellins. [*GM* 98–i (1828): 181]

42 (1813): 554–581. Review: "*The Life of John Knox, &c.* [cont.]." George Gleig, Bishop of Brechin. [Gleig's letter (signed "G—— B——") in *GM* 84–i (1814): 545; *Illust.* 7: 622, 622n]

42 (1813): 586–593. Review: "*The Life and Administration of Cardinal Wolsey. By John Galt.*" Richard Polwhele. [*Illust.* 7: 618–619]

GILMAN'S MANUSCRIPT OF "THE YELLOW WALL-PAPER": TOWARD A CRITICAL EDITION

by

SHAWN ST. JEAN*

As the recovery of women's neglected writing continues to receive the attention and energy of feminist scholars, it seems inevitable that the best of this material become subject to the same textual scrutiny and high editorial standards accorded the works of traditional canonical figures. Naturally, since forms of scrutiny and conceptions of standards vary, women's writing will also become fodder for purely textual disagreements. Charlotte Perkins Gilman's short story "The Yellow Wall-Paper" already bears out this speculation. In the 1993 annual *American Literary Scholarship*, Lawrence I. Berkove lamented that a new casebook edition,

> like all other present editions of this celebrated and much-analyzed story, . . . uses, without explanation, the questionable 1892 magazine text instead of the more accurate handwritten manuscript in the Gilman Papers at Radcliffe College. Precisely because the story has been, as the editors say, a "key feminist text" since 1973, it is baffling why so little attention has been shown to the basic scholarly functions of establishing and using the best possible text for it. (184)

A full defense of his claim that the Radcliffe holograph is "more accurate" and would prove the "best possible" copy-text for a scholarly edition was beyond the scope of Berkove's survey. Truly, with few exceptions,[1] the manuscript has received remarkably little attention by editors and scholars. The dozens of editions that critics, teachers, and students have been using for decades are all based on the first published version (*New England Magazine*, January 1892) or versions derived from it. The purposes of the present essay are to introduce new manuscript information essential to the production of *any* critical edition of "The Yellow Wall-Paper," to argue the wholly nonauthoritative character of the magazine printing (hereafter designated as NEM), and to propose that Gilman's undervalued, handwritten document (hereafter designated as MS) must supply the copy-text for a critical edition that holds the textual intentions of the author paramount.

More than a century of "The Yellow Wall-Paper"'s textual history can be interpreted as either a textbook case of corruption and disintegration, or as a case of social construction, depending on one's theoretical perspective. A

---

* My sincere thanks to Allan Dooley, David Vander Meulen, and Sidney Reid for their comments on earlier drafts of this essay.

1. Denise Knight has edited a diplomatic transcription of the Radcliffe manuscript in *"The Yellow Wall-paper" and Selected Stories of Charlotte Perkins Gilman* (Newark: University of Delaware Press, 1994), 39–53. The original resides in the Charlotte Perkins Gilman Papers, Schlesinger Library, Radcliffe College, Cambridge, Mass.

critical edition edited by Julie Bates Dock and published by Penn State University Press is due to appear in April 1998, and, judging from Dock's praise of Jerome McGann and her assessment of documentary priorities in the January 1996 issue of *PMLA*, the edition will accept a collaborative model of authorship and take NEM as its copy-text.[2] I will demonstrate that such an edition, whatever its merits, will not adequately provide a text of the story that feminists would be expected to require: one preserving Gilman's own writing prior to its appropriation by publisher's readers, editors, and compositors, most of whom were probably males.

The story appeared in at least eight editions during Gilman's lifetime, and another dozen or so before publication by the Feminist Press in 1973 cemented its position as a seminal work of the women's movement in America.[3] Working backward, collation of all later appearances during Gilman's

2. Julie Bates Dock, Daphne Ryan Allen, Jennifer Palais, and Kristen Tracy, " 'But One Expects That': Charlotte Perkins Gilman's 'The Yellow Wallpaper' and the Shifting Light of Scholarship," *PMLA* 111 (January 1996): 52–65.

3. It was thus never out of print or in need of recovery, as so many critics and editors have claimed. For example, Susan S. Lanser, "Feminist Criticism, 'The Yellow Wallpaper,' and the Politics of Color in America," *Feminist Studies* 15 (Fall 1989), begins an otherwise excellent New Historicist argument with the fable that the story was "out of print for half a century" (415). The *Instructor's Manual* to *Literature: An Introduction to Fiction, Poetry, and Drama*, Sixth Edition (New York: HarperCollins Publishers, 1995) deems such a collapsed historical record "worth recounting," presumably to composition students (82).

The only dangerous period may have been the twenty years between its book publication as *The Yellow Wall Paper* by Small, Maynard & Company in 1899 and William Dean Howells' edition in *The Great Modern American Stories: An Anthology* (New York: Boni and Liveright, 1920). However, the existence of new impressions and (re)issues of the editions listed here may establish that the story's appearances have been downright plentiful during the twentieth century. For example, the *National Union Catalog of Pre-1956 Imprints* lists 1901 and 1911 book printings by Small, Maynard, and Company. The OCLC electronic database locates a "5th Ed." of Howells' book in 1921. Unless otherwise noted in brackets [ ], the following list names editions, in the traditional sense of production from a substantially new setting of type, of "The Yellow Wall-Paper" prior to 1973.

The story was printed next during Gilman's lifetime (1860–1935) in the *New York Evening Post* of January 21, 1922. A copy of this edition was found in the Gilman Papers at Radcliffe College. The fifth edition was in *American Mystery Stories* (New York: Oxford University Press, American Branch, 1927), the sixth in *Golden Book* 18 (October 1933), a literary magazine, and the seventh in *A Book of the Short Story* (New York: American Book Company, 1934). The books containing the fifth and seventh editions are scholarly collections. The Finnish translation by Irene Tokoi appeared in *Nykyaika* 15 (June 1934), totalling eight known editions during Gilman's lifetime.

The *Short Story Index* locates two early editions after Gilman's death that do not appear in other references: in *Theme and Variation in the Short Story* (New York: The Gordon Company, 1938), and in *About Women, A Collection of Short Stories* (Cleveland: World Publishing Company, 1943).

The story enjoyed popular status as a ghost story during the time it fell from scholarly view, and according to Everett F. Bleiler's *The Guide to Supernatural Fiction* (Kent, Ohio: Kent State University Press, 1983), saw print at least eight times: in *The Haunted Omnibus* (New York: Farrar and Rinehart, 1937) [which saw reincarnation minus its Foreword, fourteen stories, and an Afterword by Edith Wharton as *Great Ghost Stories of the World, The Haunted Omnibus* (New York: Garden City Books, 1939 and New York: Blue Ribbon Books, 1941)]; *The Midnight Reader: Great Stories of Haunting and Horror* (New York: Holt,

lifetime shows that each is derived either from the 1899 Small, Maynard book edition (hereafter designated as SM, itself derived from the magazine) or NEM. I have found no diary entry or correspondence to support the possibility of Gilman's intervening (by revision or correction) in these later editions. Therefore, no appearance postdating 1899 has been judged to have any authority.[4]

Documentary evidence concerning circumstances of production of SM is scarce. Gilman was already seeing her great brainchild, *Women and Economics*, through the press with Small, Maynard & Co. during 1898, and frequently mentions reading proof for that book in her diaries.[5] From late 1898 through Spring 1899, Gilman was on a lecture tour that included stops in Illinois, Ohio, Missouri, Tennessee, Alabama, and North Carolina. From May 4, 1899, through September 1899 she was on a lecture tour in England, and SM (with variant title *The Yellow Wall Paper*) was almost certainly out by the time of her return to America. No mention of the book itself, let alone reading proof for it, appears in the diaries or correspondence of this time period. Proof was read almost exclusively at the Boston offices of Small, Maynard & Co. for her other books, but Gilman was unavailable while SM would have been at press. Finally, while the story's (and Gilman's) modest popularity in the final years of the century might have warranted a gamble on the thin volume (sold at fifty cents per copy, of which Gilman received ten percent), this venture was not nearly as important to Gilman or her publisher as her other current books. According to her diary of September 26, 1899, Small offered her terms for "another book" (presumably *Concerning Children*): "500.00 down, 15% to 5000 and then 18%." These numbers dwarf anything the little story could have made, and tend to explain why it goes unmentioned. Also, SM contains a claim to be "reprinted from *The New England Magazine* of January, 1892, by permission of the publisher, to whom the thanks of the Author are due." Collation of the two appearances confirms this claim, although some variants explainable as compositorial error appear in

---

1942) [brought out by London publishers World Distributors and Bodley Head in 1948 and 1949, respectively]; *Ghostly Tales To Be Told* (New York: Dodd, Mead, 1950); *More Macabre* (New York: Ace Books, 1961); *These Will Chill You: Twelve Terrifying Tales of Malignant Evil* (New York: Bantam Books, 1967); and *Eight Strange Tales* (Greenwich, CT: Fawcett Publications, 1972). It also appeared under similar guise in *A Chamber of Horrors Unlocked* (Boston: Little, Brown, 1965) and in *Ladies of Horror* (New York: Lothrop, Lee & Shepard Co., 1971). Some of these books were only released as paperbacks, and given the context they provide "The Yellow Wall-Paper," it is easy to imagine why they have evaded or resisted scholarly attention.

Other pre-1973 printings provide a renewed scholarly context for the story: *Points of View: An Anthology of Short Stories* (New York: Mentor 1956); *Psychopathology and Literature* (San Francisco: Chandler Publishing Co., 1960 [and 1966]); *The Writer's Signature: Idea in Story and Essay* (Glenview, IL: Scott, Foresman, and Co., 1972); and *The Oven Birds* (New York: Doubleday, 1972).

4. Consequently, no later printings derived second-hand from *these* editions (i.e. anthologies using the 1933 *Golden Book* text) carry any authority.

5. *The Diaries of Charlotte Perkins Gilman*, ed. Denise D. Knight, 2 vols. (Charlottesville: University Press of Virginia, 1994).

SM. Therefore, on the basis of internal evidence and lack of external evidence supporting authorial intervention, the 1899 book edition, SM, is treated here as a nonauthoritative derivation.

This leaves only NEM and the fair-copy MS as documents with possible authority. The situation surrounding the first publication is complex, and several circumstances that only indirectly bear on it must be appended to a narrative whose basic facts are already familiar to Gilman scholars.

We know for sure that Gilman, then Charlotte Perkins Stetson, sent a copy of the story from Pasadena, California, to William Dean Howells in Boston on August 28, 1890. This is confirmed by both her manuscript log[6] and her diary. The diary entry for August 24 states that Gilman "finish[ed] copy of Yellow Wallpaper," so she may have fair-copied an existing original for the express purpose of enlisting Howells in placing the story. This supposition is supported by an entry under "June [1890]" in the manuscript log stating that "The Yellow Wall-paper" was sent to *Scribner's*, but the entry has been lined out. The implied documentation of one manuscript in June and another completed in August suggests the existence of (at least) two manuscripts. Whether the story was originally sent to and rejected by *Scribner's*, or Gilman reconsidered before sending it, is unknown, but she evidently retained a copy while Howells had the story. No second manuscript apparently survives, but its original existence may be significant, as will be considered in the discussion of MS.

Howells passed the story on to Horace Scudder of the *Atlantic Monthly*, who attached a handwritten rejection card when he returned the manuscript to Gilman, which reads: "18 October 1890. Dear Madam: W. Howells has handed me this story. I could not forgive myself if I made others as miserable as I have made myself! Sincerely Yours, H. E. Scudder." Gilman must have been affected by this ambiguous rebuff, since she kept the card (which bears the words "(returning mss.)" in her hand) and recorded her umbrage at the incident years later in her autobiography, *The Living of Charlotte Perkins Gilman*.[7]

With the manuscript back in her hands, she sent it (or another copy) promptly out "to Mr. Austin" on October 26, according to both her diary and manuscript log. Henry Austin, whose name is attached to the name "Traveller Literary Syndicate" in the manuscript log, had written to Gilman weeks before, apparently soliciting manuscripts as a literary agent. Her diary records receipt of a letter from him (which has not been located) on September 23, and on September 27 she had sent "all this week's mss. to Mr. Austin" minus "The Yellow Wall-Paper," which was still going the Howells/Scudder route.

The autobiography records that Austin

6. "*Record of Mss.* Beginning *March 1st* 1890." Box XXVII, Vol. 23. Charlotte Perkins Gilman Papers, Schlesinger Library, Radcliffe College.

7. Charlotte Perkins Gilman, *The Living of Charlotte Perkins Gilman: An Autobiography* (New York: D. Appleton-Century Company, 1935), 118–19. Gilman must have referred directly to this card in preparing the book some forty-four years later. Except for misreading Scudder's "W. Howells" for "Mr. Howells," her transcription is exact. The card resides in the Charlotte Perkins Gilman Papers, Schlesinger Library, Radcliffe College.

placed [the story] with the *New England Magazine*. Time passed, much time, and at length I wrote to the editor of that periodical to this effect:

> Dear Sir,
>   A story of mine, "The Yellow Wallpaper," was printed in your issue of May, 1891. Since you do not pay on receipt of ms. nor on publication, nor within six months of publication, may I ask if you pay at all, and if so at what rates?

> They replied with some heat that they had paid the agent, Mr Austin. He, being taxed with it, denied having got the money. It was only forty dollars anyway! As a matter of fact I never got a cent for it till later publishers brought it out in book form, and very little then. But it made a tremendous impression. (119)

Gilman's original letter to *The New England Magazine* does not survive, nor does their reply. The author is obviously relying on her memory of these events, as evidenced by her quoting her letter "to this effect" and her inaccurate recollection of the publication date, which was actually January, 1892. As for Austin's role in the placement of the story, there would normally be no reason to doubt Gilman's word if it were not that a slightly different account descends to us.

Howells reprinted "The Yellow Wall-Paper" in his 1920 collection *The Great Modern American Stories: An Anthology*.[8] In "A Reminiscent Introduction," he recalls

> It wanted at least two generations to freeze our young blood with Mrs. Perkins Gilman's story of *The Yellow Wall Paper*, of which Horace Scudder (then of *The Atlantic*) said in refusing it that it was so terribly good that it ought never to be printed. But terrible and too wholly dire as it was, I could not rest until I had corrupted the editor of *The New England Magazine* into publishing it. (vii)

Since Gilman's account of Austin's agency appears to conflict with Howells' self-promotion, and since hers is supported by some (though hardly conclusive) documentary evidence and his by none at all, it would be tempting to accept the former, though one would wonder why Howells would misrepresent the facts, even under the guise of "reminiscence." However, given his affinity for dramatic phrases here and throughout the "Introduction," it would be difficult to define "corrupted the editor" without some additional information. Fortunately, indirect information sheds some light on this whole situation, demonstrating that Howells' and Gilman's accounts are not mutually exclusive, and more importantly, that the manuscript Howells "shiver[ed] over" was Gilman's only means of controlling the text of her story.

First we must step back in order to sort out the relationships of several people. On March 1st, 1890, while Gilman was composing "The Yellow Wall-Paper," her manuscript log records that she submitted a poem, "Similar Cases," to *The Nationalist*, a periodical edited by, as it turns out, one Henry Willard Austin. The poem was published just over a month later in the April *Nationalist*. Meanwhile, on March 11, Gilman sent her short story "The Giant

---

8. Howells requested on October 7, 1919, to "use your terrible story of 'The Yellow Wall Paper' in a book I am making for Messrs. Boni & Liveright and thinking of calling 'Little American Masterpieces of Fiction.' Correspondence with William Dean Howells. Folder 120. Charlotte Perkins Gilman Papers, Schlesinger Library, Radcliffe College.

Wistaria" to *The New England Magazine*, edited jointly by Edward Everett Hale and Edwin Doak Mead. The manuscript log records that "Wistaria" was sent "via Walter" (Charles Walter Stetson, the husband from whom Gilman was then amicably separated, who was living in Providence, R.I., at the time).

Later, in early September and while Howells was perusing a holograph of "The Yellow Wall-paper," "Similar Cases" was reprinted in *The New England Magazine*. This demand for the poem was certainly a windfall for an unknown writer, though further entries in Gilman's records explain it. On September 16, Gilman sent another poem, "An Anti-Nationalist Wail," "to Uncle Edward Hale," and it was promptly published in December's *New England Magazine*. Scattered entries in both Gilman's and Stetson's diaries confirm that "Edward Everett Hale and his wife, Emily Baldwin Perkins Hale (the sister of Frederick Perkins, Charlotte's father), frequently invited Charlotte to visit them in Boston" where Gilman always seemed to enjoy herself immensely.[9] Gilman apparently meant to make the most of this relationship-through-marriage: on October 26 she sent "Mer-songs, etc. to E. E. Hale" (diary), otherwise known as "Uncle Edward (Traveller Literary Syndicate)" (ms. log). The "Mer-songs" weren't accepted, but her short story, "The Giant Wistaria," was, and appeared in the June 1891 issue of *The New England Magazine*. By then Hale had left the publication, but retained close ties with Mead, who remained. With the publication of "The Yellow Wall-paper" in January 1892, that would make a total of two poems and two short stories placed there in a sixteen month period, during which time her "Uncle Edward" was either co-editor or a friend of the editor there.

The linking of "Uncle Edward" to "Traveller Literary Syndicate" provokes interest. The specific business name, about which nothing has been discovered, sounds much like one of the literary agencies whose advertisements offered to "undertake every kind of work required between author and publisher" and some of which are glued to the inside back-cover of Gilman's manuscript log. She has there clipped ads for "The Writer's Literary Bureau" and "The Cooperative Literary Press," along with a clipped letterhead from the "American Press Association." Recalling that, according to her diary, Gilman had received a letter from "Mr. Henry Austin, 'Traveller Literary Syndicated' " on September 23, 1890, one is reminded that Henry Willard Austin published Gilman's first poem and Hale reprinted it in short order. It seems reasonable to conclude that Henry Willard Austin and Henry Austin were the same person, and that an agency (the formality of which is not known) consisting of Austin and Hale (and perhaps others) was formed. The letter Gilman received from Austin does not survive, but he was evidently soliciting manuscripts for publication: four days later she prepared and sent "all this week's mss. to Mr. Austin," and "The Yellow Wall-paper" followed them when Gilman received the manuscript back with Scudder's rejection on or before October 26.

9. *Endure: The Diaries of Charles Walter Stetson*, ed. Mary A. Hill (Philadelphia: Temple University Press, 1985).

The extent of Gilman's familiarity with Austin is not known. That the agent was indeed the same man who edited *The Nationalist* is further supported by Gilman's diary entry of February 14, 1891: Henry Willard Austin's slim book of poetry, *Vagabond Verses*, arrived in Gilman's mail as a gift from author to author. Austin evidently admired "Similar Cases" (as did Howells and Hale) and hoped for mutual appreciation.

This is the same man who, Gilman claimed, may have later stolen her payment for NEM. That she indeed never received payment seems almost certain: first, a page headed "1892 June" in her manuscript log reads "I have out, printed and unpaid" followed by a list of 27 items, some of which have been crossed out (apparently as payment came in). The second entry is for "The Yellow Wallpaper New Eng. Mag. March 1892" and has not been crossed out. Gilman was so impecunious at the time that she recorded the smallest amounts of received money in her diary, and nothing is mentioned in connection with the story.

However, the young author did receive a check for $14.00 from *The New England Magazine* on August 18, 1891, two months after the publication of "The Giant Wistaria" and five months before NEM appeared. It seems far more likely that this was payment for "Wistaria" (which does not appear in the manuscript log as "unpaid") than an advance for NEM. Besides, Gilman claimed in her autobiography that the latter story's publication was a matter of forty dollars.

And what role did Howells really play? As editor/critic Dock has pointed out, *New England Magazine* co-editor Edwin Doak Mead was Howells' younger cousin-by-marriage, and had been brought to Boston by Howells as a teenager (58). Howells' "Reminiscent Introduction" is cryptic at best, and could be taken for a claim that *he* received Scudder's rejection and then exerted pressure on his cousin to print the story. This scenario is not actually incompatible with Gilman's account, and the "handy compromise" critics Thomas L. Erksine and Connie L. Richards outlined (and that Dock seems to deplore as irresponsible scholarship) goes farthest in resolving the facts with the perspectives of all concerned.[10] Scudder likely spoke directly to Howells about the story's inappropriateness for the *Atlantic Monthly*,[11] and Howells learned somehow (through Mead, Hale, Austin, or Gilman herself) that the story had gone on to Mead's office. If he put in a word for the story, Gilman may not have known about it or felt it important enough to mention in the autobiography, given her publishing history and pre-existing connections at *The New England Magazine*. Conversely, Howells may not have reckoned properly with Gilman's own connections and given himself more than his share of credit. And, of course, the story has its own estimable merit.

10. *Charlotte Perkins Gilman, "The Yellow Wallpaper,"* ed. Thomas L. Erskine and Connie L. Richards (New Brunswick: Rutgers University Press, 1993), 7.

11. See Joanne B. Karpinski, "When the Marriage of True Minds Admits Impediments: Charlotte Perkins Gilman and William Dean Howells," *Patrons and Protegees*, ed. Shirley Marchalonis (New Brunswick: Rutgers University Press, 1988), 227, for a discussion of the social pressures bearing on the *Atlantic Monthly* at the time of Howells' and Scudder's editorships.

All these circumstances are significant beyond satisfying the curiosity of Gilman scholars: they are crucial to the textual situation of "The Yellow Wall-Paper." An overall picture emerges. The text of "The Yellow Wall-Paper" as transmitted via manuscript through *The New England Magazine* seems to have gone beyond Gilman's control: the story was placed through an intermediary agent(s) who, enabled by personal ties, circumvented usual submission procedures. These procedures would normally have included an author's continued textual control after acceptance. However, no proofs are mentioned in any source, and Gilman lived in California, 3000 miles away from the publisher, at the time and was beholden to the agency of her husband and others when dealing with Boston's literary community: MS bears the return address of Gilman's husband, Walter, in Providence, not Charlotte's in Pasadena. As to internal evidence of authorial control, NEM's variants from MS are almost uniformly corruptions and can be attributed to compositor error or editorial intervention. Finally, Gilman was never compensated for the work.

I believe "The Yellow Wall-Paper" embodies an instance of what Fredson Bowers has called a "single authority textual situation."[12] That is, only one document survives over which Gilman can be demonstrated to have had textual control. If, indeed, demonstration could be made that Gilman corrected proofs for NEM or a later edition of the story, then even if the proofs did not survive, that appearance would gain authority and a critical edition would probably need to be edited eclectically. Since preponderant evidence suggests that Gilman did not correct proofs at all, "The Yellow Wall-Paper" fits the situation Bowers describes in which "The ideal copy-text will ordinarily remain any preserved holograph manuscript [MS] close to the print derived from it."[13] It remains possible, however, that the copy-text itself does not fully reflect Gilman's textual intentions. (The deviations may include such simple matters as slips of the pen or transcriptional errors that entered as she copied from an earlier draft.) The challenge for the editor is to assess Gilman's textual intentions and to adopt readings that most accurately reflect them. Exercising critical judgment based on an understanding of Gilman, the editor may in fact find helpful suggestions in the readings of later editions, even though these texts do not in themselves possess authority.

Some subsidiary concerns must be addressed before granting the above premises. First, is MS the actual document used as printer's copy at *The New England Magazine*? Recall that in June 1890 Gilman's manuscript log indicates that she may have sent the story to *Scribner's*, and only after copying the story in late August did she send a manuscript to William Dean Howells. Logically, then, at least two manuscripts existed while only one is known to survive. The essential question becomes: If MS and the lost manuscript differed, and MS was *not* the printer's copy, must it then defer as copy-text to NEM (which may have derived from a lost document more closely reflecting Gilman's textual intentions)?[14]

12. Fredson Bowers, "Remarks on Eclectic Texts," *Proof* 4 (1975), 43, 62.
13. Bowers, pp. 66–67.
14. This problem was devised by Dock herself and related to me in private conversation.

This takes some sorting out of conflicting evidence and argument. Cursory examination of MS shows that it is certainly a fair-copy in Gilman's hand with few corrections (and those are in her own hand.) It consists of fifty-nine separate leaves, approximately six by nine inches and blue-lined. The verso sides are blank except for occasional ink blots from the facing rectos, a sign of speed in fair-copying. That it was definitely intended for circulation to publishers is confirmed by the heading of the first page:

Mrs. C. P. Stetson.   Box 401 Pasadena Cal.
(about 6000 words-)   to be returned to Mr
Charles Walter Stetson
at the Fleur-de-Lys
Providence
R.I.

This is also in Gilman's hand. The portion beginning "to be returned" refers to Gilman's husband, the sometime-agent for Gilman living in proximity to the New England publishers. This portion is rendered in red ink (as opposed to the black of the manuscript proper) and was probably inserted after the document was returned from Boston to California by Scudder. The word count (written in black ink at the time of original transcription) is, of course, to this day a requirement of many manuscripts submitted for publication.

On the other hand, the document bears none of the telltale signs of printing house handling, such as thumbprints in ink or take marks. Aside from the expected foxing (brown oxidation), some leaves have been stained brown by a chemical that does not, however, appear to be printer's ink.

Closer examination reveals that at some points the handwriting has been clarified in a distinctly different shade of black ink from the original rendering. In most cases the lazy or hasty endings of words have been redone, but in one case the change is intriguing. On MS page 17 a sentence reads "I never saw so much expression in an inanimate thing before, and we all know how much expression they have!" "They" has been crossed out and "inanimate things" has been substituted in Gilman's hand, creating a deliberate repetition. However, the magazine printing retains "they." Although this wording suggests that another manuscript was used that did not have the authorial correction, the number and nature of authorial changes in MS argue at the least that it represents an advanced stage in the composition of the story. Collation of MS and NEM reveals 73 substantive variants and 334 in accidentals (including 110 paragraph alterations), but hardly one of these 407 variations defies explanation as compositor's error, regularization, or "correction" by a printer's reader of MS or a manuscript similar to it.[15] Conversely,

15. Some variants are likely the result of typographical concerns. For example, *The New England Magazine* used a two-column type page with occasional illustrations and customarily began each piece of fiction with a large, stylized capital letter, necessitating a narrower column. The first variant from MS, "John and myself" (the complete fourth line of NEM) for "John and I", is less correct grammatically and might not have been substituted had it not supplied an appropriate number of characters for the line. "John and I" would have required a very unattractive amount of spacing, "John and I secure" would have been too tight, and "John and I se-" would have been much less desirable than the solution that

explaining many of these variants as Gilman's own changes to proof or to another manuscript would be difficult indeed.

From a practical viewpoint, however, all this hardly matters in the face of the present documentary situation. Even if a lost manuscript copy was used as printer's copy by *The New England Magazine* and subsequently discarded, MS remains the closest surviving document to it and least corrupted incarnation of Gilman's textual intentions. There seems little chance that, given the extent of variation, MS and NEM derive from a common (lost) ancestor. But even if they do (a case of radiating texts, in Bowers' term), Gilman's obvious involvement in creating the transcription (MS) and the absence of any identifiable link between her and the details of the NEM text (whose variations can be explained without her) mean that MS ought to be selected as copy-text.

The issue of tacit consent also deserves some attention. Even if we grant MS copy-text status, some would point out that no evidence exists that Gilman objected to the changes made by the magazine to her story, even expected those changes as "regulariz[ation]" (Dock 55). She then had the further opportunity (in theory if not in fact) to revise for the book publication seven years later. Howells brought the story out again, as did others, while Gilman was still alive. Should this lack of objection on the author's part count as evidence that the story was and always has been a product of social construction, of collaboration between artist and publishers? Certainly in our own time the story *is* a social artifact "produced" not only by publishers but by critics whose arguments have depended on texts that derive from the magazine edition or the Small, Maynard book edition (i.e. the widely used Feminist Press edition of 1973).

Such editions as have been produced by this line of argument (whether recognized or not) have their uses and will continue to be available. However, an edition that seeks to recover, as closely as possible, the uncontaminated textual intentions of an author will recur to G. Thomas Tanselle's distinction between what authors (especially young, poor, unrecognized ones) will *accept* from publishers with regard to treatment of their texts and what they would *prefer*.[16] Tanselle's discussion, a refutation of contrary positions by James Thorpe and Philip Gaskell, deals with accidentals, but logic extends it, in the present context, to substantives. The specifics of Gilman's situation support Tanselle's position.

Gilman appears not to have been invited by *The New England Magazine*

---

was adopted. The story's final variant, in which MS reading "I had to creep over him!" was changed to "I had to creep over him every time!" in NEM, clearly furnished the extra line needed to make the two type columns end flush. That this evenness is not merely coincidental but rather an intended typographical feature is suggested by the nearly universal occurrence of the phenomenon throughout 1891 and 1892 numbers of the magazine, where only 2 of the almost 300 articles end with uneven columns. (I am grateful to Elizabeth Lynch for determining these numbers.) The interpretive consequences of the free rein likely taken by NEM's compositor(s) in these cases are significant: both sentences are in key narrative positions that critics typically scrutinize.

16. G. Thomas Tanselle, "Greg's Theory of Copy-Text and the Editing of American Literature," *Studies in Bibliography* 28 (1975), 225.

to correct proofs. Indeed, she may not have known the story had been accepted for publication until after it came out. Her concern over variations from her text was certainly subordinated to anger that she was not paid at all for it,[17] and she would have known the futility of the former "artistic" complaint after the fact of publication. By the time of the book edition, the story was several years old, in danger of being forgotten, and was being brought out seemingly as a low-profit contribution to an author/publisher relationship that was moving in more lucrative directions. And, as has already been discussed, if Gilman had any desire to revise the story, she had little opportunity to do so while the book was initially at press. By the time Howells asked to bring the story out in late 1919 (he didn't ask for alterations either) the story was nearly thirty years old and still obscure. Until the end of her life, Gilman never conceived that the little story would herald her reputation in the future: her 1935 autobiography of 335 pages devotes only 3 to the piece. Her "consent," then, to leave the text of the story as publishers (mis)handled it seems a hybrid matter of early powerlessness and later indifference stemming from that powerlessness. With respect to authorial control, Gilman's experiences with the story certainly do not mirror those of better-known nineteenth-century authors who viewed successive printings as opportunities for revision and correction.[18] However, she may (in this case) be a more accurate representative of vast numbers of unknown writers whose relationships with publishers were more tenuous.

Finally, the most essential questions: Is MS a truly different text from NEM, one that warrants an edition based on it? Because the Feminist Press issued a new edition of the story in 1997, one that corrects the departures from NEM made unintentionally in the 1973 edition, and because Dock's critical edition using NEM as copy-text will also appear in 1998, won't more than enough "good texts" be available to scholars?

The answers lie in the variants:

So I will let it alone, and write about the house. (MS p. 4)
So I will let it alone and talk about the house. (NEM p. 648)

For the sake of her "health," the narrator has been forbidden to write but keeps a secret journal in an attempt to express herself and retain her sanity.

17. The circumstance of Gilman not receiving payment for the story has little effect on a traditional view of the textual situation, but should not be lost on those who like to believe in social construction of texts. Gilman was a writer and lecturer who relied on her craft for a living, and overwhelming evidence shows that, penniless as she was in 1892, she would never have willingly parted with "The Yellow Wall-Paper" without payment. As initiator of a collaborative process, surely her wishes rate some degree of respect. I know of no author who has ever accepted the idea of a pirate as collaborator (whether *The New England Magazine* actually pirated the story would have made precious little difference from Gilman's perspective, and she couldn't know anyway). And by definition, collaboration involves willing cooperation between participants.

18. See Allan C. Dooley, *Author and Printer in Victorian England* (Charlottesville: University Press of Virginia, 1992), and Peter L. Shillingsburg, *Pegasus in Harness: Victorian Publishing and W. M. Thackeray* (Charlottesville: University Press of Virginia, 1992) for detailed examples of such relationships involving Thackery, Tennyson, Eliot, and others.

She adopts the subterfuge precisely because spoken conversations (with her husband John, the only available interlocutor) prove repeatedly futile.

> I never saw so much expression in an inanimate thing before, and we all know how much expression [they *cancelled*] inanimate things have! (MS p. 17)
> I never saw so much expression in an inanimate thing before, and we all know how much expression they have! (NEM p. 650)

> Half the time now I am lazy, awfully lazy, and lie down [around *cancelled*] ever so much. (MS p. 25)
> Half the time now I am awfully lazy, and lie down ever so much. (NEM p. 651)

The narrator frequently repeats herself, perhaps suggesting something about her psychological makeup. The central image of the story, the wallpaper, is the "inanimate thing" referred to in the former example.

> And dear John gathered me up in his [*next word interlined*] strong arms. . . . (MS p. 17)
> And dear John gathered me up in his arms. . . . (NEM p. 652)

> He might even take me away. (MS p. 40)
> He might even want to take me away. (NEM p. 653)

> It would be a shame to break down that beautiful strong door! (MS p. 56)
> It would be a shame to break down that beautiful door! (NEM p. 656)

Before his fainting spell (or death?) at the very end of the story, the narrator associates John with strength, both physical (i.e. his ability to carry her or break down strong doors) and mental (his scientific knowledge and domination of her).

> If I had not used it that blessed child would have! (MS p. 27)
> If we had not used it, that blessed child would have! (NEM p. 652)

> So of course I said no more on that score, and he went to sleep before long. (MS p. 33)
> So of course I said no more on that score, and we went to sleep before long. (NEM p. 653)

The bedroom at the top of the mansion is sometimes occupied by both the narrator and her husband, other times by her alone when John is away all night, as she believes, attending to seriously ill patients. MS uses solitary pronouns that highlight the sense of isolation. Perhaps the magazine's agents wished to efface any suggestions of John's infidelity.

> It is the strangest yellow, that wall-paper! A sickly penetrating suggestive yellow. It makes me think. . . . (MS p. 41)
> It is the strangest yellow, that wall-paper! It makes me think. . . . (NEM p. 654)

No typographical reason is evident for the missing sentence in NEM. It may have been a compositor's eyeskip—or a wish to avoid "suggesting" anything too unpalatable.

> It must be very unpleasant to be caught creeping by daylight! (MS p. 46)
> It must be very humiliating to be caught creeping by daylight! (NEM p. 654)

Clearly two different feelings are being contemplated here. Of course, the narrator is "caught creeping" defiantly in the final scene, and may have been planning the confrontation with John for some time. If anything, she develops an air of pride in her creeping.

It is very seldom that mere ordinary people like John and I secure ancestral halls for the summer. (MS p. 1)
It is very seldom that mere ordinary people like John and myself secure ancestral halls for the summer. (NEM p. 647)

Besides I don't want anybody to get that woman out at night but me. (MS p. 47)
Besides, I don't want anybody to get that woman out at night but myself. (NEM p. 654)

Though pronoun choice is often considered insignificant, occasionally it may be exploited to good effect or at least interpreted as if it had been. Catherine Golden, apparently without knowledge of the alterations from manuscript, devotes considerable attention to the story's use of "I," "one," "he," etc.: "In introducing 'myself' and 'John,' the narrator intensifies her awkward positioning in her sentence and society; she is not even on par with 'ordinary people like John.' "[19]
These few substantive variants readily indicate the disparity of the two texts, which contain dozens more. However, they are far less germane to the question of copy-text than the accidentals of MS and NEM, and I present them merely to indicate the essential need for a critical edition based on the manuscript. A copy-text is chosen for the texture of its accidentals; editors disagreeing with or ignoring this crucial assumption will certainly produce different kinds of critical texts. Indeed, all or some of the above substantives from MS could be adopted into an edition, like Dock's, based on a later text, but such a procedure would efface hundreds of authoritative accidentals. Preservation of an author's unique accidental usages, in essence, was a main point of W. W. Greg's famous essay.[20]
Like Dock, some have claimed that Gilman's accidental usages were (or were expected to be) uninformed, uneven, and only improved by intervention of her publishers and their agents.[21] But other scholars who have had the opportunity of examining MS have insisted that the author knew what she

19. "The Writing of 'The Yellow Wallpaper': A Double Palimpsest," *Studies in American Fiction* 17:2 (Autumn 1989), 195 (193–201).
20. W. W. Greg, "The Rationale of Copy-Text," *Studies in Bibliography* 3 (1950), 19–36.
21. Dock reasons according to the model espoused by Phillip Gaskell and others: "Gilman's manuscript has no necessary textual priority, for she would have expected editors to regularize punctuation in accordance with standards of her day. Moreover, Gilman offered no objection to the minor variations from her manuscript, as far as we have been able to discover. In the absence of evidence that Gilman opposed printing-house changes, the first printing stands as the version that best embodies the story Gilman presented to her contemporaries" (55). In my view, Dock fails to acknowledge that "minor variations" are in the eye of the beholder, that Gilman had no means or opportunity of opposing them anyway, and that absence of evidence proves very little.
At least one scholar has claimed the author was less than competent in the matter of accidentals. Biographer Ann J. Lane, in her "Preface" to *To Herland and Beyond* (New York: Pantheon Books, 1990), xiii, states in passing that "The casual relationship to the rules of spelling and grammar evidenced in Charlotte Gilman's writings reflects both her limited formal education and her later articulated belief that such rules were not especially important."

was doing at least as well as the staff of *The New England Magazine*.[22] As with any author's work, evidence for both positions exists and the question becomes one of preponderance. Again, the proof is in the pudding.

The most significant accidental variants (actually semi-substantives) are the 110 alterations to Gilman's paragraphing, 87 of which were breaks where none exist in MS and 23 of which deleted breaks present in MS.[23] Where MS presents a coherent-looking, well-paragraphed narrative that becomes more and more fragmented as the narrator grows agitated, NEM presents an entirely fragmented, rambling account in which, from the first, the narrator appears unable to hold her thoughts together. No wonder that most critics have buttressed their interpretative arguments by altering her husband John's diagnosis of the narrator's "slight hysterical tendency" (NEM p. 648) to one of outright insanity.[24]

Most of the remaining accidentals are comma, dash, or italic additions and deletions, only some of which clarify the text and most of which alter Gilman's emphases. Others are expansions of Gilman's contractions, as "would not" for "wouldn't," probably done purely for form's sake and inconsistently done at that. There are few, if any, spelling variants. More significant punctuation variants, as changes from periods to exclamation points (occasionally vice-versa), are less frequent but, with the fragmented paragraphing of NEM, help support John's diagnosis of the narrator as a

22. Richard Feldstein, "Reader, Text, and Ambiguous Referentiality in 'The Yellow Wall-Paper,'" *The Captive Imagination: A Casebook on The Yellow Wallpaper* ed. Catherine Golden (New York: Feminist Press, 1992), devises an ingenious explanation for Gilman's varying use of "wallpaper," "wall paper," and "wall-paper." He points out that in NEM "there was a perceptible, though random, pattern of word usage: initially, there are three references to *wall-paper*; then, inexplicably, *wallpaper* appears five times before the pattern reverses itself and *wall-paper* is used four times. . . . From Gilman's original manuscript, however, it is apparent that the word(s) *wall(-)paper* were conceived as a shifter calculated to create ambiguity about a referent that resists analysis, even as the narrator resists her husband's diagnosis and prescription for cure" (308). In other words, Gilman's fluid spelling "in defiance of any unvarying pattern of logic" helped establish the themes of the story. Feldstein's notion argues strongly against regularization of Gilman's accidentals (308–309).

Alfred Bendixen once suggested to me, in accounting for variant forms of "wall-paper," that NEM might have been typeset by multiple compositors. The "random pattern" Feldstein discerned would be consistent with a manuscript division into three "takes" of 19–20 ms. pages each. Further investigation into the theory, which would involve a full comparison of other accidentals in the story and probably surrounding stories in the magazine as well, is beyond the scope of this essay.

23. Disregard for an author's paragraphing was not confined to Gilman's experience. In 1914, Theodore Dreiser sent the handwritten manuscript of *The "Genius"* to a typist: "One of the most pervasive variants in the typescript is the alteration of Dreiser's paragraphing in the holograph, either by dividing a single paragraph into two or more or by combining separate paragraphs into one. . . . the original form is well-nigh always restored [through proofing] in the published version." Louis J. Oldani, "Dreiser's 'Genius' in the Making: Composition and Revision." *Studies in Bibliography*, 47 (1994), 240.

24. Feldstein, informed by his knowledge of MS, surveys some of these arguments and takes exception: "If we read 'The Yellow Wall-Paper' ironically and not simply as a case history of one woman's mental derangement, the narrator's madness becomes questionable, and the question of madness itself, an issue raised as a means of problematizing such a reading" (311).

hysterical female. Other punctuation variants positively confuse the story, as when the narrator confronts John and makes her mysterious declaration at the end:

"I've got out at last," said I, "In spite of you and Jane! (MS p. 656)
"I've got out at last," said I, "In spite of you and Jane? (NEM p. 58)

Since the name Jane has not appeared previously to this climactic moment, its referent (the narrator's own name, a nickname for John's sister "Jennie," all women, the narrator's "domestic" self, an alter ego created by delusion, etc.) has been a crux of speculation among critics of the story. NEM's introduction of a question mark converts Gilman's ambiguity into downright nonsense, and even noncritical editors have invariably emended it to a period or exclamation mark.

In short, MS contains hundreds of authorial usages, both substantive and accidental, for which no editor in the Greg-Bowers tradition could reasonably justify emendation to NEM's nonauthorial variants. Taken together, MS's usages do present a different enough text to warrant an edition, or "version" as social constructionists have it. If NEM were used as copy-text, a considerable number of Gilman's preferred readings, especially in the matter of accidentals, would never find their way into the reading text and would (at best) be relegated to the apparatus.

To return and sum up, then, as to how the textual situation of "The Yellow Wall-Paper" has been affected by addition of this new information to old. After Scudder returned her manuscript, Gilman's last act of control over her text was to send it to an agent. Its placement in *The New England Magazine* was effected in some way that precluded any further intervention on the author's part. She did not even authorize its unpaid publication, which subtly altered hundreds of her usages and may have fundamentally changed the work. Although she did authorize later appearances, she never made an effort to regain control but, indeed, had little incentive to do so. Therefore, a critical text should be based on the only surviving authoritative document, the Radcliffe holograph, and should admit only emendations that reflect Gilman's textual intentions more accurately than the obvious errors in MS.

MILTON IN THE *GENTLEMAN'S MAGAZINE*: A CORRECTION TO DE MONTLUZIN

by

John T. Shawcross

In her recent article on "Attributions of Authorship in the *Gentleman's Magazine*" (*Studies in Bibliography* 50 [1997]: 322–358), Emily Lorraine de Montluzin tentatively attributes an item that was actually produced a number of years earlier by another writer who has long been identified. *Gentleman's Magazine* in its issues of October 1746 (16: 548–549), December 1746 (16: 661), and December 1750 (20: 564–565) reproduced eight Latin translations of John Milton's *Paradise Lost* I, 1–64. Among them is one entitled "Paradisus Amissa. Lib. I. Authore M. B." (October, p. 549), which de Montluzin suggests (p. 345) was by Moses Browne. This is in error and thus Browne's name should be deleted from the list of contributors, p. 356.

The translator was Michael Bold, whose *Paradisus Amissa. Poema, Anglicè Scriptum a Johane Milton. Nunc autem ex Auctoris Exemplari Latinè redditum. Per M. B. Liber Primus*, was published, with Latin and English facing texts, in London in 1702. An issue with a different Latin title page also appeared that year, a reissue with a cancel title page came out in 1717, and a new edition was published in 1736. A survey of these publications, of the history of the attribution, of the misidentification of the translator's first name as "Matthew," and of other works possibly by Bold appear in "A Note on Milton's Latin Translator, M. B," which I contributed to *Milton Quarterly* 21.2 (May 1987): 65–66. In addition to the information there it might be noted that entry 348 in "The Catalogue of the Library of Thomas Percy" from Sotheby & Co. (23 June 1969) reports Laurence Atterbury's manuscript note identifying the translator.

Notes on Contributors

G. Thomas Tanselle is Vice President of the John Simon Guggenheim Memorial Foundation and Adjunct Professor of English at Columbia University. A new collection of his essays, entitled *Literature and Artifacts*, will be published by the Society this year.

Conor Fahy is Emeritus Professor of Italian in the University of London. He has published widely on Italian Renaissance printing. His edition of the first Italian printers' manual, Z. Campanini, *Istruzioni pratiche ad un novello capo-stampa*, 1789, has recently appeared.

Joseph A. Dane is the author of *Who is Buried in Chaucer's Tomb?— Studies in the Reception of Chaucer's Book* (1998) and bibliographical studies in recent and forthcoming issues of *Gutenberg Jahrbuch, Huntington Library Quarterly, The Library, PBSA*, and *Scriptorium*.

Anne Middleton teaches in the English Department at the University of California, Berkeley. *Piers Plowman* is the focus of her work, which currently concerns the intersections of governmental and clerical institutions with literary cultures of later fourteenth-century England.

Laurie E. Maguire is Associate Professor of English at the University of Ottawa. She is the author of *Shakespearean Suspect Texts: The 'Bad' Quartos and their Contexts* (Cambridge University Press, 1996) and of several articles on textual and feminist issues in early modern drama.

David L. Gants is Assistant Professor of English at the University of Georgia, where he teaches courses in Humanities Computing and the Literature of the English Renaissance. He is the Electronic Editor of the Cambridge University Press Works of Ben Jonson and co-director of the Georgia On-line Teaching Initiative, a project supporting the integration of emerging technologies with traditional pedagogies.

Mark Bland received his doctorate from the University of Oxford in 1995. He works on the printing-house of John Windet and William Stansby, and the textual and bibliographical problems involved in editing Jonson. He has recently been appointed Rare Books Librarian at Stanford University Library.

James McLaverty, Lecturer in English at the University of Keele, held a Fellowship at the Centre for the Book, British Library, in 1997. He is working on a study of Pope, print, and meaning, and preparing the late David Fleeman's bibliography of Samuel Johnson for the press.

B. J. McMullin is a Reader in the Department of Librarianship, Archives and Records, Monash University, Melbourne, Australia. He is preparing bibliographies of the Oxford and Cambridge Bible Presses in the seventeenth and eighteenth centuries.

Judith Milhous is Distinguished Professor of Theatre in the Ph.D. Program in Theatre, City University of New York, Graduate Center. She is currently at work on Volume II of *Italian Opera in Late Eighteenth-Century London* (Oxford University Press).

Robert D. Hume is Evan Pugh Professor of English Literature at the Pennsylvania State University. His most recent book, *Reconstructing Contexts: The Aims and Principles of Archaeo-Historicism*, is forthcoming shortly from Oxford University Press.

Mark L. Reed is Lineberger Professor in the Humanities, emeritus, at the University of North Carolina, Chapel Hill. He is Associate Editor of The Cornell Wordsworth, and is working on a "Soho" bibliography of Wordsworth.

Emily Lorraine de Montluzin is Professor of History at Francis Marion University in Florence, South Carolina. She is the author of *The Anti-Jacobins, 1798–1800: The Early Contributors to the "Anti-Jacobin Review"* (1988) as well as two electronic books, *Attributions of Authorship in the* Gentleman's Magazine, *1731–1868: A Supplement to Kuist*, and *Attributions of Authorship in the* Gentleman's Magazine, *1731–1768: A Synthesis of Finds Appearing neither in Kuist's* Nichols File *nor in de Montluzin's* Supplement To Kuist (both published by the Bibliographical Society of the University of Virginia, 1997).

Shawn St. Jean is a Teaching Fellow at Kent State University, where he is completing his doctoral dissertation on Theodore Dreiser and paganism. He has published articles on Dreiser, Joyce, Thoreau, and American gangster films. His current research involves theories of electronic critical editions.

John T. Shawcross is Professor Emeritus of English, University of Kentucky. His forthcoming bibliography of John Milton's works and Miltoniana for 1624–1799 revises and extends his former seventeenth-century compilation.

BIBLIOGRAPHICAL SOCIETY OF THE UNIVERSITY OF VIRGINIA

OFFICERS

President, G. THOMAS TANSELLE, John Simon Guggenheim Memorial Foundation, 90 Park Avenue, New York, New York 10016

Vice President, KENDON L. STUBBS, University of Virginia Library, Charlottesville, Virginia 22903

Secretary-Treasurer, PENELOPE F. WEISS, University of Virginia Library, Charlottesville, Virginia 22903

Editor, DAVID L. VANDER MEULEN, English Department, 219 Bryan Hall, University of Virginia, Charlottesville, Virginia 22903

Executive Secretary, PENELOPE F. WEISS, University of Virginia Library, Charlottesville, Virginia 22903

Hon. Secretary-Treasurer for the British Isles, R. J. GOULDEN, The British Library, Humanities and Social Sciences, Great Russell Street, London WC1B 3DG, England

Hon. Secretary-Treasurer for Australia and New Zealand, Brian N. Gerrard, 25 Leeds Road, Mount Waverley, Victoria 3149, Australia

Hon. Secretary-Treasurer for Japan, HIROSHI YAMASHITA, Institute of Modern Languages and Cultures, University of Tsukuba, Tsukuba-shi 305, Japan

COUNCIL

DAVID SEAMAN	(1998)	RUTHE R. BATTESTIN	(2001)
KENDON L. STUBBS	(1999)	KATHRYN MORGAN	(2002)
TERRY BELANGER	(2000)	KARIN WITTENBORG	(2003)

G. THOMAS TANSELLE (2004)

Honorary Councilor: MRS. LINTON R. MASSEY

PAST PRESIDENTS

CHALMERS L. GEMMILL, ATCHESON L. HENCH, LINTON R. MASSEY, KENDON L. STUBBS, I. B. CAUTHEN, JR.

Studies in Bibliography is issued annually by the Society in addition to various bibliographical pamphlets and monographs.

Membership in the Society is solicited according to the following categories:
    Subscribing Members ($35.00 per year)
    Student Members ($17.50 per year)
    Contributing Members ($125 or more per year)
    Patrons ($250 or more per year)
    Benefactors ($500 or more per year)
Contributing Members, Patrons, and Benefactors receive all publications of the Society and by their contributions assist in furthering the Society's work. The names of individual and institutional members in these three categories are listed annually in *Studies in Bibliography*.

Articles and notes are invited by the Editor. Preferably these should conform to the recommendations of the Modern Language Association of America. All copy, *including quotations and notes*, should be double-spaced. The Society will consider the publication of bibliographical monographs for separate issue.

All matters pertaining to business affairs, including applications for membership, should be sent to the Executive Secretary, Penelope F. Weiss, University of Virginia Library, Charlottesville, Virginia 22903.

AVAILABLE PUBLICATIONS

Accessible on the World Wide Web

The following publications are available without charge through the home page of the Bibliographical Society of the University of Virginia,
http://etext.lib.virginia.edu/bsuva/

STUDIES IN BIBLIOGRAPHY, vols. 1–49, with Cumulative Table of Contents.

de Montluzin, Emily Lorraine. ATTRIBUTIONS OF AUTHORSHIP IN THE *Gentleman's Magazine*, 1731–1868: A SUPPLEMENT TO KUIST.

Evans, G. Blakemore, ed., SHAKESPEAREAN PROMPT-BOOKS OF THE SEVENTEENTH CENTURY, vols. 1–8.

Distributed by the Society

The following publications are available from the office of the Bibliographical Society of the University of Virginia, Alderman Library, Charlottesville, VA 22903. Members receive a 40 per cent discount from the list prices. Postage is additional.

New Publications

Faulkner, William, MOSQUITOES: A FACSIMILE AND TRANSCRIPTION OF THE UNIVERSITY OF VIRGINIA HOLOGRAPH MANUSCRIPT, Thomas L. McHaney and David L. Vander Meulen, eds. $75.00 ($45.00 to members).

Tanselle, G. Thomas, LITERATURE AND ARTIFACTS. $60.00 ($36.00 to members).

Vander Meulen, David L., ed., THE BIBLIOGRAPHICAL SOCIETY OF THE UNIVERSITY OF VIRGINIA: THE FIRST FIFTY YEARS. $50.00 ($30.00 to members).

Currently in Print

Bristol, Roger P., SUPPLEMENT TO EVANS' *American Bibliography*. $50.00 ($30.00 to members).

Bristol, Roger P., INDEX TO SUPPLEMENT TO EVANS' *American Bibliography*. $20.00.

Cauthen, Irby B., Jr., ed., TWO MEMENTOES FROM THE POE-INGRAM COLLECTION: AN ANNIVERSARY KEEPSAKE FOR MEMBERS OF THE BIBLIOGRAPHICAL SOCIETY OF THE UNIVERSITY OF VIRGINIA 1946–1971. $10.00 ($6.00 to members).

Eddy, Donald D., and Fleeman, J. D., A PRELIMINARY HANDLIST OF BOOKS TO WHICH DR. SAMUEL JOHNSON SUBSCRIBED. Occasional Publication 2. $10.00 ($6.00 to members).

Evans, G. Blakemore, ed., SHAKESPEAREAN PROMPT-BOOKS OF THE SEVENTEENTH CENTURY. Vol. V: Text of the Smock Alley *Macbeth*. $35.00 ($21.00 to members). Vol. VI: Text of the Smock Alley *Othello*. $35.00 ($21.00 to members). Vol. VII: Text of the Smock Alley *A Midsummer Night's Dream*. $50.00 ($30.00 to members). Vol. VIII: *King Lear, Henry VIII, The Merry Wives of Windsor, Twelfth Night, The Comedy of Errors, The Winter's Tale*. $75.00 ($45.00 to members).

A KEEPSAKE TO HONOR FREDSON BOWERS. $10.00 ($6.00 to members).

Ribble, Frederick G., and Ribble, Anne G., FIELDING'S LIBRARY: AN ANNOTATED CATALOGUE. $30.00 ($18.00 to members).

Tanselle, G. Thomas, THE LIFE AND WORK OF FREDSON BOWERS. Occasional Publication 1. $30.00 ($18.00 to members).

Vander Meulen, David L., and Tanselle, G. Thomas, eds., SAMUEL JOHNSON'S TRANSLATION OF SALLUST: A FACSIMILE AND TRANSCRIPTION OF THE HYDE MANUSCRIPT. Occasional Publication 3. $25.00 ($15.00 to members).

Distributed by the University Press of Virginia

The following publications of the Society are available from the University Press of Virginia, Box 3608, University Station, Charlottesville, Virginia 22903. Members identifying themselves as such receive a 20 per cent discount on these publications. Postage is additional.

Blehl, Vincent Ferrer, S.J., JOHN HENRY NEWMAN, A BIBLIOGRAPHICAL CATALOGUE OF HIS WRITINGS. $25.00.

Boughn, Michael, H. D.: A BIBLIOGRAPHY, 1905–1990. $39.50.

Dameron, J. Lasley, and Cauthen, Irby B., Jr., EDGAR ALLAN POE: A BIBLIOGRAPHY OF CRITICISM 1827–1967. $40.00.

Fry, Donald, *Beowulf* AND *The Fight at Finnsburh*: A BIBLIOGRAPHY. $25.00.

Grimshaw, James A., ROBERT PENN WARREN: A DESCRIPTIVE BIBLIOGRAPHY, 1922–1979. $40.00.

Hodnett, Edward, AESOP IN ENGLAND. $20.00.

Pound, Ezra, A QUINZAINE FOR THIS YULE. $10.00.

Ross, Charles L., THE COMPOSITION OF *The Rainbow* AND *Women in Love*. $25.00.

Roth, Barry, AN ANNOTATED BIBLIOGRAPHY OF JANE AUSTEN STUDIES, 1973–83. $35.00.

STUDIES IN BIBLIOGRAPHY, Volumes 1–51. $40.00 each. (Volumes 1, 2, 6, 10 and 48 out of print).

Tanselle, G. Thomas, TEXTUAL CRITICISM AND SCHOLARLY EDITING. $40.00.

Tucker, Edward, THE SHAPING OF LONGFELLOW'S *John Endicott*. A Textual History, Including Two Early Versions. $26.50.

Vander Meulen, David L., POPE'S DUNCIAD OF 1728: A HISTORY AND FACSIMILE. $40.00.

Wiesenfarth, Joseph, GEORGE ELIOT: A WRITER'S NOTEBOOK, 1854–1879 AND UNCOLLECTED WRITINGS. $35.00.

West, James L. W., III, A SISTER CARRIE PORTFOLIO. $25.00.

Wright, Stuart and West, James L. W., III, REYNOLDS PRICE: A BIBLIOGRAPHY, 1949–1984. $25.00.

Wright, Stuart, PETER TAYLOR: A DESCRIPTIVE BIBLIOGRAPHY, 1934–87. $40.00.

This book was printed by letterpress from type cast on the Linotype by Heritage Printers, Inc. of Charlotte, North Carolina. The typeface is Baskerville, a design by John Baskerville (1706–1775), English printer and type-founder. Linotype Baskerville is a weight-for-weight and curve-for-curve copy of Baskerville's celebrated printing type. The pattern for the cutting was a complete font of (approximately) 14 point, cast from Baskerville's own matrices—exhumed at Paris, France, in 1929. The paper is 70-pound Glatfelter, an acid-free paper with a useful life of 300 years.